K

Charles White was born in Dublin in 1942. He lives with his wife who is a chiropodist. They have two children. He ran the first ever course on the History of Rock n' Roll at Scarborough College of Arts & Technology and opened the first ever Rock n' Roll Museum. He broadcasts regularly on BBC Radio and has had his own television programme 'My Show'. He has been dubbed 'Dr Rock' by the British Press. He writes for 'Now Dig This', *The Independent. Sunday Times, Rolling Stone*, and *The Tatler* have featured his work. In 1992 he was consultant to the Mojo Working rock series on Channel Four.

BY THE SAME AUTHOR

The Life and Times of Little Richard (1984)

KILLER!

Jerry Lee Lewis
and Charles White

ARROW

This edition published by Arrow Books Limited 1996

1 3 5 7 9 10 8 6 4 2

First published in the United Kingdom in 1995 by
Century
Random House UK Ltd, 20 Vauxhall Bridge Road,
London SW1V 2SA

Arrow Books Ltd
Random House UK Ltd, 20 Vauxhall Bridge Road,
London SW1V 2SA

Random House Australia (Pty) Limited
20 Alfred Street, Milsons Point, Sydney
New South Wales 2061, Australia

Random House New Zealand Limited
18 Poland Road, Glenfield
Auckland 10, New Zealand

Random House South Africa (Pty) Limited
PO Box 337, Bergvlei, South Africa

Random House UK Limited Reg No 954009

A CIP catalogue record for this book
is available from the British Library

Papers used by Random House UK Limited are natural,
recyclable products made from wood grown in sustainable
forests. The manufacturing processes conform to the en-
vironmental regulations of the country of origin.

ISBN 0 09 930385X

Printed and bound in the United Kingdom by
BPC Paperbacks Ltd,
a member of The British Printing Company Ltd

Contents

Contents

This book is dedicated to the greatest parents a man could wish for – to my mother, Mary Ethel (Mamie), and my father, Elmo Lewis; to my wife, Kerrie; to my late sons, Jerry Lee Lewis Jr. and Steve Allen Lewis; to my surviving children, Jerry Lee Lewis III and Phoebe Allen Lewis.

Acknowledgements

In 1962, backstage at the De Montfort Hall, Leicester, Jud Phillips, then manager of Jerry Lee Lewis, introduced me to Jerry Lee – 'This kid is gonna give you a big write-up.' Thirty years later Jerry Lee has done me the great honour of allowing me to write his official autobiography. It would take another volume to mention everybody who has communicated with me about Jerry Lee. The following acknowledgements are imperative:

To Jerry Lee Lewis, whose musical genius, humour and generosity have inspired this book. To the Lewis family, especially Kerrie for her belief in my role as biographer; Linda Gail for her endless help, and Eddie Braddock; Frankie Jean and Marion; Phoebe Lewis and Jerry Lee Lewis, III.

Kenny Lovelace, J.W. Whitten.

Chief music consultant – Tony Wilkinson.

U.S. consultants – Greg Allen Robson of *Rock 103* (Memphis); George Klein, Memphis DJ; Jay Halsey, award-winning musicologist, for Ferriday research and Sam Phillips interview; Gary Skala of Chicago for overall U.S. research. Southern music adviser – Fergus Nolan.

Sam Phillips, Barbara Pitman (the First Lady of Sun), Roland Janes, Jimmy Van Eaton, Stan Kesler and Eddie Bond (all Memphis). Morris 'Tarp' Tarrant (Mississippi). Rita Gillespie, Rodney and Sharon Pearson, Maggie and Bill Lynch, Little Richard, Ari Bass (all Los Angeles). Phil Silverman, Drew Williamson, Joe Musella (New York). Myra Williams (Georgia). Al Embry, Shelby Singleton (all Nashville). Professor B. Lee Cooper (Olivet College, Michigan). Special thanks to Jim Newcombe and Ronnie Hawkins (Canada).

Discography, UK researcher and transcription editor – Peter Checksfield.

Dave, Chris and Geoff Webb and family. Terry Adams, Barrie Gamblin, John Pearce, Tony Houlton, Brian Padfield, Steve Rowland, Albert Lee, Chas Hodges, Don and Phil Everly, Cliff White, Carl Perkins, Jack Clement.

Photographic adviser – Adrian Gatie. U.S. photos – Linda Gail Lewis, Rita Gillespie, Morris 'Tarp' Tarrant, Al Embry, Billy Miller of *Kicks* magazine, New York. U.K. photos – Colin Phillips, Brian Smith, Paul Sandford, Jim Newcombe, Dave Webb, Gordon 'the Socks' Begley. Dublin photos – Kyran O'Brien. Germany photos – Christoph Ebner and Rob Swinerton.

Film advisers – Trevor Langton and Brian Smith.

Legal adviser – Freddie Drabble and Kim Schuerman U.S.A.

Typing – Joanne and Dianne of the Duplicating Bureau, Barbara Price, Eileen Buss, Barry Hampshire.

Invaluable inspiration from *Fireball Mail* and Wim de Boer, and from Colin Phillips, U.K. president of *Lewis Scene*. Stuart Colman, Adam Komorowski, Bill Miller. The Sons of Neptune – Chris Found, Cecil, Brian Dew, Stuart Carlisle, Capt. Sydney Smith, Freddie Drabble. Liam and Patricia Hourican, Anthony Brophy and Julia, Alan Ayckbourn and Heather Stoney, Mick and Kath Price, Peter and Judy Ward.

Mick Close, Phil Davies, Gordon McGregor of the King's Hotel and John Allen.

Fellow writers who have inspired me – Nick Tosches, Colin Escott, Robert Hillburn, Jim Sullivan, Paul Gambaccini, John Grissim, Peter Doggett, Van Morrison.

The essential books – *Hellfire* by Nick Tosches, *Good Rockin' Tonite* by Colin Escott and Martin Hawkins, *Ferriday, Louisiana* by Elaine Dundy, *Rock on Film* by David Ehrenstein and Bill Reed, *Jerry Lee Lewis* by Alan Clark, *Jerry Lee Lewis 1969-1972, 1973-1977, The Killer Session Files* by Colin Escott, *Rockin' My Life Away* by Jimmy Gutterman, *Nashville Babylon* by Randall Rieses, *Great Balls Of Fire* by Myra Lewis and Murray Silver Jnr., *The Country Music Encyclopedia, Nashville: Music City USA* by John Lomax III, *Encyclopedia of Southern Culture* by Charles Regan Wilson and William Ferris, *To Cross a River* by Jimmy Swaggart, *Forgiven* by Charles E. Shepard, *Off the Record* by Joe Smith, *Teenage Idol* by Philip Bashe, *Jerry Lee Lewis Rocks* by Robert Palmer, *Whole Lotta Shakin' Goin' On* by Robert Cain. Thanks to Tony Wilkinson for the use of his library.

Radio – Sammy Jackson (KNER, Houston), Spencer Leigh (BBC Radio Merseyside), Stuart Colman (Capital Radio, London), Drew Williamson (WPJB, New York).

Newspapers and magazines – Suzanne Dolezal (*Detroit Free Press*), Richard Ben Cramer (*Rolling Stone*), Robert Hillburn (*LA Times*), Larry Nager and Laurel Campbell (*The Commercial Appeal*, Memphis).

Chart advisers – Barrie Gamblin and Bill Williams.

Richard Weize Bear Family. Peter Guralnick, Woody Wilson. Tadgh O'Coughlan, Joe Moran. John Stafford for Carl Perkins interview. Rockin' Johnas

Sipkema (Holland), Petter Bakke and Stephen Akles (Norway), John Brenda, Hans Jabell (Sweden). Desmond and Linda Johnson, John Dyer, Dave Decon. Dr Gerry Molloy of Dublin. Patrick Argent, graphic designer. Julian Browne, Marcel Guilliou, Ned Thacker, Giles Smith, Sharon Sheeley.

Thanks to Roger Osborne, my agent, for patience, guidance and extraordinary help, and to my editor Mark Booth for believing in *Killer*. Nick Smurthwaite, copy-editor. Liam White for writing, transcription, advice and general help – you will be an author some day.

Finally to my beloved wife, who has allowed her kitchen, dining room and most of the house to be taken over by books, tapes, videos and endless pieces of paper, and who has also worked overtime in the practice – eternal love and thanks.

Introduction

Jerry Lee Lewis is the last American wildman. The tapestry of his life is founded on his musical genius, which is supreme; his repertoire is a storehouse of vital 20th-century American music with which even the Smithsonian Institute would find it hard to compete. On stage he can sing literally thousands of songs redefining and re-interpreting them every time he plays. This is not a show, it is real life. The most fundamental conventions of show business fall by the wayside as he acts out his life through his music. It is a life that reads like a mixture of Shakespeare and Tennessee Williams – murder stories – death – insanity – bigamy – drug abuse – violence – bankruptcy – vandalism – racism – arrogance – egotism – genius. All these are part of Jerry Lee's incredible life and style.

His personal life has been pulverised by uncontrolled sexuality, drug and alcohol abuse and tainted by death. He has been through more tragedy than Shakespeare could conceive, losing two sons and two wives in tragic accidents, and both parents to cancer.

These mammoth events have absorbed the media ever since the British press arched its pompous nose at Jerry's marriage to his 13-year-old second cousin – a normal occurrence in the southern states in the 50s. Jerry's now infamous 'child bride' marriage has made him better known in the public consciousness than the

great musical talent which first propelled him to fame.
The recent movie *Great Balls of Fire* has further perpet-
uated the mythic aura that surrounds Jerry, that of a
man who loves young girls and sets Steinways on fire.
Jerry is no angel and indeed did once set a piano on
fire. However, there are hundreds of recordings to
prove that he has played pianos superbly, a point of
little interest to the mass media. The true Jerry Lee
story comes out of the searing environs of the southern
states, where his mother's musical influence created a
passion so great that it would fill the spectrum of
American music and make Jerry Lee Lewis its greatest
living exponent.

A Jerry Lee show is not simply a show, it is a con-
frontation with life and death, a musical explosion akin
to opening your door and having Niagara Falls gush
through. Too wild to tame, too tough to die. The runway of Jerry's mind is deeply scarred by the hereditary
sins of racism and blasphemous Bible-bashing. His
double-first cousin is the notorious Jimmy Lee Swaggart, a public ego-basher in the larger-than-life
tradition, while another cousin is Mickey Gilley,
former owner of Gilley's Night Club in Texas, 'The
Largest Honky Tonk in the World'.

Swaggart leaked on to an unsuspecting world as
God's messenger via the Bible-bashing American T.V.
Network and had at one stage a viewing audience of
more than five hundred million worldwide. His fall
from grace produced the most mortifyingly embarrassing scene ever seen on T.V. Live, in front of millions of
viewers, he begged forgiveness with tears streaming
down his face before his designer-suited wife.

The media struck Jerry Lee a cruel blow again in 1984
when *Rolling Stone*, the up-market magazine for yup-
pies and ageing rockers, virtually accused him of the
murder of his fifth wife, Shawn.

'It wasn't the failed marriages that brought me down – it was the passing of caskets.'

Jerry Lee remains aloof, noble, arrogant, witty and spontaneous even when surrounded by such degradation.

Jerry Lee: 'I would have to be at least dead or 5,000 years old to do all the things they say I have done. I am what I am, I've always said what I've wanted to say, done what I wanted to do and been what I wanted to be. I've never tried to hide anything, everything I've done has been out in the open. If people don't like that then that's their problem. I've been picked on, abused, sued, jailed, ridiculed, persecuted and prosecuted, but I never let it bother me.'

Jerry Lee has truly lived his life as a man who controlled his own destiny.

The Hollywood star machine was blamed for the corruption of morals of American youth and society in the 30s and 40s, but in the 50s rock 'n' roll and its stars were to be the target. Jerry Lee was to endure and survive more attacks than anyone else. His courage, stamina and tenacity were mammoth. He never stopped touring, entertaining and giving his whole talent to his public. His spirit was the spirit that helped rock 'n' roll survive against the onslaught of the pretentious moral high ground. Jerry kept rockin 'n' rolling even though everything possible was done to stop him.

The media image has done immense harm to his career and his life, and it has deprived the world of the knowledge of his great artistry, his generosity and his humour. To know Jerry Lee is to expect the unexpected. Those who know him find him a perfect, charming, southern gentleman, yet also unpredictable and volatile.

His influence on modern music and his relationship

with fellow artists are well known, especially the media hyped 'envy' of Elvis Presley. Both Jerry and Elvis shared the same Doctor, the notorious George Nichopoulos who has twice appeared in front of the Tennessee Board of Medical Examiners for indiscriminately overprescribing drugs to both Elvis and Jerry Lee. Elvis died of a massive drug overdose in 1977.

However, although Elvis died and Jerry Lee survived, it is Jerry Lee who is remembered as the young man. Jerry Lee is still the wild tiger-suited rock 'n' roller who zapped the U.S. in the mid 1950s with such rip roaring hits as *Whole Lotta Shakin' Goin' On*, *Great Balls of Fire* and *Breathless*. Few realise that he moved on to even greater recordings. Blacklisted after the scandal in England, he made his comeback on country hits such as *Green Green Grass of Home*, *What Made Milwaukee Famous Has Made a Loser Out of Me*, *Another Place, Another Time*, *I'll Find It Where I can*, *I Wish I was 18 Again*, *Me and Bobby McGee*. He went on to record dozens of albums, featuring blues, soul, country, rhythm 'n' blues, dixieland, pop, boogie-woogie, gospel and rock 'n' roll. Anyone just has to listen to a small fraction of his recordings to realise his genius. Those who have not seen this man on stage are missing one of life's greater experiences. He is the ultimate professional and those who dismissed him as a piano-bashing hillbilly in the 50s are having to eat their words as this established musical virtuoso and showman supreme goes from strength to strength.

When John Lennon first met Jerry Lee in 1973, he fell to his knees and kissed Jerry's feet.

When you have read this book you will understand why.

Charles White, August 1993

The Killer Live

This is my life, being on stage playing the piano, giving the people a show.

Jerry Lee Lewis

The Steinway grand piano stands like a majestic battleship at the edge of the middle stage, with the drum kit high at the back facing out onto the audience like a gun turret. A set of guitars rest on their stands while a microphone beside the piano looks like a lance thrown down by some proud warrior before battle. The sound engineers dash about the stage like frightened rabbits, checking wires and speakers. Normally there is an air of tension and excitement before any concert, but tonight there is more – there is high drama and anticipation. Jerry Lee Lewis, the world's greatest piano player and showman supreme, is about to come on stage and anything could happen. Notoriously unpredictable, 'The Killer', as he is known, can pull out any style of 20th-century American music – rock 'n' roll, blues, gospel, dixieland, cajun and country, from his seemingly limitless reservoir. The back-up musicians have usually honed their act to perfection, and must be prepared to cut off in the middle of a song or make a change of tempo from slow to burn-up at 'the Killer's' whim. Each needs the stamina of an Olympic athlete and the precision of a hawk.

Generally Jerry Lee is at his peak when on stage playing, as his whole psyche is singing and playing the piano. He will tease, humour, excite, insult, bedazzle, shock and enthrall, but above all he will entertain the people with his supreme genius, talent and incredible showmanship. This is why there are few moments in theatre that capture such thrilling anticipation as this.

Two huge mirrors are brought on stage, one as a backdrop, the other to be hoisted above the piano to give the crowd a better view of his flashes across the keyboard. A member of the Jerry Lee Fan Club walks down the aisles to tell us that 'The Killer' has arrived – straight from the airport after a direct flight from Vancouver, Canada, following a hectic 76-day tour of the U.S.A.

Suddenly Kenny Lovelace, 'The Killer's' bandleader and right-hand man, walks on stage to do final sound checks to make sure all the sound systems, especially the piano, are ready for the show. He plays a few notes on the piano and gets a roar of approval from the expectant crowd. Kenny is a multi-instrumental talent, proficient on mandolin, banjo and fiddle as well as guitar. He has devoted his life to the service of Jerry Lee – not an easy task mentally or physically, for to work for Jerry Lee is to expect the unexpected.

Kenny leaves the stage and returns with the band, The Memphis Beats, including Linda Gail, Jerry Lee's beautiful sister and a solo artiste in her own right. The audience gives them a warm reception.

'Hiya all, welcome to the Jerry Lee Lewis Show, my name is Kenny Lovelace, these are the Memphis Beats with the beautiful Miss Linda Gail Lewis.' Kenny's searing stratocaster launches into the rock 'n' roll classic, *Johnny Be Good*. Even as they start the band does not know when Jerry will make his appearance, or what songs he will sing, or even at what tempo he will perform them. Linda Gail's strong voice begins to dominate as they continue with *Rollin' in my Sweet Baby's Arms*.

Halfway through the song Jerry Lee steps out of the wings dressed in a black and white striped calfskin jacket, blue jeans and white shoes. The band keep playing while the audience rise to their feet, roaring an enthusiastic welcome; 'Jerry Lee!' they cry. He walks towards the piano with the regal poise of a king who has just been crowned. He waves with his right hand and, as he sits down at the piano, he deftly drops a bottle of Jack Daniel's whiskey by the side of the piano stool, pulling the microphone between his knees. He makes a swift, short karate-like chop with his left hand and the band stop dead. There is silence, then the thunderous sound of a million keyboards as his hands pound the Steinway grand. A pause. Then a rollin' boogie riff, peppered by a drumbeat. Then the voice – 'I'm Rockin', Rockin' My Life Away', a voice strong, powerful, and matured with the hue of gallons of whiskey and tainted with the smoke of Havana cigars. His hands flash up and down, his fingers shooting notes on the keys like a machine gun in a raging battle; the right arm darts around the mike at full stretch, and his distal digits become a sledgehammer pounding the distant notes as though he is trying to destroy some rampant poisonous insect. *Stab! stab! stab!* The air is filled with a piercing triumphant note which blends in perfect time with the background. 'Jerry Lee is rocking his life away – but he is damned sure here to stay.' His left hand slices the air like a flash of lightning, and the band stops dead in their tracks.

'Take it easy on the bass, the drums are fine, the guitars are too low, I wanna hear some guitars now!'

He swigs a mouthful of Jack Daniel's as he bends down, facing away from the audience. In an aside to the band he says, 'What's the name of this place?'. Turning to the mike: 'Good evening, ladies and gentlemen, it's great to be back in the mother country, God's own country. My name is Jerry Lee Lewis from Ferriday, Louisiana. I love ya, I need ya, and I couldn't do it without ya!' The audience roars approval.

Jerry pulls out a pair of dark glasses and goes straight into *Don't Put No Headstone on My Grave* at a slow bluesy pace, then rocks it up with a strong Memphis beat. 'Don't put no headstone on my grave, I want one o' those big Mother Humpers – I want a monument. I come to the conclusion that it is for the Killer.' He finishes by lifting his right shoe up to the keyboard level, then with an air of mock rebellion he kicks the end keys. The auditorium erupts with approval. A boogie riff and Jerry starts into *Down the Line*, 'I'm Gonna Move On Down the Line', lacerating the keyboards with furious glissandi and zinging up and down wildly, yet with apparent ease, producing ecstatic rhythms and always in harmony with the solid beat of the percussion.

After his solo he shouts back to the band: 'It's guitar time now, guitars, guitars, guitars', whilst tearing off his jacket which is caught by Ken Lovelace. He proceeds to roll up his shirtsleeves and tears a piano-shaped diamond ring off his middle finger. He stops the band. 'Hello you good lookin' thing', he snarls into the mike as he bursts into *Chantilly Lace* and 'Pretty faces makes the world go around, ain't nothing in the world like a big-eyed girl makes you act so funny and spend your money, Oh Baby that's what I like', his hands bobbing up and down like a carpet beater. He goes into a slow boogie riff, 'Jerry Lee ain't never seen a woman yet that I didn't love – I love every one of them', (the crowd cheers). 'There's nothing like a woman. If God made anything better He kept it for himself, Love Thy Neighbour as Thyself, Jerry Lee is doin' the best he can – and that's a guaranteed fact – neighbours'. A voice from the crowd shouts: *'Old Black Joe.'*

'Right, brother, we'll do that little ditty for you, right now'. Jerry Lee starts the ballad slowly, 'Gone are the days when my heart was young and gay', then proceeds to rock it to pieces in the middle solo while his hands are cascading over the keyboards. He tears the piano lid off and throws it through the air, it bounces, splits and lands at the edge of the stage, the crowd goes hysterical – Jerry Lee continues playing as though in his own front room. There is a wave of approval from the crowd as he finishes the number. 'We are goin' to slow things down for you now with my dad's favourite song, written by Jimmy Rogers, the singing brake man. Could I have a drink of water?' He gestures to the side of the stage and an attendant rushes out with a white plastic beaker.

Meanwhile Jerry takes a quick drink from the Jack Daniel's bottle at the piano side whilst leaning to the monitor controls. 'You're the One Rose That's Left in My Heart' dominates the auditorium – a beautiful country song raised to a dignified human love drama by Jerry Lee's unique interpretation. This is followed by *You Win Again*, the Hank Williams classic. Jerry Lee enters the song totally, bringing in his own name, 'Jerry Lee's Woman Been Out Runnin' Round', and winding off with 'As Hank Williams once said to Miss Audery, "Woman, You Win Again".'

Jerry Lee has another drink, lights up a huge Havana cigar, takes a few puffs and places it on top of the

piano. 'It's gonna get good in a minute, I guarantee
you, neighbours! Who's gonna play this ol' piano after
the master's not here?' He winds the song up with
mockery: 'I love ya, like a hog loves slop.' The
audience laughs and cheers. 'I know I'm not a model
husband although I'd like to be, but pay day nights and
painted women do strange things to me.' And yet another country song, *There Must Be More to Love Than
This*. Midway he turns to Kenny Lovelace, 'Play your
fiddle, son. Mr. Kenneth Lovelace, ladies and gentlemen, probably one of the finest fiddle players in the
world today. You're sure comin' through, son.' Then as
he continues his piano solo – *flash! bang!* – a bulb
crashes down from the lighting system above the piano
and with a magnesium flare bursts on the edge of the
piano. Jerry carries on coolly and instantly incorporates
the incident into the lyrics – 'There must be more to
lighting systems than this.' The crowd laps it up. A man
shouts '*High School Confidential*'. Jerry responds, 'I'll
do what I want to do – I'm workin' my butt off for you
and so are the boys in the band, if you don't like it the
doors swing both ways.' The crowd applaud and cheer
once again.

Straight into a superb up-tempo version of *Me And
Bobby McGee*. He ups the tempo even more – boogie
riffs flow out of the Steinway. A ponytailed young lady
leaps on stage, avoids the stage bouncers, throws her
arms around Jerry and kisses him on the cheek as she
hands him a rose. Jerry carries on but acknowledges the
gesture. Once again he alters the lyrics to suit the occasion, 'She was sure good enough for me, Jerry Lee and
Bobby McGee.' He raises the tempo to breakneck
place, 'Somewhere near Salina, I watched her slip
away, lookin' for a home I hope she'd find, still I'd save
all my tomorrows for a single yesterday.'

'If I could hold that woman's body on top of mine.'

He takes the tempo to a high level – 'Come on, come on, come on!' he shouts to the band, who are pushed to their limits to keep up. One thinks if he raises the tempo again, they will collapse. He does. 'Freedom's just another word, for nothing left to lose, nothing ain't worth nothin' but it's free' – zing. He cuts off, then immediately zooms on at the same racing tempo – 'Just because you think you're so pretty – just because you think you're so hot, you ain't hot – just because you think you got something that no other woman ain't got' – he bounces his elbow on the keyboard and flicks up his white shoe on the keys, rolling his heel on the notes – the crowd whistles and cheers. A wave to the band and the band stops dead. He hits a slow, bluesy note and adopts a serious posture.

'I was standin' at my window on a cold and cloudy day – when I saw a hearse come rollin' for to carry my mama away' – a solemn version of *Will the Circle Be Unbroken*. 'Mr Undertaker – I said Mr Undertaker, I'm talkin' to you – why don't you drive your waggon slow, 'cause you carrying the sweetest creature and the best friend Jerry Lee ever had – my God!' There is silence in the auditorium. Jerry Lee's preacher man attitude transforms the audience from raving rockers to those who are stunned with high drama, 'My God in the sweet bye and bye.'

He winds it up and Jerry Lee the sinner man re-emerges – 'I gonna do the Mother Humper of them all for you now' – a powerful boogie riff, *thumpa, thumpa* – 'Come On Over Baby, Whole Lotta Shakin' Going On, Jerry Lee's been getting it all night long'. He hits a piercing high note which rings like a warning bell through the air. He continues to hammer it out, 'All you gotta do is stand it in one little spot, Too much gettin' it drives the stud insane.' The sexual atmosphere

causes several couples in the audience to do a slow pel-
vic wiggling jive – 'Now Let's Go!', shouts Jerry,
standing up and kicking the piano stool back. Flying
through the air, it lands and two legs break – he tears
up and down the piano like a demented wood shearer
would carve a log – but the music is superb. He turns
his back and hits the keys with his behind, grabs the
mike, stuffs it down his midriff, points to the guitars to
do their solos – the pounding rhythm continues. He
leaps on top of the piano, the crowd hail him triumphantly. 'Shake it baby, shake it!' He jumps on the keys
in his white shoes, playing the notes amazingly in time.
He jumps off and strides to the semi-demolished piano
stool, looks coy and rests it against the piano – the two
broken legs fall off. He puts them around his neck and
walks off like a victorious matador who has killed a
mad bull. The crowd rise to give him a standing ovation.

Linda Gail comes forward – 'Ladies and gentlemen,
Mr Jerry Lee Lewis, the greatest performer in the
world today.' A young man from Belgium turns to his
lady friends, 'I told you it was the greatest live show on
earth.'

CHAPTER 1

Real Wild Child

*Louisiana celebrates life with its passionate, efferves-
cent, joyous musicality. Its anthem is laissez les bon
temps rouler – let the good times roll. Louisiana people
know how to indulge the pleasures of this world – an art
handed down by the French Duke of New Orleans,
Philippe, a notorious womanizer and libertine who
ruled France from 1715 to 1723.*

*Louisianians are not interested in ideologies or princi-
ples but in the fundamentals – food, music, sex and
gambling in the Catholic south; hunting, fishing and sex
in the Protestant north.*

*The potency of the state is best expressed by its
vigorous music – blues, country, ragtime, Dixieland,
jazz, cajun, zydeco, rhythm and blues, rock 'n' roll –
which have steered the course of 20th-century music.
The fusion of races and cultures brought about an explosion of musical talents.*

*Louis Armstrong, King Oliver, Cab Calloway, Pro-
fessor Longhair ('the Bach of rock'), Fats Domino, Jelly
Roll Morton, Allen Toussaint, Dr John and Winton
Marsalis to name a few.*

- I came into this world naked, feet first and jumpin'
  and I've been jumpin' ever since. I am just what I
  am, Jerry Lee 'screw up' Lewis, if they don't like
  that, they can kiss my butt. I've always said what I

wanted to say, done what I wanted to do and been what I wanted to be. I've never tried to hide anything. I was born in Ferriday, Louisiana on 29 September 1935, a Louisiana man, a rock 'n' roll country honky tonk boogie woogie piano playing man. I got rhythm in my soul, music in my veins and a whole lotta thunder in my left hand. I can play music 'til it drives you insane 'cause I'm the rockinest mother humper that's ever been. It's a God given talent and I can play any kind of music. I ain't no hillbilly guitar picker from Nashville. I am an artist.

My family was poor, we grew up in a shack, we didn't even have a bathroom. My mother would pick cotton all day. It was real hard work for her but she was a strong woman physically and mentally. My mother was Mary Ethel, we called her Mamie, and my father was Elmo Kidd Lewis. My folks had four children, Elmo junior, my elder brother, next me, Jerry Lee, then my sisters, Frankie Jean and Linda Gail. We were real poor, but proud. Papa Lewis, my Daddy, was a farmer, a sharecropper, a carpenter, a bootlegger, a construction worker. We moved home 13 times in one year. He was musical, real good on the guitar. Sometimes he played with my uncle, Son Swaggart, at the local night club. Now uncle Son Swaggart was a powerful preacher man. I was raised in the Assembly of God Church, the same as my cousins, Mickey Gilley and Jimmy Lee Swaggart. I respect every church and I believe in salvation. I don't want to lose my soul and I don't want to go to hell.

My Daddy was a fantastic singer as well as guitar player. We would have family sessions all the time when I was a little boy, singing gospel songs. I can recall my parents singing in church and I have never heard people that sang that good in my life.

My Daddy made the best bootleg whiskey in Louisiana. I grew up with it. We always had a still in the back yard. He knew they were watching him and he knew they were going to catch him. He had to serve a year for it. At the time he felt it was worth it.

Momma named me after my uncle, Lee Calhoun, who was the richest man around – his whole back garden was covered in whiskey barrels. The revenue man busted up twenty barrels and said 'Mr Calhoun, you gonna have to pay fifteen hundred or go to jail.' He was generous but he was mean too, and he thought he could save money by going to jail. And he had this old working overall, he wore it 'til the sweat made it rot off his body.

Everybody made bootleg liquor 'cause they couldn't get whiskey anywhere else back then. Everybody had to serve six months to a year, at least in my family they did. Uncle Lee could've paid 'em some money and got out of it but he said 'I don't mind staying for six months, you gonna feed me, take care of me.'

When my Daddy was in the state penitentiary that's when the first tragedy of my life occurred. I was at home with Momma. My brother, Elmo Jnr. was out walking nearby with my cousin, Maudine, walking along composing a song – he'd already shown some talent for songwriting. We heard a terrible commotion outside, and Momma ran out and saw her son dead, lying in a ditch. He'd been hit by some drunk driving a truck. He never knew what hit him, died outright. It was a terrible shock for all of us. Momma never got over it, she relived it all the time. That's why I feel bad about alcohol. Sure I drink but I know it's wrong. Everybody always

thinks they can handle it, but nobody can handle it. I
want to see a man who can handle it. Folks say I can
handle it, but I go home and beat up the wife. You
know Satan has power next to God, and he's working pretty hard.

LINDA GAIL (sister): Elmo Junior and my cousin
were out walking and playing. Maudine saw a driver get
in his truck and, before he started off, she hopped up
on the trailer at the back. Elmo Junior went to follow
her but a car driven by a drunk driver came up real fast,
hit him and threw his body up in the air, landing in a
ditch. He was dead instantly.

That's not all. At Junior's funeral my Daddy arrived
with prison guards, chained up. They had guns,
wouldn't even let my Daddy's hand free to say goodbye
to his eldest son. Can you imagine what that did to my
Momma? They wouldn't even let my Daddy stay to
comfort Momma.

FRANKIE JEAN (sister): They brought my father
home in shackles. It broke my mother's heart. He then
received a little postcard from Elmo Jnr. after he was
dead. He said when it reached him in jail he cried and
cried, it broke his heart a thousand times.

● Momma was the main event, she was our strength,
she moulded the family. Daddy was real quiet. We'd
ask him something and he would always say 'Go to
your mother, ask your mother.' She never had no
driver's licence for forty something years, was
stopped many times and each time she charmed 'em.
This lady knew how to talk. She and my aunt Irene
[Mickey's mother] and my aunt Ada [Jimmy's grand-
mother] and my aunt Minnie Bell [Jimmy's mother],

were all good Christian women. They did a lot of fasting and praying and reading the Bible every day.

FRANKIE JEAN (sister): Mother had the gift of speaking in tongues. It came down and hit her like a bolt of lightning. It's a gift, it's one of the gifts of the Holy Spirit and just everybody doesn't get it. It's not a bunch of mumbo-jumbo, it's as if you're speaking through the Holy Spirit. You can hear the truth, you can feel the truth and you know it's the truth. I was there when they did this exorcism. It scared me so badly I didn't eat for three weeks. I felt the demon was in my throat. The preacher would say 'When the demon come out, you must be careful, 'cause they'll go in you.' I was so damn scared, I was almost dying. I would sit there and go over everything I'd ever thought bad about a person and repent immediately. I would clench the benches so hard that I'd have blisters on my hands. It was a horrible sight when they cast the demons out. Sometimes they'd come out of a leg and it'd just bleed. Folks may not believe these things, but I swear to God this be the truth.

• My cousin Carl Glasscott [nowadays known as Carl McVoy] used to sit down and play when he was about 18 years old. I was about five and I looked at him and thought 'If I could ever be that good-looking a man and play like he's playing and sing like he's singing – nothing would stop me', and that was before I ever played a piano.

  The first time I played for the choir at the Assembly of God, I walked up there in front of the congregation, there must have been about 40 people there and I thought that was really something. I was all shook up – so very politely I walked over to my

mother and I asked her, 'Momma what's the name of
the song I am supposed to sing?' She said '*What Will
My Answer Be*', so I went back and sung it all and
ever since then I've been singing. Everybody
laughed but I played well. At home after church
Momma said, 'I think Jerry Lee is a natural born
piano player'.

My parents bought my first piano for me when I
was eight years old. They mortgaged the home for it,
cost them two hundred and eighty dollars for an old
upright. Daddy carried it into the house on his back.
I still have it at home now with holes worn all
through the keys from playing it. I always thought of
the piano as the greatest instrument and the most
beautiful sounding instrument. I just love the piano.
It has eighty eight keys or strings. I love the guitar
which only has six strings but my real love is the
piano. At first the school teacher wanted me to have
lessons, so I went along and he gave me these scales
to do. When I played the song a few days later, I
said, 'Don't the song sound better like this?' and I
did it Jerry Lee-style. He kinda slapped me and said
'Don't you ever do that again'. That was the end of
my piano lessons.

LINDA GAIL (sister): My mother listened to Hank
Williams and Jimmie Rodgers and Jimmy Davies, the
singing governor of Louisiana.

We'd all sit around and sing at night. My dad would
play the guitar, Jerry would play the piano and my
sister, Frankie Jean and me and my mother would sing.
When my brother was home I wanted to be right there
by that piano, I knew something great was coming from
that. I didn't want to play with the other kids or do anything else, I just wanted to stand right there and listen.

- My style of piano playing is just Jerry Lee Lewis. It's my own. I created it. My own sound. I'd never heard any other piano players when I got a piano, so I wasn't influenced by anybody else. I taught myself everything I knew about piano. I lived so far back in the country, I don't think I knew anybody who could influence me.

I liked Al Jolson, the blue yodeller Jimmie Rodgers from Mississippi, I liked Hank Williams, and when I was a kid I followed Gene Autry. Nobody could sing like Gene Autry, especially riding a horse and singing. I never could figure that one out. Me and my cousins, Mickey and Jimmy, wore out more horses trying to sing like Gene Autry than anybody else in the world. I never missed a Gene Autry movie. For years, until I did *Great Balls of Fire* in *Jamboree* I didn't know you could pantomime a song in a movie. John Wayne's great, Roy Rogers is great, but they couldn't shine Gene Autry's boots.

My daddy loved his music especially Jimmie Rodgers, the singing brake man. His favourite song was *The One Rose That's Left in My Heart*. He had a lot of records by Hank Williams, Red Foley, Gene Autry and they were all great.

Momma loved country music, she was always singing the latest songs.

I picked Daddy's guitar during school breaks 'cause I couldn't take the piano to school. I learned to play fiddle and drums.

The first song I played all the way through on the piano was *Silent Night*. I was eight years old. I could only play it on the black notes. After I played, my Daddy started playing around on the piano and he was better than me. I was so upset that I sat down and cried. He saw what happened and he never played piano again. He didn't want to discourage me. Can you imagine that? He loved me that much. That shows you what kind of parents I had. Four years later I made my first public appearance, it was unscheduled and in a car lot. The Ferriday Ford Agency was introducing its new line of cars and the entertainment was a hill billy band. Well the piano player let me do a short set, I did an impromptu version of *Hadacol Boogie*, the first song I ever performed in public. The folks liked it so I played *Drinkin' Wine Spo-dee-o-dee*. The crowd was amused – I was only a kid. They passed the hat. I walked away from that car lot with the most money I ever had in my jeans, nearly $14, but I was more excited at hearing my voice for the first time over a P.A. system. After this Daddy drove me around on the back of our pickup truck to fairs to make money.

FRANKIE JEAN (sister): A typical day in our childhood would have been my mother working and cooking, my father out at work and Jerry Lee playing the piano all day. Sometimes he'd play it until he dropped off the stool, that's how hard he practised. Linda Gail falling on the floor, talking, laughing and giggling, fighting and cooking three or four family meals together, visitors coming, coffee, lots of black coffee. Jerry was very dependent on Mom. She had a good disposition one day, then next day she'd be very moody. Now we know that as being a manic depressive.

Jerry Lee's mother, Mamie, noticed that he too had violent mood swings, like hers, from high to low spirits with very little warning – a kind of mild manic depression. The doctor gave him something for it, but they did not consider it serious. Later he would need stronger medication.

LINDA GAIL (sister): My mother worked really hard when she was young. She used to pick cotton all day long and give the money to Jerry so he could buy nice clothes and stuff to perform in. Jerry is very generous but I don't think anyone could compare with my mother's generosity. She was strong mentally and physically. Jerry Lee's father-in-law, J. W. Brown, Myra's father, said to my mother, 'If it hadn't been for me, you'd still be on Black River.' Well, she took that as an insult, because she felt it was her raisin' my brother the way she did and him being talented that was the reason we weren't on Black River, not because of J. W. Brown, so she knocked him down with her fist, she was that strong.

When we were kids at home, the first thing I used to do when Jerry came home was I'd sit on his lap and tell him everything I knew about everybody, 'cause I was his little snitch. I'd go out and find out what his wife Myra was doing. Myra and my sister Frankie Jean would ask me not to tell. 'O.K.,' I'd say, 'Let me have a cigarette and I won't tell.' Then as soon as Jerry came in, I'd say 'Well, they smoked cigarettes and they looked at some boys.' No wonder Myra hates me!

FRANKIE JEAN (sister): Jerry was playing football one time and his side was losing the game. Jerry, he starts running, and he makes a touch down, but he jumps so hard he pulls his whole damn hip out of its socket. Then he had to have a cast all the way from his ankle up to his waist. We would help him to the piano and when I moved his leg the wrong way, he'd scream. I'm afraid I tortured him. Anyway, after about six months in the cast, he put me in a wooden stroller and said, 'I'm gonna show you something beautiful, Frankie Jean – you've never seen this spot.' He got me to this cliff overlooking a big ravine, the thing didn't look like it had a bottom to it. I said 'Jerry, you can't!' But he pushed me – and the trees and the branches, the debris was all that saved me. There was snakes down there, it was close to the river. I got out, and Jerry ran.

In the late 1940s Elmo Lewis worked on the restoration of the Angola state penitentiary as construction foreman. The family lived on site, and Jerry Lee recalls the sound of the sirens when there was a break-out. When the contract was completed, the Lewis family moved out into the country to a place called Black River, 28 miles from Ferriday. Here the family eked out a living as sharecroppers. Elmo tried to teach his son the fundamentals of agriculture, but Jerry Lee knew he would never make a farmer.

- I knew God had given me this talent. I ain't no cotton pickin' farmer. Papa tried to teach me how to drive a tractor as he needed my help on the farm. I ploughed everything up, but it was all crooked. Then he put me on the hayraker and I made a terrible mess of that too. I picked 187 pounds of cotton, from six o'clock in the morning 'til eight o'clock at night, when everybody else had picked something like 400 pounds! I never tried it no more! I had given it my best shot and that's all I had to give. I said 'I'll play piano Daddy, I just don't chop cotton.' He said 'Go home and play it, you're not gonna amount to nothing anyway.' I said 'Well if I don't, I'm not gonna amount to nothing picking no cotton.'

FRANKIE JEAN (sister): Daddy said 'I want you and
Jerry to chop this acre of cotton'. We'd chop and we'd
chop and we'd stop and I'd look at Jerry and he'd look
at me and he'd say 'I'll tell you one thing, I won't be
doing this much longer!' – but we did our best, not too
good and we never did finish the acre of cotton.

- There was a time when the whole town of Ferriday
  was flooded. I was quite small, but I remember this
  was before we had levees and high water just over-
  flowed. Jimmy Swaggart and his family were living
  just down the road and we would all go visit them in
  a boat. Papa, Momma, Frankie Jean, Linda Gail and
  myself. Momma would take us out on the Jonesville
  Highway and she would let us swim – we didn't have
  pools then. We'd go out on the flooded highway and
  have the time of our lives. We went to the movies in
  a boat, just down the street. I used to play hookey
  from school and go swimming in Lake St John. Anyway I was swimming and I got bitten by a snake.
  Some folks pulled me out. Momma went frantic:
  'Oh, my poor little boy! Elmo do something!'

ELMO (father): He was a good boy but he wouldn't go
to school too much. We would send him to school, and
when I found out he was over at the swimming pool half
the time, we were tickled to death. He'd come on the
last day and bring his report which was right up to date.

FRANKIE JEAN (sister): Jerry was lying in his bed,
waiting for Mother to bring him his breakfast, as she
always did. I go into the room 'cause he's mumbling
somethin' – he's frozen with fear. I say 'Jerry, what's
wrong?' Then I see just above him they're crawlin'
under the wallpaper – SNAKES! He was afraid to

holler any louder in case they're gonna fall down. They were rattlesnakes up in the loft. There was a tear in the wallpaper and you could see them slithering over the paper which was bulging with the weight of the snakes.

- Yeah, there were snakes up there. I didn't pay much attention to 'em back then. My Daddy went to the roof of the house and killed about 13 big rattlesnakes. He climbed up there, took a stick and killed 'em. Things like that he'd pay no attention. Thirteen big rattlesnakes, he'd climb up the top of the roof and find a big nest of 'em up there. Killed 'em all. He had some rattlers with 14, 15 rattles on them. He was great with snakes. Back then I lived in a little ol' room and one stuck his head down and looked at me. I looked at him and we didn't like each other too much!

  Daddy ran in and killed that snake with his hoe. He then got his shotgun and blew the whole damn roof off.

  This was when we lived at Black River, which was as far back in the woods as you could get. I used to love to go fishing, I'd even go fishing if they sent me to the store across the river.

  My Momma's folks, the Herrons, had a store across the river which used to save us going all the way into town. My Momma and I'd sit on the front porch of that house and I could see steamboats going by. I'd wave out and people would wave back and it'd blow its whistle. I can remember those steamboats going by and seeing those people drinking mint juleps. I said 'Momma, it'd really be something if we was sitting out on that boat wouldn't it?' Kids don't see things like that no more, there isn't anything like that no more. You'll only see that in movies.

CHAPTER 2

Hot Gospel

- I'm Dutch, Indian, English and Irish – that's a helluva mixture. I think they all come out of me in different ways.

LINDA GAIL (sister): My Daddy was partly Choctaw Indian. I am very proud of my Indian background.

FRANKIE JEAN (sister): The Lewises are Jewish people. I've traced it back to France. They're French, English and Dutch.

- Baloney! There's no Jewish blood in the family! What she's talking about [Frankie Jean] is the Jewish people we knew in Ferriday. Joe Pasternak [Hollywood producer of Jewish extraction] lived in Ferriday. He was one of the richest men in Louisiana. Him and my uncle, Lee Calhoun, was best friends.

Jerry Lee's formative years were spent mainly with his cousin, Jimmy Lee Swaggart, destined to become famous for something other than rock 'n' roll. In his biography, To Cross a River, Swaggart recalls their youth. They would often go to hear a local piano player, Old Sam, and cycle over to the Mississippi River bridge at Natchez.

JIMMY SWAGGART (cousin): Jerry Lee would climb out on the edge of the bridge and wave at passing motorists while hanging several hundred feet above the water. If he'd fallen he would have been killed. Jerry Lee was no doubt a wild, wild child.

● Jimmy Lee was into music like I was. We was raised up together, same family, same school, same church. We was more like brothers than cousins. We'd sneak over to Haney's Big House, a negra club owned by a big black man called Haney. He'd bring blues and boogie woogie cats, the best, Duke Ellington, Champion Jack Dupree, Sunnyland Slim, Albert King, B. B. King, Muddy Waters and Ray Charles, only a young guy then – a great, great cast. Sometimes Jimmy and me, we'd get in the door of this wild negra club, and they'd be drunk, dancing and goin' crazy, some out cold on the floor. Haney knew we was there. He'd say to me, 'You wanna get us all killed, yo' uncle Lee Calhoun gonna come down here, kill us both.' And Haney would throw us out pretty quick.

But Jimmy Lee and Jerry Lee had a more profound influence than music, the movies or their school days – it was the Pentecostal Church, a charismatic sect whose literal interpretation of the Bible can lead to enormous pressure on the human spirit. In the case of Jimmy Lee Swaggart, matters were simply divided into good and evil. Jimmy Lee attributes all acts in life as controlled either by God or Satan. Like Jerry Lee he had a talent for playing the piano, which of course was a gift from God. He has hinted, however, that Jerry Lee's talent betrays the hand of Satan. This is the complex religion that would dominate their lives.

FRANKIE JEAN (sister): Jimmy Lee was brain-washed by his father, Son Swaggart. Son was a pagan until Leona Sumrall arrived in Ferriday and set up the Pentecostal Holiness Assembly of God Church. The church became a hub of social and musical activity in Ferriday. Son was first attracted by the music but soon the hot gospel converted him. The language and delivery was as intense as the first message read from the Bible by Leona Sumrall, Revelations 21:8 – 'But the fearful and unbelieving and the abominable and murderers and whoremongers and sorcerers and idolators and all liars shall have their part in the lake which burneth with fire and brimstone, which is the second death.'

After his conversion, Son became an over-zealous practitioner of the faith. He wanted his boy, Jimmy Lee, to be a preacher. Extremely strict, old fashioned, no sex, no movies, no nothing. He would put boxing gloves on and put them on Jimmy, who was only a young kid, then he'd knock him out cold.

Although Jerry Lee wanted to be a preacher, too, his sense of impish devilment got the better of him and he would appear to lead Jimmy astray. Soon they were getting into mischief, stealing all sorts of things from farms, stores and they even stole from their own bene-factor, Uncle Lee Calhoun, who said no one could pull a fast one over on him. They sold him some of his own wiring back. Jimmy would always return it, Jerry Lee wouldn't. Jimmy had a conscience, Jerry Lee said, 'To hell with it, it's too late, we've stolen it now.'

CECIL HARRELSON (schoolfriend): Jerry Lee was a real skinny kid but he was extremely strong. The first time we met we got in a fight over a school dictionary. We both reached up for it at the same time. When he

pulled it out my hand, I pulled it back, then he snatched
it again. I said why don't we meet out the back after
school and settle this. Jerry Lewis said that's fine by
me. So the whole school is waiting for the big fight, but
Jerry had just got on his bicycle and gone home.

ELMO LEWIS (father): He and Cecil Harrelson was
raised together like two brothers. Jerry didn't have a
brother, his oldest brother having got killed when he
was nine years old, and so Jerry was raised with Cecil.
They was rough boys together, and we thought they
was the best boys in the neighbourhood, but Jerry told
me later, 'Daddy we was the meanest boys in town.'
They was goin' ta Juke Joints, to Clubs chasin' women.

● I met Cecil at School. We had an argument. He said
'I'll see ya after school outside, we'll settle it then.'
So of course I never turned up. Next time I saw him
he said 'Where were ya boy?' I said I plumb forgot
about it. He knew I was putting him on, so he just
laughed. We got very close and used to run around
together. Cecil's folks had money and they had a
nice home, bathroom and everything. We didn't
have none of that and they were very nice to me.
Cecil always had a car.

My grand-daddy encouraged me to fight. I was
walkin' by his house on the way home from school,
and he said, 'Hey! Boy. Come here'. He was sitting
on the porch. He musta been 75 at the time, with his
feet propped up.

'Yes! Sir. Poppa, what is it?'

'Somebody told me you had a fight.'

'Yes sir, I did. Some fella let the sun shine in my
eyes for about an hour, these people held me down.'

'Now I'll tell ya' what you should do. Tomorrow

when you catch this cat bending over the water fountain, you slip right up behind him and let him have it with a coke bottle an' he won't let the sun shine in your eyes no more.'

'I don't think I'll do that Poppa.'

'Do it.'

'Yes, Poppa, I'll do it.'

FRANKIE JEAN (sister): The Lewises are extremely proud people, almost haughty. Jerry Lee was disliked in town. My mother would pick him up and tell him, 'Don't you ever come home cryin' and tell me you don't have a friend at school.'

LINDA GAIL (sister): When my sister gets mad everybody takes off, including Jerry Lee. He laughs about that, but if my sister gets mad, he'll be the first one to leave, and I'll be right behind him. She's tough, won't put up with anything. She'll shoot first and ask questions later. I saw her shoot between a man's legs one time. If you run a store like my sister does in Ferriday, you got to have a gun to protect yourself from the people that have the guns. My brother-in-law had these two men that were going to beat him up, and Frankie went out there with her gun and told them to go. The guy said, 'I'm not going anywhere', so she shot right between his legs. She said, 'The next one's going t'be two feet higher.' My sister is just the sweetest thing in the world until you make her mad.

Jerry had one bodyguard, this guy named Dagwood, real tough guy, there's no telling how many people he killed, not afraid of anything. He was there another time when Frankie pulled a gun on some people. Jerry said, 'The best thing you can do is to run', which is what Jerry did. But anyway this Dagwood guy walked right up to Frankie and said, 'You're not going to do anything with that gun, give it to me.' She put the gun right between his eyes and cocked it. He got his butt out of there quick. He told me later: 'I never been so scared in all my life, 'cause I looked that woman in the eyes and her hand did not shake. She did not blink.'

● I would get into a lot of fights. Doc Stone [Huey P. Stone] looked after me like I was his little brother, and every time these cats jumped on me, Doc Stone would whip their butts. Along with Cecil, Doc was truly a friend to me. Doc was a strong, healthy man and still is, but he's got a high, high temper. He looked after me like a bodyguard, a guardian angel, kinda adopted me. I knew Doc before I started school, when I was only about four years old. Doc was quite a bit older than me. I was uptown with Doc once in Daddy's truck. I said, 'Doc, can you knock that parking meter off for me, I haven't got any money for it.' And Doc took his fist and he hit it, Wham! I'm talkin' about solid concrete and iron. It just bent over, and everyone came to see it. I used to brag, 'Don't mess with Jerry Lee if he's with Doc!' We both got dismissed from school the same day for fighting the teacher.

You call someone Killer 'cause it makes 'em feel good. Mother really started it. My mother called me that, she got it from the old talent shows. She'd say 'Kill 'em, Jerry! Kill 'em with your piano. They must forget where they are. You've got to make them scream. You've got to make them jump in their seats.'

CECIL HARRELSON (schoolfriend): I was working at Duke's department store and I was waiting on this coloured woman when I saw Jerry pass by and I shouted, 'Hey, Killer'. This coloured lady just about freaked out, thinking a real killer was on the loose, began to jump up and down. I told Jerry about it and we both started calling each other Killer. It came in handy later, as Jerry Lee, like me, can't remember names and you meet thousands of people in show business, so you just call everyone Killer.

• I kept playing the piano till I fell off the stool. My cousins Jimmy Lee Swaggart and Mickey Gilley, they all got a piano each, but I was the best. I got on radio WNAT at Natchez, that's when I became known in my local area. This guy, he was a disc jockey. He asked me to come over and do a 30 minute show each Saturday afternoon. Mother'd dress me up in a suit, bow tie – it wasn't as if anyone would see me! Whatever I did my folks backed me to the hilt. I knew what I could do. I wasn't scared. I had enough confidence in myself and I really wasn't worried about anyone following me. Like Hank Williams said 'Move over little dog, big dog's moving in!'

I didn't like school, so when I was 13 I worked at the Bloody Bucket; that's what I used to call it, it was really the Blue Cat Club in Natchez. They gave me $10 a night. The meanest, lowest down place in the world, fights broke out there all the time. At about ten o'clock you'd hide behind the piano. Bullets flyin', bottles flyin', women flyin', men flyin'. After it was all over they'd all start dancin' again. The trip to Natchez four nights a week got too much for me so I quit and got a gig at The Wagon Wheel. I played piano and drums with a blind cat called Paul Whithead and got $6 a night. Momma would stay up all night – she didn't like it at all. That's where I learnt *Whole Lotta Shakin' Goin' On'*. I was running a little bit late that night and I heard a drum and Paul playing the piano and singing *Whole Lotta Shakin' Goin' On* and he put the talking part in it. I knew that was a hit and I learned it. Paul played piano, trumpet and accordion. He learnt me a lot. I used to take him home every night from The Wagon Wheel and get him out of the car. He could make it from there straight on in, knew exactly where he was. His wife was blind too.

The first real date I ever had was Elizabeth Berthridge, a girl I grew up with in Ferriday. We kinda thought we was in love. We used to laugh and joke and play around quite a bit. I took her to the prom. I got all dressed up and I borrowed my Aunt Stella's new '49 Chevrolet and went to the prom. I kissed her goodnight and I swear her stepmother was watching us and thought she had my number pretty big. But she wouldn't let me have too much leverage!

My cousin Betty Jo Slamper was the first little girl who ever taught me how to really smooch. My uncle Frank Slamper was her daddy. I was somewhere around 13 years old and uncle Frank let us stay in their trailer and during the day time me and Betty Jo did some smooching.

We moved on down the road there and there was a girl named Ruth going with some fellow. I don't know, we just started messing around. We just knew we were in love. I'll never forget, this was years ago and sex was a big thing. Finally after two or three weeks I talked her into having sex with me. She said O.K. and got ready to do it, then I said 'Ruth, I don't think this is right and we shouldn't do this.'

She said 'You mean to tell me that after weeks of getting me to do this you're not gonna do it?'

*In the winter of 1951 a travelling salvation show came to
Ferriday, led by the Reverend Jewell E. Barton who
hired Jerry Lee as piano player for his sermons. It
proved to be a fateful engagement for Jerry Lee who was
instantly attracted to the Reverend's young daughter,
Dorothy.*

- Dorothy was a sweet, fine, religious young woman,
  deeply devoted to the religious aspects of life. She
  was a very, very good woman. I fell in love with her
  and we got married in February 1952 when I was 15
  and she was 16. Dorothy was also a good-looking
  girl. Sitting up in the front row of church I was singing *Peace in the Valley* and I looked at her and I
  thought 'Jesus Christ, that's the woman for me!'
  Really, it was love at first sight. I just had to get married, y'know, it got back to the sex thing again.
  Dorothy said, 'You can forget that with me 'cause
  I'll never do that 'til I get married.' I said, 'Well that
  ain't no problem.' Of course Dorothy's father
  objected, it broke his heart. She was a virgin, I was a
  virgin, and we didn't know nothing about nothing. I
  just got it into my mind that I had to get married
  'cause I wanted to go to bed with this lady. Sex is not
  what you think it's gonna be. It all goes together but
  it has to be right. I don't know what I was expecting,
  an avalanche or something. It's not that. It's something that's supposed to be sacred and Dorothy
  wasn't wild enough for ol' Jerry Lee. She lives in
  Monroe, Louisiana, now, she's done well for herself.
  She is still one of my best friends. Whenever I go
  through Monroe I see Dorothy, always have a picture taken together. She is one of the few I've loved.

FRANKIE JEAN (sister): When he met Dorothy Jerry

Lee was very young and very happy. He talked back to mother the day he married Dorothy, and Momma hit out at him and when he dodged her she broke her finger on the wall. However, she approved of Dorothy, and they were married from our house.

In 1953 Jerry Lee, persuaded by his mother and the local preacher, set out by bus to the Bible Institute in Waxahatchie, Texas, to study to become a preacher. The austere atmosphere of the Bible college was not at all conducive to Jerry Lee's exuberant personality, nor to his status as a newly married man. Dorothy returned to her parents' home, while Jerry Lee spent his time escaping from his dormitory window down hastily improvised rope ladders and sneaking off to the movies. The people in charge, realising they had a rebel on their hands, offered him the chance of redemption by inviting him to play piano at chapel evening service. He chose the Pentecostal anthem, 'My God is Real'.

- I kinda put a little feeling into it, y'know, a little Louisiana boogie woogie. The students loved it, they stamped and hollered. I felt the spirit move me so I kept goin' on the piano, singing as powerful as I could. The students all clapped and rose to their feet in joyous rapture. But the Dean expelled me afterwards, so I came home. Momma said, 'Go to the assembly on Sunday, you're a preacher now.' I read the Bible and wrote sermons, and more churches wanted me to play the piano – so, I thought, Waxahatchie can go kiss my ass. I had a different style of playing and some folk accused me of playing boogie woogie in church, like it was sacrilegious. But it wasn't boogie woogie, it's just music with a beat, spiritual music, like coloured people do. I'd say to them, 'You might as well accept it 'cause some day that's how it's gonna be.'

After a lot more boogie woogie and night clubbing Jerry Lee met his next great love, Jane Mitcham. Although still legally married to Dorothy, Jerry Lee began a passionate love affair with Jane, as colourful as it was dangerous.

- I met Jane over at WNAT, the radio station in Natchez. The radio station was locked up, so we crawled in the back window, me and Cecil Harrelson did, and there was Jane and Atlanta, the person she's married to now. I said, 'Hey, you're the girl for me!'

  Atlanta said, 'That's my girl.'

  I said, 'No, she used to be your girl.' Jane and I was just young kids. What did we know? We was havin' fun. Then she became pregnant. Boy oh boy! I was still married to Dorothy. Jane's brothers arrived in town with horsewhips and guns, so I did the decent thing. I married her.

FRANKIE JEAN (sister): Jane was my favourite. She was wild and wonderful, and she was beautiful too. I'll tell you what, she wasn't one of those 'yes' people that roll over. She would hit him and bite back at him. He admired that. She didn't take any nonsense off Mr Jerry Lee at all.

In the mid-fifties there was a musical fusion happening on various levels which was to change forever the face of popular culture. Gospel, blues, rhythm and blues (jump blues), and rockabilly led to the phenomenon which was to be called rock 'n' roll. Fats Domino, Muddy Waters,

Billy Ward and the Dominoes, Ray Charles, Louis Jordan, Amos Millburn, Roy Brown, Bill Haley – these artistes were all permeating Jerry Lee's soul. Above all there was a young man cast in a similar mould to Jerry Lee – he lost a brother, was close to his Momma, and was a member of the Pentecostal Brethren – Elvis Presley. Between trying to settle down to married life and playing at clubs, Jerry Lee was greatly excited by Elvis.

FRANKIE JEAN (sister): Elvis and Jerry Lee were very close friends – my brother really loved him. I went to Tupelo with Jerry Lee to see Elvis, and I was never so disappointed in my life at Elvis Presley wriggling around on that stage. I told Jerry he wasn't worth a thing. I said, 'You're not gonna do what he's doing, are you?'

He said, 'Are you crazy?' Jerry was so upset with me. He said he'd never take me anywhere again – 'You've insulted the king of rock 'n' roll.' The most precious thing Jerry had was his Elvis Presley shirt, and I tore the thing off him. All that was left was the collar. I wish I could go back and pick up all the pieces and sew them back together for Jerry. He loved that shirt almost as much as he loved Elvis Presley.

● Well, Elvis Presley – what can you say? Great singer an' everything, could wiggle his butt, but I think he must've got most of his stuff from coloured artistes really. I'm sure we all did. But I think Elvis was standing on the right corner at the right time when they needed a rock 'n' roll white good-lookin' kid. Sam Phillips picked him up off the street at 706 Union Avenue, took him in, capped his teeth, took the pimples off his face, cut *That's All Right Mama*, and said, 'Let's go, boy.' See, before that they were running around screamin' at coloured artistes and people didn't like that. They had to have a white kid so they used Elvis Presley.

Elvis was a strange dude, the boy just didn't have nothin' to say. He just would not stand up to his manager, Tom Parker. Parker told him when to go to the bathroom. They gave him that suite there in Las Vegas for months at a time an' he'd never leave it. He'd go from the showroom back up there, an' sometimes he'd sail notes out of the top window to communicate with people. If that won't kill you, nothin' will. You gotta talk to folks, y'know. We met over the years an' then we went our own ways.

He let them destroy the greatest musical career in history. He was scared to death of Tom Parker. He let a bunch of his cronies – they called them the Memphis Mafia – run his life, or should I say ruin his life. What a jerk! Elvis was a monkey in a cage and they were like organ-grinders and whenever he started fussin' and threatenin' to stop, they cranked the organ, started shooting little balls of Demerol into his veins. That's why they called him King Kong, the world's biggest trained monkey. I loved Elvis. He was my friend, but I'm still here and he ain't – and that makes me the king of rock 'n' roll.

CHAPTER 3

Whole Lotta Shakin'

In 1953 aged 18 with two wives and a baby on the way, Jerry Lee was still living with his parents at Black River. He felt confused about his future. Should he spread the word of the Lord, or should he exploit the God-given talent he knew would bring him fame and fortune?

Working at the Wagon Wheel, Jerry had not only to perform on drums and piano, he had to play whatever songs the people desired, ranging from blues to ragtime, Glenn Miller to Hoagy Carmichael, Artie Shaw to Bing Crosby. The band relied on tips, so the more songs they knew the more they made. Jerry Lee needed money.

Jimmy Lee, his preacher cousin, implored him to follow the Lord, but playing at church meant no money for Jerry Lee. He attempted various day jobs – working on a pipeline project (he quit after a few days), and a more successful attempt at selling sewing machines.

- I'd knock on the door and tell 'em they'd won the machine, you know. I said 'Would you sign right here and pay us $10 excise tax', and they'd sign. I had 50 of these sewing machines and I sold them all in one day. The poor people, they'd sign and I knew they weren't gonna get no hard from it, as they were a crooked company anyway. I got my $25 per machine, I put the money in my pocket and went on down the road. I did some crazy things back then.

I broke into a store and stole a gun in St Frances-
ville, Louisiana. We saw this gun and it was just
amazing. I don't even know what it was. It was just a
big old pistol, and I needed that pistol like I needed a
hole in the head. The Sheriff put me in jail for three
days. My folks practically had a heart attack. The
worst jail I ever saw in my whole life. Kids did things
like that – I kinda thought I was Jesse James, but I
soon found out I wasn't. The judge gave me a sus-
pended sentence, on probation. My folks were told
I'd get three years in Angola [state penitentiary],
and we waited for quite a while before the judge said
he was gonna put me on probation. I was really,
really nervous.

*Jerry Lee travelled even further afield to Nashville to
work for another piano player, the hillbilly, boogie woogie country star, Roy Hall.*

● Roy had a little club opposite The Bell hotel in Nashville, cost me 50c a night to stay there and he paid me
$10. I played piano and sang, and had all these hill-
billy artists come there to see me. Webb Pierce, Red
Foley, people like that, was sittin' there lookin' at
me. I met them all later through the years and they
swear they don't remember me. You see, they was
all drunk, they was knee walkin'. I didn't drink at the
time. I saved up enough money to buy me a 1939
Ford, a green one, I got in that mother and I took on
back home to Ferriday.

*Earlier, during the wilder days with Cecil, he attempted
to cut a record in summer 1951 in a 'make your own
record' booth – one was an untitled instrumental and the*

other Lefty Frizzel's 'Don't Stay Away/Till Love Grows Old'. These, I suppose, would be Jerry's first recordings.

● [On making his first demo records] I made a couple of records down in New Orleans. I paid for them myself, I paid for them all by myself. It was *If I Ever Needed You I Need You Now* and another one, *Please Don't Stay Away So Long, Darling*. Cecil Harrelson has that record now and he's told someone that he paid for that record – he's crazy, I paid for that record. That record belongs to me – he's got it, but it belongs to me.

ROY HALL (club-owner): Elvis Presley came to me for work. I fired him after one night. He weren't no good. But Jerry Lee, I hired him for $10 a night. He'd play that piano from one in the morning until daylight. We did a lot of duets together.

No thanks to Roy Hall's talent-spotting, Elvis Presley was now breaking through. He was heard throughout the south on KWKH Radio, a country programme called The Louisiana Hay Ride featuring great artistes such as Jerry's hero, Hank Williams, as well as Slim Whitman and a resident piano player called Floyd Cramer.

It was here at KWKH Studios, Shreveport, Louisiana, that Slim Whitman got the studio manager to roll the tapes on two songs, Hank Snow's 'It Don't Hurt Any-more' and 'If I Ever Needed You I Need You Now' a song by Joni James. Nothing happened to these at the time, but Jerry was excited to have at last cut some songs in a real studio.

● Yeah, I auditioned for Slim Whitman for a piano-player an' he looked at me and he said, 'Well, I'll tell you what son, don't call me, I'll call you!' And I told him about that many years after I got into the business, he used to come and do shows with me, you know, an' he said, 'Jerry Lee, you'll never convince me that I turned you down as a piano-player.' I said, 'Well, you did, you turned me down.' He said, 'Well I must've not been runnin' the show then.' It was the guy who was running *The Louisiana Hayride* that made Elvis Presley. Elvis worked *The Louisiana Hayride* for two years and that's where Elvis Presley made it from, Louisiana. He didn't make it in Tennessee or Mississippi, he made it from Louisiana. *The Louisiana Hayride*, he worked it for two years. That was from Shreveport and Bossier City, right across the river from Ferriday.

Jerry Lee hitch-hiked from Black River to Nashville to visit studios and music publishers. After weeks of rejection, he was finally shown some kindness by Del Wood, a star of the Grand Ol' Opry.

• I was just a kid that didn't have nothing and I was standing there and Del said 'What's wrong son?'

I said 'I would just give anything if I could get in backstage here and see some of the stars.'

And she said 'I'll take you in'. You know, nobody had ever done nothing like that for me before.

I said, 'I've been in Nashville, Tennessee for three months and I can't get anybody to pay any attention to me' . . . She took me in and introduced me to all these stars.

He visited R.C.A. Studios and played piano for them, only to be told 'Guitars are king here in music city

U.S.A.' Jerry Lee said he could play guitar, but the piano was his instrument. He was low in spirits. On the way back he wrote 'End of the Road' – 'Well the way is dark, night is long/I don't care if I never get home/I'm waitin' at the end of the road'. The long haul back down to Black River seemed endless. On his return, Jerry Lee read in a magazine about Sam and Jud Phillips and their Sun Records, the first people to record Elvis Presley. He decided he would audition for them.

FRANKIE JEAN (sister): I remember the first time Jerry went to Sun to audition, we didn't have any eggs to eat for six weeks. We gathered those eggs from the hen house every day, to sell them to get money. We got all the money together and off Daddy and Jerry went. Mother prayed the whole way and lit a candle.

● We sold 33 dozen eggs so I could go to Memphis to audition for Jack Clement who worked for Sam Phillips at the time. Jack said rock 'n' roll was finished with – Elvis had got it sewn up. I said I disagreed and set out to prove him wrong. I went back about a month later and I met Jack coming out the door. He said 'Sam Phillips heard your tapes and he wants to cut a record.'

JACK CLEMENT (record producer): Jerry Lee just walked into Sun Records one day. I was back in the control room when Sally Wilburn, who worked up front, came back and said, ' There's this guy out there who says he plays piano like Chet Atkins'.

I said, 'I'd like to hear that – send him on back.' So he came in and said he could play *Wildwood Flower* and stuff like that. So he sang me some wonderful country songs and I said, 'Hey, let me tape some of this.' It was mostly the George Jones stuff like *Seasons Of My Heart, Window Up Above* – that's where he was at. But at this time country music wasn't really happening, everybody was rockin' and rollin'. We did cut some country at Sun but it wasn't Nashville-style – mostly it was rock 'n' roll. So I asked him if he did any rock 'n' roll. He told me no but he would go back home and work something up. So he left and I had that tape of him. Later, Sam came in and I played it for him. He loved it and asked where the guy on the tape was. I told him he was back down in Louisiana, and Sam said, 'Why didn't you sign him up?' Actually, we didn't really sign anybody up, we'd just make some tapes until we got something we liked then we'd put it out – then they'd sign up. I'd played that tape to everybody that walked in there. I loved him singing that George Jones stuff. George Jones was really the only country guy that was really happening, the rest was dead as shit, but I loved the way he sang country. Jerry Lee had written a rock 'n' roll song called *End Of The Road*. Then he played me a version of *You're The Only Star In My Blue Heaven* in 4/4 time rather than 3/4 and I loved it. That's what we cut – those songs and *Crazy Arms* which didn't have anything on it but piano – a spinnet piano, and a cymbal – that's all. It was his first release and although the song had already been a hit for six months by Ray Price, it sold around a hundred and twenty thousand.

SAM PHILLIPS (Mr Sun Records): This man Jerry Lee Lewis was determined to meet Sam Phillips and audition. That was when I was on the road a lot, some six to seven thousand miles a week. I had to record the records, get them off the press, get the matrix made, I even had to get the labels made 'cause they didn't make them all at the same place. We was a small outfit, living from hand to mouth almost. I mean you got an artiste to pay back. You just have to do the best you can – that's what I done. So Jerry had a little difficulty getting to me, but I had the good sense to open that door and let him walk through it. Jerry and me had a spiritual camaraderie right off 'cause we were both southern boys. I don't know anywhere else this could have happened. All this rhythm and blues came out of black people from the south, you know, practically all of it, so these are the ingredients I saw in Jerry Lee Lewis in abundance. There was no question in my mind at all that Jerry Lee was a person of just incredible talent and ability. I always consider myself like those old medicines, you put a little bit of wine, a little bit of whiskey, a little bit of this and that, they called it the elixir. I've always liked to consider myself a kind of elixir, 'cause I could look into these things. I could look into the soul of Jerry Lee Lewis, he knew that.

ROLAND JANES (session musician for Sun Records): I first met Jerry Lee in 1956. Sam wanted to cut some tapes with him. So Jack asked me if I would play guitar for the session. That turned into an all-day session, we put down several different songs. I got on great with Jerry Lee musically. I never heard anyone play as well as him. The closest I could compare him would be Del Wood with a little Moon Mulligan. Then again, he did it his own way, didn't sound like anyone else, especially when he plays the piano, the way he holds his head. He'd just sit down at the piano and blow me away. The great thing about Jerry is, and what a lot of people overlook, is that he plays as well with his left hand as he does with his right. With Jerry you never knew what you were gonna record or when you were gonna record it. We may be working on one song and Jerry would start another song. It was very loose. Generally most of the stuff was spontaneous. With Jerry Lee you could cut a song, let's say six times, and we may do three of 'em where he'd take all the solos, and three where I might take all the solos. I never knew what he was gonna do. I don't think he knew himself! But I always felt Jerry Lee didn't really need anybody. I think he was good enough to sell millions of records by himself. Whatever he did, we just played to complement him.

Jay Brown, Jerry Lee's first cousin and an accomplished rhythm bass guitarist, looked after Jerry Lee when he first came to Memphis.

JAY BROWN (cousin): I met Jerry when he was a child, but I never knew him until I saw him one night when he was playing drums. I went up to this club, Natchez on the Hill, and as I walked in I could hear him playing. Boy, they were sounding good. Jerry was playing drums, this blind man was playing piano and some other guy was playing guitar. I went up and introduced myself, 'Jerry, I'm your cousin from Memphis, I been hearing a lot about you.' We were just knocking around for several months before we did any recording. After I got the electric bass guitar I started playing behind Jerry's piano. I guess I was starting to take the place of the drums, we had no drums when we were playing at home.

JIMMY VAN EATON (session musician): Most artistes who came to the Sun studio had their own band. Jerry Lee didn't, he only had his cousin, Jay Brown on bass. We were playin' gigs with Bill Lee Riley at the time. I came down the morning that Jerry did *Crazy Arms* and happened to become part of it. It was very spontaneous and I think a rare combination of Jerry Lee, Roland and myself. You could go in the studio with better singers and better arrangers, but with the combination of Jerry Lee, Roland, J. W. and myself, it seemed like every time we played, something came out of it. You couldn't over-dub then, you either got it or you didn't. They only had one quarter-inch tape. Sam Phillips was sometimes the engineer, but most of the time it was Jack Clement. They encouraged you to do your own thing because that's probably better than they could suggest anyway. I started out with Jerry Lee, and woulda liked to have stayed with Jerry but he's not the easiest guy in the world to go on the road with.

Sun Records was to become the most important indepen-dent label in the history of recording. At first Sam Phillips and brother Jud concentrated on blues, rhythm & blues, then country and pop, but it was as a vehicle for rock 'n' roll music that it had its biggest impact. The first artistes on Sun included Rosco Gordon, and Howlin' Wolf, idol of the Rolling Stones.

The jewels in the Sun crown really started to shine in the mid fifties when Sam, with his genius for star and song spotting, collected artistes such as Carl Perkins, Johnny Cash, Warren Smith, Billy Lee Riley, Carl Mann, Charlie Rich, Roy Orbison and, greatest of all, Elvis Presley. At the time of Jerry Lee's arrival in Mem-phis, Elvis had just left Sun – Sam Phillips 'sold' him for thirty-five thousand dollars – for a major recording contract with R.C.A.

BARBARA PITMAN (Sun recording artist): Jerry Lee tried to get a job at the Cotton Club when he first came to Memphis. He was booed off the stage. But it was incredible how he improved so quickly. I always knew he was going to be a star, and I knew he'd screw up, too. Let's face it, you went to Sun Records if you went anywhere, 'cause it was the only recording studio in Memphis at that time. Sam was probably responsible for launching Carl Perkins and Elvis. Jack Clement really formed Johnny Cash's style and he also deserves a lot of the credit for Jerry Lee. Sam didn't even want Jerry Lee. At the very beginning Sam said, 'I've just had Elvis, I don't want another one.' So Jack went over to a little club in Marion, Arkansas, and recorded *Crazy Arms* in there and brought it back to put it out behind Sam's back.

SAM PHILLIPS (Mr Sun Records): I had grown up listening to the Grand Ol' Opry on the radio and I'm usually not too excited about things unless I hear something that is, well, unique. As soon as I heard Jerry Lee's audition tape I said, 'Who *is* this cat?', because it was all there in abundance – as spontaneous as anything I had ever listened to. I didn't care how raw it was. I didn't give a damn how unpolished it was, in fact I kinda liked that. I thought of myself as a jeweller, so the rougher it was the more it intrigued me. But to hear that core, that soul, that heart and that freedom flowing around . . . that's the way I listened to people and knew they was special.

I mean there was a certain awe and respect these people had for me and there was a certain awe and respect that I had for these unproven people as performing artistes. When Jerry Lee and me went out to do a session, you better believe that we could read each other. One way or the other when you heard Jerry

Lee Lewis you knew who it was, even if you only heard
him the one time.

We released *Crazy Arms* in December 1956 and it became a huge regional hit, even though it had already
been a big hit for Ray Price earlier in 1956.

CHUCK SEALS: I co-wrote *Crazy Arms* in '54 with
Ralph Mooney [steel guitar player for Waylon Jen-
nings]. When Jerry Lee recorded it I was tickled to
death. There have been some three hundred and fifty
artistes record *Crazy Arms*. I've paid for a few homes
with that song!

*'Crazy Arms' was billed as 'Jerry Lee Lewis and his
Pumping Piano', a term he picked up while he played
with Roy Hall in Nashville. It was a song Jerry Lee
played spontaneously, with stylish electric guitar riffs à
la Roland Janes and the refreshing imaginative frills of
Jimmy Van Eaton's improvised drum playing. Jimmy
Van Eaton must rate as the first great rock 'n' roll drummer. Both he and Roland Janes were session musicians
for Sam Phillips, and played in Billy Lee Riley's rock 'n'
roll band, The Little Green Men. Jerry Lee would spend
the next few months in exactly the same role. He was a
touring piano player with Billy Lee Riley, then played
on session for Riley, notably on Flyin' Saucers Rock 'n'
Roll. Then Sam Phillips had Jerry work as a session
man with Carl Perkins, and also with Johnny Cash and
Warren Smith. Jerry Lee enhanced such Carl Perkins
tracks as 'Put Your Cat Clothes On' and the classic
'Matchbox' (later to influence the Beatles).*

- I never played piano for nobody but Carl Perkins
  and it was *True Love*, that was it. That's the only
  record I played on. They say that I played on Billy

Lee Riley's *Flyin' Saucers*, and three Carl Perkins records. But I only played on one of 'em. I done *Matchbox* myself. I never played on his record of *Matchbox*. Sam asked me whether I'd do that. He needed a little bit of background and afterwards he speeded it up and made Carl's voice sound a little different. Carl got upset about it.

It was at one of these sessions that the historic 'Million Dollar Quartet' recording took place on 4 December 1956. The story went that Elvis Presley had returned to Sun Records to collect a cheque and he bumped into Johnny Cash, Carl Perkins and Jerry Lee Lewis. They all gathered around the studio piano and had a sing-song. It was not until the late seventies, and confirmation of the existence of the tapes, that anyone believed this chance meeting had taken place, let alone been committed to tape.

CARL PERKINS (interviewed in 1977): We were in the studio to cut *Matchbox* and *Your True Love*. Elvis had been out on the road and he came back to visit us at Sun Records while I was cutting *Matchbox*. Jerry Lee was playing on that session – this was before Jerry had had any sort of hit record. As a matter of fact, this was the first time I'd met Jerry, and when we got to the studio we had no intention of adding piano to our sound, but this blond-haired kid was doing things on the piano that I didn't believe could be done. So Sam [Phillips] and I talked it over and we used Jerry on both *Matchbox* and *Your True Love*. Johnny Cash had dropped by the studio too but he'd gone before the session ended. Elvis, Jerry and me started doing some old gospel things – just relaxing and having a good time. There is about an hour and twenty minutes of it. I've heard it and I have the tapes in my possession, but they're held up in court at the moment because I feel the tapes belong to me. I paid for that session. It will come out eventually – the records are already pressed up, thousands of them are in the warehouse right now ready to come out. The main reason I stepped in was because Shelby Singleton, the man who bought Sun Records, was thinking of taking the tapes into the studio and bringing Nashville musicians in to make them sound up to date. So I called up R.C.A. Victor's people who told me we had to stop him. I was just concerned that they were going to put Nashville pickers on and ruin its originality. So as a result, we got into a court hearing. My lawyer said, 'Carl, those tapes belong to you if you can prove that you paid for that session'.

- This was the first time I met Elvis. Carl Perkins had a recording session that day. I just dropped by and Sam says, would you mind hanging around a little 'til Elvis gets here? He drove up in a big white Lincoln and he hugged my neck as nice as could be. Me and Elvis we just took over. We started to sing, we went from piano to guitar to piano. He was tryin' to sing like Hank Snow. Johnny Cash did try to sing on it, Carl tried to, they tried to join in but every time they'd try to take over, me and Elvis we'd take over, that was it. I could see what was goin' on – Sam Phillips plotted that whole day. If R.C.A. had known what Elvis was doin', they'd have had a heart attack. [Elvis was under contract to R.C.A., Victor at the time.]

JACK CLEMENT (Sun Records producer): Carl Perkins had invited Johnny Cash to his session and then

Elvis and Jerry Lee just happened to show up at the same time. Anyhow, they were all talking about blue-grass and this and that. Elvis sat at the piano, Carl had his guitar, Johnny Cash stayed for an hour, but then he left to go Christmas shopping with his wife, before the session started in earnest. At first Jerry Lee sang along with the group, which was like a barber shop quartet, singing a mixture of gospel, country, pop and rock 'n' roll, stuff like *There'll be Peace in the Valley, Down by the Riverside, Don't Forbid Me, Brown-Eyed Handsome Man*. Then Jerry Lee took over the piano and began to dominate the session. Among the other songs they played were *Paralysed, When the Saints, End of the Road*, and Jerry's Boogie. I was the one who thought somebody ought to put a tape on and record all that stuff. So I went to the control room and put on a monotape which would run for thirty minutes, and every thirty minutes I would put on another roll. We ended up with about two or three hours of stuff.

The Million Dollar Quartet first emerged in bootleg form from Miami, Florida. The records were distributed in truckloads by Richard Minor, a well known boot-legger with Mafia connections. The first completely legitimate release was by R.C.A. records in 1991.

• I could go and see Elvis, or he'd come and see me, and he'd say 'Come on Jerry, play the piano, just play a couple of songs', and he'd get me down at that piano and he wouldn't let me get up. He begged me to keep playing. He loved it. He said 'You've got more talent in your little finger than I've got in my whole body'. He said that to Sam Phillips too – he recognised that, he knew it. The first time I heard an Elvis Presley record I was living in Louisiana. He was singing *Blue Moon of Kentucky*, and I thought, 'I don't know who this dude is, but somebody done opened the door.' He was something else.

We had some good times together. I went to a party at Jack Clement's house with Elvis and we rode our motorcycles down the street. Buck naked. And this policeman on a horse sees us. It was three o'clock in the morning. He never caught us. If anybody had seen us, they never would have bought another record!

Jerry Lee was asked to do his first tour with Carl Perkins, Johnny Cash and Roy Orbison. On the first date in Swift Current, Canada, Cash recalls Jerry was 'real quiet, just played a piano, no showing off'. Later Jerry Lee complained to Carl Perkins that his movement on stage was restricted by having to sit at the piano. Perkins suggested he try playing standing up.

• I thought I'd just stand up one time, right? Well, my foot got caught in the piano stool and it fell over, and the people just went wild. I guess it looked as if I'd kicked the stool out of the way. I've been doin' it ever since. My God, it's been costly!

To me a piano is like a lady, you have to show it who's boss! I was playing Yorktown, Virginia, one time, and the piano they'd set up for me was a big old baby grand and it didn't have too many notes workin' on it. I started playing it and I said, 'Jesus, this is ridiculous', and I got real mad and started kicking it, 'cause I'm a pretty serious person when it comes to my piano. I kicked it out of the club, down the sidewalk, and I kicked it into the ocean. I swear to God this is true! I think they set me up with this piano as a joke but the joke was on them when the thing sunk in the ocean. The audience followed me along the dock. I said, 'If it don't float then Jaws done got it!'

Sam Phillips was fully aware of Jerry Lee's talent and asked Jack Clement to write a song for him. Jack found inspiration while paying tribute to mother nature in the toilet. 'If you see a turd in your toilet bowl/Baby it'll be me and I'll be lookin' at you.' He converted this to the rock 'n' roll song 'If you see a lump in your sugar bowl/ It'll be me and I'll be looking at you.' It was at this session that he wanted Jerry Lee to record this as his next release. At the end of the session, urged on by Jimmy Van Eaton and Jay Brown, Jerry burst into 'Whole Lotta Shakin' Goin' On'.

It was the relaxed atmosphere at Sun that captured Jerry Lee's spontaneity. Another studio would have laid down strict routine and musical arrangement.

I said come on over, Baby, we got chicken in the barn,

Come on over, Mamma, really got the bull by the horn.

We ain't fakin', whole lot of shakin' goin' on.

Jerry Lee and Jay were excited about 'Shakin'', but Sam felt that the song was risqué. Elvis Presley was already causing a commotion, and the squeaky clean image of American society projected by the media was being undermined by movies like Rebel Without a Cause and The Wild One in which Marlon Brando is asked 'What are you rebelling against?' 'What ya got?' comes the reply.

Rock 'n' roll represented mobility, sex, self-expression, love, comfort, no longer some unattainable dream but freely available to all now.

The establishment, the church, pillars of society poured scorn on rock 'n' roll, but their contempt was under-scored with fear. Elvis was wild but a mere pussy-cat compared to Jerry Lee.

J. W. BROWN (cousin): When Sam first heard *Whole Lotta Shakin'* he said 'It sounds pretty good but it ain't no A-side.'

He wanted *It'll be me* on the A-Side and he said 'Just to show you you don't know what your talkin' about I'm gonna put that *Whole Lotta Shakin'* on the B-side.' *It'll be me* never got played the first time they heard *Whole Lotta Shakin'*. I still think it's the greatest sound I've heard come out of the little Sun Studio.

'Whole Lotta Shakin' Goin' On' was first recorded by Big Maybelle, in March 1955, and it was also recorded by the Commadores in Nashville in December 1955. When first copyrighted on Village Music it was called 'A Whole Lot o' Ruckus' on the first version by Big Maybelle with Dave Williams, a black rhythm and blues singer, credited as writer. However, it is Roy Hall who claimed to have written the song while on a fishing trip with his friend Dave 'Curly' Williams.

CURLY WILLIAMS: We was down at Pahokee, Florida, out at Lake Okeechobee. We was drunk writin' songs. This guy would ring a bell on the other side of the island to get us to come to dinner. I said 'What's goin' on?' The coloured boy shouted 'We got twenty-one drums, we got an old basshorn and they even keeps time on a ding-dong'. These were the original opening lines, which Jerry Lee ignored when cutting his version.

• That's the mother-humper of them all! I wrote

Whole Lotta Shakin'. I re-wrote the whole song. They oughta give me credit for writin' the thing. I worked for Roy Hall; he recorded the song but he got it from me. I picked it up from Johnny Littlejohn at the Wagon Wheel when I was a little kid in Natchez. When I came out with the record and it sold millions of copies, *everybody* claimed that they wrote it.

It was Jud Phillips from Sun Records who saw the commercial potential of 'Whole Lotta Shakin'', ignoring the fact that many radio and T.V. stations across the country had banned it on the grounds of its raunchy lyrics. He proposed taking 20-year-old Jerry Lee to New York to get him and the song on network television.

JUD PHILLIPS: When I saw the action in Jerry and realised it was not a gimmick, I went to him and said I would like to take him to New York. Ed Sullivan turned us down. So I got a hold of Henry Frankel, talent co-ordinator for NBC, and I got him to get a hold of Jules Green, who was Steve Allen's manager. Henry set up a meeting and Jules said, 'We'll give him fifteen minutes and see what he's got'. He wasn't too impressed when I told him *Whole Lotta Shakin'* had only sold thirty thousand copies. So I said, 'I brought my product with me, he's leaning up against the wall over there.' Jerry was just as unconcerned as he could be, you know. Then he went over and sat down and started playing, *Whole Lotta Shakin'*. Jules still had his feet up on his desk, showing no interest at all. When Jerry cut loose on *Whole Lotta Shakin'*, he and Henry both got up, went around behind the piano. Then Jules said 'I'll give you five hundred dollars right now if you take him back to the room and let nobody see him 'til nine

o'clock in the morning, when Steve [Allen] gets in.' So
the next morning Steve came in and he dug it. I told
him, 'All I'm asking is give this man three minutes of
T.V. exposure and any audience that you have at the
time he starts, you'll have them when he finishes.' So
they finally decided to let us do this and they took an
option for two more shows.

So Jerry went out on national T.V. on 28 July 1957 on
the Steve Allen Show. He pulverized the viewing
audience with an explosive performance. All the practice, all the showmanship, all the wild sexuality erupted
on to the T.V. screen like a volcano.

STEVE ALLEN (television presenter): I love quality,
and Jerry Lee sure had it. The response was incredible,
we had him back and he blew away everyone's viewing
figures, including Ed Sullivan's. Jerry Lee was a star
from then on.

● It was the first nationwide show I'd done, my first
  break on television. Someone said 'He shouldn't
  kick the stool back and act like this', and Mr Allen
  said, 'I think it's great, kick the stool back, do what
  you want with it.' Milton Berle was sitting in the
  front row – this was during rehearsals – and he said
  'When he kicks the stool back, you take it and throw
  it to the camera, and it'll look like you're throwing it
  back at him.'

J. W. BROWN (cousin): After the Steve Allen Show
we toured everywhere. We went from Chicago to
Miami to California – you name it, we were just all
over. The media had some power then, I'll tell you.
They had banned the record, y'know. All over the

country Sam Phillips had 'em all piled up in his warehouse. They couldn't see *Whole Lotta Shakin'* 'cause it said 'Shake It, Baby, Shake It'. Sam felt the record was no good, but Steve Allen didn't even think about listenin' to it to see if it had any bad words or anything. So when he did it on the show, they just turned around and re-released the record.

It was Jud's idea to take Jerry Lee to New York. Jud was a car salesman at the time. Jud started touring with us and managing Jerry. Sam did not have the confidence in Jerry that Jud had. So when Jud broke *Whole Lotta Shakin'* Sam knew he had a winner then – this was Sun's first million seller, and it sold millions and millions. They couldn't ship 'em out fast enough.

Other Sun Records stars such as Johnny Cash, Roy Orbison and Billy Lee Riley felt that Sam Phillips was pushing Jerry's records at their expense. Billy Lee Riley was once rumoured to have gone in search of Sam Phillips for not promoting his records, brandishing a tomahawk.

Riley never managed to make the big time despite being a great singer able to accommodate rock 'n' roll, blues and country with consummate ease. A tendency to self-destruct held him back. The story is often told of how orders for his version of 'Red Hot' were cancelled by Sam so that distributors could get behind 'Great Balls of Fire' instead.

Once, in a drunken fit of vengeance he commenced a demolition job on the Sun studios equipment, pouring wine over the tape machine. Sam Phillips casually walked into the studio with a bottle, and ushered Riley into the back office where they proceeded to talk and drink until sunrise. Billy left feeling on top of the world. As it happened Sam released Jerry's and Billy's records at the same time with the result that Lewis's 'Breathless' received all the effort and attention and Riley's 'Wouldn't You Know' was still-born and struggled to sell just over three thousand copies.

CHAPTER 4

Great Balls of Fire

While his musical career was taking off, Jerry Lee's private life was crash landing. He had neglected his second wife, Jane, to the point where she felt he had deserted her. She had already left Jerry's parental home on Black River to live with her sister. In an attempt to make Jerry jealous by attracting another man, Jane had become pregnant again. Meanwhile Jerry, staying in Memphis with his cousin J. W. Brown, had fallen for his second cousin Myra Brown, aged 13.

FRANKIE JEAN (sister): Jerry had been staying with Myra's family in Memphis for about a year. Jerry was very easily enticed by women and they'd leave this 13-year-old girl in the house wearing these skimpy little pyjamas. So Jerry took up with Myra and that was it. He left Jane and his son, though Mother begged him not to. Myra hated Mother from day one. Her family made fun of us, said we were hillbillies. We didn't have any manners, didn't know how to hold our napkins. See, they're from Memphis. They treated Jerry like a king. He didn't know what they were saying about his parents behind his back.

- Myra and me, we got together in the back seat of my car. I knew she wasn't a virgin. I must be the onliest man in the world that married his 13-year-old cousin and she wasn't a virgin, can you believe that? Momma pleaded with me not to marry her. But I wanted her and I'm a stubborn mother-humper. Besides, I loved Myra.

ROLAND JANES: I understood where Jerry Lee and Myra were coming from, but I could also see how some people would react. The way I saw it, it was quite normal for that part of Louisiana. My mother married at 14. The thing about Myra that a lot of people don't realise was that she was very mature for her age, and Jerry was almost child-like in his approach to everything. He was more like an 18-year-old kid. So they were closer together than most people realise.

MYRA WILLIAMS: As a kid I was crazy about Jerry. I thought he was so cute and talented. I would bring friends home from school and have him play the piano for them. I'd brag and say, 'This is my cousin . . . he and my Daddy have a band together and someday they're going to be famous'. They worked little clubs in Arkansas, Alabama, Mississippi, anywhere they could, and still drive back home after the show, 'cause they were only making one hundred dollars, split three ways. But that was all about to change because Jerry's first record had just been released – it was going to change our lives.

He treated me nice and whenever I missed the school bus he'd take me to school. If he was going to Sun studios he'd ask if I wanted to come along, and sometimes Elvis would be there, or Carl Perkins or Roy Orbison. It was a very exciting time. I didn't know how Jerry really felt about me until one day he took a friend of his to the courthouse. Her name was Glenda Burgess, and she signed my name to a marriage licence application and Jerry brought this little piece of paper home to me. I thought it was a joke and he said, 'Myra, this is serious, I love you and I want to marry you.' I told him I was too young, that my Daddy would kill him. But the more I argued with him the more I realised here was a man offering me everything I had ever wanted. I had no aspirations of college or a career. I wanted a husband, a home and a baby in a high chair. But no-one that age is ready to make a decision like that. It's like pulling fruit from the tree before it's ripe. However, with the clear, cunning logic of a child I made a decision I have had to defend and explain from that day to this. We all expected the Russians to destroy the world with the atomic bomb, so I took my chance on Jerry.

My parents were as surprised as I was. When my Daddy found out Jerry and I were married he loaded his gun and went out looking for his new son-in-law. Jerry had taken the first plane out of Memphis. When Daddy couldn't find him he went to the district attorney's office. The D.A. said, 'No, don't shoot him Mr Brown, let's put him in jail.' But when Daddy realised Jerry might go to jail for 20 years, he came home and did the next best thing. He gave his daughter a whippin'.

For a while Myra and Jerry Lee were deliriously happy, like two kids in a sandpit, despite the open hostility of the Lewis women who insisted that Myra had lured their precious Jerry away from Jane.

MYRA WILLIAMS: They were jealous of me. They hated me, and what's worse, Jerry didn't do anything to stop them. He didn't realise his loyalty should have been to me. We bought a house and I learned to cook.

Jerry was about to start making big money, so we had no problems. We spent all our time together. We ate chocolate cake for breakfast, lunch and supper, 'cause that's the only thing I could cook. Life with Jerry was full of playfulness, but not everything was fun. He wanted me all for himself. He wouldn't let me cut my hair or wear make-up, nothing to make me look the least bit attractive. I had gone from being a cute, perky teenager to a well-scrubbed, dowdy housewife, and my self-esteem plummeted. If I saw Priscilla [Presley] coming, I would run a mile. She was so beautiful and so well made-up that my pride wouldn't allow me to be in the same room as her. It's a pity – she and I could have been friends. We had so much in common. Both living with the same pain.

ROLAND JANES: We had a lot of fun on the road. There would always be four or five people in the car, long trips, never less than 150 miles and some nights several hundred miles. To keep from getting on each others' nerves, we developed this little game. We would sit there and puff cigars and blow smoke in each others' faces with the window rolled up. The first one who could not stand it any longer, and went to the window for air, lost. Anybody in the car could call on anybody else in the car to smile. If you didn't smile, it cost you a buck. You had to put a buck in a box. We had a lot of silly things like that. Each one of us carried a weapon. At any time a fight could erupt. When I say weapon, my weapon was a bottle of black shoe polish. Jerry had a couple of cans of shaving cream spray. One time, at a service station, we were all shooting this stuff at each other, the guy at the station called the cops. Jerry is the greatest put-on artist in the world. He would put people on to the extent they'd get mad, and they'd never know he was just putting them on. When he would go for gas they used to kid Jerry about his long blond hair, call him 'Blondie'. Something about Jerry that a lot of people don't realise is that he will punch you in the nose. He's a tough guy. Now he didn't go up picking on people but he would defend himself in a second. He did not back off from anybody.

The success of 'Whole Lotta Shakin'' meant the offers came rolling in from all parts of the U.S.A. It also meant that Jerry Lee had to go back in the studio to cut a follow-up to 'Whole Lotta Shakin'' because of the tremendous demand.

• I can cut it anywhere, even in an old barn. Just gimme a decent piano, a good engineer and a microphone and I'll get the sound. *Whole Lotta Shakin'* was like a country song with a good tune, but I put the beat to it and rocked it and put the real feel to it. Steve Allen told the world 'Jerry Lee Lewis plays the piano with more feeling than anyone I've ever heard'. But when you record a session in Memphis it's a completely different sound, low down and bluesy. I don't like over-dubbing, I don't dig it at all. You just don't get the same feel, the soul you can put in it, that you can get from musicians live at the time. If you're makin' love to a woman, you don't over-dub it, you gotta do it right there and then.

The man who coined the phrase 'rock 'n' roll' in 1952 was the D.J. Alan Freed, who prided himself on discovering new talent – of which there was a plentiful supply throughout the 1950s. Freed was to help Lewis not only by playing his records, but also by featuring him in his touring shows.

- Without Alan Freed back in those days you had
  nothin'. I mean you could have had Dick Clark,
  that's great, but if you didn't have Alan Freed you
  were pissing into the wind. Alan Freed was the man
  who made it happen. He'd say to me, 'Y'know, all
  I'm trying to do is what is right by you, Jerry Lee.
  I've introduced Chuck Berry, Buddy Holly, The
  Drifters, Jerry Lee Lewis. I think rock 'n' roll is the
  right way to do it.'

  Looking back, I didn't know how to deal with success. I didn't know what was going on. I never was
  the smartest person in the world. I just played my
  piano and sang my songs and left the business to
  people like Sam and Jud Phillips and Alan Freed.
  Brainy people. Without the disc jockeys, people like
  me couldn't have made it.

  Success for me started with *Crazy Arms*, my first
  record. *Whole Lotta Shakin'* was my second record,
  and it was banned for eight months. No one would
  have any part of it. Then we got it on the Steve Allen
  Show, and it broke nationwide.

*By 1958 the moral protectors of America started to smear
rock 'n' roll. D.J.s were seen to smash rock 'n' roll
records on T.V., shouting 'Rock 'n' roll has got to go'.
Preachers condemned it as a corruption that would lead
to black men dancing with white women. One D.J. in
Boston, Joe Smith, was accused of spreading venereal
disease by playing Elvis Presley records. Alan Freed was
fearless about the music he loved, secure in the knowledge that the public flocked to see his rock 'n' roll shows
all over the U.S.*

*In May 1958 Alan Freed was advised not to bring his
rock 'n' roll show to Boston, Massachusetts, by the
Archdiocese of that Catholic city. FBI memoranda since*

*released show that he was going to be jailed if he did so.
Two things contributed to the dramatic events that were
to occur at Boston – the establishment swing against rock
'n' roll, and the rivalry between Jerry Lee Lewis and
Chuck Berry that built up during a Freed tour of Ohio.*

● Chuck always wanted to close the show, even though
  I had star billing. He was warming up the audience
  for me to go on, and he was gonna close it. So I took
  me a coke bottle and the audience thought it was
  water, but it was gasoline. I sprayed it across the
  piano, took a match and Whoosh! 'O.K. Chuck, it's
  your turn!' But he just laughed. The audience went
  crazy, loved it.

  My Momma thought Chuck Berry was the king of
  rock 'n' roll. I said 'What about me Momma?' She
  said 'I'm not putting you in the same league – Chuck
  Berry is Chuck Berry!'

*But the trouble really started when Elmo Lewis took ex-
ception to seeing Chuck Berry with a white girl. Elmo
insisted on being on stage during the Boston show, and
at one point he pulled a gun on Chuck Berry. Meanwhile
Berry was holding a knife at Jerry Lee's neck. The police
were called and formed a barricade. Alan Freed, the presenter, pleaded with the police to let the show go on.
Then Freed appealed to the crowd. 'We're not going to
let them get away with this!' The crowd roared their support, whereupon Freed was arrested for inciting a riot,
and spent the next three days in jail. The tour was cancelled, and Freed was dropped by the rock 'n' roll radio
station, WINS.*

● Chuck and my Daddy kept mumbling and looking
  for a fight. I don't know exactly what was said, but

he run after Chuck for two or three blocks, and me and Alan Freed were running behind them. And Daddy was saying, 'You know what we do with cats like you down in Ferriday. We chop the heads off them and throw it in a boot hole.' It got blown out of proportion, but I believe he would have done it if he'd caught him. We came downstairs next morning and there sat Chuck and Daddy having breakfast, no problem at all. I know Chuck pretty well now, but it took me years to know him. He's more sharp than a lot of people think he is. It's pretty hard to pin Chuck down. He was cheated out of a lot of money, but he's come out of it pretty good. Chuck is the greatest rock 'n' roll songwriter that's ever been – like Hank Williams was in the country field of music.

In August 1957, shortly after the Steve Allen Show, Jerry Lee got his first movie offer – to appear in a projected film called Jamboree. Fats Domino, Charlie Gracie, Jimmy Bowen and Buddy Knox had already been signed up but Jerry Lee, the new sensation, got top billing. These movies were essentially to promote music sales and to give the fans a chance to see their favourite rock 'n' roll idols. Unlike the big productions of the era, The Ten Commandments and The Robe for example, which had a cast of thousands and took years to make, rock 'n' roll movies were done quickly and on a shoestring budget. The story lines were often moronic and instantly forgettable, but the fans were usually oblivious to anything but the music.

The chosen track for Jerry Lee's movie was to be 'Great Balls of Fire', the song offered to Jerry Lee via Sam Phillips after Otis Blackwell saw Jerry Lee on the Steve Allen Show. Otis had already written 'All Shook Up' and 'Don't Be Cruel' for Elvis Presley. He got the title 'Great Balls of Fire' from Jack Hammer, a New York writer, in return for a fifty per cent share of the composer rights. If Jerry Lee was never to record again, these two classic rock 'n' roll numbers – 'Whole Lotta Shakin' Goin' On' and 'Great Balls of Fire', both of which went gold – had already assured him a place in the rock 'n' roll hall of fame.

SAM PHILLIPS (Mr Sun Records): You just listen to *Great Balls of Fire*! The punctuation on that thing, and the interpretation of every word and every syllable in each word. You can re-cut tracks like *Great Balls of Fire* and *Whole Lotta Shakin'* with big digital sounds and all that shit, but that won't get it. Just go back to the original and listen to the spontaneity. How are you going to improve on perfection? It is just a classic.

If you can't get the spontaneity out of a person, they can sing like a mocking bird and it ain't worth a crap to me. I want to get the individuality of that man's soul or I haven't done my job, period. Jerry Lee was, like me, a very religious person in his own way. I don't care what he does, he has that spiritual and religious essence about him.

GEORGE KLEIN (close friend of Elvis and well known Memphis D.J.): Elvis invited Jerry Lee to Graceland when he got back from making *Love Me Tender* In Hollywood. We all sat around as Jerry played the piano and sang. Elvis asked Jerry to play one song in particular, *Come What May*, over and over. You could see Elvis loved Jerry Lee, and so did we. After Jerry Lee had gone, we were all talkin' about him. Elvis got quite jealous, ya'know, and said 'I don't know why you don't work for Jerry Lee if he's so great.'

- Elvis was a good person. People didn't know Elvis like I knew him. He said 'Jerry Lee, play it one more'. I said 'Elvis, it's 5 o'clock in the morning'. He said, 'Do that song, *I am yours, you are mine/Come what may*.' He was home from Hollywood after his first movie. You can tell he wasn't into it at all. He done pretty good on that first movie, *Love Me Tender*. He asked me what I thought of his movie. I said 'Well, Elvis, I'll tell you. You ain't no Clark Gable. I think that's all I've got to say. When you can beat Clark Gable, I'll let you know, but until you do that, stick to rock 'n' roll.'

  Elvis Presley battled to be number one and he didn't want anyone to beat him. He knew Jerry Lee Lewis was dangerous when he heard *Mean Woman Blues*. He was number three with *Mean Woman Blues* and I came out with my version on an EP – two records on each side – and hit number one. I was coming up to Sun Records one day and I saw this Cadillac coming right up to me, right up to my bumper, and it was Elvis. He jumped right out of the car and said, 'I'm gonna sue you for *Mean Woman Blues*!' It scared me at first, I thought he was serious. Then he started laughing. He was kidding!

  I didn't pay any attention to beating anybody, beating Elvis Presley. I never even thought about that. I was just trying to make it. Elvis Presley *was* rock 'n' roll to me. I mean, how was you going to beat Elvis Presley? I never even thought about that. I worshipped him.

Fame and acclaim continued to gather momentum. Sam Phillips considered Jerry Lee 'a more talented and capable performer than Elvis'. Jerry Lee received his

*biggest pay cheque yet from Sam Phillips – forty thou-
sand dollars for 'Whole Lotta Shakin''. Phillips told
Jerry Lee he would soon be making ten thousand dollars
a night, more money than he'd ever dreamed of.*

- It was a great feeling. I could see a nice Cadillac in a
  car window somewhere and go in and buy me one –
  that was really something.

  When Mr Phillips gave me my first royalty check
  for *Whole Lotta Shakin'*, he put on an extra thousand dollars. There was money coming in from every
  direction, y'know, and I'd never had no money
  before. I really didn't know what to do with that
  much money. I went on home and bought my kinfolk
  anything they wanted. It was great. They didn't want
  for nothing. Momma and Daddy were really proud
  of me. They were the greatest parents anyone could
  ever hope to have.

  When you become rich or famous real quick, it's
  kind of hard for people to relate to you. I was just
  Jerry Lee Lewis, same as I was before I left Ferriday,
  Louisiana, before I ever put a record out. I thought
  the same way, felt the same way. I went home to
  Ferriday and I saw Mack Stone, Doc's brother, coming from town, walking back home. I had me a new
  Eldorado Cadillac. I said 'Hey, Mack, let me give
  you a ride' and he looked at me and just kept walking. So I repeated the offer and he came over and
  said 'You sure?' He said he didn't understand how a
  person as big as I was has any business to stop and
  pick someone like him up.

  Jimmy Lee came over and asked me if I would get
  him a car. He didn't have a car. I took him over to
  Natchez to buy him a new one. I took him to the
  Ford place but Jimmy said he didn't want no Ford,

so I got him a new Oldsmobile. He was more than happy with it.

LINDA GAIL (sister): As soon as Jerry became famous we all moved out of Black River straight back to Ferriday. Jerry bought mother everything she wanted. He was so generous, always has been with money. The people in Ferriday did not know how to take it – they were really jealous. People thought we were strange because we was kind of like the Beverly Hillbillies. Of course the whole family was really proud of Jerry. It was thrilling for us, we never had anything financially then all of a sudden Jerry Lee is a very wealthy young man and we had everything we wanted. New homes, new cars, new clothes – Jerry shared everything with us.

Although he enjoyed the material trappings of his meteoric success, Jerry Lee began to have nagging doubts about the morality of rock 'n' roll, especially when it came to 'Great Balls of Fire', which reached No. 1 in 1958. It was considered by many to be sexually provocative, not to say blatantly immoral.

• God gave me my talent. I don't question God. I never have. I never will. I wasn't put here to question God. I don't think I've done no wrong. They said *Great Balls of Fire* was pure sex, well it is, but it's sex in my way, and sex in my way is not dirty. It's pure. It's what I feel. Sex between a man and his wife whom God has joined together is a beautiful thing. They said *Whole Lotta Shakin'* was risqué. I did them songs with my heart. It's the only way I know. I don't think God will judge me harshly. I've brought comfort to a lot of folks. Christians and atheists, they all love *Whole Lotta Shakin'*. Vivien Leigh said *Great balls of fire* four or five times in *Gone With The Wind*. I never accepted that *Great Balls of Fire* was a vulgar record. I finally had it explained to me – *Kiss me baby/Feels good* – but to me, it was still just innocent fun. Now in *Whole Lotta Shakin'* – *Stand it in one little spot/Wiggle it around just a little bit* – that's sexy, that's why they banned it.

On the touring rock 'n' roll shows in the mid-fifties, Jerry Lee met many of the greats of rock 'n' roll and became a friend to them.

● Buddy Holly was one of the most genuine people I knew. He could have made it a lot bigger than what he made it without them two dudes with him, Joe B. and Jerry Alison. I'm going back to 1957 now, and they was all arguing about who's going to close the show and I never said nothin'. I ended up closing the show, but Buddy Holly ended up nearly taking it all away from me – he got like four encores. Buddy Holly was one of my best friends. He didn't curse, he didn't smoke, he didn't drink, he didn't fool around with girls. I said 'What *do* you do?' When he got married, he called me and said, 'Jerry Lee I'm fixing to get married, what do you think about it?' And I said, 'Do you love her?' and he said, 'Yeah, I think I really love that girl', so I said, 'If you've fallen in love with her, you marry her'. A few weeks after that he was dead.

Jim Reeves was a great friend of mine, too, we had some good times together. You had to get to know Gentleman Jim – he was a hard person to get to know. He'd just sit in the corner in a chair and not say anything. But if you got to know him like I got to know him . . . We done a record hop together one night and got through by about 9 o'clock at night, and we went on to every club in the town and sang all night and we had a ball! It wasn't too long after that he was dead, got killed in an airplane crash. It took 'em three days to find the plane, and it was only three or four blocks from the airport. Weird isn't it?

I played with Patsy Cline maybe on the night before she died. She was one of my best friends. I told her she should give up flying on a plane and she didn't really want to get on it too much, but obviously they all got on it. Hawk Shaw Hawkins got on it, Lloyd Cowboy Copas, Randy Hughes, he was on that plane. Patsy Cline had a great sense of humour, she was a knockout. In Little Rock, Arkansas, she whipped me off to the toilets, shoved me in a stall, locked it and told me the craziest joke you ever heard in your life. It was the first time I'd ever met her and she just cracked up laughing. She'd do her show, go round and sit out front for me, when I was doin' mine.

Jackie Wilson was a gentleman. I never heard anybody say a bad thing about Jackie Wilson – and never heard him say a bad thing about nobody. He sure could dance and sure could sing, one of the greatest I've ever seen. He would slide across the floor like a bullet and spin so fast you couldn't hardly see him. James Brown is good but Jackie could outdo him. I done a Jackie Wilson tour one time, strictly for the south. Strictly to a coloured audience and ain't nobody else would have done that but me. Jackie was closing the show and before the tour was over, I was closing the show – to his audience, to his people.

You're not gonna beat people like Ray Charles – where you gonna find another Ray Charles? There's only one Ray Charles. Sam Cooke, he could sing like a mocking bird – he just opened his mouth and it rolled out. We done so many tours together, we had some good times together and there's not but one o' those people. They come along once in a lifetime, and you better get them while you can 'cause they're not going to be around forever. I mean when they're gone, you really gonna miss them. You don't miss the water till the well runs dry.

I think Little Richard is one of the greatest rock 'n' roll singers in the world, fine piano player too – he proved that in the beginning with *Long Tall Sally* and *Tutti Frutti* and all those records. Nobody's gonna beat those Little Richard records. I never had any problem with Little Richard, always worked together very good.

I still like Bo Diddley. If he ever gets outta the chord of E he might get dangerous. One of the first tours we done was down in Florida with Gene Vincent, not too long after that he had an accident on his motorcycle and hurt his leg. It would have been just as good as his other one, if he'd just stayed off that machine. A month later he tore it all to pieces again on a motorcycle, but he was back on stage with a cast on his leg. He just kept on until he ruined his leg completely. He said 'I gotta get with it'. Gene got really depressed.

Bill Haley was a very nice person, he was a gentleman. *Rock Around the Clock* was magic, still exciting today, one of the first classic rock 'n' roll records.

With the success of 'Whole Lotta Shakin'', which eventually reached the six million mark, topping the country &

*western and rhythm & blues charts simultaneously,
'Great Balls of Fire' zoomed to No. 2 on the U.S. charts
and No. 1 on the U.K. charts. It sold one million in its
first 10 days of release. The B-side, Hank Williams's
'You Win Again' also sold a million.*

*Jerry Lee worked at New York's famous Apollo, in
Harlem, a bold decision in view of his reputation as a
wild redneck.*

- It was a bet between Jud Phillips and Harry Bal-
  sheim of the William Morris Agency that I couldn't
  work the Apollo – Jud said I could. I knew there was
  a lot of coloured people in Harlem. You could feel
  the tension in the club. I introduced the band. The
  audience went serious. They lookin' at me like I was
  crazy. Then this huge thick-set guy on the front, he
  burst out laughin'. I went into *Whole Lotta Shakin'* –
  and that was it – six shows a day for nine days,
  packed out each show.

NEW YORK TIMES (review, 2 October 1957): There
is a lot of animal vigour in the Jerry Lee Lewis Trio . . .
Lewis, in the spotlight, carries the act. He has a style
similar to that of Presley, using the piano, though, to
beat on rather than a guitar. And beating on the piano
is putting it mildly. Rather he pounds, but to his credit
he never misses a note or slips the beat, which all in all
adds up to a showmanlike display. He would be wise to
cut out some of his antics, for example, that of combing
his hair after a frenetic number, and blowing his comb
free in the direction of the audience. He could be the
hillbilly he boasts that he is with good manners too.

The trio sing and play *Crazy, Mean Woman, Great
Balls of Fire* and *Whole Lotta Shakin'* to good effect.

On 3 November 1957, Oscar Davis takes on Jerry Lee's management – being well connected with Hollywood. His big buddy was Mike Todd, producer and husband to be of Elizabeth Taylor, then widely regarded as the world's most beautiful woman. Oscar brought Jerry Lee to Hollywood and introduced him to Elizabeth Taylor.

- I kept winking at her but I never got through! She only give me a smile. She and Mike Todd were to-gether at the MGM lot when we were filming *High School Confidential*. Mr Todd said, 'Jerry, would you mind escorting Liz around for a while for me, while me and Oscar go for a few drinks down-town.' You know I'm lookin' at Elizabeth Taylor. The most beautiful woman I've seen in my life!! There wasn't a flaw anywhere! She had on black shoes, black stock-ings, a black dress and – a white blouse! And I'm looking at Elizabeth Taylor. She looked at me and she said, 'What do you think about that MGM lot?' I said, 'I don't know, what do you think of it?' She said 'I think it ain't worth a shit.' That's what she said. I said 'I'm glad my Momma didn't hear you say that.' I was twenty-one and she was twenty-three and there I was trying to escort Elizabeth Taylor round. 'I ain't much of a talker, Miss Taylor', I said. And she said 'Don't worry about it.'

High School Confidential starred Russ Tamblyn, Jan Sterling, Mamie Van Doren and Jackie Coogan. Russ Tamblyn is called in to clean up a high school deeply in-volved in the three ds – drag racing, drugs and depravity. Jerry Lee zaps into the high school playground belting out 'Bopping at the High School Hop' on the back of a truck. The loose plot that followed was built around blonde bombshell Mamie Van Doren, oozing sexuality like a volcano in high heels.

Jimmy Van Eaton, Jerry Lee's drummer, was excluded from the two movies Jamboree *and* High School Confidential *after it emerged he'd been fooling around with Jerry Lee's second wife, Jane. Russ Smith, Jerry's road drummer, appeared in the two movies.*

- It really wasn't Jimmy's fault. My wife, Jane, I believe she could run a person into a ditch to make sure she went to bed with 'em. That's the way I think she was. I never held that against Jimmy at all. He thought I did, but I never did. I went after her about it, but I didn't hold it against Jimmy – he was just a kid.

Jerry Lee's next record, also written by Otis Blackwell, 'Breathless', became an instant hit. The quality of Jerry Lee's recordings at this stage was unsurpassable, with Roland Janes on guitar and the sharp rim-shots of Jimmy Van Eaton on drums, Jerry Lee's powerful vocals and his unique piano style.

Meanwhile Elvis Presley was drafted into the U.S. Army. Little Richard was called by the Lord to be a religious minister and quit rock 'n' roll after his Australian tour. Soon Jerry Lee and Ricky Nelson would be the only rivals for the title King of Rock 'n' Roll – and the younger man showed little inclination to enter into a battle with the man they called Killer.

CHAPTER 5

Scandal, Scandal, Scandal

- You're supposed to marry and settle down, I guess, raise a family and sit by the fireplace, chew tobacco and spit, watch T.V. and sit there and be an idiot. But me, I'm a rock 'n' roller, I play my piano and sing, make love to the best-looking women I can find and drink good, good whiskey.

The youth of England in 1958 was hungry for American pop culture. The cult of the teenager had arrived from the States somewhere mid-decade and awoken England's young generation from the gloom of post-war austerity. To see Bill Haley and the Comets in Rock Around the Clock, and James Dean in Rebel Without a Cause, was to realise that adolescence was more than just a matter of marking time before adulthood.

Inevitably there were middle-aged pillars of the establishment to condemn rock 'n' roll as silly and irresponsible. But that only served to enhance its appeal. To the starry-eyed English teenager of the late 50s figures like Elvis Presley and Marlon Brando were impossibly glamorous. The idea that one of these icons of the new dawn, Jerry Lee Lewis – the Killer himself – was actually coming to England was unthinkable!

But on 22 May 1958 the Louisiana Fireball arrived at Heathrow Airport for a 37-day tour, his first outside the States.

The touring entourage consisted of Jerry Lee, Myra, her father Jay Brown and her mother Lois, with her three-year-old son Rusty, Jerry's sister Frankie Jean, drummer Russ Smith and Oscar Davis.

They left New York on 21 May, making an emergency stop at Shannon Airport in Ireland because of engine trouble. After an early breakfast and a change of aircraft, they were on their way to Merrie England. As they disembarked at Heathrow, Oscar led Jerry towards the reporters, keeping the rest of the party at a distance behind. Jerry Lee breezed through with an air of total command. As Lois and Myra moved through the airport a young reporter, Paul Tanfield, asked Myra:

'Who are you, Miss?'

'Jerry's wife,' replied Myra.

Oscar spotted Myra talking to the reporter and rushed her into the waiting car.

Another reporter had asked Jerry who the girls were.

'My sister Frankie, J.W.'s wife Lois, and my 15-year-old cousin Myra,' he replied matter-of-factly.

The Britain of 1958 was a proud, conservative country which felt safe and secure through its great achievements in history: most recently, victory in World War II and domination in the world of science and invention. Penicillin, television and the jet engine all came from the U.K., which was also still proud of its empire, its image as the standard-bearer of democracy and all it had given the world. The class system was still in order and among the thinking classes the attitude still prevailed that, in Oscar Wilde's phrase, America was 'the only country to go from savagery to decadence without experiencing civilisation'.

Nevertheless, even though the BBC still dominated world broadcasting, supplying over 700 programmes worldwide in 1958, the U.S.A., through its powerful *entertainment industry, was having a major impact on British culture and indeed the whole world. Rock 'n' roll was exercising an enormous influence on the teenage population and on youth culture. The media, the politicians, the clergy and the educational system scorned it, regarding it as nothing more than a cheap gimmick – transient trivia. One award-winning press photograph showed two teddy boys (portrayed as the moronic vanguards of rock 'n' roll) standing looking at an exhibit of two stuffed gorillas; the caption read, cynically: 'Darwin's Theory' – implying that rock 'n' roll was the music of the savage and the jungle. Lord Boothby, a pillar of the establishment, condemned rock 'n' roll as silly on the famous BBC programme 'What's My Line?', and stated that the teddy boys should be made to join the army and get sent to Cairo. The British press were starved of scandal – their 'vicar runs off with tart' and even stories of queer politicians were languishing in the realms of ponderous monotony. Jerry Lee's arrival in England was to be the equivalent of Attila the Hun attending a Buckingham Palace garden party.*

The first show in Edmonton on 24 May was a big success. The fans were ecstatic and everything looked set for a successful tour.

The press, however, continued to quiz the band members and management about Myra.

'How young?' a member of the press asked Jerry.

'About 13.'

Meanwhile the American press did some research in conjunction with the U.K. press. A press conference was called at the Westbury Hotel where the party was staying. Jerry Lee had been married twice before and had not got a proper divorce from either one.

Jerry casually confessed to the press, 'I was a bigamist at the age of 16. I have not told the full truth about my

*marriages before. I have a three-year-old son called
Jerry Lee by my second wife, Jane. My second marriage
was not legal under United States law. I married
Dorothy Barton when I was 14. I didn't know what I was
doing. I had to marry Jane, her brothers were huntin' me
with hide whips. Dorothy was a good girl but I decided
to leave her after a year because I was too young for
marriage. Then I met Jane. She was as wild as the wind.
I married her one week before my divorce from
Dorothy. I didn't know. So I married her bigamously.
There it is. That's the truth. I hadn't wanted to tell it but
now it's all come out. I was a young fool. My father
should have put his foot on my neck and beaten a worm
out of me. Everybody thinks I'm a ladies' man. I'm not.
I'm a good boy and I want everyone to know that. My
wife Myra and I are very happy. I am buying her a wedding ring very soon, a diamond one, here in London.*

- I was a 21-year-old kid, and I didn't know whether I
  was comin' or goin'. We were just kids in love at the
  time. It didn't matter to me. I was getting to sell
  more records than Elvis. He had gone into the army
  and I was hitting big, but there were a lot of narrow-
  minded people who thought I was corrupting the
  youth. I'd figured out my style, I done it my way and
  I was very hard-headed.

MYRA WILLIAMS: They went crazy when they
found out I was Jerry's wife and how young I was. I
didn't realise there was such a difference in attitude between England and America. Jerry thought it would be
O.K. to say I was 15, but next day all the papers said
here he was with his child bride. Then they did some
checking and it came out that I was really 13. Then they
found out I was his second cousin and that he wasn't

legally divorced from his second wife. It was a full-blown disaster. I was this frightened, fragile little thing who happened to be his wife. We kept thinking the scandal would go away, the next day it would stop, someone else will be on the front page tomorrow, but it never stopped. It put an end to his tour and it put an end to his career for the next 10 years.

By the time we left England we wanted to go home more than they wanted us to go. We couldn't wait to get back to America, our home, where they would welcome us with open arms. But that's not the way it happened 'cause the opponents of rock 'n' roll said, 'See. We told you it was wicked, look what it does!' Preachers denounced Jerry from pulpits, they burned his records in the streets, housewives called radio stations to protest, the sponsors became nervous. Jerry was blacklisted. Jerry had been a star less than a year and now, thanks to the news media, he was a has-been. The British press was no worse than the American press, only at home we had nowhere to run. We were held up as a joke. There were lots of Myra jokes going around, 'I hear they had a double ring ceremony? Yeah, a wedding ring and a teething ring'. That sort of stuff. No one knows the struggle we had after this. Jerry went from making ten thousand dollars a night to one hundred bucks, split three ways after expenses.

- One newspaper said I'd married my 9-year-old cousin, another one said it was my 12-year-old sister. Hell, they had *me* confused who I'd married for a while! It got so ridiculous there was ten thousand people outside my hotel waiting to get a look at me. Like I was some monster. I was eating in my room and went over to open a window – this was two or three storeys up – and there was a man hanging on a rope with a camera. I raised the window, dragged him in, and said, 'Here man, get your picture.' The publicity and the crowds got so much that, in the end, my promoter said, 'Let's go home.' We came back to Idlewild [now Kennedy] Airport, and I had a bigger reception waiting for me than Clark Gable in his prime.

The 37-day tour of the U.K. had been arranged by the respected William Morris Agency. The promoter and Jerry Lee's manager, Oscar Davis, who had organised the trip, was noted in the business; he had acquired an excellent reputation through handling Hank Williams, Jerry Lee's No. 1 idol, and for introducing Col. Tom Parker to Elvis Presley. The proposed fee for the tour was $100,000 and Jerry Lee would gain a guaranteed $26,000 from it – a fortune in those days!

Oscar was a shrewd manager and he knew that Jerry was his own man. He also knew that Jerry had been told by all concerned to keep his marriage to Myra a secret.

OSCAR DAVIS (manager): They were shocked in England to see such a young girl. Myra looked about 10 at that time. We held a press conference at the West-bury Hotel. Everyone in the music press was there. I stood with Jerry and we talked to about 30 reporters. Then a couple of reporters broke away and asked me about Jerry being married three times and I said, 'No, he's kidding'. I looked Jerry in the eye and said 'Did you tell these people you've been married three times?' and he said 'Yes I have!' and went bam-bam-bam, nam-ing all the girls. I guess Jerry thought nothing over there [U.K.] would matter over here [U.S.A.], but the story soon broke all over the U.S., and we had quite a furore on our hands.

The tour was cancelled, following the fourth concert in Kilburn. The Rank Organisation who had booked Jerry for 27 one-night appearances issued a statement saying they had cancelled the contract because of 'unfavourable audience reaction and for other reasons'.

When someone in the audience yelled 'Go home, go home', Jerry Lee shouted back 'Somebody put the lid on that garbage can.' Oscar Davis, desperate to salvage something from the wreckage, called up his old partner, Tom Parker (then Elvis Presley's manager) and asked him if he had any ideas. He suggested, jokingly, that Jerry Lee should wheel a pram out on stage during the act with Myra in it. The idea was so ludicrous it fuelled speculation that Parker had deliberately tried to sabotage Jerry Lee's U.K. tour in order to safeguard Presley's position as 'King' of rock 'n' roll.

Meanwhile Davis attempted a more practical solution to the problem of shoring up Jerry Lee's plummeting credibility.

OSCAR DAVIS (manager): I thought the best thing would be to have a marriage ceremony between Jerry Lee and Myra so that the public didn't think there was something sinful about their union. I went to the U.S. Consul in London, but they wouldn't help because of all the bad publicity we'd already had. I suggested various other options to Jerry, but he is a rank individual, a rebel, you know. Even today no one can really control Jerry.

Such was the impact of the scandal that the matter was debated in the House of Commons on 25 June 1958. The following is an extract from Hansard, the parliamentary journal: –

*Sir F. Medlicott asked the Minister of Labour on what
grounds the United States singer Mr Jerry Lee Lewis was
recently given a permit to enter this country, for a six
week tour of theatres and music halls.*

*Mr Iain MacLeod: 'A permit was issued for this man
under quota arrangements which have been agreed by
my Department and the Variety and Allied Entertainment Council of Great Britain for the Employment of
Foreign Variety Artistes.'*

*Sir F. Medlicott: 'Is my right Hon. friend aware that
great offence was caused to many people by the arrival
of this man, with his 13-year-old bride, especially bear-
ing in mind the difficulty that others have in obtaining
permission to work here? Will he remember also that we
have more than enough 'rock 'n' roll' entertainers of our
own without importing them from overseas?'*

*Mr Iain MacLeod: 'This was of course a thoroughly
unpleasant case, which was ended by the cancellation of
the contract and the disappearance of the man. But at the
time the matter was before my officers it was purely a
question of a permit for employment, and his case was
treated under the ordinary arrangements which apply to
anybody.'*

TOM JONES (singer): When Jerry came to England
rock 'n' roll was just beginning and we were amazed by
his talent, his great piano playing and showmanship. I
was a big fan, but the press went over the top on this
child bride incident and it all got really vicious. He
didn't think he was doing anything wrong, and he
wasn't.

LINDA GAIL (sister): The tour had a devastating
effect on the family, especially my mother. She had
pleaded with Jerry not to take Myra to England. It

affected her health and shortened her life. Myra was not a virgin when she married Jerry. She had been raped by a next door neighbour before she met Jerry.

- Jud Phillips told me before we ever left Memphis, 'If you do this tour and introduce your wife, you're gonna blow the greatest talent down the toilet that's ever been known in the history of music.' I told him Myra was my wife and I was going to introduce her as my wife. And I did.

SHELBY SINGLETON (record producer and current owner of Sun Records): No one can control Jerry Lee, and an act that has a manager has to let the manager be the guiding force behind it. The artist or the act has to be told what to do. Jerry Lee is the type of person who refuses to take direction and he does exactly what he wants to do, when he wants to do it. It's that simple. No matter who the manager is with Jerry Lee, you can be his booking agent or you can be his adviser, but in this business you could never be his manager because he wouldn't listen to you.

- I never did have the business sense to deal with lawyers or managers. I didn't think that was right because I had to do my own thing, my own way – and I still have to do that. If I got someone telling me how to spend my money, how to make my money, what I can drink, what I can take, what I can't, where I can go, what I can fly on, that's bullshit. I can't work that way.

In the winter of 1957/58, Jerry Lee played an engagement at the Paramount Theatre, New York, that sold out for 12 days. His third hit, 'Breathless', had increased his

*popularity even more and he played to an audience of
five thousand five times a day. It broke all previous
attendance records – including those of Johnnie Ray and
Frank Sinatra. His ego was gigantic and he used it to put
the world on. What saved him was the ability to laugh at
himself.*

CHAS HODGES (of *Chas & Dave*): I first heard him
on Radio Luxembourg. Even allowing for the sound
fluctuations peculiar to that station I knew it wasn't
Dean Martin's sidekick I was listening to. I never had a
record player at the time, only a wind-up gramophone.
My friend in my skiffle group bought *Great Balls of
Fire*. He said the B-side *Mean Woman Blues* was
better. He kept trying to describe it, not very success-
fully. What I heard in his front room that day in 1957 on
a 78 record, it changed my life. What's more, it determined the direction my life was going to go.

In May 1958 he was advertised to play at the Regal,
Edmonton and that's where I saw him. Yellow hair, red
suit, wild! I remember no catcalls. Only a wild reception. The catcalls must have come a couple of days
later, after the bad publicity. I wrote down the set he
played. I've still got it.

The only heckling I heard was from a girl who cried
out 'The drummer's too loud!' Jerry Lee told the drummer to quieten down a bit and the show continued. He
played *High School Confidential* but called it *High
School Hop*. I remember it got so fast, the drummer
couldn't keep up with eights to the bar and had to make
do with fours. Later, I got the drummer in our skiffle
group to play the same way.

CHAPTER 6

I'm Comin' Home

Dear Friends

I have in recent weeks been the center of a fantastic amount of publicity of which none has been good. But there must be a little good even in the worst people, and according to the press releases originating in London, I am the worst and am not even deserving of one decent press release.

Now this whole thing started because I tried and did tell the truth. I told the story of my past life, as I thought it had been straightened out and that I would not hurt anybody in being man enough to tell the truth.

I confess that my life has been stormy. I confess further that since I have become a public figure I sincerely wanted to be worthy of the decent admiration of all the people, young and old, that admired or liked what talent (if any) I have. That is, after all, all that I have in a professional way to offer.

If you don't believe that the accuracy of things can get mixed up when you are in the public eye, then I hope you never have to travel this road I'm on.

There were some legal misunderstandings in this matter that inadvertently made me look as though I invented the word indecency. If nothing else, I feel I should be given credit for the fact that I have at least a little common sense and that if I had not thought the legal aspects of this matter were not completely straight, I certainly would not have made a move until they were.

I did not want to hurt Jane Mitcham, nor did I want to hurt my family and children. I went to court and did not contest Jane's divorce actions, and she was awarded $750 a month for child support and alimony. Jane and I parted from the courtroom as friends and, as a matter of fact, chatted before, during and after the trial with no animosity whatsoever.

In the belief that for once my life was straightened out, I invited my mother and daddy and little sister to make the trip to England. Unfortunately, Mother and Daddy felt that the trip would be too long and hard for them and didn't go, but my sister did go along with Myra's little brother and mother.

I hope that if I am washed up as an entertainer it won't be because of this bad publicity, because I can cry and wish all I want to, but I can't control the press or the sensationalism that these people will go to to get a scandal started to sell papers. If you don't believe me, please ask any of the other people that have been victims of the same.

Sincerely,

Jerry Lee Lewis

This 'open letter to the music industry' appeared in Billboard magazine on 9 June 1958 as part of a five-page advertisement intended to rebuild Jerry Lee's career.

In the same month, Jerry re-married Myra in a ceremony of impeccable legality to ease the pressure of the bad publicity, and his record 'High School Confidential' made the U.S. top hundred at No. 21. But Sun Records, shocked by the U.K. furore, hesitated to push Jerry's records, and the D.J.s began to freeze him out.

Jerry Lee was returning to the States confident that he would pick up where he left off regardless of events across the Atlantic. This was not to be. Waiting at Idlewild airport, New York, was the full force of the American media, every bit as eager for scandal as their English counterparts.

T.V. reporter to Jerry Lee: 'What about this reception in London, can you tell us about that?'

'Yes, sir, we had a very good reception, people treated us really nice.'

Reporter: 'Is that so? Well, the papers over there reported that you were greeted with silence and catcalls from the audience.'

'I can't agree with them there, sir, the audience were very nice and very good.'

- I've been picked on, abused, sued, jailed, ridiculed, persecuted and prosecuted, but I never let it bother me. I've learned that people are narrow-minded and they don't know me, they don't know my feelings. Who knows anybody's feelings? As long as they don't do anything wrong, I think a person's private life is really their own. I don't care what a person does in his private life. It's nobody's business. Who can cast the first stone, ya'know? I can't tell you what to do. I can't tell you who to marry.

Jerry Lee and Myra were portrayed by the kinder press as a pair of cooing turtle doves oblivious to reality, both feet firmly planted on Mars. The language between them seldom progressed beyond the goochie-goochie stage. In

*an article in Confidential magazine, the couple were
shown at a funfair, riding on a merry-go-round and eating pink candyfloss. Myra carried a cuddly toy. They
could have been two kids playing truant from school.*

'I happened to meet a girl I fell in love with,' Jerry told
reporter Renee Francine at the Coney Island Hotel. 'I
knew Myra was the special girl I was looking for. No
matter what anybody said or did, I knew I was going to
marry her because that was the natural thing to do. She
washes my hair, she washes my feet, she powders me
and puts me to bed.'

*The record industry slammed the door on Jerry Lee,
but he was able to persuade Sun Records into releasing a
gimmicky record, 'The Return of Jerry Lee' to cash in
on the adverse publicity and laugh the incident off. It
was put together by Jack Clement, interspersing extracts
from his previous Sun hits with questions from George
Klein, a Memphis D.J.*

Klein: 'How does it feel to be back home?'

'Ooh! It feels good.' [from 'Great Balls of Fire']

Klein: 'How did you manage to get a marriage licence
with your wife being so young?'

'I told a little lie.' [from 'I'm Feeling Sorry']

*The record failed despite an exuberant piece of Jerry Lee
indulgence on the B-side, 'Lewis Boogie'.*

MYRA WILLIAMS (third wife): They pulled his
records, banned them. He wasn't allowed on any T.V.
stations, and his career simply took a nosedive. I felt so
guilt-ridden, the fact that they were doing this to Jerry
because of me. I wanted just to throw up my arms and
say 'Stop! You're crucifying an innocent man!' The

only thing he's guilty of is loving and marrying a very young girl. I felt so protective of Jerry.

FRANKIE JEAN (sister): Myra and Jerry got married again for the press. They did it all over again. I kept saying, 'Jerry, mother told you not to marry your cousin, she begged you not to!' and Myra was very irate at me. I'm not saying I like her and I'm not saying I dislike her. She didn't like my mother. She had no charm, she couldn't sing, she couldn't hold a candle to mother's mind. Jerry's mother always came first. How could you expect Myra to like it? I wouldn't have liked her either if I'd been her daughter-in-law. But Jerry Lee humiliated his family. I'm not saying what he did was a crime, but it devastated us. He went from ten thousand dollars a night to five hundred dollars a night. Our furniture and air conditioning was repossessed. They even took a baby bed!

My mother told Jerry Lee, 'You've got to fight. If you give up now, I won't have a son. I'll lie down and die with you.' Jerry Lee said, 'Momma, you're right', and he cried like a baby. There was hardly any food, there was no furniture and, of course, Jerry was so embarrassed, so humiliated. You can imagine how he felt, being the big provider and giving all these things to his Momma.

MYRA WILLIAMS (third wife): I always believed things were gonna change. The two of us had the same belief, that tomorrow it would be O.K. I think that's how the two of us were able to hang on and fight back. Jerry tried so hard to get back to the top, he pushed himself to the limits. He cut some great records but the D.J.s wouldn't play them. After Jerry had a hit in 1968 I think he became extremely bitter. He realised when he

looked back that he had lost 10 years for no good
reason.

*The records that followed were 'Lovin' up a Storm/Big
Blond Baby'; 'Let's Talk About Us/Ballad of Billy Joe';
'Little Queenie/I Could Never be Ashamed of You';
'John Henry/Hang up my Rock 'n' Roll Shoes'; 'When I
Get Paid/Love Made a Fool of Me'. He even cut an in-
strumental record under a pseudonym, The Hawk,
rocking up Glenn Miller's 'In the Mood' with B-side, 'I
Get the Blues When It Rains'.*

*Jerry Lee feels he was badly let down by Sam Phillips, a
man he had admired and respected so much in the past.*

- I put Sam on a pedestal, y'know, and over the years
  in my opinion the man turned out to be immoral, a
  liar and a thief. Sam Phillips, my idol – that's what he
  turned out to be. I don't know what Mr Gene Autry
  turned out to be 'cos I wasn't around him too much,
  but Sam Phillips, who I put my trust in, that's what
  he became. He stole from me. He took my money
  and he's been taking it over 30 years. Sam Phillips
  gave me three checks – he gave me a check for three
  hundred dollars one time, one for forty thousand
  dollars one time, and another for thirty-nine thousand dollars, and that was it. He never paid me on
  Breathless and he never paid me on *High School
  Confidential*. All of them hit records. All of 'em
  belonged to Sam. And he don't ever call me up, he
  won't ever write me a letter. Never gave me a royalty
  statement, never gave me a penny since then, man,
  for 30-something years.
     Breathless was a three million seller record. I
  wasn't even given a royalty statement, much less a

nickel. Those two records sold millions and I was never even recognised or given a penny for that. All these recordings that Sam took like *One Minute Past Eternity, I Can't Seem to Say Goodbye*, several songs were No. 1 records years later. After I had left him they went to Mercury. He still has a pile of unsold records. And hell, he has no right to sell Jerry Lee Lewis anyway. He can sell all he wants to sell, but selling Jerry Lee records, he's still going to have to pay. He's got to pay me, not shelve the singles.

Sam kept me back a long time, six or seven years. He would release a record on me and wouldn't try to push it, wouldn't even distribute it. Fulfilling his contract he called it – writing it off for income tax, that's what I call it.

SAM PHILLIPS (Mr Sun Records): He's a devil to talk that way. Jerry Lee is no damn fool but business was not his forte. I never worked harder in my life on any artiste than I did for Jerry Lee. Believe me, I had no rougher time in business than I had in trying to do the right thing, the calm thing, the patient thing. To see this incredible talented artist maybe put away ... Man, when you don't know what the end result is gonna be that's when you have to push back a little bit and say, let me see now, we are approaching an iceberg here that can sink the whole ship. I'm not scared of anybody, but the worse thing I could do was force this issue of people buying Jerry Lee's records right at this time. The one thing we don't need to do is to start throwing records out there because we need to meet a certain quota of income.

I never over-released my artists because, remember, we were bringing into existence a brand new type of music here. We were bringing in a new clientele. These

were little suckling babes in the entertainment world.
You're building a career, trying to sell a whole new
approach to entertainment through the process of
music. The worst thing you can do is try to make a business out of it instead of developing the artistic patience
– you need to get this process going.

I talked to all the distributors. I told them, he ain't
down for the ten-count, he'll be back. I stayed in the
background and I talked to these people. I had to be
faithful to my distributors because they helped us do a
lot of things. I didn't go to them on my hands and
knees, I talked to them honestly.

I didn't want to lose Jerry Lee. I cared about what
happened to him. I loved my artistes. We were close.
We didn't fraternise a lot but we were close. I didn't
have plenty of people around me. I liked to stay close
to my artistes. I believe Jerry Lee has said that I kept
him down during his bad time. Well, that ain't how I
see it. But I'm willing to accept that it is due to a lack of
me conveying directly to him all of the intricacies that
was going on in order not to ruin him for ever with the
distributors and the D.J.s. I could have killed his career
for sure.

I'm not trying to say my record is perfect or anything.
I've made as many mistakes as I have successes, I
guess. If I knew of anything I could have done, I damn
sure would have done it.

*Sam Phillips kept unreleased recordings in the vaults for
years after Jerry Lee left Sun Records in 1963. He did not
think they were viable at the time. According to Jerry
Lee he cut enough tracks for some 15 albums.*

*Despite Sun's apparent loss of interest in Jerry Lee,
his releases gathered a momentum of their own. His
cover version of the Ray Charles classic 'What'd I say',*

given the unique Jerry Lee treatment, made the hit parade on both sides of the Atlantic with very little help from Sun. As 'High School Confidential' peaked at No. 12 in the U.S. Top 100, Myra gave birth to Lewis's second son on 28 February 1959. He was born at 6.33 a.m. in Ferriday, Jerry Lee's hometown, and weighed in at seven pounds, three ounces. Jerry Lee and Myra named him Steve Allen Lewis as a gesture of gratitude to Steve Allen, the T.V. personality who gave Jerry his first big T.V. exposure.

Whilst in Ferriday Jerry Lee bumped into his childhood friend Cecil Harrelson, and invited him to become his road manager. He needed all the friends he could muster to rebuild his career.

• When the D.J.s stopped playing my records I never said anything. There was no hard feelings. What could I do? Holler and scream at them? For a while they weren't playing Elvis, Chuck Berry or anyone. You'd think rock 'n' roll had died in the night. I'd just take a record to them and say, 'If you want to play it, I sure would appreciate it.' All they played was all them Bobbys – Bobby Vee, Bobby Vinton, Bobby Rydell, Bobby Darin. If your name was Bobby you were in with a sporting chance.

I now had my wife and my little boy, Steve Allen. I was happy and doing good. I must be the only artiste in the world who's been down as many times as I have. I mean down to rock bottom. I was making ten thousand dollars a night and I got knocked down to two hundred and fifty a night, then built myself back up. Now I couldn't care less. Money don't mean nothing to me, 'cause that ain't where it's at. I'd rather have friendship. People are crazy. Money, money, money, that's all they want. Cut your throat

for 50 cents. Life is too short to worry your brains
over makin' a buck.

*During the down years of 1958–68 Jerry Lee toured con-
stantly. Under the pressure of constant travelling,
one-night stands and lack of hit records Jerry turned increasingly to the bottle and pep pills.*

- I'd be on the road with the band and we'd take some
  biphetamin to life us up, then we'd try placidyls to
  bring us down.

*On Easter Sunday 1962, Myra prepared to give Steve
Allen a family Easter surrounded by Easter bunnies and
Easter eggs. Together with Elmo, Steve Allen's grandpa,
they were set to really make it a great day for the child.
Jerry, exhausted from drink and travel, was asleep when
Cecil called his hotel room to tell him he had to ring the
Memphis Hospital.*

*It was evening. The new swimming pool, not yet ready to
use, had partially filled with muddy water due to a heavy
downpour. Steve Allen had wandered out of the house
alone, his hands sticky with candy, and started to play at
the edge of the pool. He slipped into the murky waters
and drowned instantly. Myra, noticing his absence,
called out but there was no response. She saw the pool
was full of dirty water and screamed, sensing disaster. A
neighbour came running, went into the pool from the
shallow to the deep end and found the child in five feet of
water. Mouth to mouth resuscitation was tried – a neighbour thought the child breathed for a mini-second. The
local doctor opened the child's chest with a pocket knife
for heart massage.*

It was Easter Sunday and Jerry Lee felt God was

punishing him for his sinful ways. Jesus died for the sins of mankind so that we might be saved, and he rose up on Easter Sunday.

At the funeral Jerry Lee accepted the death of his son as the will of God.

Even after this tragedy Jerry Lee announced that he would go ahead with a scheduled tour of England, four years after his disastrous first visit.

Jerry Lee's notoriety hadn't done any harm to record sales, and all his singles in this period had been hits in the U.K.

Though the start of the tour was only a few days after Steve Allen's funeral, Jerry Lee seemed eager to plunge himself back into work. Myra followed him to London a week later, wearing black ribbons and clutching a bible.

They were apprehensive about the kind of reception they would experience this time round. They needn't have worried.

- On the opening night in Newcastle they wanted to carry me shoulder high. I never had a reception like it, not even when I was red hot in the States. We were so inundated with fans we had to bolt the back-stage dressing rooms. The fans were practically breaking the doors down. Poor old Cecil couldn't get in because the doorman thought he was a fan. 'But I work for the guy!' he kept insisting. It sounds funny now, but it wasn't at the time.

A tall blond spectre appears in the wings dressed in a dark suit and white shirt and black tie. Zap! He slides across the stage, some 17 feet, landing on his knees. He hits the keyboards of the large grand piano on the beat and goes straight into 'Down the Line' – 'If you can't be my lovin' baby/You ain't got the style/I'm gonna get me some lovin'/That'll drive a cool cat wild'. Flaying the keys up and down like a wood carver. Next follows a fast and furious rendition of 'Breakup'. Jerry stops after the first verse, tells the drummer he is not happy with the beat. Jumping off his stool he takes the drum sticks, demonstrates the correct rhythm – back to his piano he starts into 'Breakup' again.

'It's great to be back in England. I've had my sorrows lately but I'm goin' to drown my sorrows in my music and give it all I got.'

CHAPTER 7

The Greatest Live Show
on Earth

*In Europe Jerry Lee was hot. His loyal following mani-
fested itself in two strong fan clubs. One called Fireball
Mail (after the Ferriday Fireball) was run from Holland
by Wim De Boer – still going strong today, thirty years
after its foundation. The other was The Shaking Keyboard, today called The Lewis Scene and run from the
U.K. by Colin Phillips. The fan clubs linked up with
their U.S. counterparts run by Kay Martin and Jerry
Lee's greatest fan and loyal friend Gary Skala. The fans
were like a well oiled P.R. machine, urging promoters to
tour Jerry Lee, writing to T.V. and radio stations to
show and play his music on air as much as possible.
Jerry got to know many of them as close friends. Many
of them would gladly have laid down their lives for him.*

*Don Arden, the U.K. promoter, well pleased with the
1962 tour, now set himself a more ambitious logistical
puzzle – Rock Across the Channel. The trip would be
from Southend, Essex (near London) to Boulogne,
France. The worthy fans were to see Jerry Lee performing on board the cross channel boat, The Royal
Daffodil.*

*Jerry was supported by the Flee Rakers, Nero and The
Gladiators and Johnny Angel. Fans swarmed from
London to catch the rockin' boat. British Rail supplied
special trains, but many arrived late leaving hundreds of
fans smouldering with rage as they saw The Royal Daffodil disappear over the horizon. Jerry Lee had travelled*

all night with Tarp Tarrant, his new drummer. Tarp was trying to sleep while Jerry obliged his fans, answering questions, signing autographs.

When the boat docked in Boulogne, Jerry Lee, wearing dark glasses and a white mac, was greeted by the mayor of Boulogne and a French rock band. He led his fans along the promenade like a proud general to the local casino.

The French police, alarmed by the possibility of a rock 'n' roll riot, surrounded the casino. Grim faced gendarmes arrested a few fierce-looking Teddy Boys who turned out to be only teddy bears. They then marched Jerry Lee and the rock 'n' roll fans back to The Royal Daffodil.

PAUL SANDFORD (eyewitness): On the return journey Jerry Lee performed for one and a half hours on the upper deck, surrounded by what seemed like an entire boat load of fans. This was the first time I'd seen and heard him perform songs outside his usual show repertoire, numbers like *C.C. Rider, In the Mood, I Get the Blues When It Rains, Lewis Boogie* and *Bonnie B.* We heard them all for the first time in Europe that night.

Back in England Jerry Lee appeared on the BBC's radio show Saturday Club which helped establish The Beatles, and on the T.V. show, Ready, Steady, Go with the Rolling Stones. However, it was on his return trip to the U.K. in 1964 that Jerry Lee made his greatest visual impact on a T.V. special for Granada.

Producer Johnny Hamp psyched up the fans by playing wild rock 'n' roll before introducing the top U.K. group The Animals who burst into Chuck Berry's

'Around and Around'. Instant excitement. Gene Vincent followed with raving versions of 'Long Tall Sally', 'You are my Sunshine', and his big hit, 'Be-Bop-A-Lula'. Reeling with joy, the audience's attention was suddenly switched to a grand piano perched 20 feet above floor level where Jerry Lee prepared to unleash 'Great Balls of Fire'. While playing he was lowered into the throng, banging his white boots on the keys. He slowed the pace for his favourite Hank Williams number, 'You Win Again'. Jerry intros into 'Whole Lotta Shakin'', tears off his jacket after the first verse, flings it into the seething mass. Next he kicks over the stool. The piano and Jerry start to ascend, fans jump on to the platform. Jerry Lee climbs on top of the piano, mike in hand as hundreds of fans try to shake his hand and touch him. His blond curly hair takes on a Medusa-like form, the mike in hand like a prophet's staff – the imagery produced is a cross between the tortured souls in a Hieronymus Bosch painting reaching from hell towards heaven, and the macho movie heroism of John Wayne raising the U.S. flag on the hills of a fallen enemy – the sands of Iwo Jima.

Clips from this highly successful T.V. special are still used today on rock documentaries and programmes on Jerry Lee's life. It has been shown worldwide on several occasions.

Back in the States, Jerry Lee finally signed with Smash, a subsidiary of Mercury Records, in September 1963, after a protracted wrangle with Sam Phillips over distribution and royalty payments. Phillips had shaken up the record industry with his small, independent Sun label in Memphis. Now he wanted a special clause in Lewis's Mercury contract, protecting his stake in the man he virtually discovered. But by that time Jerry Lee was thoroughly disillusioned with Phillips and eager to move on.

- He held me to that contract with Sun for five long years, knowing all the time he had no distributors for my records. Why he done that I don't understand, but he did. He recorded some stuff just before the contract ran out. He said I owed him a session. I said I didn't owe him nothin' but I'd do it anyway.

Jerry also had a new manager, Frank Casone, a night club owner in Memphis, who had allegedly evaded a murder charge. In one fell swoop, Frank wowed the still influential Mamie and told Jerry Lee he should play in a movie version of Hank Williams's life story. He also got Jerry Lee a contract playing in the Thunderbird Lounge. Elvis Presley had flopped with his first Las Vegas appearance, so Jerry was very impressed by Mr Frank Casone.

But the relationship soured all too quickly, and the two men found themselves fighting an ugly battle in the courts. Lewis claimed Casone had induced him by trickery and misrepresentation to sign a contract in July 1963. The contract provided Casone with receipt of 25 per cent of royalties and personal appearances and 50 per cent of movie and T.V. fees. Casone had already sued Lewis, charging breach of contract.

Basically, Jerry Lee claimed he had not received two hundred and fifty thousand dollars in the two year period and that by demanding Jerry Lee be paid five thousand dollars a week, Casone had damaged Jerry Lee's career. The first ruling favoured Casone by concluding that Lewis had breached the contract four months previously by not allowing Casone to serve as his manager. Eventually the matter was settled out of court. Jerry Lee paid four thousand dollars, with Casone still insisting he deserved a seven thousand settlement.

- Tarp Tarrant started working for me when he was 16
years old. He was a little wild, you couldn't really
hold him down, but he was a great drummer. He
done some really great stuff. He'd go at it so crazy
you'd think he would fall off them drums – and he
did a couple of times and hurt himself real bad. We
wore out two or three cars a year touring with the
band. You wouldn't believe the miles we ate up,
some four hundred thousand miles a year, something
like that. In 1963 we got through five cars.

TARP TARRANT (drummer): I started playing
drums in Georgia when I was 10. My first band was a
school rock 'n' roll band. We did cover versions of
Eddie Cochran, Chuck Berry, Little Richard and Jerry
Lee Lewis. We didn't do no Elvis, 'cause we thought he
was too lovey-dovey. We loved the hard rock image.
We was the cool cats with ducktails, y'know.

When I first heard *Great Balls of Fire* and *Whole
Lotta Shakin'* I just totally freaked out. I thought
'Someday I gotta play with these guys, I gotta be what
they need.'

I got a call to go to Sun Records to audition as drummer in Jerry Lee's band. I went in and played *Great
Balls of Fire* and *Whole Lotta Shakin'*. Just a few bars
of each with Jerry trippin' around the middle. I just
picked right up on it. Sam Phillips broke in on the mike
and said, 'Hey, I think the kid's got a good foot, you
oughta hire him.' Jerry Lee didn't say nothing. Cecil
[Harrelson] didn't say nothing. Jerry just stopped playing, and I got my sticks and said, 'Nice meeting you, sir,
Mr Lewis.' I didn't hear nothing 'til that phone call inviting me to join the band.

Touring was tough, at times. We were in cars and

trailers, driving everywhere. We set up our own equipment, then we played four hours. We'd start 9 o'clock, finish at one. Jerry would come on at 10 and do an hour show, then we'd come back and play another set, and Jerry'd come back on at 12 and do *another* set. My relationship with Jerry Lee Lewis was simple as this: we loved each other then, we love each other now. I taught his boy to play drums. Jerry said, 'I'm thinking about putting Jerry Jnr. on the road, playin' drums; you got two days to get him in shape.' We worked near 10 hours a day practising. He was very young, had a lot of talent. I loved Jerry Jnr. just like I do my own son – very dear and close to me.

Jerry Lee could get mad about a lot of things. He would make a phone call home and things wouldn't be going right and he'd come and take it out on us, the band. I would retreat to my own crutch, drugs 'n' alcohol, an' goin' out an' getting arrested to get me some attention. I thought I was doing a great job. I knew I was doing a great job. Jerry is human like the rest of us. He gets tired and he is a man of extremes. He's like me – his own worst enemy. My doctor said, 'You don't know when to quit.' Life to me is not worth living if you don't live every day, every minute, to the fullest extent.

Speed is like riding a Harley at a hundred and ninety miles an hour on a straight highway, just as fast as it'll go. Your hair blowin' in the breeze. All the hairs stand up on your arms. It's outta sight. I started takin' downers so I could go to sleep. Y'know, I used to take so much speed that I just stayed up and up. I'd be walkin' into walls. So I started getting valium and placidyl and qualudes. I got a good mix goin'. So what I'll do is, I'll get enough downers to get me to sleep then enough uppers to keep me up, an' I won't have to worry about the in-between.

Would I do it again? I'd use the speed. But I did enjoy it very much, and I remember it like it was yesterday. It did control my life, and my family, for, I guess, 12, 15, 20 years. I was controlled by the uppers and the downers.

The worst thing was that it led to prison. Five years out of my life, away from my family, away from my freedom. Freedom – the most precious thing in the world. People don't realise that until they have it taken off them. You can't just get up and go to the icebox for a glass of milk, or get a cookie. Every time you go to the toilet somebody walks by with a flashlight and shines it in there on you, and you've gotta be counted four or five times a day. It ain't no good feelin'.

Jerry Lee Lewis was getting rough on the band – a few times he would call home an' things weren't going right. But, yeah, we had to bear with him.

Once you become a performer, in the limelight, whether you're Babe Ruth or Elvis, you've got to be in perfect health. You've go to be up, alert. You've gotta be like your album covers. It's impossible to ask of any human being. If I'm paying $15 a ticket, I don't care if you're in Detroit last night or your wife is sick. When you come on stage you better be showin' me something for my money.

We were a commodity, we were a hot item. The Memphis Beats had to be somebody special, else they wouldn't be with Jerry Lee Lewis – that's the way it is. To this day, I feel that I'm the best drummer he ever had, and I believe with all my heart that I made that man sound better live, on stage, than any drummer has ever made him sound.

I love Jerry Lee Lewis with all my heart, but a lot of things happened in our business relationship where money was concerned – before it got to me and when it came to him. It was put to him in such a way that he had no choice. There was times I didn't receive the amounts, or the credits, I deserved. The money don't mean anything to me. I think God had something in mind for me. I'm 49 years old today, and I'm in real good health, real good shape.

Two D.J.s played a very large part in building up rock 'n' roll stars in the 1950s – Alan Freed who first used the term on his radio show, Moondog's Rock and Roll Party; and on T.V., Dick Clark with his daily show, American Bandstand, which had viewing figures in excess of twenty million. It was only when a public inquiry into 'payola' – i.e. accepting bribes to promote particular records – looked into the relationship between the D.J.s and the record industry that it emerged just how influential the likes of Freed and Clark were. It was claimed that Connie Francis, Bobby Darin and Fabian owed their success almost entirely to Clark's patronage. A record company executive estimated that simply by playing a record every day for a week Clark was able to boost sales by a quarter of a million. He also owned a record-pressing factory, a music publishers and a management company. Clark was cleared of any payola charges, but Freed, who died in 1965, admitted that he accepted bribes and was unceremoniously dropped by the New York radio station he'd helped to put on the map.

• In the early days if Alan Freed didn't play your record, you didn't have a hit. I first met Alan in New York in 1957 when I did *The Steve Allen Show*. We did some tours with his roadshow. He was straightforward and one of my best friends. He never lied about anything. When they had the inquiry into payola in Washington everyone was saying 'I never took no payola,' and Alan Freed said, 'Yeah, I took payola.' If that had been me, I would have pleaded the fifth amendment.

We grew up together in a way, me and Alan and Elvis and Dick Clark. We changed the world musically. If you didn't have Dick Clark on your side, you were as good as finished. We were the first band ever to play live on *American Bandstand*. Mostly he had people lip-synching to their records. I wouldn't do that.

TARP TARRANT (drummer): We were on tour with Dick Clark one time, with Joey D and the Starlighters, Frankie Avalon, Paul Anka and Fabian. Something had happened to Fabian and he couldn't make the show, so they was out there makin' a bunch of apologies for Fabian, and Jerry Lee was raving, 'I'm ready to go on! We've got five hundred miles to drive!' So he came rushin' out the dressing room with Dick Clark standing there. Jerry said 'Look, either we go on now, or we're outta here. I don't care.' Dick knew he meant business so he put us on. He didn't mess with Jerry ever again. That's why I've got the greatest respect in the world for the man – he came to do a show, he was ready, y'know, and there was no nonsense about it. I've seen him come on stage, stoned drunk as a bicycle. I been there with him. I've fell off the drums. I fell 20 feet off a foot stage once, blood running everywhere. I remember one time in Nashville, Tennessee, I believe it was. I was high as a rat. I tell you, all of a sudden the whole world left and I left with it. They took me to the emergency room, and some guy said 'This guy's so full of drugs and alcohol we can't see if there's anything wrong with him or not'.

Myra and Jerry were living at Coro Lake, where Myra
was still suffering from deep depression following the
death of Steve Allen. Jerry Lee's continuous touring
only served to emphasise her loneliness. Added to this
was the feeling she had that Jerry and the Lewis clan still
blamed her for the death of Steve Allen. Myra felt utterly
neglected, even though she was pregnant again.

On 29 August 1963, Phoebe Allen Lewis was born.
Jerry Lee was performing in Hot Springs, Arkansas. At
first Myra could not reach him to tell him the good news.
When she did finally reach him, he was not interested
because Jerry Lee had wanted a boy. Even on his return
home Jerry Lee practically ignored his baby girl. Myra
suspected that Jerry Lee's mother, Mamie and Linda
Gail, who did not like Myra, had hinted to Jerry Lee that
the child was not his.

Soon, however, Jerry Lee became the doting father –
'Phoebe is the closest thing to me on this earth' – and he
would refer to Phoebe as 'my heart'.

Jerry returned to Europe in 1964. He cut a terrific
album live at the Star Club in Hamburg with a British
group, The Nashville Teens of 'Tobacco Road' fame.
Shelby Singleton decided to record a live performance
with Jerry Lee and his touring band, who were able to
cope with his habit of playing what he wants, when he
wants and at the varying tempos of his mood.

BUCK HUTCHESON (rhythm guitar in Lewis's band):
We was playing Houston, Texas, with the Everly
Brothers. They were real big, they had *Cathy's Clown*,
Let It Be Me, all of them. The promoter gave them the
closing spot. Jerry said he would teach them a lesson
they won't forget. We stayed on stage an hour and
a half and you ain't seen nothing like it. The Everly
Brothers came on stage and people got up and started

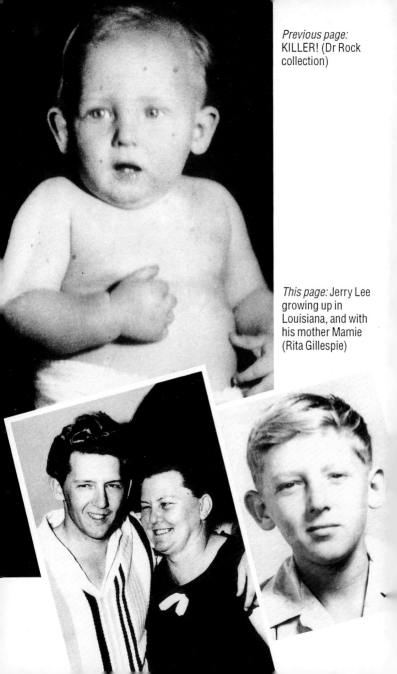

Previous page:
KILLER! (Dr Rock collection)

This page: Jerry Lee growing up in Louisiana, and with his mother Mamie (Rita Gillespie)

Left: Jerry Lee with the Rev. Edenfield, 1954 (Dr Rock collection)

Below: Family portrait at Black River. Left to right, Mamie, Jerry Lee (aged 16), Frankie Jean, Linda Gail, Elmo. (Linda Gail Lewis)

Far left: Jerry Lee and Myra, 1958 (Billy Miller, *Kicks* Magazine)

Left: In the movie *High School Confidential*, 1958 (MGM)

Below: On stage, Memphis, 1958 (Tony Wilkinson collection)

Whole Lotta Shakin' – in action in New
York, Café de Paris, June 1958 (Billy Miller,
Kicks Magazine)

Above: Live, New York, 1958

Right: In England, 1963, and on the way to France via the Royal Daffodil (Dezo Hoffman Ltd)

leaving. They thought the show was over. Nobody, and I mean nobody, ain't ever put on a show like that. I ain't saying anything bad about the Everly Brothers – they're great. But if I was an entertainer there's no way I'd follow Jerry Lee Lewis. You can't do it. I don't care who you are!

When we did the Greatest Live Show On Earth album in Birmingham, Alabama, the electricity was there. When that man came on stage he was glowing, he had a halo around him. You ought to have seen it!

PHIL EVERLY (singer): Jerry Lee is one of a kind. As soon as you have one of a kind you have that kind of importance. It's as unique as they get – he is the pillar, the bridge between country music and rock 'n' roll.

DON EVERLY (singer): Jerry Lee is an original. There is nobody like him – an original if there ever was one. His music is great – terribly important. Lord knows, he lived a rock 'n' roll lifestyle to the ultimate.

Fifteen thousand people came to hear Jerry Lee record the album at the Municipal Auditorium in Birmingham. It was the first important rock 'n' roll concert properly recorded. Highlights are 'Memphis Tennessee', 'Who Will The Next Fool Be', 'Together Again' and 'High Heel Sneakers', which was released as a single. If it failed to be the success it deserved – though it did enter the U.S. album Top 40 – the mainstream D.J.s were to blame.

● Shelby had microphones set up all across the stage. It was the first time anyone had set up a live recording like that. We really got some momentum goin' out there, and it all had to be captured in that one take. No second chances. I think Shelby edited out some of the talking, but that was all. Tarp was on drums – he'd just started working for me then. Herman Hawkins, we called him Hawk, he could play some bass fiddle. Buck Hutcheson was on guitar and me on piano – that's all we needed. We were on the runway. We were revving up and we were ready to take off! Buck loved his guitar and he loved the girls. The thing about him, me, Tarp and Hawk was we was all the same way. Totally electric.

When Jerry Lee returned to the U.K. in November 1964 he appeared in a cheap movie entitled Be My Guest, singing 'My Baby Don't Love No One But Me'. It starred David Hemmings and Avril Angers, with musical contributions from The Nashville Teens, The Zephyrs, Kenny and the Wranglers and the Nite Shades – all since gone from obscurity to oblivion.

But there was one unknown singer from the U.K. whose destiny was to be anything but obscure. Tom Jones has often said that he owes his inspiration to Jerry Lee and Little Richard.

TOM JONES (singer): I was in New York in 1966 and one of the first things I did was to find a record store where I could buy Jerry Lee's album, *Country Songs for City Folks*. That's when I first heard *Green Green Grass of Home*, and I wanted to record it straight away. When I went back to England, I met Jerry at the airport and we became friends. I joined him on stage at Bradford where we sang *Green Green Grass of Home* together. I wanted Jerry to play piano on my recording but he'd already returned to the States. It was a huge hit for me in 1966, stayed at No. 1 for seven weeks.

- The first time I met Tom Jones I was walking along a London street with my old friend Cecil Harrelson and this guy pulls up alongside in a jaguar and says, 'Jerry Lee, Jerry Lee, I'm your number one fan! I'm in your fan club!' That's how I met old Tom. We had some great times together. We'd get drunk and argue, but when we sobered up we was always good buddies.

While the British film industry had conspicuously failed to produce a credible rock 'n' roll movie, the U.K. was at least able to boast one of the great rock 'n' roll producers, Jack Good, whose T.V. music shows were always in a class of their own. Jack Good was born in London in 1930, educated at Oxford University, and studied acting at the London Academy of Music and Drama. He worked for the pioneering Six-Five Special for the BBC, and then Oh Boy! for ITV in the late 50s. He moved to the States in 1962 to produce first Hullaballoo, followed by Shindig, featuring some of the hottest music around.

Sometimes Good's imagination was inclined to run away with him.

JACK GOOD (T.V. producer): I went to London Airport to greet Gene Vincent – it was just a bunch of huge air hangars at the time. This plane came in; they had steps coming down from the door, and down came this thin, frail, rather quiet fellow in a baseball jacket. I thought, is this the great Gene Vincent – surely not? I looked at his face – yes, it is Gene Vincent. He came up to me: 'Hello sir! I'm very happy and proud to make your acquaintance.' I thought, this won't do – I can't have anybody who's happy and proud to make my acquaintance. I want a rocker. He's got to be a rocker – he's got to say, 'Hey man, what's happenin', cut the cackle and get on with the show.' I was deeply disturbed. I thought this guy was going to be the greatest flick-knife boy, the rip-it-up, rock 'n' roll screamin' end, and he was a polite young man from Virginia. So we fixed him. When he came down the steps of the plane he had on these leg irons. So he didn't come down like anyone else, he hobbled down. At the time I was the biggest Shakespearian fan ever – hobbling means Richard III. Then I thought, we'll give him a hump back – no, we can't really do that, Richard III but he's got to be moody like Hamlet. We'll cover him in black from head to foot and have him hobble more, wear a medallion around his neck and black gloves, 'cause I once played a part called Lightbourne, a murderer with gloves on. I thought, that's very sinister, he plays everything with gloves on. So I got this kit for him – he'd never heard of Shakespeare or anything like that – so I got these steps and he hobbled very well.

- Jack was a great person and producer and a great friend to me – he recognised my talent from the beginning. He had me on his *Shindig* show many times – 'I got my hair bleached pure white blond for the teenagers,' Jack and I laughed. I had done the *Return of Rock* album for Smash, and *The Greatest Live Show On Earth*, which was a fantastic album, was also out at the time. Jack did everything he could to help me. He had me on *Shindig* playin' *Rockin' Pneumonia & Boogie Woogie Flu* on a harpsichord. Fun, fun days, man, fun days.

One of Jack Good's dreams had always been to write and produce a rock 'n' roll musical based on Othello. Finally, in 1967, his dream came true and he persuaded film composer Ray Pohlman to write the music for Catch

My Soul. He wanted Little Richard to play Othello, with Jerry Lee Lewis as Iago – the rock 'n' roll dream ticket.

JACK GOOD (T.V. producer): I took Little Richard to see Laurence Olivier's film of *Othello*. Richard was wearing huge wigs at the time and, inside the cinema, I had to ask him to remove his wig because the lady seated behind couldn't see the screen. He did as I asked, then put a brown paper bag on his head. After the movie Richard said, 'Hey man, that was cool! But I thought I knew all the black actors!' I said, 'He's not a black actor, he's white and he's English.' He looked at me with his great saucer eyes and said, 'Man, where does he get his action from?'

But the producer of Catch My Soul remained unconvinced that Little Richard was the right man for the job. Othello was eventually played by the veteran black actor William Marshall. However, the producer was as keen as Jack Good to cast Jerry Lee as the villainous and conniving Iago.

JACK GOOD (T.V. producer): He was the wild man of rock 'n' roll, but I knew he would work well for someone who respected what he did, and I'd always loved what he did. He really rose to the challenge. He learnt his lines before anyone else. When we were rehearsing, after he'd finished speaking, he would always look at me as if to say, 'I told you I could do it.' I had to say, 'No Jerry, don't look at me, look at the person you're talking to.' But I was happy for him to improvise. I didn't want him to be completely hamstrung by all the usual theatrical conventions. Jerry is one of those people who exists like fixed points on the compass by which everything else must be judged. He's really himself. He's not trying to be anybody else. Thirty-one years of southern individuality was not about to be bent out of shape by 500 years of dramatic tradition.

Variety found Jerry Lee's Iago 'an often chilling contemporary schemer', while the Los Angeles Times noted that 'Iago becomes Lewis as much as Lewis becomes Iago'.

• It was the hardest work I ever did. When the script was brought to me I thought, there's no way a southern boy from Louisiana is going to be able to play this dude. Jack said, 'I'm telling you it'll be great. You can pull it off.' So I took him at his word, and he was right. We worked six weeks just rehearsing, then six weeks doing it in Los Angeles. Jack wanted to take it to Broadway, but I didn't think I could go any further with it. We proved we could do it and that was great. As soon as it was over I flew back to Memphis, got my band together and went back on the road, 'cause I had another hit with *Another Place, Another Time*.

For some years his marriage to Myra had been a travesty. The tragic death of Steve Allen had driven a wedge between them – Jerry Lee persisted in blaming her for the boy's death. But as early as 1957, the year of their marriage, he'd tormented Myra by telling her he was in love with another woman.

Myra filed for divorce on 10 December 1970, citing physical abuse and mental cruelty. She accused Jerry Lee of drinking constantly and acting improperly with other women. During the proceedings she alleged that he would threaten to hire people to throw her in the river or throw acid in her face. On one occasion, she claimed, he had thrown a plate of spaghetti at her, knocking her to the ground.

But Jerry Lee's worst accusation by far was that she had been personally responsible for the death of their son in 1962.

CHAPTER 8

The Mercury Sessions

The song that was to change Jerry Lee's fortune and put him back on the tracks was 'Another Place, Another Time', a slow country ballad by Jerry Foster and Bill Rice, which reached No. 1 in the U.S. country charts, and took Jerry Lee off in a whole new direction.

- I had the audience kinda mixed up for a while. They knew I was a rock 'n' roll singer so they didn't know what to make of all this country stuff. On tour we always went back to *Great Balls of Fire* and *Whole Lotta Shakin'*. No matter how many country hits I had I always went back to rock 'n' roll 'cause that's what people want, and that's what I do best.

The songs that followed were about the drama of every-day middle-American life. Jerry Lee put his own personal experience and pain into songs like 'What's Made Milwaukee Famous (Has Made a Loser Out of Me)', 'She Still Comes Around to Love What's Left of Me', 'To Make Love Sweeter For You' and 'Today I Started Loving You Again'. On the album Together he was joined by his kid sister Linda Gail, by now an established country singer in her own right, for country classics such as 'Jackson', 'We Live in Two Different Worlds' and 'Don't Let Me Cross Over'.

Linda Gail had been touring with Jerry Lee since her

*early teens – she is 14 years younger – but their close har-
mony on stage was not always reflected by their
behaviour behind the scenes.*

LINDA GAIL (sister): We had this really crummy
dressing room in the basement of a night club where we
were performing. There was a flight of stairs outside the
door, and when you got to the top you were on stage.
Anyway we had a terrible fight and I spit in Jerry's face,
then ran up the stairs, on to the stage so he couldn't get
me back. We were meant to be singing *Roll Over
Beethoven*, which we'd released as a single, but he
wouldn't sing with me. It was terrible. It was his way of
getting even. And it worked 'cause I felt such a fool
singing out there all on my own.

● Linda disagreed with me one night over what key a
   song was in. I said, 'Listen, if you're so smart, why
   don't you sit down and play,' and she did. She played
   a mix of boogie woogie, blues and country. I could
   hardly believe it – the gal could get it! Not only that,
   she took most of my band off me. She's doin' her
   own thing and finding out she can be just as great as
   she wants to be.

*Once he had established his versatility, Jerry Lee
recorded a wide variety of country music, notably three
songs by Kris Kristofferson – 'Me and Bobby McGee',
'Help Me Make it Through the Night', and 'Once More
With Feeling'. 'Me and Bobby McGee' was his biggest
hit single for 13 years.*

KRIS KRISTOFFERSON (singer): I consider Jerry
Lee Lewis one of the great singers of all time. I think
you can put him up there with opera singers. This guy's

a natural resource who is inclined to self destruct. He
had a way of transforming my songs into something I
couldn't believe I was hearing. I loved what he did with
Me and Bobby McGee. He was late for the session
when they did the recording. They had all these
musicians lined up. Now in Nashville they don't have
three songs in three hours – someone's gonna lose their
job. In comes Jerry Lee and Jerry Kennedy, the producer, says 'How are we gonna do it, Killer?' and Jerry
Lee says 'Like this.' He sat down at the piano and he
just destroyed it, it was a wonderful version. He hated
Janis Joplin's version of it, and he told me he cut his
version to show 'that woman how it should be done'.

Janis Joplin claimed Jerry Lee Lewis and Kris Kristof-
ferson were the only two men she knew who could drink
her under the table.

LINDA GAIL (sister): Jerry Lee was on stage in Louisiana and Janis Joplin joined him on stage to sing *Me*
and Bobby McGee, as they'd both recorded it. Earlier,
in the dressing room, she'd been bragging about her relationship with Kris Kristofferson. Anyway, Jerry sure
didn't like her, and he told her she was out of line when
she boasted about whipping her audience into a riot.
She was drinking and carrying on. Jerry said to her, 'If
you're gonna act like a man, I'll treat you like one.' He
slapped her and threw her out of the dressing room.

● The material I cut for Mercury suited me at the time.
  It was a way to get in through the back door, to get
  the disc jockeys to play my records again. I went
  through the country field, though to me I was still a
  rock 'n' roller. I was just taking their material and
  doing it because I knew they were good first-class

songs. That's the way I did them. I delivered them in my own way. I lived a lot of those songs. As the years go by you get into it – you've lived it. People from all over the world have told me my records have raised their spirits, inspired them, helped make life easier for them – and they've done the same thing for me. I listen to other peoples' records all over the world, have done all my life. But I would rather listen to Jerry Lee Lewis records. Not because they are my own records, but 'cause I hear more meaning to it, the deliverance of the vocal or something in the words. It's more substantial. The piano playing and the singing go together and it all speaks to me.

Jerry Kennedy played a big part in recording my country music. But the guy running the board was a genius – Tom Sparkman – one of the best board men I've ever known in my life. Sharp and snappy, that's what Tom Sparkman is. He just mixed it and cut it. I mean you got the records – he was on all the Mercury albums. He done all that except *Middle Age Crazy*, a classic song, the only song I ever recorded where he put the soundtrack down by himself. I wasn't even there.

On over two hundred recordings Lewis manages to bring his own name – Jerry Lee, Rockin' Jerry, or simply The Killer – into the lyrics of whatever song he is interpreting at the time. Those who appreciate Jerry Lee see this as a great artiste moulding a song to his style . . . others might be tempted to see it as another manifestation of a giant ego on the rampage.

• Sure I make a song my own. I use my own name . . . Yeah, ol' Jerry Lee makes his presence felt. One day when I was recording, Jerry Kennedy came up and said, 'That's a good song, isn't it? Thank God we finally got one without mentioning your name! It really made me mad.' I told him I didn't know I did that, and after that I didn't mention my name in a song no more. I guess I just got into the habit of doing it. Sometimes I'd cuss a little, too. They'd get uptight about that.

In May 1970 Mercury released Live at The International, capturing Jerry Lee's act at The International Hotel, Las Vegas. It was while he was performing there that he encountered one of his lifelong heroes, John Wayne.

● He was walking around with a bunch of bodyguards where I was playing, going off to make an announcement or something. To me, anyone who walks up and down, or worse, out the door, while I'm playing, upsets me. So I hollered, 'Hey, you wanna find a seat, or get out the door. I'm trying to do a show here, boy!' I knew who he was. I'll call a star down like anyone else if they're messing up my show. He was walking through my crowd but no-one turned to look at him. My fans are so loyal – they wouldn't let ol' Jerry Lee down.

Jerry Lee was riding high on his success in the country market and still very much in demand in the rock field. Festivals such as Newport, Rhode Island Folk Festival in summer 1965 led to the Monterex Pop Festival, California 1967. Festival fever spread to Hyde Park, London in summer 1969, then to the famous Woodstock Music and Arts Fair a month later. The first major festival Jerry Lee played was the Toronto Peace Festival, along with

John Lennon and the Plastic Ono Band, Little Richard, Chuck Berry, Bo Diddley and Gene Vincent.

The promoters were anxious as to what Jerry Lee would play – country or rock 'n' roll. Anxious also was the movie director D. A. Pennebaker, a movie director and documentary film maker, who had signed up Jerry Lee and the rest of the rock 'n' roll giants to do a movie of the Toronto show, released as Keep on Rockin' 1972. Jerry came on stage casually dressed in slacks and a tee shirt and did a superb rock 'n' roll set, throwing in three Elvis Presley songs, 'Don't Be Cruel', 'Hound Dog' and 'Mystery Train' on which he played guitar. To cap it all he did his crowd pleasers 'Great Balls of Fire' and 'Whole Lotta Shakin''. He bowed politely to the crowd, telling them 'I love ya like a hog loves slops'.

In the summer of 1972, Jerry Lee was to appear at Wembley Stadium in the London Rock 'n' Roll Show which was to be filmed. The crowd waited an hour before Lewis appeared in red slacks and red tee shirt. He walked casually to the huge Steinway on the stage, and as he thundered into 'Great Balls of Fire' the whole stadium erupted. He followed this with 'High School Confidential', 'You Can Have Her', 'Chantilly Lace' and other greatest hits. All the while he was being eagerly photographed by someone in the wings. Jerry Lee was used to being photographed on stage, but on this occasion the face behind the lens looked strangely familiar.

• He was rolling about on the floor, taking pictures from every angle. I said to one of the band, 'Who is that cat?' And it was him, y'know, Mick Jagger. He came backstage after the show and told me what a big fan he was. He said he had all my albums. 'What I don't understand is why people don't dig these songs like *Think About It Darling, Would You Take*

Another Chance on Me, and *What's Made Milwaukee Famous*, songs like that. I said, 'Well, Mick,
that's the way it is ... I don't know, but I know it's
not rock 'n' roll!'

*Mamie Lewis was at Monument Studios, Nashville on 9
March 1971 to hear Jerry Lee record Cecil Harrelson's
and Linda Gail's song 'Gather Round Children' from
the album There Must Be More To Love Than This.
Jerry often brought the whole Lewis entourage –
parents, sisters, cousins, girlfriends, club owners, disc
jockeys – to witness a recording session. The part of the
studio where these guests sat was known as the 'peanut
gallery'. Jerry Lee's Momma jumped up and sang the
chorus of 'Gather Round Children'. A few weeks later
she was admitted to hospital in Houston, Texas, and
diagnosed as having cancer. Myra now wanted a
divorce. To cap it all Jerry's uncle, Lee Calhoun, whose
advice Jerry Lee had sought so often, had recently
passed away.*

- I prayed to God for Momma. I quit all the pills, the
  dope, the booze, the women. I started singing gospel
  again and I cut a gospel album with the help of Linda
  Gail. Momma's cancer started to get better.

*The day after Easter 1971, while Jerry was mourning the
anniversary of his son Steve Allen's death, his beloved
Momma passed away. He had not visited her during her
illness, finding the idea of her dying unbearable.*

LINDA GAIL (sister): He blamed himself for her illness, and he thought there was hope when there was
none. I knew it was only a matter of months. The
specialist in Houston gave her a one in a thousand

chance of survival. Jerry continued to blame himself and does to this day.

The effect on Jerry Lee was enormous and Linda Gail had a nervous breakdown. Jerry Lee's next album Touching Home contained the song 'Mother the Queen of my Heart'.

- Every time you, so to speak, pass the coffin, it rips 25 per cent out of you, but you have to accept it, have to keep fighting, have to keep singing. You just have to learn to handle it. It did affect family life in a way. The day she died, my father kinda went astray to a certain extent. I got blamed for that. I got blamed for a lot of things people did – I'll give you an example. My Daddy went to a rock 'n' roll show, and he saw all these girls screaming and carrying on, and when I came off stage, he said 'How can you take that? All those beautiful girls screaming at you?' I said 'They just like the music.' And he said 'They want more than that.' He said he couldn't handle it. He fell by the wayside after that, and when he did, my mother divorced him. But she never stopped loving him and he never stopped loving her. I had the greatest mother in the whole world. My parents were the greatest people in the world. They did everything, backed me up 100 per cent. When I made it big I never let them down. I took care of them. We were a very close knit family.

My Dad could be a wild cat and he knew how to get out of a jam, too. Once he was getting off a plane. We were arguing about something and we'd all been drinking. Daddy jumped in the limousine, took off with it and ran it into a ditch. When the cops came, he jumped into the back seat of the car. He told the cops, 'You can't trust any of these drivers, can you?' The cop said, 'What'd he look like, Mr Lewis?' and he said, 'I don't know. Jerry hires these limousine drivers, you know how they are!' My Daddy got away with it. That was a great day!

Jaren Gunn Pate, the former wife of Russell Pate, a Tennessee walking horse trainer, was a sheriff's secretary at Memphis Police Department in December 1970 when she came across The Killer, who was still reeling from his divorce from Myra.

● There was a lot of love there [sighs]. Love is always the inexplicable factor . . . Jaren was a very sexy lady and she wanted to marry me.

LINDA GAIL (sister): Jerry married her 'cause he was impressed with her influence in town. She knew all the law people – judges, senators – and she was into drugs. She got Jerry really heavily into drugs – they were stoned most of the time.

● That's baloney, she wanted to marry me. I said, 'Girl, you gotta know what you're doin', you gotta lot to take on when you marry The Killer – you better know what you've got.' Jaren knew a lot of politicians and she knew sheriffs and such like – that never impressed me at all. Jaren impressed me as a very smart-thinking girl. But her being in strong in the political side of life – I never got into that with her. She was just a very nervous person. She wanted something and her mother insisted that I meet her – it was her mother's fault. Once I met Jaren, she never let up until she got married.
   That's like the rest of 'em – they never let up until

they got married, and every one of 'em had to get
married to Jerry Lee Lewis. I told 'em, I said, 'You
really don't need and you don't want to really be
married to Jerry Lee Lewis, you just think you do!' I
said, ' You people should really get this out of your
mind!' And every one of 'em talked me into it, as
God is my witness, and every time they did, I
believed in what they were saying.

   We had a private ceremony – Sheriff William Morris and Sheriff Roy Nixon, mainly Jaren's friends,
came along. That girl sure did want to marry Jerry
Lee. We went out on tour – Toronto, Buffalo, New
York, Akron Ohio. Jaren didn't like to tour, so I just
bought her a house and let her settle there.

*Jerry Lee was only married a short time when his former
wife, Myra, brought a contempt citation against him for
$19,000 alimony. The judge, Howard Vorder Bruegge,
issued a stern warning to him. 'Mr Lewis has the keys to
the jail in his pocket. I don't want him back here trou-
bling the court again.'*

   *Myra, now Myra Gail Malito (she had married the
private detective whom she had employed to investigate
Jerry Lee's infidelities), received a cheque at the last
minute under the decree. Jerry was to pay $250 a month
child support and $10,000 alimony in instalments over
five years. Asked by the press how he could afford a new
limousine, horses and a plane, Jerry Lee replied, 'Before
you criticise, accuse or abuse, walk a mile in my shoes.'*

   *The relationship between Jerry and Jaren was turbu-
lent, to say the least. It was announced on 27 April 1972,
while Jerry was on his U.K. tour, that he was the father
of a five pound, nine ounce baby girl. Jaren Lewis gave
birth at 4.59 p.m. at Baptist Hospital.*

JAREN LEWIS: I haven't named the baby yet. We were hoping for a boy and didn't have any names for girls. I'll discuss it with Jerry – but we'll probably name her Lori Leigh Lewis.

● Thank God, Jaren and the baby are in good condition. It doesn't really matter as long as they are both healthy.

Jerry Lee was speaking from his hotel room in Birmingham, England. Although Jaren and Jerry were together quite a lot before they married, Jerry bought a house in Collierville and left her alone there most of the time. He befriended the beautiful Charlotte Bumpus, who became his mistress and with whom he lived while married to Jaren.

It was just a short while before Jaren asked for separate maintenance. On 1 December 1973 she asked that the singer be required to pay her bills, allowing her to live away from him. At this stage there was no mention of divorce – in fact they separated after two weeks of marriage.

Jaren, Jerry Lee's fourth wife, drowned in a swimming pool on 8 June 1982.

● We obviously drifted apart before her tragedy. Yeah, it's sad – that's sad, it really is. It got sad – it just wasn't workin'. We finally just cut it off and I got a phone call one day to say she fell into the swimming pool over at a girlfriend's house and drowned. She – I don't know – she must have taken some sleeping pills or something, and didn't know it. I know Jaren wouldn't have committed suicide. It had to be an accident. I was at home when it happened, and they called me an' I couldn't believe it. She was dead. Sad, poor woman.

Jerry Lee has claimed in the past that Jaren's daughter Lori Leigh is not his child.

- No way. She was born six and a half months after we got married and she was a fine five and a half pound baby girl. Born six and a half months after we got married. I take care of my children, there's no doubt about that. Any child that's really my child. There's no problem – I would give them anything I've got. But if there's a child that's not my child, I just can't accept that. I don't think it's right, and I don't think it's right for somebody to try to make me accept that. There should have been something done about that, though – back then! Something should have been said and done, but that never took place.

But a Mississippi court, asked to decide the issue, found in favour of Lori Leigh and ordered Jerry Lee to pay maintenance.

In January 1973 Jerry Lee arrived in London with Jerry Lee Jnr. and his friend Kenny Lovelace to embark on a proposed double album to be produced for Mercury by Californian Steve Rowland.

STEVE ROWLAND (record producer): Everybody told me I was a fool to take on the job, they said I'd never get on with Jerry Lee. I flew out to Memphis from London to meet Jerry Lee as I was going to produce the London session album with 25 top rock musicians. On arrival in Memphis I felt I had flown into a 1950s' B movie. All the women had bouffant hairdos.

They drove me to a club to meet Jerry Lee. He was surrounded by bums and bleeders sucking him dry. As I sat down at this table this guy pulls a gun out, lays it on the table, and says, 'Hey boy, you that limey that's gonna record The Killer? Ya better learn ya stuff boy, ya hear?'

Jerry Lee arrives and he's fine, full of fun. 'Jest get me a good piano and a good engineer and let The Killer rock 'n' roll for ya . . . all you gotta do is roll those tapes, brother.'

On my return to London I went straight to Harrods, ordered a couple of cases of Wild Turkey bourbon and a box of best Cuban cigars. Then the pressure started. First we had a death threat from the Hells Angels, who did not want The Killer recording with 'long haired hippies', so security had to be stepped up. The studio was fitted out at my request with a 12 foot long Bechstein (there was two thousand pounds worth of damage to it after Jerry Lee had finished rockin' it). Everyone wanted to do the album – Barry Gibb, Rory Gallagher, Eric Clapton, Stevie Winwood, etc. I did the studio work in shifts so if Jerry Lee wore out one lot then the next bunch could come in.

So gathered together was the cream of English rock culture – Rory Gallagher, Peter Frampton, Albert Lee, Joe Jammer, Kenny Jones (of the Who), Johnny Guastafson (of John Lennon), Alvin Lee, the whole of Heads, Hands and Feet. Chas Hodges (later of Chas and Dave) came along – he had worked with Jerry Lee in the old days. John Lennon wanted to come but was worried about his U.S. visa. Jerry Lee Jnr. looked on the trip as a vacation to Europe. The staff of Jerry Lee Enterprises were really Jerry Lee's closest friends – Cecil Harrelson, Rita Gillespie, Eddie Kilroy and Jud Phillips.

On Monday, 9 January at 3 p.m., Jerry arrived at Advision Studios, which were booked from 2 p.m. 'til midnight each day. The night before Jerry Lee went to see The Godfather at a Soho cinema, then on to his favourite Chinese restaurant, The Lotus House, in the Edgware Road.

STEVE ROWLAND (record producer): I put Jerry Lee on a Rhodes electric keyboard in the studio. He played great but the notes bled so there is a blur on the recording. Then he didn't want to rock 'n' roll, he wanted to do country. Suddenly he would call out, 'You cats know *No Headstone on My Grave*?' There was more trouble when Jerry Lee Jnr. cussed out Peter Frampton: 'You can't play guitar worth a flip.'

ALBERT LEE (session musician): He was drinking heavily at the time and he had a bottle of whisky on the piano at all times and some big Havana cigars. God help you if you touched his bottle or his cigars. You couldn't push him into anything. Nothing was more than two, three or four takes at the most. He was on form. He knew he had to deliver the goods. He played hard on that piano when he was ready. He had that arrogance and drive but you never knew if he was really serious or putting it on, living the Killer image. The last few days he was drinking really heavily and eventually he didn't turn up at all. That's why there are two instrumentals on the album.

At that time Albert Lee was playing with a band called Heads, Hands and Feet – an archetypal 1970s band with long hair, flared jeans and the next spliff never far from their thoughts. Also in the band was Chas Hodges, who had played with Jerry Lee on his previous visits to

*London, as had Albert Lee. It was suggested to pro-
ducer Steve Rowland they be hired to make Lewis feel
more at home.*

CHAS HODGES (musician): Jerry Lee – with his
brashness and entourage – gave the session 'stardom',
but in truth he was like a fish out of water. If it wasn't
for me and Albert in particular, I don't think the album
would exist today. We kept it together. He was given
songs to learn like *Heard it thru' the Grapevine*, which
just wasn't him. He got drunker in the embarrassment
of trying to learn songs in front of everybody. But he
had a friend in us. We knew his talent. In front of us he
had no need to prove himself. But he still got progres-
sively drunker over the days. On the first day he called
for a bottle of wine halfway through the session. On the
sixth day he arrived with a near empty bottle of whisky.
On the seventh day he never turned up at all. Despite
everything, not a bad album was turned out. It could
have been better, but it wasn't bad. The Jerry Lee Tribute on which I played piano was done on the seventh
day, simply because he never turned up. But yes, I do
retain some fond memories of those London sessions:
Sixty Minute Man, when he felt really at home; *Bad
Moon Rising*, when I was singing harmony next to him
for my own amusement, and he called to the producer
to give me a mike so I could sing on the record.

STEVE ROWLAND (record producer): Jerry drove
the musicians hard. One drummer complained he
played so much his hands were raw and blistered. I had
some back-up singers: people like Madeleine Bell and
Dinah Hightower. One of Jerry's rednecks said, 'Jerry
Lee ain't gonna sing with no negras', and things nearly

came to blows. I had to call a halt and have a serious discussion with him.

I had a beautiful girlfriend at the time, he would say to her 'Hey, honey, what you doin' with this boy? Honey, what are you doin'?'

- I walked in. I seen all these cats standin' around. They had real long hair an' everything. So I turned to Junior and I said 'Boy, have I made a mistake by comin' over here.' I sat down at the piano, put my headphones on, and started to record. These kids, there wasn't any one of them smokin' any pot, wasn't any one of them takin' any pills or liquor. They were clean, real nice, and they were the greatest musicians I ever heard.

On release, the album zoomed up the U.S. charts to number 37, Jerry Lee's best national chart result. And it produced another hit, 'Drinkin' Wine Spo-Dee O'Dee'.

To follow up the success of the London session, Mercury turned to the southern states. The album Southern Roots featured Steve Cropper, Duck Dunn, Tony Joe White, Carl Perkins, Wayne Jackson, The Memphis Horns and Kenny Lovelace.

Jerry Lee needed a lot of propping up at this time. The session turned into a drunken party lasting two long weeks. Carloads of relatives, friends, cousins, girls, beer, whisky, pills and pot would arrive at the studio each day. Huey Meaux, the producer, has 52 gold records to his credit including Johnny Preston's 'Running Bear' and Sir Douglas Quintet's 'She's About a Mover'. Mercury gave Meaux thirty thousand dollars to do the album. He brought in 36 musicians, including Booker T and the MGs, and Al Jackson.

HUEY MEAUX (record producer): Jerry Lee is a
genius, but we'd cuss each other out all the time 'cause
we're both from Louisiana. A lot of people wanted to
see me and Jerry work together. They knew I was hot-
headed and independent, and they knew Jerry Lee was
the same way. They wanted to see the explosions. I
could work with Jerry Lee Lewis all day and all night
but it takes you a year to get over him. He's crazy and
he's one of a kind. You've got to have a lot of soul to
put up with Jerry Lee for two weeks. I produced his
cousin, Mickey Gilley, before anybody else did – but he
was really a cheap imitation. If it hadn't been for Jerry
goofing off so much, Mickey would never have happened. People were always hungry for Jerry Lee's
pumping piano sound.

I had spent three months pickin' the songs for *Southern Roots* – and when we went in the studio, Jerry Lee
doesn't do one of them. You record what Jerry Lee
sings. Most of the time he starts playing and if you want
to record an album, you turn the tape on and you go
along with it. Then you slice out what you want. That
piano is his wife, man, and if you don't mike that
mother, then you ain't got Jerry Lee. The piano is Jerry
Lee and Jerry Lee is the piano. He loves to play and
he's great. I told him he was singing like bad one time
and he said, 'This is the Killer singin', man . . . if you
wanna take my place, you'd better get better.'

*Huey knew humour was the best way to get through to
Jerry Lee and since they both came from the same part
of the world, he found this a lot easier than most. The
following repartee is extracted from the original tape of
the Southern Roots session. Jerry Lee is at the piano in
the studio, Huey in the control room, twiddling the
knobs:*

Here I am making you a million an' you puttin' me down.

Huey: Well, y'know what we gonna spend it on, don't-cha?

Yeah, women!

Huey: That's it.

If he wasn't such a damn good cat an' knowed so much about music, I'd kill him.

Huey: Mercy, you wouldn't talk like that if you weren't my friend.

I am your friend . . . but you'd still look funny in a coffin.

Huey: Dead! That's the last step ain't it?

Well, Jud'll embalm ya!
(Jud was lying drunk and unconscious on the floor.)

Huey: Jud didn't put it on me . . . don't wake him up, man.

If you give me any crap I'll marry me another wife.

Huey: You might as well write another song.

I knew I'd say something I could agree with ya on . . . All right, here we go.

(The tape is rolling, Jerry Lee breaks into 'I Sure Miss Those Good Ol' Days.)

HUEY MEAUX (record producer): Me and Jerry Lee walked on the edge. Sometimes we went over. We said things that people would like to say but were afraid to say – people don't pay no mind to a few dirty words these days. The track *Meat Man* was risqué because it coincided with that plane crash in the Andes where the survivors ate the flesh of their dead fellow passengers. It didn't get a lot of air play 'cause of that.

• The album could have been better . . . I just didn't have my act together. When Jerry Lee does his best shows there is nobody can beat him. But when he does a bad show it's terrible. I gotta be the world's worst critic of myself, but after a while I started putting myself down bad. I didn't like what was going on. Jud was well oiled on all these sessions. When we were cutting the album, *Killer Rocks On*, just before Jud passed out on the floor, he'd say, 'You gotta do *Chantilly Lace*.' I told him I don't even know *Chantilly Lace*. So he said I should make it up. I did one take on it and I made the words up as I went along. I rewrote the whole song!

When we was recordin' *Southern Roots* I took Huey out in the car with me one night, and I was doin' 120 miles an hour. I said 'Huey, you about to die', and he was as white as a sheet. He said 'Jerry, if you slow down I'll do anything in the world for you.' I said 'Naaw, I think we'll just go out in a blaze of glory!' Looking back, I shoulda been scared myself.

SAM PHILLIPS (Mr Sun Records): I don't care if he is doin' something so slow you can't even walk to it. Jerry Lee's still rockin'. If you listen to the progression of his chords and everything – I'm not talking about finger flying – Jerry Lee is rocking, even if you barely notice it. Fortunately the Smash and Mercury recordings leave a great legacy of Jerry Lee material for posterity, even though the public rarely gets to hear the bulk of this superb material. Just as Little Richard is always asked to sing *Tutti Frutti* and *Long Tall Sally*, Jerry Lee is always associated with *Great Balls of Fire* and *Whole Lotta Shakin'*. Thankfully there exists on Mercury albums songs such as *The Session, Southern Roots, Odd Man In, Country Memories, Keep On Rockin', Boogie Woogie Country Man*, each one a monument to Jerry Lee's enormous talent.

While Jerry Lee and Linda Gail were working at the prestigious Roxy Club in Los Angeles they received a stream of celebrity visitors, including the late John Lennon, a long-time Jerry Lee fan.

LINDA GAIL (sister): After the show Lennon came into our dressing room backstage. Instead of saying 'Hello, glad to meet you', he walked over to Jerry who was sitting cross-legged with trainers on, and got down on his knees and kissed the bottom of his shoe. I swear to God! Sure, Jerry used to cuss out the Beatles but after John Lennon kissed his feet he was all for 'em.

● It's true John Lennon fell down and kissed my feet at the Roxy. He was very big then. He said something like 'I want to thank you for making it possible for me and the boys to be rock 'n' roll stars', which was the ultimate compliment. You couldn't beat that. My son, Junior, said 'D'you know who that is!?'

I knew John and the boys way back even before Ringo was their drummer. They were only kids then, and I said to Cecil 'Listen to those kids, they can sing.' He didn't think they'd make it 'cause they didn't have the right manager. But I knew they'd make it one way or another. John was such a smooth, brainy kid, always way ahead of people, and Ringo backed up those guys so perfect on drums. I told Cecil, 'They're gonna be the biggest thing you ever seen.' They knocked Elvis and Jerry Lee right outta the saddle.

CHAPTER 9

God and 'The Ferriday Three'

Memphis, like most southern cities and towns, has a tremendous array of beautiful churches of all denominations. They stand as a majestic symbol of the God-loving and Christian people who dwell in the Bible belt. The old-time religion rules many communities. The absolute authority of the Bible is interpreted by the various factions of Christianity according to their background, their educational standards and their wealth. The complexity of the Bible guarantees eternal conflict, and the main river of moderation is often overwhelmed by the flash floods of extremism.

The 'snake handlers', a sect which started at the same time as the fundamentalist movement, interpret Mark 16:18, 'Thou shalt take up serpents', as a direction to use poisonous snakes in religious services. At their services, which are usually held twice a week, the congregation play loud music and handle venomous snakes – rattlesnakes and copperheads – with complete abandon. Worshippers toss the snakes to each other. Those who are bitten are considered to be weak in their faith in the Holy Ghost – the victims do not generally seek medical help, preferring to trust in the Lord for their healing. At least 63 men and women have died from snakebites sustained during these religious meetings.

These really are the far-out fringes of Christian lunacy. 'Thou shalt take up serpents', it says in the Bible,

*so members of this sect do just that; wives who are sus-
pected of adultery are obliged to put their hands into a
swarm of poisonous snakes to prove their innocence,
and in some cases children do so to prove the strength of
their faith. Many die as a result (faith is the ability to
believe that which you know to be untrue, cynics would
say). The snake sect represents the distant fringe of the
charismatic movement and the fundamentalist Christians, and their activities are used by others to condemn
fundamentalism. Bob Jones Jnr., son of the founder of
the Bob Jones University in South Carolina, a fundamentalist establishment that sends graduate students to
Harvard and Yale, says, 'Ya know, people have this idea
that fundamentalists are down-at-heel, unkempt and un-
educated. They think we're crude, that we're snake
handlers. We don't believe in speaking in tongues and so
on. We believe the apostolic gifts were drawn when the
Scripture was done. We define a fundamentalist as someone who believes in the authority of the Bible, proclaims
the Bible, defends the Bible and tries to obey the Bible.'*

*The Rev. Son Swaggart tells of the Leona and Mother
Sumrall, founders of the Assembly of God church in
Ferriday in 1936, and of how they won the admiration of
that small community with their passion for God: even
Jerry Lee's uncle, Lee Calhoun, was moved to help them
in his own way. Son was Jimmy Lee Swaggart's father,
and Lee was the main benefactor of the Lewis clan. Lee
Calhoun had married Stella Herron, the sister of Jerry
Lee's mother, Mamie, who in turn was sister to Minnie
Belle.*

*These three ladies were to embrace the Pentecostal
faith with extraordinary vigour and they would impart
their faith to Jerry Lee, Jimmy Lee and Mickey Gilley
with enormous passion. Born in March 1936, Mickey is
the son of Irene and Arthur Gilley – Irene being the*

eldest sister of Lewis's father, Elmo. Mickey was raised in that boisterous little town of Ferriday, Louisiana, along with his cousins, Jerry Lee Lewis and Jimmy Lee Swaggart – this trio became known as 'The Ferriday Three'. All went on to their own greatness, but Gilley was the last to achieve fame. His turn in the spotlight did not come about until he was approaching his mid-thirties. Out of the threesome, he is generally considered as being the most normal, with the other two being regarded as larger than life.

Along with his cousins and their mothers, he performed at the Assembly of God church, playing guitar to Lewis's piano, and was zealously infused with the Pentecostal faith. As with his cousins, the church was the keystone of his upbringing and the birthplace of his talent. Furthermore, all three married for the first time within a year of each other, all of them to partners who also attended the Assembly of God.

However, in August 1957, after witnessing Jerry Lee's success at a concert, Mickey decided to cut his first record, 'Ooh Wee Baby', which bombed without trace just as 'Great Balls of Fire' blazed its way through the charts. Mickey changed labels and tried again, without success – also crucially failing to impress Dick Clark into giving him a slot on 'American Bandstand'. To his credit, Gilley persevered, crafting his musical style in long residences at small clubs around Houston through the sixties.

Mickey's determination eventually paid off when he attracted the attention of Sherwood Cryer, a somewhat eccentric millionaire and owner of honky-tonk night-clubs. Gilley's talent impressed Cryer sufficiently to have his Pasadena club refurbished and reopened as 'Gilley's' – with a half share for Mickey and salaries for himself and the band. This served as a good base for Gilley to

*expand his power, which eventually established Gilley's
for a time as the largest nightclub in the world.*

*An article in 'Esquire' magazine, about the honky-
tonk sub-culture, inspired the John Travolta film 'Urban
Cowboy'. The film was basically set in Gilley's and captured the lifestyles and atmosphere of the place. The
honky-tonk style of music enjoyed a surge of popularity,
selling staggering amounts of Gilley's records, who sub-
sequently opened another Gilley's in Nashville.*

*Cryer's oddball business acumen truly paid off in in-
vesting in Gilley, one of 'The Ferriday Three', that
spring of talent first tapped in the Assembly of God. The
intense counsel and nurturing of the three cousins'
mothers has seen them all vigorously pursue their own
respective directions in life. Gilley openly admits to
being a mama's boy, and also has fond memories of his
Aunt Mamie, Jerry's mother.*

MICKEY GILLEY (cousin): Mamie Lewis was my
aunt: it's hard to describe her . . . she was a giant. She
went to the Assembly of God church. She seemed to be
a very loving, sweet person, a very caring mother. The
times I stayed at Jerry's house she was just like a
mother to me.

I think Jerry Lee was probably closer to his mother
than his father. Jerry's very close to his family as a
whole, but I think he probably felt more for his mother
than anybody.

FRANKIE JEAN (sister): When Mickey Gilley used to
come and stay, he used to wake up shaking like a leaf,
the sheets soaked with sweat. He had terrifying night-
mares of demons and hell like we were taught about at
the Assembly of God – when he woke, he'd be saying:

'I'm damned, I'm a sinner, I'm going to hell' – absolutely convinced that he was. Poor kid, he was very young.

Gilley is now established, well off and not tormented by demons. He has had his fair share of ups and downs and, whilst being well balanced, can show anger. His relationship with Lewis can still be fraught at times, but each seems to hold each other in high regard if the truth be known. After all, they are family.

Jerry Lee is at his most intense when discussing religion: 'Do not use the word "religion" – it doesn't mean the word "religion" in the Bible.' His moods can vary – putting people on, sending people up about their beliefs: 'Are you sanctified, boy?' he demands of a young studio assistant, 'Do you love God?'

'Yes, sir,' replies the young man.

Jerry Lee: 'What denomination are you, boy?'

'I'm a Baptist Christian, sir,' he replies politely.

Jerry Lee: 'I knew you were messed up, boy. I'm only putting you on, young man – really.' (Laughs.)

Camera crew in Norway to Jerry lee Lewis: 'Do you believe in God?'

Jerry Lee Lewis: 'God – I wouldn't be here without God.'

Camera crew: 'Do you believe in the Bible?'

'Yes sir, I'm a preacher. Do not covet your neighbour's wife. Love your neighbour as yourself – I'm doin' the best I can – be kind to rock 'n' roll singers.' (Laughs.)

But when Jerry Lee discusses God seriously he stands erect and looks you straight in the eye, his eyes fixed on you.

● If you don't get yourself right with God, then you're

going to go to hell, whether you like it or not – that's it, that's the Bible, that's the word of God and I believe it. Right now I know how to live and I know what's right and what's wrong. I've been wrong cussing, carrying on, screwing women – people just don't want to believe this hell bit, they don't want to believe it. They just don't like it at all. I'll tell you something else: a person, a being, a God creates somebody and then lets 'em burn – it just don't make any sense, does it? But it doesn't make sense for 'em to take his son, nail him to the cross with a crown of thorns on his head, being spit on, nail spikes to his hands. You know the only thing in heaven that's made by man are the scars on the hands of Jesus – that's the only thing he has made. And the only reason we're here now is because Christ died for us and he was tempted for 40 days and nights himself by Satan, and he was tempted, he thought and he thought, and he was crucified. God turned his back on him. He said, 'My God, my God, why have you forsaken me . . . I know my Bible.'

True, Jerry Lee does know his Bible. But it is his earthly cousin Jimmy Lee who has constantly reminded Jerry Lee of his sinful ways.

JIMMY LEE SWAGGART (cousin): Jerry told me he was going to have hit records and make millions of dollars. So I said to him 'What about your soul?' He didn't answer me.

Jimmy Lee constantly projected the image of the saint in comparison to Jerry Lee the sinner.

JIMMY LEE SWAGGART (cousin): I'm going to

heaven to be with the Lord. Jerry Lee, unless he changes his ways, is on his way to Satan's hell.

Jerry was playing honky-tonks when he was 14. If I had even thought about doing that, my father would have taken me to the wood shed. Jerry Lee's parents did not discipline him at all. Perhaps that's why we are so different.

Jimmy Lee Swaggart became the most popular television evangelist in the world. At the peak of his success he claimed a world-wide audience of more than 500 million, transmitted on over 3000 stations and into 145 countries. 'People can see me in over half the homes on this planet,' he would brag. He was also making $150 million per annum and built a massive Bible college and headquarters to run his world-wide religious organisation in Baton Rouge, Louisiana.

Jimmy Lee learnt his art of preaching the hard way, as Jerry Lee had learnt his facing the public, by years of gruelling travel in rough conditions, supported by his loyal and devoted wife, Frances, to get his biblical message across. He felt, and would explain to his congregations, that Jerry Lee was suffering from demonic anointing.

In the late sixties Jimmy Lee made his first radio broadcast and realised the power of the media. The early years of driving endlessly from one poor country town to another with no guarantee of payment were soon to end. He had become a great orator, a skilled master of delivering the gospel message. On church platforms he would stalk the boards like a steaming panther in heat, using every gesture and wrenching every emotion out of each biblical phrase – he spoke directly to God and oozed repressed sexuality. There has been for some time a feverish plague of Bible-bashers in the U.S. Many of them would make St Peter seem like an agnostic, but with the new dawn of media religion, especially T.V. in general and the P.T.L. ('Praise the Lord') T.V. network in particular, Bible-bashers appeared to become more concerned about the dollar collection than about the harvest of souls.

Soon the T.V. stations across the U.S. had attracted the most repugnant, noxious, crass and scurrilous charlatans posing as preachers. One Nashville- based station had a couple who owned a Bible company sitting in their home, which appeared to be decorated with a kaleidoscope effect after a vomit-inducing traumatic experience. Staring into the camera with a sanctimonious air they declared that their Bible was for 'white folk and black folk, as King Solomon was a black man after all, ya know. So we're sellin' ya this Bible with a cedar box for $25' – the lady then flicks the cover open to expose a sheet of red cellophane. She stares again into the camera, her sincerity melting as ice in boiling water. 'This represents the blood of Jesus,' she says as the camera picks up the expression of phoniness. No wonder graffiti in a New York suburb at the time read: 'God knows we exist but he ain't no longer interested.' Yet the T.V. Bible-bashers were to grow enormously powerful and would soon be corrupted by their own power.

The first to fall was the Rev. Marvin Gorman, a T.V. ministry preacher with the Assemblies of God. Gorman confided his adultery to Swaggart, who promptly denounced him. He was dismissed from the Assemblies of God altogether. Jimmy Lee and his arch-rival Jim Bakker used this episode to condemn each other. Jimmy Lee was to insist that Gorman surrender his minister's credentials and begin a two-year rehabilitation, as demanded by the Assemblies of God.

JIM BAKKER (T.V. evangelist): I think we ought to

bring stoning back'. He referred to Jimmy Lee as 'the man who is destroying the man who is pointing the finger'.

It got hotter: Bakker became further enraged by Jimmy Lee Swaggart's success and, probably seeing in Jimmy Lee a reflection of his own contemptuous hypocrisy, called him 'a cruel prophet of doom and gloom'. There is no doubt that Jimmy Lee was a humourless, pompous and self-righteous Bible-basher. Soon God or Satan or both would have enough of the Bakkers and of Jimmy Lee Swaggart.

First came Jim Bakker's downfall. The 'Charlotte Observer' got a telephone call from a woman called Jessica Hahn, who said that on 6 December 198– she was introduced to Bakker in Room 536 at Sheraton Sand Key Resort, Florida. 'He disrobed, seduced and sodomized her . . . did then physically enter the private recess of her body with genitals.'

The Bakkers, Jim and Tammy, fell from their false pedestal. He was imprisoned for fraud – $14 million dollars had disappeared. 'The devil got into the computer,' he insisted.

Jimmy Lee's fall had to be spectacular. He had condemned sex, any form of sex outside marriage, even touching and kissing. Lipstick, powder and paint were condemned. Catholicism was a 'monstrosity of heresy': the Kennedys and the most saintly lady on the planet, Mother Teresa, would 'burn in hell'; and, of course, he would always refer to the man he had the most complexities about, Jerry Lee: 'Jerry Lee is damned.' Jimmy Lee could not cope with honesty about his own destiny.

- I'm a rock 'n' roll singer, I like good whiskey, good looking women and good music – there's nothing

like a woman. I mean, if God made anything better
He kept it for Himself – He gave man a woman to
love – and I've done the best I can do. Love women,
never seen a woman yet that I didn't love – who are
my favourite women? Any of 'em. Jimmy judges
people – 'Judge not lest ye shall be judged.' He puts
himself up there – no man should judge another
man's soul.

When the Lord's book is opened, we will stand
before Him and be judged. God gave me my talent.
He will judge me. No man or woman can. I don't
question God, but I don't think I'll have much of an
argument with God. Satan don't scare me worth a
damn. Satan won't bother me.

JIMMY LEE: I will not be satisfied until I know Jerry
Lee has entered the kingdom of heaven.

Jimmy Lee's blast furnace delivery about the everlasting
flames of hell, the evils of sex, drugs and rock 'n' roll
and the ultimate heresy, Catholicism, were to build up in
his image a character so pure and impossible to contain
in human flesh that it was bound to collapse sooner or
later.

LINDA GAIL (sister): Jimmy Lee created a situation
that he could not live up to – he made it impossible to
live what he was preaching.

Just as the devil got into Jim Bakker's computer, the
devil was to enter Jimmy Lee's trousers and go straight
to ecstasy control, turning his penile tissue into an un-
controllable boa constrictor. With Marvin Gorman and
Jim Bakker disgraced, Jimmy Lee would have the whole
harvest to reap.

Judgement time had arrived for Jimmy Lee. His pride was at its zenith: 'I have sold more long-playing albums than any gospel singer on the face of the earth.' (He has recorded forty-six gospel albums, although the gospel music encyclopaedia states 38 albums and 6 million copies, backed mainly by the Sweet Comfort Band.) One of his first albums, 'God Took Away My Yesterdays', was made at Sun Records, produced and engineered by Elvis Presley's guitarist Scotty Moore.

He claimed to be 'The most powerful preacher in the world'. He claimed on T.V. he was watched by half the world. He had ignored two fundaments of Christian beliefs – the sin of pride and the virtue of forgiveness. He had not forgiven Marvin Gorman – a preacher who had become bankrupt – and he had a swollen, irrepressible pride about himself.

Suddenly on Palm Sunday 1987 there was talk of Jimmy Lee consorting with prostitutes in the Airline Highway area of New Orleans. At first no one could believe it and regarded it as a joke, especially in the Bible-bashing arena. But Peggy Carriere would testify to a T.V. reporter for WBRZ Baton Rouge that Jimmy, with an obvious erection, would arrive at the Texas Motel in a plush tan Lincoln. She saw him twice in the same car wearing red joggin' shorts, V-neck shirt, tennis shoes and white socks. I told this guy, 'You know who that is, don't you? That's Jimmy Lee Swaggart – he just gave my old lady twenty dollars for a head job.'

The Travel Inn on Airline Highway was to be the scene of Jimmy Lee's downfall. He was cruising the area for cheap tricks – sexual favours for $10 and $20 from prostitutes – when he honed in on Debra Murphee, a prostitute who also had on her list Randy Gorman, son of Marvin. Debra casually mentioned to Randy that Jimmy Lee was a client – who liked cheap tricks. Debra *was to sell the story to 'Penthouse', and also appeared on national T.V. on the Phil Donahue show. Jimmy Lee had set himself up for a huge downfall.*

JIMMY LEE: Pornography titillates and captivates the sickest of the sick and makes them slaves to their own consuming lusts.

Before the scandal, Jimmy Lee had time to think. The result was to be the most embarrassing T.V. scene ever, in front of his wife Frances and a huge audience. He declared: 'My sin was done in secret but God said to me – I will do what I do before the whole world. I have sinned against you, my Lord, and I would ask that your precious blood would wash and cleanse every stain until it is in the seas of God's forgetfulness never to be remembered against me any more.'

He wept bitterly – he held out his arms and Frances, his wife, threw her arms around him uttering: 'I forgive you.' Three months later he was back on T.V., against the wishes of a one-year ban by his Church. Later still he would be caught again with a prostitute in California. 'Brother Swaggart!' cried out a man at one of his sermons. 'Brother Swaggart, your hypocrisy is scornful of the government of God. Liar! Hypocrite!' 'Hypocritical scum,' said a lady caller to the Phil Donahue show – but Jimmy Lee goes on. 'I'll rise again – ain't no power on earth can keep me down.'

Jimmy Lee knew he was going to be exposed several months before it was made public. The seeds of his mental turmoil were sown long before his desire to fornicate with prostitutes. He even presumed in his own autobiography, 'To Cross a River' that preachers who reach a threshold of notoriety 'can't stand fame, it goes to their head'. They start to think they are God, but Jimmy

Lee was adamant that Satan could not seduce him into immorality. The build-up of his self-righteousness and over-the-top puritanical putridity reached a new level of neurosis as he realised he was about to be shown up as a charlatan. He vigorously renewed his attacks on pornography, stating that the supreme court was not doing enough to eliminate its publication. He intensified his attacks on dancing – ballroom dancing, he declared, as men and women glide cheek to cheek, is harmful, while ballet classes and aerobic dancing are totally licentious.

Shortly before his 'sin' would be made known to the mass public he was with his friend, President Ortega, in Managua, Nicaragua, preaching to 25,000 people in Revolution Square. He attacked Jews and Catholics, saying that they could not enter heaven unless they were born again fundamentalists. He in turn was attacked as being a false prophet.

JIMMY LEE: This is what's fun about being a Pentecostal – the world already thinks you're crazy. The people on the block think you're dealing with half a deck, so you have nothing to lose.

Why did Jimmy Lee allow such a degrading episode to happen? He was shrewd, popular, successful and he had a beautiful wife ('Frances is band box dainty from her pert features to her white silk blouse under her white bolero embroidered with black sequins, to her black silk skirt and her trim patent leather pumps, she is the last word in southern chic' – quote from Elaine Dundy's 'Ferriday Louisiana'). He had a beautiful home, cars, God.

The early bashings he received from his father, Son, described by Frankie Jean as 'child molesting', will not have had a totally good effect on his well-being. As a

*youngster he would walk away from a movie box office
while Jerry Lee would rush in to see the movie. God
would speak to him to tell him it was sinful – 'I didn't
know it was an angel who used to break the projector.'
He would not look at a dirty book; when shown one, he
would say 'I forgive you – I forgive you.' According to
Frankie Jean, he would never try to look up little girls'
dresses like any normal boy – he would not kiss or chase
girls at all.*

*So Jimmy had suppressed nature's strongest urge of
all, and mother nature can only take so much.*

- I believe everybody got to die and face God some
  day, and I hope and pray that I'll go to heaven when
  I die. We don't know what God's gonna do. We
  know there's a supreme being – we believe there is a
  God. He holds the key. I believe God lets us live
  with reason. I believe there's something more to be
  lived for, I would imagine. I want to live as old as I
  can and God knows this. I think this is our main purpose in life; to live as long as we can and do as much
  as we can to help people, to give as much of our
  talent as we can in the best way we know how to give
  it.

    Jimmy Lee did say I was doing wrong and I was
  goin' to hell. I don't think he had the right to do that
  – I don't think anybody has the right to get up an' tell
  anybody, 'Hey you – you're going to hell' – or 'You
  ain't goin' to heaven if ya don't do exactly what I tell
  ya to do, walk like I tell ya ta walk.' This was apparently his problem. I don't think you've got that
  right and it will catch up with you eventually. Jimmy's a great guy. I don't see him as often as I used to
  or I'd like to.

    Sure we foul up sometimes down through life and

we make our mistakes, but God's always there to forgive us. I don't mean I've tamed myself down or anything like that. I should be playing in church – that's what I should be doing, that's my first love. I'm talking about my belief in God, in the Son of God, the Holy Ghost and the Gospel. The greatest honour that a person can have in this life is to be a fully-fledged Christian and be baptised in the Holy Spirit and have the evidence coming through speaking in tongues. The Holy Ghost will not dwell in an unclean temple, but Jerry Lee is not your average run-of-the-mill talent and for some reason or other the Holy Ghost has always abided in me. There's a reason for that – I've been a real fighter for the Holy Ghost. I have felt its power – most people don't even know what they're talking about when they talk about the Holy Spirit.

Jimmy Lee's problems, now I got blamed for them. I'm a big drain on Jimmy Lee. He loves his cousin very much and he believes in me. For years he's been on at folks trying to get me to preach. Now I think he understands why I didn't. If Jerry is going to preach it he is going to live it.

Jimmy Lee wasn't fooling me for a minute – I knew Jimmy, knew him from the beginning. All he was fooling were the people. I knew a time would come when I'd get blamed for Jimmy Lee's downfall.

[On Jimmy Lee Swaggart]: I knew what he was doing. I knew where he was coming from, I knew where he was going, and I knew exactly where he was gonna land! [laughs] I just knew him that well. He stuck with judging people all the time, preaching real strong, he preached something, it got so strict and preached so hard that he found he couldn't live it himself. He couldn't be God – he's a human being

like everybody else, I guess. That's what happened.
It's very sad, after 28 years. I think he meant well,
but he had a bad way of doing it. That's the end now.
You gotta be what you are. I'm not a hypocritical
person, I am what I am, I know what I am, and I've
never hid nothing from nobody in my life. Everything I've ever done I've made sure the public knew
about it like that. I didn't stall on nothing. If I married somebody, everybody knew it so they could get
upset and get over it! [laughs] I didn't know it'd take
so long for some of 'em to get over things.

*'No one ever went broke by underestimating the poor
taste of the public' is an American business maxim.*

LINDA GAIL (sister): Jimmy Lee is back on U.S.
national T.V., still preachin' and as big as ever – it
seems as though preachers can get away with it more
than most.

*Little old ladies may still be sending T.V. preachers their
social security cheques – there will always be a false Mes-
siah about. As the Surgeon General warns us about the
dangers of smoking to our health, so should there be at
least a biblical warning at the end of every religious tele-
cast. 'Beware of false prophets which will come to you in
sheep's clothing for inwardly they are ravening wolves'
(Matthew 7,15). There is a crucial difference between
Jerry Lee and Jimmy Lee – Jerry Lee is proud and arrogant, as is Jimmy Lee, but Jimmy lacks the humour and
self-mockery that characterises Jerry Lee.*

● My music is gospel music – everything I sing is influenced by gospel music. I *am* gospel music – it

depends on what kind of gospel you're talkin' about. The gospel, I might rewrite the whole deal – I mean, the Episcopalians, they come off the Catholic Church, and the Catholics, they come from Rome, and of course we have the Church of God and the Assembly of God – brother – because there was just one Church called the Assembly of God and they went to court and the judge split it up because one of 'em believed in wearin' rings and one didn't and one believed in wearin' lipstick and one didn't. So he split it up. [Mock judge voice]: 'I'm tellin' you what, boys! I'm calling *you* Assembly of God and *you* Church of God. Now get outta here.'

I was a preacher one time, scared the pants off every congregation. I'll tell you a true story. I was doing a tour in Australia. One time many years before I'd held a revival meeting in Hammond, Louisiana and a guy had come up to me wanting to whip me for some reason, but instead of doin' that he'd listened to my sermon, come down to the altar and got saved. So years and years passed and I'm there in Australia, walking out of the auditorium with a fifth of liquor and a glass in my hand and this guy walks up to me and says, 'I just wanna shake your hand, I got the Baptism of the Holy Ghost under your ministry in Hammond, Louisiana', and I'm standing there with a fifth of whiskey in my hand.

The Gospel, it's hard to understand. You get this Church, this Church, this Church and everybody's got different beliefs, you know. To understand the Bible, which I think is the greatest history book in the world – I can understand my cousin Jimmy Lee Swaggart, he believed I believed. He was raised the way I was, too, but for some reason or another I can

believe that I love God, Jesus Christ, the Holy Ghost
as much as anybody. I do my rock 'n' roll or whatever you want to call it, my country music, my blues,
my gospel – Jerry Lee Lewis' music. Jimmy Lee said,
'You should join up with me and do this', and I said
'You've got a good point, Jimmy – but you know,
maybe someone out there wants to hear 'Whole
Lotta Shakin' Goin' On'. Now if that's the work of
the devil – and it could be – I've made a mistake.
And I don't think I'm that dumb. I don't know, I
couldn't really picture Jesus Christ singing 'Whole
Lotta Shakin' Goin' On' – but then again we're not
Jesus Christ. Who is to say? Who is to judge?

My Daddy taught me how to sing – and my
Mamma, too. And I remember these folks in church
– my mother plucked a guitar and my Daddy'd sing –
it was fantastic, it was great. And my aunt Minnie
Bell Swaggart was my mother's sister and my aunt
Fannie Glascock, who is Carl McVoy's mother, and
my aunt Stella Calhoun – you're talking about four
Heron sisters – apparently they must have come
from Ireland. You could hear these ladies for three
miles singing these great spiritual songs, and you
could hear and you could feel the presence of God
Almighty. And, y'know, in church it was something
else, and you could hear the people talkin' in
tongues – they could call it unknown tongues, they
could call it tongues, they could call it anything they
want to – but you could check this out of your book
of facts, you could go ahead and check. . . . Paul was
one of the greatest Christians that God ever gave the
energy to preach the gospel, and he ain't got a lot to
say about the Holy Ghost. These people try to get
around the Holy Ghost, and they kick it and they
blaspheme it and they won't deal with it – they can't

understand. They don't like the speaking in other tongues, as the spirit gives utterance. They rewrite the second Book of Acts – they rewrite it. They don't want this, and as God is my witness this is the downfall of every human being walking on two feet or no feet . . . HALLELUJAH!

I just went to Bible School, and I couldn't get away from the music.

CHAPTER 10

Rockin' My Life Away

In September 1970, Jerry Lee Jnr. Lewis's son by Jane Mitcham and now aged 16, joined his Daddy's touring band, playing tambourine and back-up singing. Soon he would come under the wing of Jerry Lee's talented young drummer, Tarp Tarrant.

● I was surprised when Junior started playing the drums. He'd never had any lessons, but he had spunk and that's what it takes. I was a little nervous at first when he started playing but after I heard a few licks I knew he could do it. After all, I never took any piano lessons and I ain't done so bad.

Tarp turned him on to drugs. If I hadn't liked Tarp so much I would have killed him. Tarp learned bad habits from me too, I guess, shooting holes in the walls and stuff. But I took offence at what he done to Junior. I was gonna come down heavy on Tarp, but Momma said, 'Hey, wait a minute, Tarp ain't much older than Junior.' I got to thinking about it and she was right. They were like two children together. You can't blame it on one only a bit older than the other.

TARP TARRANT (drummer): I taught JLL Jnr. to play drums right there in that living room on a Thursday night and a Friday night, and Saturday night he opened at the Coliseum with us. He was good – when I

said something, he would listen. We'd come in from a
tour and Jerry said, 'Look, I'm thinking about putting
Jerry Jnr. on the road playin' drums. You got two days
to get him in shape, just to play steady backbeat behind
you.' I said, 'Jerry, I can't do it in two days.' He said,
'You got two days!' I said, 'Yes sir!' I brought Jerry Jnr.
out here and we worked and we worked – we worked
near ten hours a day practisin'. Talk about gettin' mad
– Jerry got mad! I used to end up throwin' sticks against
that wall, and he'd get up and storm out of the room.
He was young, had a lot of talent, he was a beautiful
kid y'know – he didn't want to be a drummer at that
time in his life, but his Dad wanted him to play and, tell
you what, he turned out to be a hell-acious drummer.
I'm very thankful to say that he was playin' my licks, he
was playin' stuff no one else knows that I taught him to
play, unless they've heard it on one of my records and
tried to duplicate it. He would listen, he showed me a
lot of respect and I had a lot of respect for him. I loved
Jerry Jnr. just like I do my own son, very near and dear
and close to me.

LINDA GAIL (sister): Junior was just the sweetest
kid, laughing and smiling all the time. He had a wonderful personality.

Junior's drug problem was beginning when Mamie be-
came terminally ill in Houston. Linda Gail left the
touring show to look after her mother, while Jerry Lee
also stayed home to plan a gospel album.
  By 1973 Junior appeared to be rid of his drug prob-
lems and was developing into a fine musician. Then on
13 November 1973 Jerry Lee received a blow even more
devastating than his mother's death two years earlier.
Junior was killed in a traffic accident near Cockrum,

Mississippi. He'd been towing a late model Ford behind his jeep from Cockrum toward Hernando on the Holly Springs Highway when he lost control and veered off the road. Nobody knows precisely what happened because Junior was alone when the accident took place. But the sheriff who discovered the wreckage gave his opinion that, in taking a curve, the towed car had hit the abutment of a bridge and jack-knifed into the jeep, which then overturned, killing the driver instantly. Junior had recently celebrated his 19th birthday.

This latest tragedy plunged Lewis into the blackest period of his life, when his only comforts were drugs, liquor, sex and, of course, rock 'n' roll. His mind-boggling itinerary for that year included engagements in some 20 states and four foreign countries. At the beginning of the seventies Jerry Lee was an enormous success in the country and western music charts. He had come back on the rebound wave of U.S. music trends. Rock 'n' roll pushed country music very much into the background in the late fifties, but now country music was coming back revitalised by the music it had tried to suppress. (Elvis Presley was only acclaimed as a country artist after his death, and Nashville producers would not allow drums in the studio up to the dawn of rock 'n' roll – they regarded drums as 'being associated with negro music'. Jerry Lee was the man who changed this more than anyone.)

American D.J.s cut Jerry Lee from their play lists because of the Myra scandal, but with his characteristic mixture of tenacity, dignity and arrogance – above all, supreme confidence in his own God-given talent – he kept on travelling and touring, rebuilding his reputation the hard way. The Killer has criss-crossed the world as many times as T.W.A., always giving excitement and value for money, acting out every emotional nuance of

*each song so that it becomes a musical playlet. On stage
Jerry Lee would dramatise the most simple song. On
'Please Release Me Let Me Go' he would immerse himself totally in the lyrics – 'Woman you got to let the Killer
go, I want to love again.' Not only that, but he would en-
rich the song by embellishing the lyrics with his unique
frills and glissandi on the keyboards.*

*His touring schedules were exhausting. Even to read
them leaves you reeling with the gruelling sense of what a
living legend had to endure to please his public.*

JERRY LEE LEWIS ITINERARY 1973

Jan. 8–11	*Advisions Recording Studio, London, England.*
Jan. 20	*Grand Ole Opry, Nashville.*
Jan. 28	*Greenville, South Carolina.*
Jan 29	*Greensboro, North Carolina.*
February	*Cincinnati.*
February	*Richmond, Virginia*
March 3	*Grammy Awards, Los Angeles*
March 22	*Bananafish Garden, Brooklyn. Taping 'In Concert'.*
March 23	*Hampton, Virginia.*
March 24	*Coliseum, Charlotte, North Carolina.*
April 1	*Dallas, Tx. George Wallace Fundraiser.*
April 7	*Taping 'Midnight Special', NBC Burbank, California.*
April 10	*'Wembley Stadium Documentary'. BBC TV England.*
April 27	*'Midnight Special' US TV.*
April 28	*University of Maryland, Silver Springs, MD.*

April: one week	*Bachelors III Club, Fort Lauderdale, Florida.*
May 11	*'In Concert' ABC US TV. Taped 22 March.*
June 2	*'Artist of the Year Award', Memphis.*
June 19–21	*The Boston Club, Boston, Massachusetts.*
June: three days	*Bahamas.*
July 4–6	*Steel Pier, Atlantic City, New Jersey.*
July 10–12	*Mercury Studio, Nashville.*
July 14	*Phillips Studio, Memphis.*
July 15	*American Legion Park, Culpeper, Virginia.*
July 21	*Rockland Warrior Stadium, Haberstraw, New York.*
July 31	*Honolulu, Hawaii.*
July	*Mill Run Theatre, Chicago.*
July	*Greely, Colorado.*
August 25	*Colorado State Fair, Pueblo, Colorado.*
August 28	*Michigan State Fair, Detroit, Michigan.*
Sept. 8	*Park La Courneuve, Paris, France.*
Sept. 9	*Hanover, West Germany.*
Sept. 13	*Coliseum, Lubbock, Texas.*
Sept. 14	*Tarrant County Convention Center, Fort Worth, Texas.*
Sept. 15	*Merrywater Post Pavilion, Columbia, Maryland.*
Sept. 16	*Hofheinz Pavilion, Houston, Texas.*
Sept. 23	*'Sonny & Cher Comedy Hour', CBS US TV.*
Sept. 24–26	*Recording Studio*

Sept. 30	*Spectrum, Philadelphia, Pennsylvania.*
Sept.	*Los Angeles. Taping 'Police Story'.*
October 6	*Myrid, Oklahoma City, Oklahoma.*
October 7	*Corpus Christi, Texas.*
October 12	*Madison Square Garden, New York City.*
October 13	*Coliseum, Miami, Florida.*
October 15	*Gardens, Boston, Massachusetts.*
October 26	*Bowling Green, Kentucky.*
October 27	*Des Moines, Iowa.*
Nov. 9	*Pershing Auditorium, Lincoln, Nebraska.*
Nov. 10	*Auditorium, Minneapolis, Minnesota.*
Nov. 9–10	*'Midnight Special' US TV.*
Nov. 11	*Capitol Centre, Washington DC.*
Nov. 20	*'Police Story – Collision Course', US TV.*
Nov. 21	*Sacramento, California.*
Nov. 22	*San Francisco, California.*
Nov. 23	*Fresno, California.*
Nov. 23	*Jerry Lee's Nite Lighters Club, Memphis, Tennessee.*
Nov. 24	*Los Angeles, California.*
Nov. 25	*San Diego, California.*
Nov. 25	*Indianapolis, Indiana.*

It was also the year he made his long-awaited debut at that mecca of country music, the Grand Ol' Opry in Nashville, Tennessee. The Opry had always frowned on Lewis because of his media-projected image, and he'd always had reservations about appearing there because they'd expect him to perform country music only.

So when the time came, would the Killer stick to the

C & W songs he'd made his own, or would the Killer break loose and start pounding them keys?

GLORIA YOUNG (lifelong fan): I think it was 11.30 before the Killer came on stage – I'd dozed off listening to some country dude. You'd better believe I woke up like a shot when I heard the strains of *Another Place, Another Time*. John, my husband, and I sat there in disbelief as we listened to Jerry go from gospel to country to some of the rockinest songs he sings – *Whole Lotta Shakin', Great Balls of Fire, Good Golly Miss Molly*. Who else could go on stage at the Opry and go from *Tutti Frutti* to *I'm So Lonesome I Could Cry* and have the crowd whooping for more?

John Lomax III, writing in his book 'Nashville Music City U.S.A.', observes:

JOHN LOMAX III: Quite possibly the foremost-rock-country-blues musician of the twentieth century, Lewis is also seriously tormented. One of the most charismatic performers to ever grace a stage or deface a piano, Jerry Lee has influenced every rock and country player who has ever sat behind a keyboard. He lives according to his own rules and, as a result, he has been continually at odds with women, alcohol, amphetamines, the police, and the IRS [tax authorities]. He is probably the all-time leader in legal fees. When word leaked out of his marriage to his 13-year-old cousin, Myra Gail, he was practically deported from England. Lewis spent ten years in social exile before making a comeback in 1968. Lewis belongs in the Hall of Fame but will never be selected.

John Pugh of Music City News agreed that Jerry Lee's

long-awaited debut at the Opry was an event worth wait-ing for.

JOHN PUGH (critic): He killed 'em with music that's an extension of his gigantic personality, an embodiment of his turbulent lifestyle, a vocal and visual picture of a man's entire existence. From *Me and Bobby McGee* to *Chantilly Lace*, from *Another Place, Another Time* to *Johnny B. Goode*, from *Waiting For a Train* to *Whole Lotta Shakin'*, he displayed his berserkly hypnotic music that could only be played and sung by the most unique music personality America has ever produced. And for one of the few times in his life Jerry Lee con-sented to do an encore. Three of them. He killed them with his showmanship. Playing the piano with almost every part of his anatomy, shaking his legs back and forth at the piano stool like a man who can't hold it an-other minute, flinging off his modern art sport coat, he was never more in his glory. It was all there in spades; the arrogant manner, the haughty demeanour, the regal aura that have probably caused Jerry Lee Lewis to be both praised and damned more than any other entertainer.

But another side of Jerry Lee was also revealed at the Opry. After a few numbers he stopped his show and called Opry pianist Del Wood out on stage. Following a short but moving speech on Mrs Wood's graciousness and compassion, he invited her to duet with him on the ragtime piano song, 'Down Yonder'. It was an unforget-table sight – Jerry Lee Lewis, the hedonistic Killer, playing alongside Del Wood, one of the greatest ladies of country music. Finishing their number, they sponta-neously embraced as the applause rose to a tumult.

So the Killer not only conquered the Opry but also re-paid Del Wood, his old friend, for her kindness to him. The Killer felt he had earned the supreme honour from the Country Music Hall of Fame, but they wanted Jerry Lee to change his ways.

- They had voting in the, like R.C.A. Victor, Columbia, Mercury, everybody had so many votes I was offered all the awards one year. This man Dick Blake tells me, 'Jerry, if you cut your drinking a little bit and stop cussing so much on the stage and carrying on, I got a deal for you – you can get all the awards all this year.' I said, 'Now you have insulted me more than anybody has ever insulted me in my life. If you wasn't a good friend of mine I'd whoop your butt right now.'

- I saw some bootleg tapes of mine at a garage. Yeah, well that was between Nashville and Memphis. I stopped off at this place to get some gas, me and the boys, and they had all these records on a big stand out of all my tapes and everything on 'em. I saw all my records and I said, 'Hey, man, where'd you get these tapes from?' and it goes way back to when these big tapes were played in the car – eight-track, four-track, whatever – anyway, I took 'em and I threw them out on the ground, poured gasoline all over 'em and burned 'em up and he said, 'Now what am I gonna do, Jerry Lee, when the man comes back in here and wants to know where his money is for the tapes?' I said, 'Well, I don't know. Just tell him the Killer was here, checkin' out' – it's not really funny, but it's true.

  I tell you about the bootleg records – who owns the bootleg records? I said Columbia Records own bootleg records, RCA-Victor owns bootleg records, Sam Phillips and Shelby Singleton own the bootleg records. That's it on the bootleg records. I wouldn't touch any of them with a ten-foot pole, it's the truth. There might be a few people around here who put out a few records or bootleg records of a show or something like that, but your big bootleg records they come straight from the horse's mouth, I've always known that. Reaping the harvest. They call the record in, re-mix it and put it out again on another label, same people, and sell them again to fans. Yeah, same records, re-done, re-mixed, put out in a different way, on a different label. They sell them again to the poor people who buy them – that really burns me up, man.'

Immaculately dressed in classy suits and shirts, the image of Jerry Lee in 1975 was that of a man who lived the rock 'n' roll ethos to the ultimate extreme. At first Jerry Lee would play the southern country gentleman, but as the toll of touring and tragedy mounted up he tanked up on booze and played to his media image, giving his audience the works.

They came to see the man who could out-drink, out-drug, out-fight, out-rock, out-do anyone at anything. They wanted the Killer, they wanted to see the piano lid flying across the stage, the piano stool being kicked in the air, the piano being set alight – they wanted the Killer to take them away from their mundane lives, and they knew he would give it all he'd got.

At the Berlin Rock Festival the German audience, clad in leather motorcycle gear, had come to be rock 'n' rolled to pieces. Jerry Lee teased them as they waited for wild rock 'n' roll. He casually walked out, pulled the mike between his legs and started into a slow country version of 'What's Made Milwaukee Famous Has Made a Loser Outa Me'. The black leather-clad rock 'n' rollers started to chant: 'We want rock 'n' roll!' Jerry Lee carried on, completely ignoring them – they chanted again. Jerry Lee: 'What's made Milwaukee Famous has made Hitler kids out of you'. He eased into another slow country number, 'One Has My Name' and the chanting 'We want rock 'n' roll' continued. Jerry Lee stops. 'Yar nuthin' but a bunch of Hitler kids, and if ya don't like what I'm doin' the door swings both ways – cause you're lookin' at the finest piano player that was ever born.' Jerry Lee leaves the stage. There is silence – the packed arena becomes like an undiscovered Egyptian tomb.

A few minutes elapse – Jerry Lee comes back on stage, the crowd erupt with applause, he sits down once again and plays 'Green Green Grass of Home'. Then he bursts into a rockin' riff followed by a pulverising boogie-ridden version of 'Down the Line'. The crowd go crazy.

- I never did claim to be no king of rock 'n' roll or the greatest in the business. All I said was, 'I'm simply the best'. If I went on stage and didn't know what I could do, I would be nervous. I've never been nervous when I go on stage in my life. When I've had problems with the sound system and pianos and things I've got a little upset over that, but not nervous, no. I always enjoy looking at the fans, the people, and I can tell they're enjoying it and like it. And I enjoy entertaining myself, too – I love music. As long as I have a good band kicking behind me I like to get out there with the folks.

  I could always handle my liquor. I could never stand anybody like that around me. I mean, it would kill a normal guy, you've got to admit. Yeh, it would probably kill a normal person – but it was a phase in my life I went through there. I'd done a lot of drinking and a lot of hard living, so to speak – well, some people would think it was hard living. A couple of bottles a day sometimes, maybe. I'll just tell you what some of the musicians say. They thought I was doing some heavy drinking. I was putting them on a little bit, yeh. At one time I kept a bottle with me. They thought everybody would be drinking out of the bottle. I'd have a couple of bottles, you know, and they thought I was drinking only whiskey. At the time in my life when I was drinking that whiskey I drank it like water. It was like drinking Coca-Cola – I'd just guzzle it down and I'd go on and do my show. I've always done a great show – Jerry Lee Lewis was never staggering, mis-talking, misrepresenting a song or his stage work or his records with whiskey.

[Drinking with Merle Haggard]: Oh, I know Merle very well, I've known him a few years. Yeh, I got him drinking – he had gotten out of the penitentiary, I think. I don't know what he was in there for – like we all been there a couple of times. He got back on the road, he made a big hit with *Swinging Doors* and I met Merle in Richmond, Virginia – we were doing a show there and he stayed to himself, he wouldn't talk to nobody. I went in the dressing room and started talking with him and I nudged him and I said, 'Do you drink at all?' He said, 'No, I don't.' He said, 'I don't drink, Jerry.' I said, 'Okay, I thought you might want to take a shot of this Crown Royal with me.' He said, 'Well, I might try some', and before I knew it we done that bottle and walked by the stage and busted it there in front of everybody and that really got off with him. Yeh, he busted the whiskey. We kept drinking every day after that. Oh how long we've been – oh, it's been twenty years. I said, 'Well, you really oughta do that one Merle, that's gonna really identify you.' I said, 'That's gonna crucify you, boy.'

[Drinking with Bob Hope]: He was a pro all the way, still is. I'll never forget, the first time I met him in person, we was doing the March of Dimes benefit show and they had Bob Hope and wanted Jerry Lee Lewis to host it. Well, I'm not cut out for hosting a show, that's not my ball game. I was handling it pretty good, I could've done it, but I asked, 'Is there anything to drink here?' and Bob Hope said, 'Yeah, I have a fifth of vodka right here.' I brought it up and I'd take a drink, he'd take a drink, I'd take a drink, he'd take a drink, I'd take a drink, he'd take a drink. Then all of a sudden I was seeing four Bob Hopes and he was laughing and looking at me and you couldn't even tell if he'd had a drink! I said, 'You gotta do something', so they got someone else up there (to host the show), a coloured man who sang *Tobacco Road* [Lou Rawls]. He was a pro, he stepped up there and took my place. I'm glad he did 'cause I would've fallen off.

In November 1978 Jerry Lee left Mercury.

● One of the last things they done on me was *Middle Age Crazy*, and that's why I left the company then. I saw a man take a song and put a track down on it and I didn't even like it at the time, and when I went in a month later and put my voice on it and I heard it I said, 'Man, that's great, isn't it.' It kinda scared me – that's not the way I record. You're losing out on something when you record like that. But it was a great record.

He signed up with Elektra Records and had a hit with 'Rockin' My Life Away'. The producer at Elektra was Bones Howe, who had his roots in rock 'n' roll and had worked with Elvis.

BONES HOWE (producer): I was looking forward to meeting the man of whom Kris Kristofferson said, 'Jerry Lee should be given an award for simply being himself'. This is my first album with Jerry Lee Lewis and it's a terrific thrill to work with someone who's as talented and as dynamic as Jerry Lee. When Jerry Lee came to L.A. to record I told him, 'Jerry Lee, we've got four days – we're going to do an album in four days.' He said, 'What are the other two days for?' 'Well, because we never worked together before, we may need a couple of days to get acquainted.'

We went into the studio for four days and we cut 16 songs. Jerry learnt all the songs in the studio, we arranged them in the studio and we recorded them all in one or two takes. Jerry Lee was surrounded by great musicians like Hal Blaine and James Burton [Hal has played on seven Grammy-winning records]; James was the great rock lead guitar on the Ricky Nelson hits and the Johnny Rivers Go-Go days. We recorded the same way that all the great rock hits were cut in the 50s; the band was there, the singer was there and everything happened in the studio at once, with no overdubbing. Jerry Lee played and sang, and all the excitement of the spontaneous recording comes through on the tape. All the songs on this album were chosen in the studio. The ones that Jerry Lee didn't already know, he learnt from demo records that I brought in. I played the song *Rita May* to him, without telling him who it was by, and when it was over he said, 'Who wrote that?' I said, 'Bob Dylan'. He said, 'He's great, I'll cut anything he wrote.'

'As he got into the limo he shook hands with me and said, "I don't care what you do with these records as long as *I Wish I Was 18 Again* is on one side of the first record that comes out." There's a lot of improvisation on these records. At one point in *Everyday I Have to Cry* Jerry Lee spontaneously, in the middle of the take, made up a verse about his five wives. 'Every day I have to cry – once there was Dorothy and then came Jane, look out Myra you look insane – come on Jaren, you're struttin' your stuff, I think I'll take another 'cause I can't get enough.' *Rockin' My Life Away* fades out, Jerry Lee says, 'What a mother humper, son, if that don't sell a million I'll kiss your butt on the courthouse square and let Jud Phillips draw the crowd.'

Bones Howe did a great job on the first Elektra album, which captures Jerry Lee's style and greatness and stands today as a classic rock 'n' roll album.

- Why didn't I do a second album? I'd like to know that myself. It wasn't my fault or my idea – I was ready to record, I was on top of the deal. When I cut that first album, my Daddy was passing away at the same time. Yeh, we got through the last song and I was told my Daddy died and I went on home. It wasn't my fault Elektra couldn't come through. They had given me a three hundred thousand dollar guarantee an album and they got mad about that – they don't want to stick up to the contract, that's what it was. They wanted to bring it down to about one hundred and fifty thousand dollars an album, but the deal was three hundred thousand dollars an album. They wanted to cut me off, you know. I said, 'I don't need your record label that bad, and you don't need me if you feel that way.'

Eddie Kilroy was to cut the next session in Nashville. He produced the classic versions of 'When Two Worlds Collide', 'Thirty-Nine and Holding' and the unique interpretation of 'Over the Rainbow'. Jerry Lee made the song his own, even though it was a well-used standard.

At this time not only was the Killer a danger to himself but he was becoming a danger to those around him, accidentally shooting his bass player Norman Owens in the chest while blasting a coke bottle in Jaren's living room in Collierville, Tenn. And, in 1976, Jerry Lee was arrested outside Elvis Presley's home, Graceland, brandishing a Derringer pistol, only hours after driving his Rolls Royce into a ditch whilst drunk.

- I took this bottle of champagne and decided to go and see Elvis. Man, I was really loaded. Someone had given me this pistol as a present and I put it on the dashboard where it could be seen, otherwise the law will arrest you for concealing a weapon. Anyway I hit the gate in my Lincoln and a guard run out. The pistol had fallen on the floor. He saw the pistol and said to me, 'Are you gonna shoot Elvis?' I said, 'What would I be here for if I didn't come to shoot him?' Next thing I knew there were six squad cars around me and they put the cuffs on me and took my butt off to jail. Elvis came and got me out. He said, 'What are you doin'?' I said, 'I'm trying to get in your gate!'

  Why has the media always picked on me like that? I mean, like they said I broke into Elvis' front gate – bullcrap!! – how you gonna break into Elvis Presley's front gate to begin with? That's stupid to even think about. Elvis called me – he called me and he even had his girlfriend to call me, and they finally caught me at the Vapors in Memphis, and I talked with a lady on the phone, and she said, 'Well, Elvis has called and called and called, he wants you to come by, he's really depressed and he wants to talk to you.' Well, they caught me really knee-walking drunk – I was drinkin' champagne that night. I said, 'I'll be there'.

Charlie Foren comes up to me when I walk out of the car. He said, 'Jerry, I want to give you somethin' for playing all these benefit shows', and he gave me this pistol – it was a .38 Derringer pistol, a nickel-plated, beautiful pistol, and I took it and I laid it up on the dashboard. He said, 'Naw, put it in your glove compartment – and it's not against the law.' So I put it in my glove compartment and he said, 'Naw, I'm wrong, you put it on your dashboard.' I said, 'Well, make up your mind, man.' I think he was drunk, too – so I took it and I put it on the dashboard and I went down to Elvis' house and I was really loaded – I ain't gonna lie about that.

He had just put a new man on the gate, and I whipped in, in that Lincoln limousine of mine, and I swear that the front of that limousine was like it was three miles long, and I hit the gate and it went like this – it was like Elvis was doing a show and the guy comes over and says, 'Who are you?' I said, 'I'm Jerry Lee – I'm supposed to be here to meet Elvis.' He said, 'What are you doin' with that pistol on your dashboard?' [laughs] And by this time it had finally fell off on to the floor. He said, 'Did you come here to shoot Elvis?' I said, 'Well, what would I be here for if I didn't come to shoot him?' The next thing I knew there were six squad cars around me and they took me to jail. [laughs] And it was funny, I couldn't believe anybody could be that stupid or that envious of what was goin' on – I am what I am, I do what I do, I play my piano, I sing my songs. If Elvis don't like it or he didn't like it – I do what I do and I'm the best at what I do.

Sure, well, Elvis always wanted me to come around and play the piano – he loved my piano playing. He should have known that from the beginning – as a matter of fact he did – when he was doin' that live album where he didn't know the tape was on, and I didn't either. Elvis sat at the piano for two hours and he finally said, 'Hey, Jerry Lee, I think everybody ought to know how to play a piano.' I said, 'Well, I bin tryin' to tell you that for two hours' [laughs]. 'Really think about it.'

Elvis was a fine person. I knew him very well and the books you read about him that his so-called friends put out on him and stuff like that, I think most of it is a bunch of baloney. He had a weight problem, he may have taken some diet pills or something to help him lose weight, but that's not what killed Elvis. What killed Elvis was loneliness and friends that he thought he had around him weren't friends – they got to him. I could see it happening. I should've went up to talk with Elvis – as a matter of fact he called me at least 15 times. I don't know, I just couldn't picture Elvis dying, or in that bad a shape. I didn't take the time I should have to go and talk with him, 'cause he would listen to me. When he opened up in Las Vegas and he hadn't worked for 12 years on stage, he called me and said, 'Jerry, I want you to come here. I want you to come here and tell me the truth about my show.'

They said I tried to kill Elvis. Elvis called me and said, 'Jerry, I'm so depressed, you gotta come talk to me.' Elvis Presley and me were just like this – the

best of friends that ever was, swear to God, tell you
the truth.

This is one of the greatest people I've ever known,
one of the greatest persons – this guy was unbeliev-
able. Well, Elvis opened the door, man, but he
couldn't follow Jerry Lee on stage – no siree.

*Jerry Lee and Elvis really loved each other – they had so
much in common. They were both southern boys, they
were both mamma's boys, they both had the same
nature, the same religious background, and they were
both rock 'n' roll legends.*

- Elvis was my friend and you'd better believe it. Elvis
  Presley loved Jerry Lee Lewis. Elvis was a good person – we had a good time together. We were two of
  the same kind.

*But Jerry Lee and Elvis did collide, and Jerry Lee got
disillusioned with his rock 'n' roll brother.*

KENNY LOVELACE (band leader): It was '69, we
were in Columbus, Ohio, in a hotel and we had one
night off. Elvis was in Las Vegas getting ready for his
opening show the next night. We knew nothing about
it. Jerry knew he was going to open in Las Vegas, but
wasn't aware Elvis was trying to contact him. So Elvis
called the hotel. Jerry was asleep when he phoned, so
Elvis left a message for Jerry to call him back at the
International Hotel. When Jerry got up he returned
Elvis' call. Elvis was in the steam room, so Jerry left a
message. He had returned his call. When Elvis got out
of the steam room he called Jerry back and said, 'I'd
really like to have you come and see my show tonight if

you can.' Jerry said, 'We got one night off, you got it.' Elvis said, 'Fantastic, I'll see you tomorrow night.'

Well, Jerry asked me to go and Cecil Harrelson and Dick West. We got to Las Vegas and checked in at the hotel, and at showtime they had a nice booth – a perfect seat – reserved for us. Come showtime they introduced Elvis. He looked great and did a fantastic show. About middleways through his show, Elvis said, 'Ladies and gentlemen, I've got a real good friend of mine in the audience I'd like to recognise tonight, who came to see my show and I think he's a fantastic entertainer. I want you to give a nice round of applause to Mr Jerry Lee Lewis.'

Jerry stood up and took a bow, and the crowd gave him a standing ovation. There were many celebrities there and they all gave Jerry a standing ovation. After the show we all went back to Elvis' dressing room. He had out the red carpet with champagne for us. I was talking to Elvis' guitarist, James Burton, and Jerry and Elvis were talking together. After a while Elvis said he had a piano in the room. 'Hey Jerry, would you mind getting up and playing a couple of tunes on the piano?' And Jerry replied, 'No. I'd be glad to.'

So Jerry goes over to the piano and starts hitting a few notes, and Elvis strolls over and leans on the piano and looks down, and Jerry's doing all these licks and Elvis starts shaking his head and says, 'Man, what a piano player.'

It was great. Col. Parker was there and Elvis' Dad too. Elvis was a good person, and it's really a shame what happened to him. I think Jerry and Elvis had a lot of respect for each other. I think they were good friends. They just didn't get to see enough of each other.

Elvis called Jerry frequently. Jerry and I and the

band were invited to meet Elvis in Vegas at the International. Elvis got a piano in so Jerry Lee could play for him. He loved Jerry's playing and singing. Jerry and he were both gospel fans.

Jerry played *I'll Fly Away, Will the Circle Be Unbroken, How Great Thou Art* – gospel material. He ribbed and joked with Elvis, and Elvis enjoyed his company. He said to Elvis, 'You don't know what your doin', you're just Colonel Parker's puppet.'

'Well,' said Elvis. 'If I'm so dumb and you're so smart, how is that I'm playing the main room and you're playin' the lounge?'

Jerry Lee respected Elvis until their get-together in Vegas and until he saw how Col. Parker controlled him.

- [When Elvis was fine]: Yeh, I got on with him. When I said we had a ball, I mean the fun, let me get this right. That was having a ball. Don't get me wrong here. The best memory I have of Elvis, when I knew him, is when he had to be overseas to do his eighteen months over there and he came back. At the old club in Vegas we were together quite a bit. We had some good times, it was good fun. That was when he looked good and carried himself real well, but he was always worried about somebody stealing his style, he continuously worried about that, I don't know why. He wasn't as confident on stage apparently as I was. I knew I could do it, you know. Yeh, that's the way I see it anyway. If I didn't know what I could do when I go on stage, if I didn't know what I could do, I would be nervous – if I had to go out there and do something I didn't know what I was doing. That's why he invited me to Vegas when he hadn't performed. He wanted my advice as a friend.

[On drink and Elvis and drugs]: Yeah, I've always
felt like I could have helped Elvis but I tried to a
couple of times – he didn't wanna accept it – and
when he did call me up, wanted me to come over and
talk with him, and two or three times he called me
and I wouldn't. If I had really felt like I really should
have went, I believe I should have went. I started to
go a couple of times, but I don't know – he requested
that I never bring the subject up to him again and I
didn't think I'd better do that. I didn't want another
argument with him. It's so sad – very sad, but obviously he loved me too, you see. It was a shame, it
was all the way round a shame, 'cause the people he
had workin' with him they double-crossed him, they
kept us apart a lot. If Elvis tried to get to me or
somethin' they wouldn't let him, and if I tried to get
to him or somethin' they wouldn't let it happen.
They were jealous of us all. We didn't know what
was goin' on, and there I was runnin' wide open. I
went everywhere I wanted to go and done everything
I wanted to do, and Elvis he's just sat up there in the
house lookin' all alone. This stuff – he gets mad, and
takes his pistol out 'n shoots two television sets, stuff
like that, y'know – poor boy. But I tell you what, the
doctor, there was one doctor who had, he had a surgery but it was false – he just prescribed drugs for
Elvis and just sent 'em off all the time. Yeah, Doctor
Painless. Doctor Painless [laughter] I saw him on
television one night – *Johnny Carson Show*, I believe
it was – he said, 'Well, they call me doctor painless
'cause I don't like to see people in pain' [laughter].
He said, 'I'll give them anything they want – I don't
wanna see 'em in pain.' I never run into him before,
he was a doctor, a real doctor, he was, yeah, but he
was supposed to be a dental guy, but he had no chair

[laughter], he had no equipment, he could write prescriptions out – just write prescriptions all the time.

The death of Elvis was a tragedy – a lot of people blame Dr Nick, I know. I stand up for Dr Nick and say he did his job, but I think with Elvis it seems he got approached from other sources. He worked with Elvis a long time, he was Elvis' doctor and, I don't know, I heard all sorts of different things. I knew Dr Nick real well and I knew Elvis real well – I really couldn't picture it, what they were saying. I knew Elvis got tied up with some other doctor and he had doctors flying in every direction, when he did I think Dr Nick said to him, 'If you need me again I'll be in Memphis.' I feel it was unfair the way they interpreted Dr Nick, the way he treated Elvis, because a lot of fans of Presley blame Dr Nick for his death, they say that he over-prescribed. I think they're wrong over that. If I thought they were right I'd say so. I've studied Dr Nick, I've studied him very close. I've had a talk with Dr Nick about this. No, it's not true. He never would give me anything, an aspirin maybe, never give me no hard dope or anything, that was out of the question. If I was dying, or cut one of my legs off, he might give me a Demerol shot – I had to be hurting, I had to be hurting really bad – but that was it. No hard dope, no. Yeh, he is a good man, a very honest, very faithful person. I couldn't breathe, but when I found out he was with me I was fine. He saved me at least twice. I don't know what I'd do without Dr Nick. When you need him, he's there. He didn't kill Elvis – it was others who gave him too much.

The crucifixion of Jerry Lee's career by the media continued long after Elvis' death. U.S. and U.K. tabloids exceeded their normal hysteria in June 1988. Lisa Marie Presley, Elvis' daughter and only child, was in Las Vegas for business discussions with Tom Parker. She paid a social call on Jerry Lee and his wife, Kerrie. They were all seen at a local hotel having dinner in a sociable fashion, which the media interpreted with such headlines as 'King of Rock's daughter in bizarre pact with pop wild man', followed by a text which implied that Jerry Lee and 'grasping' Lisa Marie had teamed up in a plot to bankrupt and humiliate Tom Parker.

- [On meeting Lisa Marie Presley]: I met Lisa Marie in Las Vegas – she came to my show there. Yeah, well there she was, she was a grown girl and she was standing by herself, and we were talking and talking. I knew her when she was a baby, but I hadn't known her since she'd grown up. She talked about her Dad quite a bit. They kept on trying to push something into people's minds about something going on that wasn't going on. This guy wanted an interview and I gave him an interview, and he kept on about me and Lisa Marie, and I said, 'I'm gonna tell you something: you'll never know and nobody'll ever know between Lisa Marie and me what happened.' He looked funny about that, you know, he wrote it up big time. According to one journalist I said I was gonna marry her and get all Elvis' millions – obviously putting them on, or did I say it at all now? I don't think I said that, y'know. I might have said it jokingly – I could have . . . anyway, he kept on about Lisa Marie, and I told him, 'I'll tell something about Lisa Marie, you or the world will never know what happened between me and Lisa Marie – you can think what you wanna think, say what you wanna say.' They wanted more scandal about big bad Jerry

Lee at it again. That is so ridiculous – I mean, poor little girl, she's just 19 or 20 years old, and with her mother. They were with Jerry Schilling, who was a good friend of her father, and I never saw Lisa Marie or even hardly talked to her by herself – behind stage at the show for just a minute, and I think we all went out to a party one night, and another fellow that she had was with us. They just wanted a bit of scandal. Yeah, they really pushed it on. That was so silly, I mean they really got ridiculous. Elvis Presley was a dear friend, so to speak, of mine and it's really stupid to put me with his daughter. They printed a lot of things that were not true – I've read some pretty crazy things. I just gave up on reading them. I got to where I wouldn't even read them, it got so ridiculous, really crazy some of them. I know I may have been, so to speak, a rebel – they probably thought James Dean and Elvis were pretty wild till I came on the scene, and they started on my case. Who's this guy and a piano stool? He's got real wild.

So the image of Jerry Lee and Elvis as rival enemies is totally false – they were close.

KERRIE LEWIS (sixth wife): When Jerry is watching T.V. and Elvis comes on he calls Lee, 'Hey, Lee, that's my buddy Elvis. They say I tried to kill him. Don't believe it, Lee, he was my friend.'

One outstanding question remains. Why did Elvis go into the army while Jerry Lee remained rock 'n' rollin'?

● I said to Elvis, 'You must be crazy, man. Sure I got my call-up papers – never even filled 'em in.

In 1977 Elvis died from a massive overdose. Jerry Lee had just finished a set in a small Mississippi club when he heard the news on the night of 16 August 1977. The door of his dressing room burst open and in charged a T.V. news team, demanding a comment. With ill-judged and probably drunken flippancy, Lewis responded directly, 'I'm glad he's dead. Now I'm the king.'

One might speculate here that the only reason Jerry Lee survived the ravages of his phenomenal drug intake was that he started so young. His body developed drug tolerance early on.

The only stable thing in Jerry Lee's life was the adoration and loyalty of his fans. He rewarded them by giving away as much of himself as he could, undergoing impossible touring schedules to satisfy his growing need for applause.

- I was working at *The Wagon Wheel*, and truck drivers would come in and say, 'I'd like to hear a song'. I'd say 'You gonna put something in the kitty?' They'd say 'No, but I've got something for you right here'. They'd hand you a whole bunch of these brown amphetamines. They'd bring your energy back. You think you're really going strong, but that's a bunch of baloney. If you take two or three of them you could go on for four hours no problem, but then you want to go on and take some more, and then you're out in left field. I stayed up 12 days and 12 nights. That was so stupid, wasn't it? We never stopped, kept clubs open all day and all night. Dared not close them up! The women was there for the taking, and I was there for the giving! The greatest times I've had in my life. It was remarkable, all these mean dudes hanging around – they'd have a few drinks, then want a fight or something. If I got all this on film people would've been standing nine blocks away to get in the movie theatre.

Buck Hutcheson was hanging in there with me. Buck told me one time how I gave him one of those blue and yellow pills [Dezmetol]. He loved 'em too and he took it and it got stuck halfway in his throat. It wouldn't come up and it wouldn't go down, and it stayed there for two weeks! Those were the greatest times, the greatest days. I wouldn't do it any other way. I wouldn't do it any different.

Amphetamine abuse can make sleep impossible for several days, leaving you hallucinating and walking into walls. One option is to reach for the depressants, then the vicious circle of uppers and downers accelerates, requiring increasing doses. Over decades of touring, the constant concentration of strong drugs in the stomach took a heavy toll on Jerry Lee's body.

When Lewis failed to appear in court after being arrested outside Elvis Presley's home brandishing a Derringer pistol, it was because he was in hospital undergoing treatment for a peptic ulcer. Less than two months later he was back in hospital having his gall bladder removed. While they were at it, doctors had to deal with a collapsed right lung, a case of pleurisy, and injuries to the back and neck sustained in a car crash three months earlier.

One of Jerry Lee's closest brushes with death came when it took surgeons four hours to repair a gaping gash in his corroded stomach – he was given a five per cent chance of survival. Thousands of well-wishers from all over the world, many offering to give blood, jammed the hospital switchboard. Frequent callers include Carl Perkins, Willie Nelson, Tom Jones, Kris Kristofferson, Johnny Cash, Glen Campbell, Stevie Wonder, Charley

Pride, Mickey Gilley and Elton John. Merle Haggard, Conway Twitty and Emmylou Harris stopped in the middle of a concert to call up the hospital and check how 'the Killer' was doing. When asked to pray for his recovery, a crowd of over seventy thousand maintained a solemn silence for two minutes.

- Oh yeah, I don't think there was any doubt, my doctor told me I didn't have a chance. I said, 'Doc, could you give me a Demerol shot? It might blow this train up.' He said, 'Give him anything he wants, it won't make no difference anyhow'. I felt a lot better. They operated on me three times in two days.

J. W. WHITTEN (Jerry Lee's tour manager): When we got him out of hospital the first thing he did was run over to the piano to see if he could still play it! The first thing he did, he cracked me up. He said 'I just want to see if I can still play.' I said 'You still got it!'

Three months later Lewis was out of hospital and rockin' again at a celebration of his 46th birthday. The same night, mysteriously, his Eldorado Cadillac was burnt out irreparably. Not that Lewis was fazed – a new Rolls Royce convertible had been ordered for his return.

Also that year Jerry Lee's physician, Dr Nichopoulos, was charged and tried for over-prescribing drugs to, among others, Lewis and Elvis Presley; but he was eventually acquitted. The doctor testified that, to his knowledge, Lewis took 30 pills a day. In a single month in 1988, Lewis reportedly received 71 doses of methadone, 86 doses of the sleeping pill Halcion, 40 Didrex (amphetamine) and at least 17 injections of Demerol or a Demerol/methadone mixture. Dr David Knott, a witness, testified that Jerry Lee was addicted to amphetamines and sedatives to the point of 'physiological and psychological reliance'. Withdrawal produced a schizophrenic reaction.

KERRIE LEWIS (sixth wife): It was 1985, the year Rick Nelson died. Jerry Lee was a walking death. He showed me his arm and it was all bubbled up like a soft ball. He had been shooting up in the vein. This girl he had left on tour with turned out to be a junkie and she'd shown him how to shoot to the vein. It must have been four in the morning when I called Dr Nick and told him that he'd better get up here. I told him Jerry was so bad, that I was frightened they would commit him. Dr Nick literally cut his arm open and sucked all the poison out. Jerry has a scar to this day. Dr Nick gave him shots for the fever and the infection and stayed with him until the fever had completely gone. He came up every day after that to change Jerry's bandages. I mean everybody talks about him like he killed Elvis, yet he did something like that. I mean he saved Jerry's life, man!'

• I stayed up 12 days and 12 nights without closing my eyes. I said 'Boy, I have broke all records!' And I did. I got in the shower, turned the shower on, and I'm standing there, and I'm not feeling nothing! Nothing! The water's pouring on me and I'm not feeling nothing! I got out of the shower, sat on the bed, punched myself. I was numb. There was nothing I could do. Booze and drugs, the whole lot. I'll tell you what, I'll never try it again! Next time I'm just gonna stay out for 11 days and nights!

I had a plane in those days and I'd do a concert, fly back to Memphis, spend some time in a club. Used to do that year in and year out. We was just starting to rock when we got back to Memphis – we was just gettin' in gear. They'd open up Hernando's Hideaway! Open up Nellie Jackson's! Open up Bad Bob's! The Killer is back in town! Everybody was on their toes. There'd be naked women dancin' on every table. I'd be sitting there with my boots on, spinnin' these records, man. Them gals, there'd be about 20 of 'em in there, 19 or 20, and they'd be beautiful, beautiful, beautiful. I'd get all those girls from the clubs, like G.G's. They'd come round to the party and they'd strip off, get up on the tables and they'd just dance and have a ball man, drinkin' whisky like water! Man, listenin' to that great music and enjoyin' it and the women is just everywhere, dancin' and floatin' it right in your face! That was when you could get amphetamines, before they took amphetamines off the market. You could get some real pills! I mean strong, strong, strong. Yeah, but they made amphetamines with a sedative in it. A downer in it and an upper in it. You could eat on it, sleep on it or whatever. They took that off the market because it was too good. They left all the downer pills on the market, the worst pills. The Placidyls, the pain pills or Valium, or Demerol pain pills. Yeah, you think you are movin' in high gear and you're not, you're movin' in slow-motion. The next thing you know you're . . . keeling over. That's what killed Elvis Presley. We just had to settle for what we could get and they started takin' them downers. It didn't take 'em long to figure that out. The amphetamines you bought then had the downer in it. All you had to do was lay down, relax and close your eyes and in 30 minutes you was just snoring. If you get amphetamines now, there's just nothing to it. It's just straight amphetamine. They're gone. From about 1969–70 they've been gone. I accused Richard Nixon of being

on 'em. I think he took all the Desmetol himself.
That was the greatest pill ever made, Desmetol.
Man, I could become Superman in three minutes!
But you had to know how to take 'em, couldn't take
too many of 'em. You could take maybe two or three
at the most. These things that you get now, you can't
get no good pills no more and what you can get, I'm
scared of. Every now and then they sneak in some
good pills, that's what people tell me. I don't know.
I'd have a bottle of whisky and you can't go too long
on a whisky. I can go about two or three hours and
I'm ready to conk out, if I haven't got any pills to
take. I like to talk and drink.

*The routine and everyday hell-raising lasted, this time,
until 1984. This year saw him undergoing treatment for
another bleeding stomach ulcer, and more dramatically,
his being brought back to life twice in an ambulance on
the way to Memphis. Jerry had taken about 17 muscle re-
laxant tablets, prescribed to his wife-to-be Kerrie
McCarver. Early in 1985, Jerry was back in hospital with
yet another bleeding ulcer. Surgery removed 40 per cent
of his stomach to ensure the new ulcer was destroyed, as
well as the ulcer from the previous year.*

KERRIE LEWIS (sixth wife): He had a major drug
problem when I married him. I mean he was on about
15 different kinds of sleeping pills, 15 different kinds of
'speed'. I would say it was like three or four months
into the marriage before I actually knew what he took,
when he took it, how he took it and where he got it.
'Cause 'til then he kept everything hidden. I mean it
wasn't a case of here's your sleeping pills, baby, here's
all your medicines. He kept everything under wraps.
Basically, Jerry is a very private person and he didn't

want anybody to know. I mean he hid it in plastic bags behind the toilet, or in the water tank – you would not believe the places he would find to hide the stuff. I really didn't know how bad it was at this point. We had a canopy bed. One day he was out of town and I was cleaning up. I got up on there and, my God, there was more needles than I'd seen in my entire life. They were not dry needles, they were fresh needles. And that's how I found out he was on them as bad as he was. I mean, he was so messed up and demanding like four more bottles and I would say 'Four more bottles of what?'

He was working all the time when we first got married, all the time. And what would happen, he would get his 'medicine' on the road – that's why I never saw any transactions or how he got it. I just knew he was on something. And Jerry had this attaché suitcase he carried with a combination lock on it. And you just did not go in his case! Then it got to the stage where he would be totally out of it, and then he'd say 'Go and get me so and so out of my bag' and I would ask him the combination and that's how I got to know it. It was basically years of abuse. So I went to see Dr Nick and I said, Jerry Lee is on drugs and he is going through a really bad time and he's having a hard time trying to get off them. I don't know what to do. Can you help me? He said he couldn't help unless Jerry was prepared to make up his mind to stop. In the end Jerry went to a load of different places and none of them worked. Then we went on tour, and he passed out on stage in Belfast. We were in England when he decided that he was going to get off the drugs. I don't think it was 'cause it was affecting his performance. It was more a case of he was tired and he was ready to do it. Now I told him, 'You are going to have to wait 'til the end of the tour.' At that time we didn't know he had a very bad bleeding ulcer. I knew he couldn't just come off from it without help. The doctor told me that it could cause cramping, you know, anything could happen. I told Jerry all this but he was adamant. It was something about this tour. He was going to do it on this tour; he was going to prove he could do it on this tour. I could tell he was getting sick. He had a hard time breathing and this was only about the third or fourth day of the tour. I mean, I was a basket case. I had not been sleeping. I was scared to go to sleep 'cause I was watching him all the time. There were times when I would fall asleep at his feet just to feel his pulse. I thought if I slept on his feet and ankles I could feel his pulse, you know? Anyway it was like two or three days before the Ireland thing and I had just had it with him. He was getting worse. By this time he was spitting up blood. I said he was going to kill himself if he didn't get help. I know it seems crazy that at last he wanted to come off the drugs, but this was not the way to do it! I told him that I was going home and that I was not prepared to sit here and watch him dying.

At this point I was so mentally and physically exhausted that I couldn't even pack our cases. He got up the morning I was leaving and we had a big fight. It was about an hour before I left England that I got a phone call telling me that Jerry had collapsed in Belfast, going down the stairs. I was on the next shuttle flight there. I stayed in the room with him and never left his side. I was so scared at all the machine guns outside, 'cause I'd never seen anything like that in my life before. Anyway, we got through it and we got home and he went through surgery. We moved out of our ranch to a penthouse in downtown Memphis, just to get away from everything. Then one day he was really really sick and was having a hard time breathing.

We were watching T.V. I was sitting right there by Jerry, on the floor. He was trying to smoke his pipe, and I said to him to please put that thing down. He started coughing and he just threw his head back and he'd gone kinda stiff. I couldn't get his mouth open and I thought if I could only break his teeth then I could get his mouth open and get the pipe out. So I took the ring off my finger and I laid him out. His caps didn't break but they kinda fell out. God, what if he had swallowed them! I heard the caps pop. I hit him so hard that he gasped and I shoved the pipe in his mouth and shook it around. The next thing I knew I was covered in blood. He started haemorrhaging and I just kept hitting him on the back. I called the medics and they were there in two seconds.

It really scared me so I called the ambulance. He had been throwing up a lot and I kept it so that the ambulance men could see it. They said it looked like a bleeding ulcer. Of course Jerry was insistent that he was going to be all right, so one of the medics got down on his knees and he said, 'Jerry, I love you and you are dying! You have got to get to hospital, let me take you.' Jerry would not go. Anyway, this medic gave me his number and told me to call him direct should anything happen, and he told me that he would be there in two minutes if I should need him. It wasn't 10 minutes when I had to call him back. They told me he was going to go any time. Now it was 6.30 at night when we walked out of that penthouse and by four o'clock in the morning I had not heard anything. I thought he was dying. My father went to the hospital and demanded they tell us what was going on. Half an hour later they called us up to the emergency room and told us to call his family 'cause he wouldn't last 24 hours. I just fainted right then and there. That was the end for me.

Lewis's frenetic lifestyle also meant ever more frequent clashes with the law. In 1975 his private touring jet was seized at Stapleton Airport, Denver, Colorado, after a routine search by customs officials had yielded half an ounce of cocaine, two ounces of procaine and 11 different kinds of amphetamines. As the entire band and crew were on the plane at the time, however, charges were not pressed. It was impossible to pin responsibility on to any one person.

The previous year, a business neighbour of Jerry Lee's in Memphis had called the police when he discovered 25 bullet holes in the walls separating his office from Lewis's. It transpired that a firm previously based on the other side of Jerry Lee's office had moved because of bullets coming through the walls, adding that one bullet narrowly missed a female employee's head.

- Where would a southern boy be without his pistol? I mean, we'd all have .38 pistols and be shooting the walls out. People crawling under the bullets on their belly and bullets bouncing around everywhere – the whole wall was just shot through! And there'd be six squad cars all lined up outside, not knowing what to do. They were too scared to do anything. They checked back with the Mayor and checked back with the sheriff, you know. They just didn't know what to do. 'Should we break in, should we do this?' And they'd say, 'You know how he is. You go in there with Jerry Lee, you'd better be prepared to kill somebody, 'cause he'll nail you!' And they were right! I would've nailed them. One of them quarterbacks, Roy Dean, he was a big ol' star, you know. They brought him in there and he had a little cap on his head. I shook hands with him, then I looked up at him and Pow! I shot the cap right off his head. He just froze, he didn't know what to think.

People can put it down and say what they want to, but if they missed out on the Jerry Lee Lewis days they missed the greatest life and the greatest rock 'n' roll and country and western singing, loving, kissing, smooching and carrying on like a man ought to! Tennessee is where the women are women and the men are proud of it!

We'd go in a club in New York or somewhere and we just took it over. 'Jerry Lee Lewis is here!' I had these guys with me who'd just whoop anybody in the world. Meanest people in the south, but good people. If anybody fooled with Jerry Lee Lewis or said something wrong, they were dead meat. It was different back then. I had it big time under control. I mean I had it ALL under control: the aeroplanes, the fighting, the money, the women, the women, the cars, the women, the women, the women, but we had them under control. Yes sir, and if they couldn't hack it, if they couldn't hang in there, we just dismissed 'em.

I could smoke a joint or something and I'd become the President. I'd start ordering folks around. I can't handle that stuff. I've got about thirty minutes to really enjoy it but all of a sudden it starts to get really crazy! You can even hear a gnat crawl across the floor, y'know. If you're listening to a record you can hear everything in that record so perfect. You can hear the bass, the drums, you can hear it just like you're in this big stereo or something. I have two or three puffs and I can get up there, and I think I'm sounding pretty good at first. But when you start re-writing *Great Balls of Fire* and you think you're doing it better than the record, it's time to back off. I cut a song smoking pot one time, and afterwards I

said, 'Well, I finally beat *Whole Lotta Shakin'*!' I
went back there the next day and I erased it. It was
awful. I just can't handle it. Sex is fantastic, only
you're fooling yourself again. You are pretty well in
control with that. At least I was. But I've always
been in control. I'd just rock 'n' roll, that's what it
boils down to. Rock 'n' roll covers a lot of territory.
It brings everything out, it sure does. One minute
people are screaming, then they're crying, next
minute they want to shake your hand, the next they
want to knock your head off, the next minute they
love you, the next they don't want you. Rock 'n' roll,
that's right.

*In September 1976, the year after his touring jet was
seized in Denver, the Killer also had a four hundred
thousand dollar suit filed against him after a shooting incident in which his bass player, Butch Owens, was
injured. Criminal charges of firing a firearm inside the
city limits and of disorderly conduct were brought
against Lewis. He forfeited a $50 bond on each charge
rather than appear before the magistrate. Owens claimed
in the civil suit that Lewis was drunk when he pulled the
.357 Magnum and told him: 'Look down the barrel of
this.' Lewis then took aim at a Coca-Cola bottle and
said, 'I'm gonna shoot that glass or my name ain't Jerry
Lee Lewis.' Owens also testified that immediately after
the shooting, as he lay bleeding from the upper left por-
tion of his chest (where two fragments of the bullet had
hit him), Jaren, the then Mrs Lewis, asked him. 'Did
you have to get my white carpet bloody?'*

● . . . I swore before God one night when we were out
   in California doin' a tour, 'Butch, when I get you
   back to Memphis I'm gonna shoot you.' I believe he

was giving Rusty some bad dope – Rusty Brown [J. W. Brown's son, Myra's brother], he was just a kid, about the same age as Junior. When we got back to Memphis – I was at Jaren's house at the time – Butch came on over with Dagwood Mann, a good friend of mine. Dagwood said, 'Jerry, there is a gun here with a hair trigger on it.' I'm looking for a hair on it, so I take the gun and I just touch it . . . Boom! It went off and hit a Coke bottle right in front of me. A piece of the glass hit Butch in the arm – went all the way through it – and he stuttered, 'Uh, uh, uh, I'm shot!' and he fell down on the floor. He sued me for fifty thousand dollars and he collected. But he was wrong because I couldn't believe that I had promised I was going to do that to him. The moral of the story is not to have a hair trigger pistol.

In 1986 Jerry was inducted into the Rock 'n' Roll Hall of Fame

● I was the first artist to be inducted into the Rock 'n' Roll Hall of Fame. I worked hard, Killer. I am rock 'n' roll, not rockabilly. I messed up a little bit, they say, but I'm still rock 'n' roll from the top of my head to the bottom of my toes. Hallelujah!

Other inductees were the great founding artists of rock 'n' roll Elvis Presley, Chuck Berry, Little Richard, Fats Domino, the Everly Brothers, Buddy Holly, Ray Charles, James Brown and Sam Cooke.
His live concerts still drew the crowds.

JIM SULLIVAN (*Cream* magazine): Jerry Lee still cuts it and connects. He doesn't make you think, 'Oh, those were the days,' he makes you think, 'This stuff still kicks butt and still makes sense' – he shouts, he's fifty-one and still lighting 16 candles, shaking nerves and rattling brains.

'Sixteen Candles' was a song he recorded for 'The Class of '55', a reunion album which was meant to celebrate the million dollar quartet. It brought together Carl Perkins, Roy Orbison, Johnny Cash and of course Jerry Lee, and was produced by Chips Moman.

The album was good, the outstanding tracks were Jerry Lee's 'Sixteen Candles' and Roy Orbison's 'Coming Home'. Jerry Lee is reputed to have brought a gun into the studio and thrown a bottle at Chips Moman, the producer.

- Yeah, I did throw a bottle at a producer and took a gun, yeh! Chips Moman. Well, we got into it pretty good, he thought he knew it all. I expressed my opinion and he got mad, I got a little mad, he was sitting over cross the desk and he jumped up and I jumped up, like we was gonna fight or something, and he said, 'Well, I'd hit you,' he said, 'but I just got too much respect for you.' I said, 'You'd better believe that, you better have more respect, but I tell you one thing – you ain't fooling with one of your musicians here boy.' Oh, it was over a song or something to do with some money. It was over several different things – money, song, sessions, productions, the whole deal, yeh. Moman says it weren't kept, that's right. Moman says it weren't kept.

- That old marine tried to put the Killer down. Worst album I ever heard except for my parts! [laughs]

   [On *The Class of '55* album]: Like that *Class of '55* album we did with Roy Orbison, Johnny Cash and

Carl Perkins and Jerry. That was done in two days –
that was too soon. 'Cause you had four different
artists and four different egos and it could've been a
great album. It wasn't a bad album, it just could've
been better, that's what I'm saying.

The *Four Legends* album that Webb Price got me
to do with Faron Young and Mel Tillis, now that's a
good album. Webb Pierce was one of the best people
in the world. He was a great man, a dedicated man;
he wasn't a haughty, stuck-up man, he was a gentleman. Webb just wanted to do it – he wanted to do it
himself. He got a big kick out of doing it and he enjoyed it. He had more money than he could ever
spend – he had an eight-million-dollar home in Nashville, y'know, and it wasn't that. It was just he
wanted to do this album, and *Softly and Tenderly
Jesus Is Calling* was one of the songs we did. He requested that that be played at his funeral, and Mack
Vickery took the record and played it at his funeral.
It was done for Webb, just a personal kind of thing –
that was the *Four Legends* album.

*Mervyn Conn, U.K. promoter, got Jerry Lee over to
Europe annually for the Wembley Country Music Festival and a major European tour.*

J. W. WHITTEN (on Jerry's European tours): He
always put more into the shows in Europe because of
the fans. You'd think he'd never be able to go back out
there, especially after he had that gall bladder operation. He went on tour two days after he got out of the
hospital, and with all the pressure I thought we'd see
his insides rip out of the stitches. The first couple of
shows were excellent, but everyone wants to see him
kick back the stool and get on top of the piano. That's a

big treat for them over there, especially for the teddy boys. He's never ceased to amaze me. I know a lot of times he's been sick and not felt like working, but you'd never know it when he gets out on stage 'cause he always gives 110 per cent.

The tours are rarely without excitement or incident.

TERRY ADAMS (Jerry Lee's London friend and cab driver): Jerry had done two concerts and was coming to London. He wanted a piano in his suite to entertain his friends and close fans. Well, we got a piano up to the sixth floor and moved it into this suite. But the suite was too small so Jerry moved to the next one. The piano wouldn't fit through the door, so we thought what can we do – it wouldn't fit in the lift. Jerry Lee walked out on to the balcony and said, 'Let's move it across to the other window.' It was six floors up, re-member. So we got some pulleys, blocks 'n' tackles and we strung the thing all across the side of the hotel. All these people were gettin' dressed, gettin' ready to go out or whatever, and suddenly this baby grand comes lurching across the skyline! [laughs] You know when the Killer's in town!

• We were staying in a hotel and there was a piano in one room making too much noise for the customers or something. We actually moved the piano out of the window – I don't know how we got it around – and to another room. We didn't take it out on to the hall, but outside through the window. We roped it up and took it over to another room – ask Terry and them about that. That was in London, England, and we went and played piano all night.

TERRY ADAMS: Jerry played the piano from about 2 a.m. straight to 11 a.m. – I left about 7.30 a.m., I was knocked out by it all.

Several gigs towards the end of the eighties failed to happen. Fans became hesitant. However, a major concert that was put off and off finally occurred at the Hammersmith Odeon on 21 November 1989. After an abrupt cancellation a few weeks earlier, the clan gathered in West London to attend the ritual of a Lewis concert. What was generally known was that it was going to be filmed for television transmission and that there were to be 'Special Guests'. Word quickly spread that The Killer was in attendance and that the rehearsals sounded great. The faithful were reassured.

Inside the theatre the houselights dimmed and an air of expectation arose from the masses as long-time Lewis bandleader Kenny Lovelace stepped forward to introduce the all-star band consisting of himself, the legendary guitarist James Burton, U.K. rocker Dave Edmunds, Phil Chin (bass player for Rod Stewart) and noted Lewis sideman Jim Isbell on drums. After four numbers performed in a desultory manner, the group then marched off stage with no announcements.

What was happening? Had Lewis cancelled? Or was it the interval? Following a seemingly interminable period, a solitary figure strode on stage, sat down at the piano and proceeded to play and sing some mean boogie-woogie. The multitude erupted. J.L.L. was here to perform for them and their greetings, mixed with a degree of relief, sounded like a Watusi war chant.

The aforementioned all-star band straggled on to the stage, one member seemingly adjusting his flies, and picked up their instruments. The complete outfit then pounded full tilt into 'I Don't Want to Be Lonely

Tonight'. Lewis, in typical fashion, called for a guitar solo and proceeded to drown it out with inspired piano playing, letting his fingers seemingly dance along the keys. The number terminated with the piano lid being forcibly removed and discarded.

Then ensued a spoken introduction mentioning the ill-fated '58 tour and commenting that he had got 'some scars from women's wars'. This was all boding well, as the faithful knew that, when Lewis was brooding over the ladies of the world, his performance was generally uplifted.

'Mean Woman Blues' followed, and this time J.L.L. took exception to the cameraman recording the event for British satellite television, declaring that he was here to play for the people in the theatre and not them. This was received with rapture by the converted; they always knew he was their man, but here was proof positive. The cameramen thereafter kept a respectful distance.

After 'I Am What I Am', during which the drummer bore the brunt of the aggression being exhibited – on this occasion for not keeping up in the desired tempo – it was into a storming 'Goodnight Irene'. Suddenly a figure appeared from the right-hand side of the stage and commenced dueting on vocals. Many in the audience did not recognise Van Morrison. This galvanised Lewis, who then commenced a wonderful and lengthy instrumental introduction to 'What'd I Say', leaving a bemused Morrison standing there idly tapping his trouser leg. Eventually the cue to join in was given, vocals were swapped and Morrison departed the stage, leaving J.L.L. to complete the number with piano-playing pyrotechnics. This was true Lewis, and the intensity was a joy to behold.

Number followed number, and the stage started to bear a varying collection of ragbag and motley British

*musicians who had come along to pay homage. Permu-
tations included Brian May (Queen), Stuart Adamson
(Big Country), Dave Davies (The Kinks) and John
Lodge (The Moody Blues). Far from being impressed,
this served to provide Lewis with maniacal energy as he
proceeded to drive the songs along with a ferocity behol-
den of a man about to meet his Maker. Who were these
young whippersnappers? They were merely here to pay
their dues and ensure that the recording could be sold to
American television.*

*By now the show had developed into a rock 'n' roll
show of classic proportions. Jerry Lee was performing
with an evangelical vehemence that his cousin Jimmy
Swaggart would be unable to better. He played sitting
down, standing up, with his hands, his feet, his backside
– but above all with feeling. At one point Lewis yelled
out 'This is great!' Rock 'n' roll standards – done J.L.L.
style – followed rock 'n' roll standards. 'Great Balls of
Fire', 'Hang Up My Rock 'n' Roll Shoes'. 'Good Golly
Miss Molly', 'Jailhouse Rock', 'Tutti Frutti' – they all
roared down the line like an express train tearing across
the French countryside.*

*After a rousing and hardly bettered version of 'Wild
One', with the piano stool sent flying and the keyboard
being ravished and raked arm over arm, the evening was
brought to a close. The appreciative crowd were on their
feet bawling for more, but it was not to be. It had been 90
minutes of truly vintage Lewis.*

*In the summer of 1991, Jerry Lee Lewis was to head-
line a Wembley country weekend.*

JOHN DYER: Great – well, almost. Would he turn
up? That was the question. Racked with drugs, booze
and God know what else, Lewis could no longer be relied on. Fans were camped out at Heathrow – would he

or would he not turn up? The phone went, a fan somewhat excitedly informed us, 'He's here.' Jerry Lee
Lewis fans must be the most loyal, not to say fanatic, of
all fans. Its eight years since he had a recording
contract, but little details like that don't bother the
Killer's fans. The decision was taken, hesitantly, to go.

Having arrived at Wembley, assurance was sought
before entering. Sitting through six hours of country
was just about bearable if Jerry Lee was at the end.
There was no way I was going in without a guarantee
that he would appear, I tried to reassure myself. It was
no good: the required assurance was unobtainable. All
my brave words fell away, and in I went. Once inside
things weren't as bad as feared. At least there were
plenty of places to escape the middle of the road
(country?) crap. Watching the supporting acts a few
minutes at a time, I couldn't help wondering why there
is an inverse relationship between the amount of
country uniforms and talent? Sixteen years later, it
seemed longer – there must be a factory producing
bland musicians. Supermarkets of the world, take heart
– your tapes need never be blank. Lewis' band were on
stage, but still no Jerry Lee. The compere was going on
and on – there were obviously some backstage problems. As the minutes rolled on the compere's patter got
faster and faster. His by now all too obvious panic was
conveyed to an increasingly restive audience. At one
point he looked to the band for reassurance, only to
find them more worried than him. Kenny Lovelace,
perhaps because of long experience, looked the most
worried of all. Then the nod was given, the compere
stopped mid-joke. The great Jerry Lee Lewis! That was
it, the compere was off, in more ways than one.

All should have been all right, but Jerry Lee was
seriously ill. God, he looked awful – white as a sail, fat,

his face drawn, a unique and very worrying combination. Straight to the piano. This is where fans' judgement must be taken with a large dose of scepticism, but reality cannot be denied, he was awesome. Backed only by bass, guitar and drums he took Wembley apart, piece by piece, as he went relentlessly straight from one number to the next, without even stopping to say hello. The audience's surprise at his choice of material was second only to that of the band. That's only the half of it – the audience, the band and, I suspect, Lewis himself, have no idea what or how he will do any number. No matter how many times he's done a number before, he never does it the same twice. One, two or two thousand times, it makes no difference, it's always a one-off. Miss an interpretation one night and you've missed it forever!

That's all part of the legend, his genius (a meaningless cliché nowadays as almost every piece of hype testifies) was on display. Of course Jerry Lee did almost everything but country, rhythm & blues, rock 'n' roll, soul, blues and Jerry Lee Lewis music. There is a unique combination of different musical formats that are put together by him, that can only be described as Jerry Lee Lewis music. If you want country, go to one of his rock 'n' roll shows.

A dramatic and haunting moment occurred about two-thirds into the set. The stage was in complete darkness; only one cruel stark spotlight illuminated Lewis' frail frame. He was doing the old gospel number *Will the Circle Be Unbroken* when suddenly he stopped playing and raised his right hand. There was a long, long pause; the skin on his face was so tightly stretched that you thought for a moment that he was unable to get the words out. Then looking skywards, hand still raised in a prayer-like position, he slowly pleaded:

'Please misteeeer undertaker SLOW your wagon down.' The band almost stopped . . . Wembley did, as a collective shiver went down its back. It was an unconscious moment of great theatre.

Then there was, of course, the movie based on Myra and Murray Silver's book, 'Great Balls of Fire'.

- She wanted to call it *Balls of Fire*. I said 'Myra, let's get it right now! GREAT *Balls of Fire!*' [laughs]

AL EMBRY (the booking agent of Jerry Lee at the time of the movie): Dennis Quaid only saw Jerry Lee when he was goofin' around. He never saw the real Jerry Lee. That's what he picked upon – a goofin' Jerry Lee.

Actor Mickey Rourke was getting psyched up for the part, but Dennis Quaid got the role. Adam Fields was to be producer, Jim McBride director.

- A true film of my life would take centuries or at least five *Gone with the Winds*. They wanted Dennis Quaid to do the music. Now how can anyone outdo Jerry Lee?

ADAM FIELDS (producer): I had Dennis Quaid wanting to sing and play Jerry Lee, and I never thought Jerry Lee in his fifties could capture Jerry Lee in his twenties.

Jerry Lee called and said, 'Look, let me come in and show you what I can do. And if I can't sing better than I did in 1956, I have no business being here.'

Fields was still marvelling at Jerry Lee's magnanimous

*offer when the bad boy of rock 'n' roll added an ultima-
tum. He said, 'If you don't let me do it, I'm gonna kill
you.'*

ADAM FIELDS (producer): I thought, 'Well, that's a
convincing argument.'

LINDA GAIL (sister): When Jerry Lee said he was
going to do the soundtrack I thought, 'No way, José'.
However, he was terrific – it was as good as the Sun
recordings.

*This, the soundtrack that Jerry Lee insisted he do, was to
be the best aspect of the movie. It was superb. New York
critic Susan Korones and other critics saw Quaid's por-
trayal as infantile: 'There are two ways to portray Jerry
Lee, the silly way and the serious way. McBride and
Fields took the silly way – to failure.' The soundtrack by
the Killer, however, won acclaim.*

*On seeing the script Jerry Lee said: 'Lies! Lies! Lies!'
Even Myra, on whose book it was based, said, 'What
have you done?'*

*The whole movie was really like a long advertisement
for vanilla shakes with rock 'n' roll music.*

- [On the movie and on Dennis Quaid]: He just didn't
  handle it right at all. He handled it the way they told
  him to handle it, I guess. It is so embarrassing to me,
  you know. The music was terrific, I insisted on doing
  that. I thought, 'The only thing you are going to get
  out of this movie is the music', but when I saw them
  doing some acting my face turned red. It embarrassed me so bad I would never go back and catch
  another scene. I said, 'that's it, off.' It's not Dennis'

fault – he was being told what to do by a stupid director, Jim McBride. He ought to be a Jim Dandy – he
was nuts, I know that. Me and him got in a fight two
or three times. He's a real smart idiot; he thought he
knew everything and didn't even know where you
ate. You ain't in Hollywood, California – you're in
Memphis. I had a pretty good go at him, snatched
him around by his collar a couple of times and got his
attention. Yeh, he told me one night, 'Now what is it
you just don't like about my life?' 'One thing I don't
like about it,' I said, 'they are nothing but a bunch of
liars, I don't even like you asking the question.' I
pushed my finger on him, you know. I said, 'You're
talking lies. You think you know what you're doing
but you can't direct anything. And you've got a producer who doesn't know where he's at.' No, he
didn't know what was going on at all. He thought he
knew everything but he didn't know nothing. I think
it was his first thing he produced ever – and last
thing, nearly. Yeh, he was just a naughty boy, a kid.
Dennis Quaid did his best but he didn't get it –
couldn't have with that script, really.

WINONA RYDER (who played Myra): I loved the
role of Myra in *Great Balls of Fire*.

*She had the major threshold of credibility in the movie,
only matched by Trey Wilson as Sam Phillips.*
  *Another piece of media hype occurred when the
tabloid press splashed another sensation: 'Jerry Lee
bolts outa Betty Ford Clinic'. The story was that Jerry
Lee had checked into the famous clinic to dry out from
drug addiction. The tone of the story was: 'Jerry flees
clinic'.*
  'This ain't no place for the Killer, I ain't cleaning my

*room or stickin' to no routine, I'm outa here [Jerry Lee
tells a cab driver]. Here's fifty bucks. Just get me outa
here fast and don't spare the horses.'*

But, as always, there are two sides to the story.

KERRIE LEWIS (sixth wife): I was pregnant with Lee
and I told Jerry I was not raising our child around
drugs, so he went into several clinics with no results.
We were told about the Betty Ford clinic and Jerry
agreed to go. Roger Cappittini with the *Inquirer* was a
friend of ours and wanted to do a positive story on Jerry
getting help, so they sent a reporter on the plane with
us. Jerry looks at it as a weakness on his part because
he couldn't do it on his own. He was embarrassed about
it. Believe me it was not a set-up! I slept on a hard cot
for a week and came home with toxaemia and had to go
into the hospital myself for five days! Jerry stayed in the
Eisenhower hospital for a week and the Betty Ford
clinic two days. He left when they told him he had to
make up his own bed. He couldn't understand what
that had to do with him getting off drugs.

CHAPTER 11

Killer!

(On stage at Gilley's nightclub, Texas, March 1984, after singing *Over the Rainbow*): Somewhere over the rainbow, bluebirds fly. That's right. As long as there's a whole lotta shakin' goin' on, I will live on. I was born in Ferriday, Louisiana, nineteen hundred and thirty-five, been in the business professionally now nearly thirty years, not counting the years I threw in complimentary. I have worked hard and I've loved it. I've not done it for money, I've not done it for greed – I've done it because I love to play this piano and sing my songs. I have been brow-beaten, ridiculed, accused of things that are the most ridiculous crimes that they have said I've done and I don't appreciate it at all, and I want you to know that I love you and God bless you, I appreciate you people coming to see me tonight. Matter of fact, I thank God I'm breathing – that shows you I'm innocent. [Sings *You Win Again*]

On 7 June 1983 Jerry Lee married his fifth wife and companion of four months, Shawn Michelle Stephens, then aged 26, tanned, blonde and sassy, at his ranch in Nesbit, Mississippi. Shawn was the daughter of Thomas Stephens, an iron worker, and Janice Stephens, a commercial traveller for Polaroid.

SHAWN LEWIS: We had a good childhood really, me

and my three sisters. We were tomboys, not timid little girlies. We didn't play with dolls, we ripped their heads off. Naturally I became interested in boys, the guys liked me. When my sister and I went to a Tigers baseball game, this pitcher guy could not keep his eyes off us. I flirted with the guys I liked. Any girl does, naturally. The guy that first bowled me over was a well built car worker called Scott Bonn. I had no particular career in mind. I liked the good times so I was feelin' great when I landed a job at the Hyatt Regency Hotel night club in Detroit – a plush club with a fine night show: people like Billy Eckstein. I was a 'Dib Girl', like a bunny girl. Customers gave me money and cocaine. My sister Denise and I tried cocaine and mescalin for a good buzz. My relationship with Scott was at a low ebb when I heard Jerry Lee Lewis was coming to perform at the club. The boss was worried at first, ya' know, with Jerry Lee's reputation – booze, women, guns and drugs. But he was a pussycat, not the mean critter we were led to believe. He asked the boss to supply some piano stools he could bust up as part of his act. I thought maybe I could fix up Mom (who was divorced) with Jerry Lee. I invited her to the club with this in mind, but she didn't want to know, although she said he looked lovely.

My friend, Pam Brewen, got involved with Jerry Lee's manager, J. W. Whitten, and off they went. When they came back in February 1981 Scott and I were apart and Pam told me Jerry Lee 'liked me'. 'Nothin' special,' I still thought. Pam told me about the good life – jet travel, every comfort you wanted, limousines, best hotel suites, room service, money, gifts and grand houses. I always liked the grand style and privacy of the homes at Bloomfields. I thought maybe Jerry Lee could give me what I wanted, ain't no harm in tryin'. So I

accepted his invitation to Memphis. It was so exciting,
all the travelling. Jerry took me to Europe – Germany,
England, Ireland, places I always dreamed of going to.
I was not a great Jerry Lee fan until I saw him at the
club. Then I saw how much talent he had and later how
he was worshipped in Europe. He wooed me with his
music, too. He was kind. That's what I really loved.
The down side, the touring, was hell at times. I took
stimulants and depressants to keep up with the hectic
life he led. Jerry Lee's medical condition, a kind of
manic depression, required drugs. The scary part was
watching him inject himself in the stomach. He'd swal-
low 30 desoxyns [metamphetamines] before a show,
plus dexedrines by the fistful. He swallowed pill after
pill, whatever he needed to control his stamina.

JOEL SHULMAKER (member of Jerry's band):
Shawn and Jerry were happy. They were close, real
close. They had their fights, but who doesn't?

*The wedding ceremony was performed at Jerry's ranch
in Nesbit, Mississippi by Justice W.E. 'Bill' Bailey of
South Haven, and attended by 30 friends and relatives. It
began at 5.15 p.m. and was over by 5.30. Jerry Lee's
band were there; so too was Dr George C. Nichopoulos,
the late Elvis Presley's physician.*

*Jerry Lee took the vows and embellished them with his
own words, promising to love and honour his new bride
'until the day I die'.*

*The following Thursday Jerry, Shawn and the band
headed for Los Angeles. The hectic touring continued.
On 20 August the couple were back in Memphis.*

• We'd been out dancing and having a good time at
  Hernando's Hideaway every night, so we decided to

stay in and enjoy our home. We watched T.V. and
went for a swim. We had a fight. Shawn said 'I have
taken too many sleeping pills.' I thought she was
teasing me. Well, I told her, 'Girl, you better tell me
right now, or I'll call the ambulance', and she said 'I
didn't take that many. Don't worry about it.' I was
concerned because she was possibly pregnant and we
desperately wanted a child. I had lost two precious
sons. 'You better make your peace with God if
you're O.K., honey'. She just waved her hand. We
went to bed. I kept checking her throughout the
night. In the morning I tried to wake Shawn. She
seemed lifeless and I saw her lips were blue. I
dragged her through the house to walk off the effects
of the pills. I went crazy, slammed my fist on the
wall, broke a glass, called Lottie [the maid] to get an
ambulance. She had taken methadone which I was
taking to get off talwin, which I had to take for my
stomach pains. She thought they were sleeping pills.

*It was only a year since Jerry Lee's fourth wife, Jaren,
had been found dead in a friend's swimming pool. The
two were separated and seeking a divorce at the time.
But this added to Jerry Lee's murderous reputation and
invited sinister speculation on the latest scandal. Jerry
Lee gave a clear explanation of Shawn's death to the
press and demanded a thorough autopsy by Dr Jerry
Francisco, the Shelby County Medical Examiner.*

*He told the press, 'Lord, I really don't know what to
think. It is such a shock to me that I really haven't
realised this has happened . . . I'm still stunned.'*

*An initial post mortem stated that Shawn had died of a
fluid accumulation in her lungs. 'We have no evidence of
foul play,' read the report. 'There is no indication of a
violent death, there are no stab wounds, no trauma, no*

bullet wounds.' Later evidence concluded that nothing had been forced into Shawn's body.

On 28 August 1983, Shawn was buried at the Lewis family plot in Ferriday, Louisiana, far from her Michigan home. She would join Jerry Lee's mother, father, two sons and brother. The sermon was given by Jerry Lee's cousin, Gerald Lewis, who turned to Shawn's ivory casket said, 'If this beautiful young woman's heart is right with God, she is on the streets of gold today.'

The local newspaper, the Memphis Commercial Appeal, reported, 'The man who all his life has sent out engraved invitations to disasters and usually gotten prompt replies began weathering another one. He lingered at the cemetery a moment before going to the home of Frankie Jean, his sister. Another of his loves had made it home to Ferriday, where cousins sometimes marry cousins and Jerry Lee Lewis has a standing engagement.'

Later, according to the press, at Hernando's Hideaway, Jerry Lee tried to drown his sorrows in singing and playing, drinking and flirting, as if he hadn't a care in the world. A country buff shouts out, 'Killer, do my favourite 'Let's Put It Back Together'.' Jerry Lee starts the song pensive. He stops. 'How can I put it back together? She's buried. You think I'm Count Dracula?' As usual, however, the press had manipulated the facts to make a good story, even though it was actually not true.

Soon Jerry is seeing women once again and is photographed in the press with a 19-year-old cosmetic clerk, Mary Ellen Terrance, under the headline 'Jerry Lee Lewis finds love – weeks after wife's death'. He declares he is 'truly in love'. Mary Ellen also claims to be head over heels in love. She tells a journalist, 'He really is the most kindest, gentlest man I've ever met, a loving person who just every once in a while has to exert some energy *through his temper. We went to Hernando's, a quiet bar where fans don't bother him, and we partied the night away.'*

Seven months after Shawn's death, the magazine 'Rolling Stone' featured an exclusive article, *The Mysterious Death of Mrs Jerry Lee Lewis* by Richard Ben Cramer, which virtually indicted Lewis on circumstantial evidence. Cramer seemed to imply that Jerry Lee was a murderer who had bribed the police and covered up all evidence. Even the autopsy was suspect.

Jerry Lee was a soft target, they knew, as gross slanders had been printed about him in the past. The Killer's attention span for legal matters is as infinitesimal as his care for financial fastidiousness: however much the IRS and the hordes of other litigants plague him he remains utterly oblivious, and however much he has been abused and slandered and ridiculed, Jerry has never entered a courtroom as a plaintiff. Though mightily wronged, Jerry Lee Lewis has never sued anyone.

Cramer, in archetypically prejudiced preppie mode, subtly appealed to the 'Rolling Stone' readers' (mainly music industry and college students) own prejudices about the South. Stopping just short of intonating genetic defects, Cramer lampoons the southern drawl to the uttermost limits of caricature and portrays the Nesbit police as incompetent, inbred hill-billies: 'Ladies and gentlemen! The greates' ennataina inna' worl' ... caricature and portrays the Nesbit police as incompetent, inbred hill-billies: 'Ladies and gentlemen! The greates' ennataina inna' worl' ... The Killa ... Jerra Lee! ... Very little excited Jay (Clarke, highway patrolman), not even his own hair-raising habit of reading while he drove.'

This sly ruse enabled Cramer to sell his frothy, insubstantial piece – typical conspiracy theory journalism – to *the 'Rolling Stone' readership as something more. By selectively hopping around the sequence of events surrounding Shawn's death, Cramer weaves a candyfloss case of circumstantial evidence for the prosecution against Jerry Lee.*

Read on its own in ignorance of the wider circumstances, although clearly prejudiced from the start, the article is, however, highly compelling – as are the cases for proving that Elvis is alive, and that John F. Kennedy was murdered by a galactic conspiracy of aliens.

The ramifications of the 'Rolling Stone' article are still destroying Jerry Lee's image to this day; it has planted in the conscience of the world of popular music the doubt, the possibility that Jerry Lee is a murderer. It has done irreparable damage to his career. Not once does the article mention his great achievement in music. People who read it would have had little respect for Jerry Lee and would have felt he was guilty – even though foul play was never suspected and a grand jury concluded there was still no indication of foul play.

LINDA GAIL (sister): That *Rolling Stone* article was a load of bull. I was at the house, they were as happy as two kids, I had never seen Jerry so happy – they were jet-skiing on the lake, having a ball.

Jerry wouldn't kill a flea. He's like me – he gets mad and stuff and has a bad temper – but if he'd ever thought there was something wrong with that woman and he knew about it he'd have done anything to save her. He really loved her.

J. W. WHITTEN (tour manager) on the *Rolling Stone* article: They were running around talking to people who didn't even know Jerry. 'Spendingest man in the county?' Hey, he's an entertainer, he's going to have luxury cars, he's going to have a nice house. That doesn't mean he's 'the spendingest man in the county' – there's farmers down there who spend more than he does, 'cause the farmers in this area are millionaires, this is big farming country. And Riley? [the local sherrif] The reason we supported Riley? He did us no favours. Jerry gave him no money – I gave it, on Jerry's behalf. It was my money, I got the cheques, I signed them. Jerry lived in that county and I said, 'I think it's gotta be better, Jerry, if you back your sheriff. You're a citizen here and he's your sheriff, our sheriff.' And he has turned out to be a great sheriff, you can go down and get no dirt off of him. He's an honest man and there for the people of his county. And as far as the autopsy on his wife, we wanted there to be an autopsy. We paid $2800 to get that autopsy. We could've got it free down there by an amateur mortician, but Jerry wanted to know the exact reason. Paid $2800 out of his pocket. I paid it, but it's his money. There's nothing to talk about. He said, 'I want the best.' I said, 'Well, if you go out of state you have to pay.' He said, 'I don't care what it costs.'

FRANKIE JEAN (sister): They used his name, The Killer, against him when Shawn died. I think that was a cheap shot. I am not a writer, I am not anything in that style, I'm only a blue collar worker, but I could have done a better job, I could have done a more honest, more in-depth job. I could have taken thirty minutes and let the people see the truth. I'd have shown 'em things that really happened. I don't like cheap shots. He really loved Shawn – yes, oh God, yes – he was so proud of her. I met her only once and he sat in a chair and talked to me while she went to get dressed. She came out of the pool and she had to put some clothing on. Jerry told me how much he loved her. That family were terrible to Jerry after that. Jerry didn't kill her, no one killed her – she killed herself. It's one of those things that happen – it happened to Elvis. No one has killed anyone.

PHOEBE LEWIS (daughter): The *Rolling Stone* article was a vicious, horrible thing, but I don't see that it ever did him any harm. In fact, I considered many times whacking him [the author] down like a dog and beating his brains out. The fact that he got a Pulitzer prize is, y'know, pathetic. I mean, I don't even know what to say. It was just such a brutal thing. Right now, I'm just interested in how he's treated while he's still alive, and I would like to see him treated with the respect and dignity he deserves as a musician. I would like to see that continue when he's gone. I don't really like to think about him being gone, but it would be nice to pick Enyclopaedia Brittanica and look up your Daddy and see it said he's a great musician, 'cause that's what it's all about. A great man, in many ways, with faults, but a genuinely good person.

The 'Rolling Stone' story was taken up by the investigative T.V. show 20/20 which spent four months looking into Shawn's death. They were urged to do so by Shawn's family, who were not satisfied with the Mississippi Grand Jury's decision that cleared Lewis of any criminal responsibility for his wife's apparent suicide. Their aim was to get the case reopened.

J. W. WHITTEN (tour manager): You noticed they didn't want to talk to me; I was there the whole time. They tried to make it one-sided. That show got so criticised by the public because it was so one-sided. It was a flop show for them. If you notice, everyone they claimed to talk to, they mentioned no names. They really didn't say nothing negative, they put it in their own context. They tried to make me look like I was a mafia figure, but I fixed that. I made a phone call – it wasn't no big deal. I'm supposed to do that. I didn't say, 'If you don't do this . . . ' When *Rolling Stone* called me, Jerry'd never read the article. I just said, 'I never thought they'd do that kind of story on us.' The lady called me and said 'What do I think about the story'? I said, 'I haven't read it complete, I've just looked through it.' She said, 'This guy won a Pulitzer prize.' I said, 'Well, I think they should take it away from him because of this story.' It's a bad story. A bad story. (On getting Jerry's own opinion): A few people asked him but it was never printed. Two days after she died, I wasn't about to grant an interview with *Rolling Stone* or anybody. Most *Rolling Stone* stories suggested that they were staff writers – they wasn't someone from the *Boston Globe*. I tell you, 73 per cent of that was all fabrication and lies, to get the story printed. I tell you that right now. 'Cause if they hadn't put in some stories it wouldn't have got printed in the first place. They did an autopsy, they did everything in the world and had a grand jury to see if there was any criminal wrongdoings. You cannot force pills down a person's throat without it coming up in an autopsy. Let me tell you what the deal was. They had a little spat. She said, 'I'm going in there to take some sleeping pills and forget all about it – you won't have to worry about it any more.' She goes in there, he said, 'Girl, what'd you do?' She said, 'I've just taken 12 sleeping pills.' He said, 'You better not have. If you have, you better let me call somebody right now.' She said, 'I'm just kidding.' So he goes in there, opens the pill box – sleeping pills – and they're all there. But she saw the methadone bottle sitting there and, goofy with drugs, she thought they were sleeping pills. It was an accidental overdose. She said sleeping pills, he counted the sleeping pills, they were all there. He thought she was bluffing. If she'd said methadone, he'd have counted methadone.'

CHAPTER 12

Great Balls of Taxes

- Money don't mean nothing to me, 'cause that ain't where it's at. I'd rather have friendship, ya know. People are crazy: money, money, money – that's all they want. Cut your throat for 50 cents. I come into this world naked and I'll go out naked, I hope.

The staff at the Memphis offices of the Internal Revenue Service (IRS) live in dread of anyone asking for the Jerry Lee Lewis files. They are now so vast as to be almost unliftable. Apart from the long-running battles between the IRS and Lewis, there is a catalogue of litigation against him that would take days to go through. The scale of it leaves you breathless.

For years the IRS had tried to collect taxes from Lewis. Finally, every other means having failed to get a response, early in the morning of 27 February 1979 they moved in on Jerry Lee's ranch with a view to confiscating his large collection of vehicles as part payment on his increasingly mountainous tax debt. He was depressed about his father, Elmo, who had been operated on for cancer a few days before, and his drug problem was intense. As he and his then wife, Jaren, lay in bed they were totally unaware of what was about to happen.

JAREN LEWIS (fourth wife): Suddenly there was all

this noise, like all the traffic on the highway was driving into the ranch. I woke up and tried to wake Jerry. I ran to the window and saw a fleet of armed wreckers hitching up all his cars. I went back to get Jerry – he'd had some medication the night before and was still half asleep. I dragged him out of bed. Some guy handed me a document, an order from a Mississippi judge permitting the IRS to seize our property. They took Jerry's new Rolls Royce, his Eldorado Cadillac, a Corvette Stingray, a 1956 Cadillac, a 1935 Ford Convertible, a Lincoln Continental, a jeep, our tractor and our motorcycles. Twenty vehicles. How could they do this? Jerry was not aware that this was going to happen.

The property was then protected by Eve Miller of the IRS, who filed a lien in Shelby County against its disposal.

ADDRESS TO IRS AGENTS by agent W. F. Childress: Are you ready for this? We're getting ready to go get every vehicle Jerry Lee Lewis has got.

- The IRS treated me like a dog. There was nothing I could do about it. They just came to my house and took all my cars away, didn't leave me one. They should have said, 'Jerry Lee, you owe us some money', then we could have worked something out. But they came right inside my house and took my organ and my T.V. set. It was just like the Gestapo. America should wake up to the fact that these people are dangerous. They can walk in your house and take anything they want. They say I owed $167,135.72 in back taxes.

Jerry Lee left for Las Vegas for a two-week concert tour, bragging to the press that he would simply go out and buy another 20 cars. Jaren was confident they would be able to reclaim all their 'lost property'. But this was not to be. Jerry Lee continued to ignore his tax problems, and in October 1980 the IRS auctioned off over 60 personal items they had seized from his ranch. A mixture of opportunists and fans attended. Unwilling to chance a low bid taking the lot, the IRS announced it would also auction off the items individually after taking bids on the whole lot, then take the greatest amount. As well as Jerry Lee's vehicles there were jewellery, firearms and musical instruments.

As the IRS files continued to swell, Jerry blithely ignored the massive bureaucratic build-up. He told his employee Dick West, 'I ain't gonna give them no more – they've got all they're gonna get. If anybody comes messin' around with my property again they might get their head blown off.'

Perhaps the best insight into Jerry Lee's carefree attitude to money is provided by Mary Kathy Jones, who lived with the Killer for over three years in the early 1980s.

MARY 'K-K' JONES (former lover): Jerry bought me all kinds of gifts. He took me to Hawaii in 1981 and gave me fifteen thousand dollars in cash. He bought me fur coats and two cars – a Cadillac and an Eldorado – all paid for in cash. He bought numerous cars in other people's names. Money was hidden all over the house. In 1981, when we thought he was dying, he told me to get one hundred thousand dollars in cash from a shoe box and put it in a safety deposit box at a Mississippi bank under a false name.

Later Jerry Lee put the cops on to Mary, accusing her of stealing a forty thousand dollar diamond and ruby bracelet. In the ensuing case Lewis admitted that he had given her the money in cash to buy the bracelet. The case was dismissed and Mary filed a suit against Lewis, accusing him of malicious prosecution, false imprisonment and the deprivation of civil rights.

The IRS continued to show that Jerry Lee had bank accounts and cars in the names of others, including Charlotte Bumpus, identified as a business associate. Finally, in October 1984, the IRS announced that Jerry Lee was to be put on trial for tax evasion. Judge McCrae requested that seventy prospective jurors be summoned to his courtroom. From that number a dozen would be chosen. Justifying this unusual procedure, Judge McCrae said, 'I am aware that Mr Lewis has a lot of supporters in this community, but he also has a lot of detractors. I am determined to give him a fair trial. I will question all persons called to the jury box about whether they have formed any opinions, positive or negative, about Lewis.'

Prosecutor Devon Grosnell asked Judge McCrae to set two hundred and fifty thousand dollars bond [bail] for Jerry Lee, stating that he had failed to appear in other criminal and civil cases. She also cited as grounds for the high bond his 'rather serious alcohol and drugs problems' and said he had access to resources, including his Nesbit, Mississippi Ranch, that were not titled in his name. Devon Grosnell said that Jerry Lee owed the government nine hundred and ninety-four thousand dollars in back taxes, interest and penalties.

Bill Clifton, Jerry Lee's attorney, acknowledged that Lewis owed taxes and had not paid them on time, but he denied that the defendant had intentionally hidden his assets from the IRS. He said 'Jerry Lee has only a sixth grade education and he knows nothing about finances. He has always dealt in cash because that's the way he was paid out there in the boon docks for playing the piano.'

On Thursday, 18 October 1984 Jerry Lee walked triumphantly out of a Memphis courtroom, acquitted of income tax evasion. There was applause and cheering from supporters when the 'not guilty' verdict was returned.

But just because there was a 'not guilty' verdict did not mean Lewis was relieved of his debt to the IRS. He still owed them six hundred and fifty-three thousand dollars.

ANNETTE SHANNON (juror): We all knew Jerry Lee didn't pay his taxes. He was just ignorant. He should have taken care of it. I really think he was a good ol' boy who let everybody else take care of his business because he couldn't manage it himself. I felt sorry for him – not on his income tax case – but as a whole. He needs help.

Not all the jurors were quite so sympathetic. Alma Anderson, jury foreman, said the prosecution 'had good evidence but just didn't have enough proof of the hidden assets . . . my personal feeling is he's guilty but we couldn't go by that. We had to go by the evidence. If he had gone to prison, he would still have to pay his taxes.' Judge McCrae said, 'Lewis appeared to think he was above the law and didn't have to pay taxes like other people do.'

Jerry Lee's attorney, Bill Clifton, said, 'The jury looked at the total man, and they knew he was a simple man with a talent for playing the piano and nothing else.'

• These people knew beyond a shadow of a doubt that I wouldn't steal from the federal government. I knew I wasn't guilty. I depended on God, and my wife and all my friends stood by me. That Judge McCrae, I think he's got some problems. The man is bitterly against me. He said a lot of things that hurt my feelings. As for the prosecutor, Devon Grosnell, she's a demon-possessed lady. She told more lies than Carter's got liver pills.

This used to be a great country and now it's gotten ridiculous. I mean, people don't own nothin' no more. When you work your fingers to the bone for 25 years and you end up with twenty thousand dollars lyin' around the house, a few cars, most of 'em mortgaged, and then they come out here and knock your door down and take your money and your cars and drive off with them, well, you ain't got nothin'. The FBI and the IRS are the most vicious people since Adolf Hitler. They'll come out and slap your butt down in a minute, take everything you got. You don't own the britches you got on. They'll come and snatch 'em right off you.

While Jerry Lee had undoubtedly won a great victory over the tax man, many people in Memphis felt cheated and saw this as Jerry Lee getting away with something that the average person with a fraction of his debt to the IRS would have gone to prison for.

A Memphis group, Wampus Cats, cut a record 'Great Balls of Taxes' to the tune of 'Great Balls of Fire', expressing the way some Memphians felt. Lyricist Eddie Dattel wrote the song during the week of the trial. He said, 'I've never heard anything directly from Jerry Lee, but his wife Kerrie Lewis once told me that she loved it.'

GREAT BALLS OF TAXES

There is a rock 'n' roll singer
From down around Tennessee
He played the bars and the honky tonks
But he never did play for free.
'Gonna buy myself a big Cadillac'
He'd say from behind those curls
'And marry my pretty little cousin
An' take her all around the world'.

He could play that ole piano
With the heels of his leather shoes
And sing like a preacher on Sunday
Spreading the gospel news.
Rock 'n' roll was making the big time
And the Killer was sweeping the land
But the taxman sang a different tune
That's when the trouble began.

   Jerry Lee, Jerry Lee
   They had you singin' the blues
   But you don't have to feel so bad
   I hate taxes too.

Now the IRS man came to see
Just where that money went
Asking all kinds of questions
About how it all got spent.
They took his cars and motorbikes
A tractor and a colour T.V.
And held a public auction
On account of a court decree.

   CHORUS

They had a trial up in Memphis
And when it was over and done

The jury said, 'He's not guilty.
He never meant to hurt no one'.
As the courtroom became empty
And the judge was walking away
I heard the taxman whisper
'We'll meet again someday'.

   CHORUS

PHOEBE LEWIS (daughter): The fact that he's a very generous man has never been reflected. I can show it in little ways that you may or may not understand – you have to know him. He'll come into the kitchen with something in his hands, and I'll say, 'What have you got' and he'll say, 'Open the door so I can get this cricket out.' You know, he respects life, he loves life. He'd give you the shirt off his back. That may seem trite, but the thing that's so sad is that people steal from him all the time. He says to me, 'This person has taken this and this person has taken that – if they just asked me I would have given it to them.' That's my Daddy. Nobody knows him like that. The people who write bad stuff about him in the papers, I don't want them to know him – they don't deserve to know him.

CHARLIE FEATHERS (one of the founding fathers of rockabilly): Jerry Lee's a fine person. He played a benefit for me when my heart and lung operation was due, down at Bad Bob Vapors. My wife and I thought I was gonna die – Jerry Lee played like he never played before, and raised more than $30,000 towards my hospital bill. He didn't have to do it. At heart he's got a heart as big as gold, he sure has. The greatest piano player on the face of the earth.

J. W. WHITTEN (road manager): he has raised thousands and thousands of dollars for St Jude's Hospital here in Memphis – it's a world-famous children's cancer hospital. I've seen him do a concert for some elderly ladies. They hadn't collected enough cash to pay him so they wrote a cheque, and it was good. He knew they did a lot of charity work, so he tore up the cheque and he said to them, 'Keep the cash when you collect, you owe me nuthin' – It's for you.' I've seen him do shows for promoters who had not enough money to pay him and he went out and did as good a show as if they had given him a million dollars. I've seen him do this on numerous occasions. He's done charity shows in Memphis since he first hit – even when I was a kid he done George Klein's Christmas show. Aids to Goodfellows, children's charities, Alzheimer's benefits – he's given all he's got to these causes.

Jerry Lee was not the only great American entertainer to be subjected to the wrath of the IRS. Willie Nelson, the country 'outlaw' singer and composer, owed them $16 million in 1991.

WILLIE NELSON: I have the ability to make money. I have the ability to owe money. I have the ability to spend money and I'm proud of it. I'm the perfect American.

His IRS publicity did attract one unusual case. A woman claimed that on 4 January 1985 in the Biloxi, Mississippi, Hilton, she and Willie had had sexual intercourse for nine consecutive hours and that he consummated the act with a backward somersault with the woman still attached. She sued Willie for $50 million

*for a breach of promise in refusing to marry her. On
hearing this Willie replied, 'That, I guess, is about the
only true story ever written about me. My ex-wife, Shirley, said she'd be glad to testify on my behalf.'*

HERB O'MELL (Jerry Lee's advisor at the time):
What started happening, once that judgement was
passed on him, was that he would show up at a job
and the owner of the venue would say that the IRS
were there and they were going to take all the money.
So then he got a reputation of not showing up and
being unreliable. I called the IRS, the agent in charge,
and I told him: this is what we're doing, this is what
we plan to do, this is where we're going to work, this
is a schedule of events and bookings. We'll give you so
much money now and at the end of six months we'll sit
down again and see what our gross is. He was in full
agreement and said nobody had ever sat down with
him before and nobody had ever gone through that
with him before. I think Jerry Lee Lewis was happy
with it, but you can't be too sure with the Killer. He's
going to do what he wants to do when he wants to do
it, even if it's harmful to him, physically or business-
wise.

I don't think he can be managed. I think Jerry Lee
Lewis is one of the smartest people I've ever met – in
the daytime when he has all his faculties. He's very
observant and he knows a lot about people. He just
has a lot of things that he gets involved in, and he goes
nuts. I don't know whether it's drinking or if it's emotional or what it is. He gets frustrated and I think he
just breaks out.

I understand that since he got the boy [Lee], he's
got a lot better. You have to put your trust in some
people and Jerry Lee Lewis did that, and maybe – I'm

not pointing the finger – but maybe some of them were the wrong people, and they took advantage of him. If you talk to Jerry Lee Lewis you'll find that we never had that problem, we never had any money fights at all.

A lot of great artistes have had this problem. He can't handle it and he needs somebody. Two or three people asked me if I would do it again and I've said if Jerry Lee asked me, I would. But I would not tour with him. I think that's where the arguments would come from. From what I've observed, that's where all the trouble starts. I think a manager's job is long-term planning. Would it be possible to arrange again a deal with the IRS to enable Jerry Lee Lewis to resume concerts? I think I know a way, but he'd have to come to me.

The tax trial did not make the slightest difference to Jerry Lee's lifestyle or his cavalier attitude to money. He celebrated his victory over the IRS by going to Hernando's and playing 'rockin' mother humping piano till the early, early dawn'. Next morning he set off on a tour to Cleveland and Springfield, Ohio, then on to Lake Tahoe, Nevada.

Bill Clifton was left behind to deal with the mess. The IRS stated that they would continue their efforts to collect Jerry Lee's tax bill, now topping the million dollar mark. Clifton announced that he would 'sit down with Jerry Lee and discuss handling it on my terms and conditions where I can speak with authority and control'. Words like 'authority' and 'control' do not feature at all in Jerry Lee's vocabulary. The IRS files and tax demands continued to accumulate as he zoomed full steam ahead with his time-honoured celebration of rock 'n' roll irresponsibility. By 1986, after a decade plagued by health problems and IRS investigations, Jerry Lee's debts had soared to three million.

As the movie of his life 'Great Balls of Fire' was being filmed in Memphis he was filing for personal bankruptcy. As well as the IRS there were 22 other creditors. The suit was filed in the U.S. bankruptcy court for the western district of Tennessee. It was a voluntary individual petition. Jerry Lee owed George Cunningham and the Whiskey River Club in Nashville the sum of $950,000; Memphis lawyer Irving Salky the fee of $40,000; night club owner Steve Cooper $7,000; C & C Floor Covering of South Aver $300; Memphis lawyer Marvin Ratner about $5,000; the Waldorf-Astoria, New York $191; Doctors, Hospital in Memphis $15,000; St Francis Hospital about $10,000; Baptist Hospital about $3,000; and Charlie Cowan of Kansas City $51,000; etc. etc.

In 1992 a major concert at the Royal Albert Hall, London, was scratched after much ballyhoo as it was billed as the battle of the pianos with Fats Domino. Further concerts in France, Norway, Spain and Germany failed to happen, with equal annoyance to fans and promoters alike. Later dates for Dublin's new venue, The Point Theatre, where they had installed special equipment for Jerry Lee, followed by two major concerts at London's Hammersmith Odeon, were again cancelled at the last minute. His fans were feeling acutely disillusioned, as many had arranged flights from all over Europe to see 'The Killer'.

A typical promoter was loyal Norwegian fan Peter Bakke who spent two months promoting a Jerry Lee tour of Norway with his own money. The day before the first concert he received a fax saying the tour in Norway was cancelled.

Bakke's debts were insurmountable. He was a broken man.

In May 1993 the IRS broke into Jerry Lee's ranch in Nesbit, Mississippi, taking his musical instruments, the very tools of his profession – effectively preventing him from being able to pay them back.

His friend and contemporary Little Richard says 'Jerry Lee has probably been ripped off more than I have'.

• I believe Sam Phillips owes me eight million dollars, he said that to me over 20 years ago and I got plenty witnesses to it. He's going to have to be pushed into the corner to bring it out. It wouldn't be as though it was out of his pocket. I mean, he's got so much money and it would make him feel better. It would clear the air with the people, it would clear the air with him and all my fans, myself and everybody. Somebody's gonna be after this man sooner or later. You can't tell what these people might do. People can get crazier than I can when it comes to hurting an artiste they really love! I don't mean pay back exactly, but they need to settle up with me on some of this money. I don't want no fortune, or anything like that. But they should just call me up on the phone, or write me a letter and tell me that they've just looked it over and there's something they need to settle up.

I believe Sam Phillips pulled some pretty shady deals with me. In my opinion he's a very devious character on the business side. I was never much of a business man myself, and I've never sued anybody in my life. It would clear the air. A man that I admired, I guess, more than anybody in the world was Sam Phillips in the beginning. To me he was one of the greatest people, one of the sharpest geniuses I have ever met! He could take a talent and really prove what those talents could do. Then the man turns around and he makes a lie out of himself. To me he's a thief, and this really has blotted the way I thought of Sam. I just couldn't believe the way this man turned out to be that kind of person. I understood that he turned his wife out of his home and put her in a home by herself in Memphis, and he put Sally in her place in his home and he never divorced his wife. It really hurt my feelings to think that this man would do a thing like that.

Yes, if he just paid me what he owes me on *Whole Lotta Shakin'* alone over a period of 30 years, I believe it would come to a sack of money. He gave me forty thousand dollars for that one and thirty-nine thousand for *Great Balls of Fire* and he's never given me a cent since. *Breathless* was a three million seller record. I wasn't even given a royalty statement on that, much less a nickel. He went and shelved the singles that he said he sold when he sold Sun records, but he never sold Sun records to nobody. He still has a pile of unsold records.

I feel Sam and his brother Jud fouled me up bad. It's what I'd call cowardly betrayal. Yeah, cowardly but real sad. It's a shame, you know, that a person like myself with God-given talent should have made people more money than they could ever think about making – yet they don't give me my part of it. Just a little piece of what I've got comin'. Man, is this so wrong? I've done some heavy thinkin' on it in the last few months, especially since Lee's been born. If Sam's beaten me out of the money, it wasn't so bad if he was taking *me* in. But now it's like Lee and Phoebe I'm thinkin' about. That I won't stand for! I'll get him for that, one way or the other.

I don't understand that when a grand jury finds you completely innocent of all charges they still make a way to say they're right about anything you do. He's guilty, as long as we say he's guilty. Know what I'm sayin'? I'm sure the judge was probably wondering if I ever went out with his wife, or his girlfriend. Yes, the last judge I had there, Judge McCrae, he's a mean man and you can write that in quotes from Jerry Lee Lewis. An' if he don't like it, he knows where I live.

It is very unfair. They're wrong. I don't owe the government any income tax, it's the interest and penalties they've added. It's not income tax, I've paid my income tax. I'm not gonna pay that 'cause I don't think I owe it. If they ever get that outta me it'll be after I'm dead! They were picking on me, they're still picking on me. They pick on a lot of people. Something'll have to be done about them people, someday someone who gets to be President should see about the IRS, CIA, the Federal Government – they need to be put in their place and brought off us. Some cat who makes two hundred dollars a week is nagging somebody to death who's got a little money. They've got way too much power. They abuse it – and they abuse it big time. They've got the law behind them and they really abuse it. They can bang you to death with it. They're gonna bang on the wrong cat one of these days. Some of 'em are banging on the wrong one already. I'm getting tired of all those people.

Even as large as the United States is, they pushed me into a corner. And I just took so much I could take no more – from the Government, from the movie people, from record people, from the whole industry. I had to get out of there or it would have driven me crazy. I had to breathe.

The following was filed on 11 May 1992.

IN THE UNITED STATES BANKRUPTCY COURT FOR THE WESTERN DISTRICT OF TENNESSEE WESTERN DIVISION

IN RE:
JERRY LEE LEWIS,   *CASE NO. 88-28250-B*
     Debtor.   *CHAPTER 7*
JERRY LEE LEWIS,
     Plaintiff,
   v.   *ADV. PRO. NO. 92-0351*
UNITED STATES OF AMERICA,
INTERNAL REVENUE SERVICE,
           Defendant.

ANSWER
The defendant, the United States of America, by and through its attorneys, for its answer to the Complaint To Determine Dischargeability Of Debt And For Declaratory Judgment And To Determine Whether Plaintiff Made A Fraudulent Return Or Willfully Attempted In Any Manner To Evade Or Defeat Taxes (hereinafter 'Complaint'), responds to the numbered paragraphs in the Complaint, as follows:

1. Denies, except admits that the debtor, Jerry Lee Lewis, filed a petition for relief under Chapter 7 of the Bankruptcy Code (11 U.S.C) on November 8, 1989, and that the discharge of the debtor was entered on May 31, 1990.

2-3. Denies, except admits that the debtor, Jerry Lee Lewis, is indebted to the United States of America for unpaid federal income taxes and statutory additions for the years of 1977, 1978, 1979, 1980, 1982, 1983, 1984, 1985, and 1986, as of September 9, 1991, in the amount of $3,159,256.66, plus statutory additions accruing thereon according to law from September 9, 1991.

4. Denies.

5. Denies, except admits that the Internal Revenue Service has filed notices of federal tax lien against all property and rights to property of the debtor, Jerry Lee Lewis, securing payment of the unpaid federal income tax liabilities and statutory additions due and owing the United States by the debtor, Jerry Lee Lewis.

6. Denies.

FIRST AFFIRMATIVE DEFENSE
To the extent the Complaint seeks a declaratory judgment with respect to federal taxes, the Court lacks subject matter jurisdiction to entertain the Complaint pursuant to 28 U.S.C., Section 2201.

SECOND AFFIRMATIVE DEFENSE
The unpaid federal income tax liabilities and statutory additions due and owing the United States by the debtor, Jerry Lee Lewis, for the years 1977, 1978, 1979, 1980, 1982, 1983, 1984, 1985, and 1986, are nondischargeable because the debtor, Jerry Lee Lewis, willfully attempted to evade or defeat the taxes due for said years pursuant to 11 U.S.C., Section 523(a) (1) C).

THIRD AFFIRMATIVE DEFENSE
The unpaid federal income tax liabilities and statutory additions due and owing the United States by the debtor, Jerry Lee Lewis, for the years 1985 and 1986 are

nondischargeable under 11 U.S.C., Section 523 (a) (1) (A).

FOURTH AFFIRMATIVE DEFENSE
To the extent that any federal income taxes and statutory additions due and owing the United States by the debtor, Jerry Lee Lewis, are determined to be dischargeable, the federal tax lien of the United States nevertheless attaches to property claimed as exempt by the debtor pursuant to 11 U.S.C., Section 522 (c) (2) (B).

FIFTH AFFIRMATIVE DEFENSE
The plaintiff is not entitled to a jury trial in this adversary proceeding.
WHEREFORE, the United States of America, prays that the relief sought in the Complaint be denied.

> *ED BRYANT*
> *United States Attorney*
>
> *By:*
> *MICHAEL J. MARTINEAU*
> *Trial Attorney, Tax Division*
> *U.S. Department of Justice*
> *P.O. Box 227*
> *Ben Franklin Station*
> *Washington, DC 20044*
> *Telephone: (202) 307-6483*

The following was filed on 9 August 19XX.

IN THE UNITED STATES BANKRUPTCY COURT
FOR THE WESTERN DISTRICT OF TENNESSEE
WESTERN DIVISION

IN RE:
JERRY LEE LEWIS,   *CASE NO. 88-28250-B*
    Debtor.   *CHAPTER 7*
JERRY LEE LEWIS,
    Plaintiff,

    v.   *ADVERSARY. NO. 90-*
0244
UNITED STATES OF AMERICA,
INTERNAL REVENUE SERVICE,
        Defendant.

COMPLAINT

Comes now the debtor, Jerry Lee Lewis, and states to the Court as follows:

1. Debtor filed his petition for relief under Chapter 7 of the Bankruptcy code on November 8, 1988.

2. That the defendant, United States of America Internal Revenue Service, alleges that it is due the sum of $2,623,040.75 for personal income taxes which they calculate as follows:

Year	Tax	Penalty	Interest	Total
1977	–0–	–0–	74,517.42	74,517.42
1978	88,267.37	25,436.04	90,866.65	204,570.06
1979	18,605.98	41,296.65	248,271.20	308,173.83
1980	106,351.22	33,377.95	209,758.13	349,487.30
1982	299,214.37	102,381.01	353,259.14	754,854.52
1983	144,727.00	76,663.90	148,716.19	370,107.09
1984	151,977.00	42,233.46	99,634.08	293,844.54
1985	90,796.00	21,109.47	43,635.77	155,541.24
1986	69,166.00	19,141.17	23,637.04	111,944.75
Totals:	969,104.94	361,640.19	1,292,295.62	2,623,040.75

2. The defendant, United States of American Internal Revenue Service, maintains under Section 523 (a) (1)

(C) that said tax debts are nondischargeable because 'the debtor made a fraudulent return or willfully attempted in any manner to evade or defeat such taxes'.

3. The debtor/plaintiff did not make a fraudulent return or willfully attempt in any manner to evade or defeat said taxes and that said taxes are dischargeable.

4. The defendant, United States of America, Internal Revenue Service, has caused to be recorded numerous tax liens or 'Notice of Federal Tax Lien under Internal Revenue Laws' at various times and places against the debtor and/or his assets, some of which are known and some unknown to the plaintiff. That said liens are null and void, under Sections 545 and 724 of the Bankruptcy Code, as to the dischargeable taxes for which said liens were recorded. In particular, said liens are null and void as to any property acquired by the debtor after November 8, 1988, the date of the filing of the bankruptcy petition by the debtor.

WHEREFORE, PREMISES CONSIDERED, your debtor/plaintiff, Jerry Lee Lewis, prays that the Court:

1. Hold and determine that the debtor/plaintiff did not make a fraudulent return or willfully attempt in any manner to evade or defeat any taxes alleged to be owing to the defendant, and the Court therefore declare such taxes as are dischargeable to be discharged;

2. That the Court hold null and void all 'tax liens' related to the taxes found to be dischargeable; and

3. Grant such other and further relief to which the plaintiff/debtor may be entitled, and the plaintiff/debtor demands a jury to try this action.

> *NORMAN P. HAGEMEYER,*
> *Attorney for Plaintiff/Defendant*
> *969 Madison No. 1103*
> *Memphis, TN 38104*
> *901-526-0093*

CHAPTER 13

Emerald Exile

- I'm an Irishman now . . . I think I was an Irishman before I came over.

That's how Jerry Lee Lewis summarised his unexpected move to Ireland – where artistes are exempt from tax – in 1993 with his sixth wife, Kerrie, and their small son Lee. Any love and loyalty he had once had to his mother country had been flushed out of the Killer by the relentless activities of the Internal Revenue Service.

Kerrie enlisted the help of long-time fan Tadhg O'Coughlan, a resident of Dublin, and Rob Swinnerton, whom they had both met at the annual Jerry Lee Lewis Conventions in Newport, South Wales. They found them a house in Foxrock, overlooking the Wicklow Mountains. In no time the Killer was serenading the locals with My Wild Irish Rose and responding to that famous Dublin hospitality.

- Dublin reminds me of my home in Ferriday, Louisiana when I was about 10 years old. The people are so friendly and so laid back. I feel a closeness to the people here. They don't bug you. I don't think I could live anywhere else now. This is one of the finest places I've been to and I've been everywhere, man.

Is it conceivable that the original wildman of rock 'n' roll, the hell-raiser to beat 'em all, the Killer, has finally been tamed as he lurches towards 60? It seems too much to hope for, although he is the first to admit that the birth in 1987 of his son Lee – named after his revered uncle, Lee Calhoun – had a chastening effect on him. Having already lost two sons, both in tragic circumstances, he has no intention of sacrificing a third.

- I never thought those wild days would run out, but getting married to Kerrie was the greatest thing that ever happened. Then I turned round and I got me a little baby boy. So the king of rock 'n' roll is gonna have to get his act together in a different way from now on. Lee is really something: he's given me new hope, new life.

These days Lewis leads a much quieter, more domestic existence, smoking his pipe, watching T.V. and videos, playing with his son, and leaving the business decisions to Kerrie. Within a couple of months of settling in Dublin she had organised guest appearances on the U.K.-networked Aspel chat show, the popular Gay Byrne Show, and Ulster T.V.'s Kelly, another chat show.

- I've been done dirty so many times by wives and friends and business people. I don't know if I can trust anybody no more, but I can trust Kerrie. I'm just working hard to keep up with what she's doin'! Kerrie is a very good singer, too. When we got married I said, 'If you wanna keep your singing career goin' don't let me hinder it . . . you're doin' pretty good.' I think she wants to more than she don't. My advice to Kerrie is that she should follow up her career.

This was no whirlwind romance. Lewis had known Kerrie's father, D.J. Bob 'The Dude' McCarver, for years, and he first met Kerrie when she was ten years old and star-struck. She sang 'Whole Lotta Shakin'' in a Christmas show for kids called Toys for Tots, with her sisters Sherry and Dee Dee playing piano and drums. They performed at the 25th anniversary show at the Grand Ole Opry. She worked as a singer at a number of clubs frequented by Jerry Lee and his cronies – Hernando's and Vapor's. They were little more than nodding acquaintances until Jerry Lee got bored with his live-in girlfriend Mary Kathy (known as 'K-K') Jones.

KERRIE LEWIS (sixth wife): One night he showed up at the club where I was working and said, 'She's gone, I took care of that.' He picked me up off the stage and said: 'Do you want to get married?' I mean, I thought he was making fun of me 'cause I was only just separated from my first husband and no-one knew about Jerry and me. Well, through the microphone I said 'I can't marry you, Baby, I'm already married!' It really hurt him and he left – he just left. I thought it was all over 'cause he never came back to the club. So I just took it as, well, you made the break and it wasn't meant to be.

Anyway, next time I saw him he was with Shawn, the new lady in his life. We were sitting at one side of the stage and he was way over the other side of the room, so he didn't see me at all. He got up and said to everybody, 'Well I want to let you good people know I'm getting married.' Anyway, he still hasn't spotted me and he starts singing, and you know when you see something or someone and you do a double take? Well, he did just that and when he looked again I, of course, acknowledged him. Then, instead of walking straight over to his table, he comes by ours and sort of deliberately nudges me. I mean, everybody saw him do it, including Shawn, and I thought, 'What was all that about? He's just announced his plans to marry, so why play silly games with me?'

Then I thought, 'If he can play games, then so can I.' At that time I was singing *Somewhere Over the Rainbow* in my routine and I started to sing it there and then – and better than I will sing anything ever again as long as I live. It was just pure emotion. And the next thing I know he comes over to the table and says, 'If you're trying to tell me something now, I need to know now!' I really didn't know what he was getting at. I wasn't sure if he was trying to embarrass me in front of my friends or what. So I looked at him and I said, 'I have nothing to say to you.'

I didn't see him again until a couple of weeks before he got married. Then after they were married they started coming into the club again a few times, and then Shawn died of a drug overdose and he started showing up at the club all upset and saying would I please go home with him? Not for anything other than he just needed somebody to talk to. So I went home with him. He was just so down and so depressed. I mean, he just could not believe that Shawn would do something like that to him in his home. He told me he had been good to her.

I think, basically, Jerry was not the womaniser that most people thought. He just wanted a wife! Somebody to love him and take care of him, and somebody that he could love. You know, Jerry comes from an area where being a southerner really means something. And he was of the idea that he'd married this northern girl and brought her to his home, given her a big wedding and tried to be good to her, and I guess it wasn't enough, or she got into something she didn't know she was getting into. Being married to Jerry means he will beat you if you are not a strong person. He's a good man and he's a responsible person, but he is just so very demanding. Whether it be fixing him a meal or washing clothes, his attitude is 'I want it now. Get it done now, not tomorrow or in 10 minutes. I want it now!' He was very spoiled. I think it was just that Shawn didn't know him or his ways. Plus southern wives are brought up to be southern wives, and he was brought up to expect this. Shawn just didn't know what was going on in his world, although I really can't say as I wasn't there.

Kerrie's sharp humour, charm and vitality have endeared her to Dublin society and she has become a media attraction. She has been asked to sing at Bad Bob's nightclub and has received rave reviews. Kerrie has always been in the shadow of Jerry Lee, but the Irish love her in her own right.

Bono of U2, Ronnie Wood of The Stones, Van Morrison and Paddy Maloney of The Chieftains all visited to pay their respects to the Killer. The tone of the Irish media changed dramatically from cynical to respectful. Crysalis T.V. arrived to do a major documentary, the most in-depth ever done on Jerry Lee. Lewis would be required to play off the top of his head any one of hundreds of songs, and to answer questions on the most intimate details of his extraordinary life. A special piano used by Elton John on his visits to Dublin was installed in Jerry's own front room, where the interview was to take place. Everything was fine, set to go when the phone rang. IRS agents had broken into Jerry Lee's ranch in Nesbit, Mississippi, and confiscated everything – family photos, his pipes, all his musical instruments, even Lee's toys.

Jerry Lee came downstairs ready to do the T.V. documentary. Kerrie bravely kept her anguish suppressed and wished him luck as he walked towards the cameras. He proceeded to give a vintage performance. The following day Kerrie broke the news to him.

- I tried to do everything according to the law. I've given them everything I've got – which never really meant that much anyway, as long as I was good to my family, my fans, and my friends. But when they come out there with the National Guard and knock your fence and your doors down and take all your cars and your money . . . When they do it over and over and over again . . . I don't understand how these people can take privileges like that on a person. How do they get away with this? If they want our bedrooms and stuff like that, I can replace it. But I can't replace all those pictures of my grandparents and my Momma and Daddy and me, sitting on a levee when I was a baby. I can't replace that stuff!

Ireland is his home now, and he has been made to feel very welcome. But that doesn't stop the Killer feeling homesick for Louisiana, his spiritual home. The older he gets, the more he feels drawn back to the place he grew up in.

- I never thought I could live anywhere but Ferriday, Louisiana, but when I left there I never went back except for somebody getting married or buried. I expect the road's put a hat on that but I've always wanted to move back and I've been thinking of doing that in the near future. Not living there, but just having a place there. I think we'll all end up migrating back to Ferriday. I'd like to build me a home and a museum there. It's the most beautiful state, you know, Louisiana. Down in the swamps, through Louisiana, really beautiful. We used to like hunting, fishing and shooting. At four o'clock in the morning we'd go after wild duck. One day when I had a duck hunt, I was standing out in the water and it was freezing. I was standing out there waiting for a duck to fly over. I took my shotgun, put it in the car and I went home. I ain't been back since. Some of the best fishing in the world's in Louisiana. Big bass, weighing 12-15 pounds. We'd take them home and my Momma would cook them. Yeah, we used to do that or we'd throw 'em back again if nobody wanted to eat them. We just liked to catch 'em. You used to have to let him work to get him in, he'd get tired, but you try to bring him in and he'd snap your line in two. It's like where I live now in the Wicklow Mountains, beautiful fish up there. On the lake behind the house.

I'd really like to be the governor of Louisiana. I'd make a pretty good governor. I need to have a place there because the family graveyard's there. I'd love to build a game reserve in Louisiana for all the wild critters. The Jerry Lee Game Reserve, a park to protect the wild life. I don't regret any of the years that God's let me live on this earth. I've had a wonderful life, a great career. I just want to be remembered for my music.

DISCOGRAPHY

Editor: Charles White

Chief researcher & compiler: Peter Checksfield

Invaluable contributions from:

Gary Skala, U.S.A., Barrie Gamblin, U.K., Thomas Sobezak, Germany, Peter Molecz, Austria, Tony Wilkinson, U.K., Wim de Boer, editor of 'Fireball Mail', Christopher Ebner, Germany, Ari Bass U.S.A.

RECORDING SESSIONS

The following section attempts to chronicle the various recording sessions that led to the hundreds of Jerry Lee Lewis records that have been available since 1956. A sessionography lists recordings in the order they were recorded, not the order in which they were released to the public (which often has little to do with when they were cut!). We have also attempted to list all known recordings/ sessions that are unreleased. Details are often very sketchy for unreleased sessions, though when song titles are mentioned these almost certainly were recorded.

The format used herein is pretty standard. Personnel and instrumentation: Voc = vocal, pno = piano, gtr = guitar, st.gtr = steel guitar, bs = bass, dms = drums, org = organ, sax = saxophone, tpt = trumpet, tbn = trombone.

DATE OF RECORDING (Recording location). Producer (*Not* Sun, as details are very sketchy).
Master number (when known)   Song title   Record number
● = available on the Bear Family CD Box Set ('Classic Jerry Lee Lewis' BCD 15420).

The record numbers we have listed for each song represent the FIRST appearance of a given song/take on 45 rpm (or 78 rpm), 45 rpm EP (extended play single), and 33 rpm *or* CD (whichever was issued first).

We have not included recordings of live performances that have appeared on various bootlegs (though we *have* included details of Radio Transcription Discs), since (a) they were never intended for recording, much less release, and (b) the inclusion of every known tape in the hands of collectors would defeat the purpose of the listing. However, when songs/takes have *only* been issued on bootlegs, then details have been included.

The sessionography is divided into three sections:

Part One: Pre-Sun and the Sun years, 1954-1963.
Part Two: The Smash-Mercury years, 1963-1977.
Part Three: Sessions for various labels, 1977-1992.

DISCOGRAPHY

As with the sessionography, the discography is divided into three sections:

Part One: Pre-Sun and the Sun years.
Part Two: The Smash-Mercury years.
Part Three: The post-Smash-Mercury years.

The records/CD's in each section are listed in chronological release order (singles first, then EP's, then LP's/CD's).

To keep the discography relevant, a few procedures have been used to simplify matters. For the LP's/CD's, only those cuts appearing for the first time are listed (with the addition of a few important compilations such as the Sun International 'Original Golden Hits' series and the Smash/Mercury 'Best of' albums). The numerous repackagings that have appeared over the years would, if listed completely, make this section equal in size to the main text!

JERRY LEE LEWIS

Recording Sessions
1954-1992

(in chronological recording order)

PRE-SUN

NOVEMBER, 1954 (KWKH studios, Shreveport, Louisiana)

Jerry Lee Lewis (voc, pno).

I don't hurt anymore	EVCD 3001
(If I ever needed you) I need you now	EVCD 3001

1954-1956

Possible pre-Sun demos;
Jerry Lee Lewis (voc, pno).

Hadacol boogie	UNRELEASED
My God is real	UNRELEASED
Summit ridge drive	UNRELEASED
Down the road apiece	UNRELEASED

THE SUN SESSIONS

DEMONSTRATION SESSION, LATE 1956 (706 Union, Memphis)

Possibly;
Jerry Lee Lewis (voc, pno).

Seasons of my heart	UNRELEASED

NOVEMBER 14, 1956 (706 Union, Memphis)

Jerry Lee Lewis (voc, pno), Roland Janes (gtr), Jimmy Van Eaton (dms),

●Crazy arms	Sun 259,LP 1230,EPA 109
●End of the road	Sun 259
You're the only star in my blue heaven (1)	UNRELEASED
●You're the only star in my blue heaven (2)	Sun 102

●Born to lose   Sun 6467.029

DECEMBER 4, 1956 (706 Union, Memphis)

Jerry Lee Lewis (voc, pno), Elvis Presley (voc, gtr, pno), Carl Perkins (voc, gtr), Clayton Perkins (gtr), W. S. Holland (dms).

You belong to my heart	Charly CD 102
When God dips his love in my heart	Charly CD 102
Just a little talk with Jesus	Sun 1006
Walk that lonesome valley	Sun 1006
I shall not be moved	Sun 1006
Peace in the valley	Sun 1006
Down by the riverside	Sun 1006
I'm with the crowd (but oh so alone)	Sun 1006
Farther along	Sun 1006
Blessed Jesus hold my hand	Sun 1006
As we travel along the Jericho road	Sun 1006
I just can't make it by myself	Sun 1006
Little cabin on the hill	Sun 1006
Summertime has passed & gone	Sun 1006
I hear a sweet voice calling	Sun 1006
Sweetheart you done me wrong	Sun 1006
Keeper of the key	Sun 1006
Crazy arms (1)	Sun 1006
Don't forbid me	Sun 1006
Out of sight out of mind	Charly CD 102
Brown eyed handsome man (2 takes)	Charly CD 102
Don't be cruel (2 takes)	Charly CD 102
Paralysed	Charly CD 102
Don't be cruel (3rd take)	Charly CD 102
There's no place like home	Charly CD 102
When the saints go marching in	Charly CD 102
Softly & tenderly	Charly CD 102
Is it so strange	Charly CD 102
That's when your heartaches begin	Charly CD 102
Brown eyed handsome man (3rd take)	Charly CD 102
Rip it up	Charly CD 102
I'm gonna bid my blues goodbye	Charly CD 102
Crazy arms (2) (vocals off mike)	Charly CD 102
That's my desire	Charly CD 102
End of the road	Charly CD 102
Black bottom stomp (aka Jerry's boogie)	Charly CD 102

You're the only star in my blue heaven	Charly CD 102
Reconsider baby	'Elvis – The Complete 50's Masters' (Box Set)
Island of golden dreams	UNRELEASED
I was there when it happened	UNRELEASED
Strange things happening	UNRELEASED
The old rugged cross	UNRELEASED
This train is bound for glory	UNRELEASED
When I take my vacation in heaven	UNRELEASED
Tutti frutti	UNRELEASED
Blueberry hill	UNRELEASED
Will the circle be unbroken	UNRELEASED
I won't have to cross Jordan alone	UNRELEASED

LATE 1956/EARLY 1957 (706 Union, Memphis)

Jerry Lee Lewis (voc, pno), Roland Janes (gtr), J. W. Brown or Billy Riley (bs), Jimmy Van Eaton (dms).

●Silver threads amongst the gold	S.I.LP 119
●I'm throwing rice (at the girl I love)	S.I.LP 114
●I love you so much it hurts	S.I.LP 114
Deep Elem blues (1)	Charly CD 70
●Deep Elem blues (2)	S.I.LP 121
Goodnight Irene (1)	UNRELEASED
Goodnight Irene (2)	Sun 102
Goodnight Irene (3) (undubbed)	BCD 15211 (See April 4/8,1958)
●Goodnight Irene (4)	Sun 102
●Honey hush	S.I.LP 124
●The Crawdad song	S.I.LP 121
●Dixie (instrumental)	CR 30002
●The Marines' hymn (instrumental)	CR 30007

LATE 1956/EARLY 1957 (706 Union, Memphis)

Jerry Lee Lewis (vcl, pno) only.

●That lucky old sun	CR 30007

LATE 1956/1957 (706 Union, Memphis)

Personnel probably as first late 1956/early 1957 session.

●Hand me down my walking cane	S.I.LP 121
You're the only star in my blue heaven (1)	Sun Star 002 (bootleg)
●You're the only star in my blue heaven (2)	BCD 15420

You're the only star in my blue heaven (3)	S.I.LP 121
●Lewis boogie	Sun 102
●I love you because	Sun 102
●I can't help it	CR 30129
●Cold, cold heart	Sun 102
●Shame on you	6467.029
●I'll keep on loving you	S.I.LP 121
You are my sunshine (?)	S.I.LP 121
●You are my sunshine (?)	Sun 102
●Tomorrow night	6467.029
Sixty minute man (1)	Charly CD 70
●Sixty minute man (2)	Sun 102
Sixty minute man (3)	6467.029
●It all depends (undubbed)	Sun 102 (See April 4/8,1958)
I don't love nobody (1)	UNRELEASED
●I don't love nobody (2)	NY-6
●Whole lotta shakin' goin' on (1)	Sun 102
Whole lotta shakin' goin' on (2)	UNRELEASED
Whole lotta shakin' goin' on (3)	Charly CD 70
Whole lotta shakin' goin' on (4)	Sun Box 106

1957 (706 Union, Memphis)

Personnel probably as November 14, 1956.

●It'll be me (1)	Sun 102
●It'll be me (2)	BCD 15420
●It'll be me (3)	BCD 15420
It'll be me (4)	Sun 102
●It'll be me (5)	Sun 267
Ole pal of yesterday (1)	UNRELEASED
Ole pal of yesterday (2)	Sun Star 002 (bootleg)
Ole pal of yesterday (3)	Sun 102
●Ole pal of yesterday (4)	6467.029
●Whole lotta shakin' goin' on	Sun 267, EPA 107

1957 (706 Union, Memphis)

Personnel probably as November 14, 1956.

You win again (1)	UNRELEASED
●You win again (2)	Sun 102
You win again (3)	Charly CD 70
●Love letters in the sand	Sun 102

Little green valley (1)	Sun 102
●Little green valley (2)	BCD 15420
Little green valley (3)	6467.029

SUMMER, 1957 (706 Union, Memphis).

Personnel probably as November 14, 1956.

●Lewis boogie	Sun 301
●Pumpin' piano rock	6467.029
It'll be me (1)	UNRELEASED
It'll be me (2)	Charly CD 70
●It'll be me (3)	LP 1230, EPA 110

SUMMER, 1957 (706 Union, Memphis)

Personnel probably as November 14, 1956.

All night long (1)	Sun 102
●All night long (2)	6467.029
●Old time religion (1)	Sun 102
Old time religion (2)	S.I.LP 119
●When the saints go marching in (undubbed)	Sun 102 (See April 4/8, 1958)
●Carolina sunshine girl	6467.029
●Long gone lonesome blues	6467.029
●Drinkin' wine spo-dee-o-dee	S.I.LP 124
●Singing the blues	S.I.LP 124

SEPTEMBER 5, 1957 & possible other date(s) (706 Union, Memphis)

Jerry Lee Lewis (vcl, pno), Roland Janes or Sidney Manker (gtr), J. W. Brown or Billy Riley (bs), Jimmy Van Eaton or Otis Jett (dms).

●Rockin' with Red (she knows how to rock me)	Sun 102
●Matchbox (1) (undubbed)	Sun 102 (See April 4/8, 1958)
●Matchbox (2)	Sun 102
●Ubangi stomp	LP 1230, EPA 109
●Rock & roll Ruby	6467.029
●So long I'm gone	6467.029
Ooby dooby (1)	6467.029
●Ooby dooby (2)	Sun 102
I forgot to remember to forget (1) (inc.)	UNRELEASED
I forgot to remember to forget (2)	Sun 102
I forgot to remember to forget (3)	Sun Star 002 (bootleg)

Granada TV special, filmed in Manchester, England, 1964 (Brian Smith)

Ready Steady Go! TV show, England, 1964 (Rediffusion TV, London)

Above left: Linda Gail Lewis
(Tony Marsh)

Left: Kerrie Lewis: 'What other
wives? I'm the only one that's
stuck by him.'

Above: As Iago in Jack Good's
production of *Catch my Soul*.
'I never knew there were so
many words in Shakespeare.'
(Rita Gillespie)

Right: England 1972 (Brian
Watson)

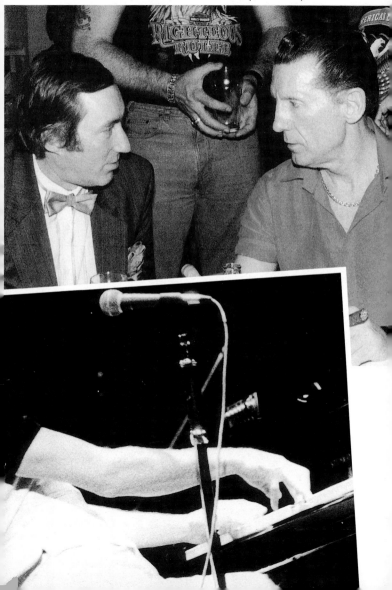

Right: The
Lewis Family
1988

Far left: Jerry Lee with his fifth wife Shawn, London, 1981 (Peter Checksfield)

Left: Jerry Lee on stage with Bruce Springsteen and Joe Ely, Dublin, June 1993 (Kyran O'Brien)

Below: With Van Morrison in an impromptu appearance at Bad Bob's, Dublin, 1993 (Kyran O'Brien)

Overleaf: Jerry Lee in uncharacteristic cowboy hat ('I'm a rockin' mutha humper from Memphis. I ain't no hillbilly guitar picker from Nashville!') 1984 (Phoebe Lewis)

I forgot to remember to forget (4)   Charly CD 70
●I forgot to remember to forget (5)   BCD 15420
●You win again (undubbed)   Sun 102 (See October, 1957)

SEPTEMBER 10, 1957 (706 Union, Memphis) (Possibly two separate sessions)

Personnel probably as first late 1956/early 1957 session.

I'm feeling sorry (5 takes)   UNRELEASED
●I'm feeling sorry (?)   BFX 15211
●I'm feeling sorry (?)   BFX 15211
I'm feeling sorry (7)   Charly CD 70
I'm feeling sorry (8)   Sun star 002 (bootleg)
●I'm feeling sorry (9)   Sun 102
●I'm feeling sorry (11)   EPA 107
●Mean woman blues   EPA 107
●Turnaround   EPA 107

OCTOBER 6-8, 1957 (706 Union, Memphis)

Personnel probably as November 14, 1956.

●Why should I cry over you   Sun 102
Great balls of fire (1)   UNRELEASED
Great balls of fire (2)   Charly CD 70
Great balls of fire (3)   UNRELEASED
Great balls of fire (4)   Sun 102
Great balls of fire (5)   UNRELEASED
Great balls of fire (6)   Sun star 002 (bootleg)
Great balls of fire (7, 8, 9, 10)   UNRELEASED
Great balls of fire (11)   J.L.L. EP 002
●Great balls of fire (12)   Sun 102
Great balls of fire (13)   UNRELEASED
●Great balls of fire (14)   Sun 281, LP 1265
●Great balls of fire (15) ('Jamboree')   W.B. JAM ½

OCTOBER, 1957 (706 Union, Memphis)

Unknown vocal group overdubbed on to raw track from September 5, 1957.

●You win again   Sun 281

JANUARY 16-18, 1958 (706 Union, Memphis)

Jerry Lee Lewis (vcl, pno), Billy Riley (gtr), J. W. Brown (bs), Jimmy Van Eaton (dms).

●Down the line (1)	BCD 15420
●Down the line (2)	Sun 102
Down the line (3)	J.L.L. EP 001
Down the line (4)	UNRELEASED
●I'm sorry, I'm not sorry	Sun 102
Down the line (5)	Sun 102
Down the line (6,7)	UNRELEASED
●Down the line (8)	Sun 288
●Sexy ways (false start)	Sun 102
●Cool, cool ways (Sexy ways)	CR 30002
●Breathless (1)	BCD 15420
Breathless (2,3)	UNRELEASED
Breathless (4)	Sun 102
●Milkshake mademoiselle (1)	Sun 102
●Milkshake mademoiselle (2)	Sun 102
Milkshake mademoiselle (3)	6467.025
●Milkshake mademoiselle (4)	Sun 102
Milkshake mademoiselle (5)	Bop Cat 100 (bootleg)
Milkshake mademoiselle (6)	Redita 103 (bootleg)

PROBABLY JANUARY 21, 1958 (706 Union, Memphis)

Personnel probably as January 16-18, 1958.

Breathless (1)	J.L.L. EP 001
Breathless (2)	UNRELEASED
Breathless (3)	Sun star 002 (bootleg)
●Breathless (4)	Sun 288

FEBRUARY 14, 1958 (706 Union, Memphis)

Personnel probably as November 14, 1956

High school confidential (7 takes)	UNRELEASED
High school confidential (2)	Sun 102
High school confidential (3)	Sun star 002 (bootleg)
●High school confidential (4)	Sun 102
●High school confidential (?)	BCD 15420
High school confidential (?)	Charly CD Box 1
●High school confidential (13)	Sun 102
High school confidential (14)	Sun LP 1004

FEBRUARY, 1958 (706 Union, Memphis)

Personnel probably as first late 1956/early 1957 session.

Put me down (1)	UNRELEASED

| Put me down (2) | Sun star 002 (bootleg) |
| ●Put me down (3) | Sun 102 |

FEBRUARY/MARCH, 1958 (706 Union, Memphis)

Jerry Lee Lewis (vcl, pno), possibly J. W. Brown (bs) & Russell Smith (dms).

●Good rockin' tonight	Sun 102
●Pink pedal pushers	S.I.LP 124
●Jailhouse rock	S.I.LP 124
●Hound dog	6467.029
●Don't be cruel	LP 1230,EPA 108
●Someday (you'll want me to want you)	CR 30002

MARCH, 1958 (706 Union, Memphis)

Personnel probably as first late 1956/early 1957 session.

●Jambalaya	LP 1230,EPA 109
●Friday night	6467.029
●Big legged woman	S.I.LP 107
●Hello hello baby	LP 1265
●Frankie & Johnny	LP 1265
●Your cheating heart	S.I.LP 114
●Lovesick blues	S.I.LP 125

APRIL 4 &/or 8, 1958 (706 Union, Memphis)

Unknown vocal chorus overdubbed on to raw tracks from 1956/1957.

●Goodnight Irene	Sun LP 1230
●When the saints go marching in	Sun LP 1230
●Matchbox	Sun LP 1230
●It all depends	Sun LP 1230

APRIL 20, 1958 (706 Union, Memphis)

Personnel probably as first late 1956/early 1957.

●Fools like me (1) (undubbed)	Sun 102 (see April, 1958 overdub session)
Fools like me (2)	BFX 15211
Carrying on (Sexy ways) (1)	6467.027
Carrying on (Sexy ways) (2)	Sun Star 002 (bootleg)
●Carrying on (Sexy ways) (3)	BCD 15420
●Crazy heart (1)	Sun 102
Crazy heart (2)	Sun star 002 (bootleg)
Crazy heart (3)	6467.029

Crazy heart (4)	CR 30006
●Put me down (1)	Sun 102
Put me down (2)	UNRELEASED
●Put me down (3)	J.L.L. EP 002
●Put me down (4)	Sun LP 1230,EPA 108

APRIL 21, 1958 (Union, Memphis)

Jerry Lee Lewis (vcl, pno), Billy Riley (gtr &/or bs), Roland Janes (bs &/or gtr), Jimmy Van Eaton (dms). Possibly another guitarist on some titles.

High school confidential (1)	UNRELEASED
High school confidential (2)	L.L.L. EP 001
●High school confidential (3)	Sun 102
High school confidential (edit of takes 1 & 3)	Sun 296, LP 1230, EPA 110
●Slippin' around	NY-6
●I'll see you in my dreams (instrumental)	Sun 102
●Wild one (Real wild child) (1)	6467.029
Wild one (Real wild child) (2)	CR 30002
●Let the good times roll	CR 30006

LATE APRIL, 1958 (706 Union, Memphis)

Unknown vocal chorus overdubbed on to raw track from April 20, 1958.

| ●Fools like me | Sun 296 |

PROBABLY MAY, 1958 (706 Union, Memphis)

Jerry Lee Lewis (vcl, pno) only.

●Memory of you	Sun 102
●Come what may	6467.029
Break up (1)	Sun star 002 (bootleg)
●Break up (2)	Sun 102
●Crazy heart	Sun 102
●Live & let live	Sun 102
●I'll make it all up to you (1)	BCD 15420
Break up (3)	UNRELEASED
I'll make it all up to you (2)	Sun 102
●Crazy arms	Sun 102
●Johnny B. Goode	Sun 102
●Settin' the woods on fire (undubbed)	BCD 15420 (see July 9, 1958)
●Break up (4)	Sun 102

MAY 30, 1958 (706 Union, Memphis)

A novelty compilation narrated by Jack Clement & d.j. George Klein, including extracts from the following previously issued titles; Great balls of fire, You win again, I'm feeling sorry, High school confidential, Mean woman blues, Don't be cruel, Breathless, Crazy arms and Whole lotta shakin' goin' on.

●The Return of Jerry Lee	Sun 301

JULY 9, 1958 (706 Union, Memphis)

Instrumental accompaniment overdubbed on to raw tracks from May '58 'solo' session. Personnel uncertain, probably Roland Janes (gtr), Jimmy Van Eaton (dms).

I'll make it all up to you	UNRELEASED
Break up	UNRELEASED
Settin' the woods on fire	S.I.LP 125

JULY 16-18, 1958 (706 Union, Memphis)

Jerry Lee Lewis (vcl, pno) except on some or all of the takes of I'll make it all up to you which have Charlie Rich on piano, Billy Riley (gtr), Jack Clement (bs), Otis Jett, Jimmy Van Eaton (dms).

Break up (7 takes)	UNRELEASED
Break up (2)	Sun 102
Break up (4)	J.L.L. EP 001
●Break up (?)	BCD 15420
●Break up (?)	BCD 15420
I'll make it all up to you (6 takes)	UNRELEASED
●I'll make it all up to you (?)	BCD 15420
I'll make it all up to you (8) (undubbed)	Sun 102 (see July 21, 1958)
●Johnny B. Goode	S.I.LP 107
●Break up (12)	Sun 303, LP 1265

JULY 21, 1958 (706 Union, Memphis)

Unknown vocal chorus overdubbed on to raw tracks from July 16-18, 1958 session.

●Break up	UNRELEASED
●I'll make it all up to you	Sun 303

NOVEMBER 5, 1958 (706 Union, Memphis)

Jerry Lee Lewis (voc, pno) except on the takes of It hurt me so, which have

Charlie Rich on piano, Martin Willis (sax), Roland Janes, Billy Riley (gtrs),
Cliff Acred (bs), Jeff Davis, Jimmy Van Eaton (dms).

Drinkin' wine spo-dee-o-dee (1)	UNRELEASED
●Drinkin' wine spo-dee-o-dee (2)	Sun 102
I'll sail my ship alone (?)	UNRELEASED
I'll sail my ship alone (2)	BFX 15211
I'll sail my ship alone (?)	Pickwick PCD 840
I'll sail my ship alone (4)	Sun 102
●I'll sail my ship alone (5)	Sun 312
I'll sail my ship alone (6)	J.L.L. EP 002
●It hurt me so (1)	Sun 102
It hurt me so (2)	Sun 102
It hurt me so (3)	UNRELEASED
It hurt me so (4)	Charly CD 70
It hurt me so (5)	UNRELEASED
It hurt me so (6) (undubbed)	UNRELEASED (see November '58 o'dub session)
You're the only star in my blue heaven (1)	Sun 102
●You're the only star in my blue heaven (2)	BCD 15420

NOVEMBER, 1958 (706 Union, Memphis)

Unknown vocal chorus overdubbed on to raw track from November 5, 1958.

●It hurt me so	Sun 312

PROBABLY DECEMBER, 1958/JANUARY, 1959 (706 Union, Memphis)

Jerry Lee Lewis (vcl, pno), probably with Roland Janes (gtr), Billy Riley (bs),
Jimmy Van Eaton (dms).

Lovin' up a storm (1,2)	UNRELEASED
●Lovin' up a storm (3)	BCD 15420
Lovin' up a storm (4)	Sun 102
Lovin' up a storm (5)	Charly CD 70
●Lovin' up a storm (6)	Sun 317
●Big blon' baby	Sun 317

PROBABLY DECEMBER, 1958/EARLY 1959 (706 Union, Memphis)

Jerry Lee Lewis (vcl), unknown pno (possibly J.L.L.), bs, dms.

●Sick & tired	6467.029
●(Just a shanty in old) shanty town	CR 30002
●Release me	6467.029

MARCH 22, 1959 (706 Union, Memphis)

Jerry Lee Lewis (vcl, pno), Brad Suggs (gtr), Cliff Acred (bs), Jimmy Van Eaton (dms).

I could never be ashamed of you (2 takes)	UNRELEASED
●I could never be ashamed of you (?)	BCD 15420
I could never be ashamed of you (3)	Sun 102
Near you (instrumental) (1)	Charly CD box 1
●Near you (instrumental) (2)	CR 30002
●I could never be ashamed of you (5)	Sun 330
●Hillbilly music	LP 1265
●My blue heaven (1)	Sun 102
My blue heaven (2)	Sun star 002 (bootleg)
●My blue heaven (3)	Sun 102
My blue heaven (4)	S.I.LP 121
Let's talk about us (1)	Sun star 002 (bootleg)
Let's talk about us (2)	Sun star 002 (bootleg)
Let's talk about us (3,4)	UNRELEASED
●Let's talk about us (5)	Sun 102
Let's talk about us (6,7,8,9)	UNRELEASED

MAY 28, 1959 (706 Union, Memphis)

Jerry Lee Lewis (vcl, pno), probably with Roland Janes (gtr), Leo Lodner (bs), Jimmy Van Eaton (dms).

●Little queenie	Sun 330

JUNE 25-26, 1959 (706 Union, Memphis)

Jerry Lee Lewis (vcl, probably piano on all tracks), Charlie Rich (vcl duet on Sail away & Am I to be the one, possibly piano on some tracks), Roland Janes, Billy Riley (gtrs), Leo Lodner (bs), Jimmy Van Eaton (dms).

●Home	LP 1265
●Will the circle be unbroken	S.I.LP 119
●The Ballad of Billy Joe	Sun 324
Let's talk about us (1,2,3,4)	UNRELEASED
Let's talk about us (5) (undubbed)	J.L.L. EP 002 (see June/ July, 1959)
Let's talk about us (6)	Sun 102
●Sail away (1)	CR 30002
Sail away (2)	SHM 864
Am I to be the one (1,2)	UNRELEASED
●Am I to be the one (3)	Sun 102

Am I to be the one (4)	S.I.LP 114
●Night train to Memphis	S.I.LP 114
●I'm the guilty one	Sun 102

PROBABLY LATE JUNE/EARLY JULY, 1959 (706 Union, Memphis)

Unknown vocal chorus overdubbed on to raw track from June 25-26, 1959.

| ●Let's talk about us | Sun 324 |

PROBABLY LATE 1959 or EARLY 1960 (639 Madison, Memphis)

Jerry Lee Lewis (vcl, pno), probably with Martin Willis (sax), Roland Janes (gtr), Leo Lodner (bs), Jimmy Van Eaton (dms).

●The Wild side of life	Power Pak 247
●Billy boy	JS-6120
●My bonnie	NY-6

PROBABLY JANUARY 21-25, 1960 (706 Union, Memphis)

Jerry Lee Lewis (voc, pno), Roland Janes (gtr), Leo Lodner or J.W. Brown (bs), Jimmy Van Eaton (dms)

●Mexicali rose (1)	Z 2003
●Mexicali rose (2)	6467.029
●Gettin' in the mood (instrumental)	Z 2003
●In the mood (instrumental)	PI 3559
●I get the blues when it rains (inst) (1)	Z 2003
●I get the blues when it rains (inst) (2)	PI 3559
Don't drop it (1)	Z 2004
●Don't drop it (2)	Sun 109
●Great speckled bird (1)	Z 2004
●Great speckled bird (2)	Z 2004
●Bonnie B. (1)	Z 2003
Bonnie B. (2)	Z 2003
Bonnie B. (3)	Z 2004
Bonnie B. (4)	Sun 109
Bonnie B. (5)	UNRELEASED
●Bonnie B. (6)	Sun 371
Baby, baby bye bye (1,2)	UNRELEASED
●Baby, baby bye bye (3)	Z 2004
Baby, baby bye bye (4)	UNRELEASED
Baby, baby bye bye (5)	Sun 109
Baby, baby bye bye (6,7)	UNRELEASED
Baby, baby bye bye (8)	Z 2003
Baby, baby bye bye (9)	Sun 109

●Baby, baby bye bye (9) (vocal group overdub)	Sun 377
Baby, baby bye bye (10)	UNRELEASED
You can't help it (I can't help it) (1)	Z 2003
You can't help it (I can't help it) (2)	Z 2004
●You can't help it (I can't help it) (3)	BCD 15420
You can't help it (I can't help it) (4)	Sun 109
●Your cheatin' heart	Z 2003
●Old black Joe (1)	Z 2004
Old black Joe (?)	Z 2003
Old black Joe (?) (undubbed)	Sun 109
●Old black Joe (?) (Vocal group overdub)	Sun 377
Old black Joe (at least 3 more takes)	UNRELEASED
As long as I live (1)	Z 2004
As long as I live (2)	Charly CD box 1
As long as I live (3)	Sun 109
As long as I live (4,5)	UNRELEASED
As long as I live (6)	Z 2003
As long as I live (7)	UNRELEASED
●As long as I live (8)	BCD 15420
●As long as I live (9)	Sun 367,LP 1265
●Hound dog	Z 2004
What'd I say (1)	Z 2004
●What'd I say (2)	Sun 109
●Keep your hands off of it (Birthday cake)	Z 2003

PROBABLY JUNE, 1960 (639 Madison, Memphis)

Jerry Lee Lewis (vcl, pno), Martin Willis or Johnny 'Ace' Cannon (sax), probably Roland Janes (gtr), Billy Riley (bs), Jimmy Van Eaton (dms).

●Hang up my rock & roll shoes	Sun 344
●John Henry	Sun 344
●What'd I say	Sun 102
●C.C. rider	S.I.LP 107
●When my blue moon turns to gold again (1)	BCD 15420
●Lewis workout (instrumental)	CR 30006
●When my blue moon turns to gold again (2)	6467.029

From here on an increasing percentage of Jerry's recordings were issued with vocal chorus, all presumably overdubbed after the original recording sessions. As no further information is available on the overdub sessions, no further reference will be made to them. We are now into the period where very few original session tapes & alternate masters have so far come to light.

MID/LATE 1960 (639 Madison, Memphis)

Jerry Lee Lewis (pno only), Linda Gail Lewis (vcl), Frankie Jean Lewis (duet vcl on Good golly miss Molly), Roland Janes, Scotty Moore (gtrs), J.W. Brown (bs), Stan Kessler (st. gtr on Love made a fool of me), Jimmy Van Eaton (dms).

Good golly miss Molly	UNRELEASED
Love made a fool of me	UNRELEASED

OCTOBER 13, 1960 (639 Madison, Memphis)

Jerry Lee Lewis (vcl), Larry Muhoberac (pno), Fred Ford, Ronnie Capone, Robert Alexius (horns), Scotty Moore, Brad Suggs (gtrs), Billy Riley (bs), Jimmy Van Eaton (dms).

●No more than I get	CR 30007
When I get paid (?)	Sun 352
●When I get paid (?)	BCD 15420
●Love made a fool of me	

Also possibly;
Is it too late	UNRELEASED
I gotta know where I stand	UNRELEASED

FEBRUARY 9, 1961 (Phillips studio, Nashville)

Jerry Lee Lewis (vcl, pno), Hank Garland, Kelton Herston (gtrs), Bob Moore (bs), Buddy Harman (dms).

●I forgot to remember to forget	CR 30007
●Cold, cold heart	Sun 364
●Livin' lovin' wreck	Sun 356
●What'd I say	Sun 356

JUNE 12, 1961 (Phillips studio, Nashville)

Jerry Lee Lewis (vcl, pno), Marvin Hughes (producer, possibly piano on some tracks), Kelton Herston, Wayne Moss (gtrs), Bob Moore (bs), Buddy Harman (dms).

●It won't happen with me (1)	Sun 364
It won't happen with me (2)	CR 30116
●C.C. rider	Sun 102
●I love you because	S.I. LP 128
●Save the last dance for me	Sun 367

JUNE 14, 1961 (639 Madison, Memphis)

Jerry Lee Lewis (vcl, pno), Johnny 'Ace' Cannon (sax), Brad Suggs (gtr),
J.W. Brown (bs), Gene Chrisman (dms).

●Hello Josephine (my girl Josephine)	LP 1265
●High powered woman	S.I. LP 1000
My blue heaven (1,2)	UNRELEASED
●My blue heaven (3)	Sun 109
●My blue heaven (4)	Sun 109
●Sweet little sixteen	BCD 15420

SEPTEMBER 21, 1961 (Phillips studio, Nashville)

Jerry Lee Lewis (vcl, pno), Cam Mullins, John Wilkin, Don Sheffield, Bill
McElhiney (horns), Jim Hall, Karl Garvin, Homer 'Boots' Randolph (saxes),
Jerry Tuttle (org), Jerry Kennedy (gtr), Bob Moore (bs), Buddy Harman
(dms).

●Ramblin' rose (1)	Sun 374
●Ramblin' rose (2)	S.I. LP 108
Ramblin' rose (3)	Sun 102
●Money	Sun 371, LP 1265
●Rockin' the boat of love	NY-6

JANUARY 4, 1962 (639 Madison, Memphis)

Jerry Lee Lewis (vcl, pno), Roland Janes, Brad Suggs (gtrs), R. W. McGhee
(bs), Al Jackson (dms).

●I've been twistin' (1)	Sun 374
I've been twistin' (2)	SHM 823
I've been twistin' (3)	Sun 102
●I've been twistin' (4)	BCD 15420
Whole lotta twistin' goin' on (1)	CR 30002
●Whole lotta twistin' goin' on (2)	S.I.LP 1000
●I know what it means (1)	Sun 396
I know what it means (2)	Sun 102
●High powered woman	CR 30006

JUNE 5, 1962 (639 Madison, Memphis)

Jerry Lee Lewis (vcl, pno), Shirley Sisk (org), Scotty Moore, Roland Janes
(gtrs), J.W. Brown (bs), Al Jackson (dms).

Sweet little sixteen (1)	UNRELEASED
Sweet little sixteen (2)	Sun star 002 (bootleg)
●Sweet little sixteen (3)	Sun 379

●Sweet little sixteen (4)	S.I. LP 107
●Hello Josephine (my girl Josephine)	S.I. LP 107
●Set my mind at ease (1)	NY-6
Set my mind at ease (2)	Pickwick PWK 015
●Waiting for a train (1)	UK Sun 1003
●Waiting for a train (2)	S.I. LP 121

JUNE 14, 1962 (639 Madison, Memphis)

Personnel as June 5, 1962.

●How's my ex treating you (1)	BCD 15420
●How's my ex treating you (2)	Sun 379
●Good rockin' tonight	S.I. LP 107
●Be bop a lula	S.I. LP 124
●Hello Josephine (my girl Josephine)	BCD 15420

SEPTEMBER 11, 1962 (Phillips studio, Nashville)

Jerry Lee Lewis (vcl, pno), Boots Randolph (sax), Kelton Herston, Fred Carter (gtrs), Floyd Chance (bs), Buddy Harman (dms).

●Good golly miss Molly (1)	Sun 109
●Good golly miss Molly (2)	Sun 382
Good golly miss Molly (3)	Charly CD box 1
●I can't trust me (in your arms anymore) (1)	Sun 382
I can't trust me (in your arms anymore) (2)	Z 2004
●My pretty quadroon	NY-6
●Waiting for a train (?)	Z 2003
Waiting for a train (?)	Sun 109
Waiting for a train (?)	Z 2004

The raw performance of I can't trust me (1) was in 1973 remixed with new instrumental accompaniment recorded at Singleton Sound Studios, Nashville, for release on S.I.45-1130.

MARCH 11, 1963 (639 Madison, Memphis)

Jerry Lee Lewis (vcl on Sun 384 only, pno throughout), Linda Gail Lewis (vcl except Teenage letter), W.R. Felts (org), Luke Wright (sax), Scotty Moore (gtr), George Webb (bs), Morris 'Tarp' Tarrant (dms).

●Seasons of my heart	Sun 384
●Teenage letter	Sun 384
Nothin' shakin' (1)	CR 30007
Nothin' shakin' (2)	Charly CD box 1
Sittin' & thinkin'	Charly CD box 1

C.C. Rider	UNRELEASED

Also possibly:

Danny boy	UNRELEASED

AUGUST 27, 1963 (639 Madison, Memphis)

Jerry Lee Lewis (vcl, pno), W.R. Felts (org), Luke Wright (sax), Scotty Moore, Roland Janes (gtrs), George Webb or Herman 'Hawk' Hawkins (bs), Morris 'Tarp' Tarrant (dms).

●Your lovin' ways	S.I. LP 128
Just who is to blame (1)	NY-6
●Just who is to blame (2)	CR 30007
●Just who is to blame (3 or later take)	BCD 15420
Hong Kong blues (?)	CR 30002
●Hong Kong blues (?)	BCD 15420
●Love on Broadway	S.I. LP 128

AUGUST 28, 1963 (639 Madison, Memphis)

Jerry Lee Lewis (vcl, pno), Scotty Moore, Roland Janes (gtrs), Herman 'Hawk' Hawkins (bs), Morris 'Tarp' Tarrant (dms).

●One minute past eternity	S.I. LP 108
●Invitation to your party (?)	BCD 15420
●Invitation to your party (?)	S.I. LP 108
●I can't seem to say goodbye	S.I. LP 114
I can't seem to say goodbye (remix)	Sun 109
Carry me back to old Virginia (1,2)	UNRELEASED
●Carry me back to old Virginia (3)	BCD 15420
●Carry me back to old Virginia (4)	BCD 15420
●Carry me back to old Virginia (?)	Sun 296
Carry me back to old Virginia (?) (remix)	Sun 109

Note: There are *unconfirmed* rumours that the following titles were also recorded during the 1956-1963 Sun period;

Reelin' & rockin' (1959)	Second chance with you (1963)
San Antonio rose (1961)	You betcha gonna like it
My babe (1962)	Shake a hand
Lovin' Cajun style (1962)	Tennessee saturday night
I get the jitters (1963)	Red sails in the sunset
Lawdy miss Clawdy (1963)	Mystery train
Shake, rattle & roll (1963)	Don't forbid me
Mule skinner blues (1963)	I know the say
Hard headed woman (1963)	Wee wee hours (instrumental)

Blue moon of Kentucky (1963)
Summertime blues
April in September
Beach party
Ooh! my soul
Kaw-Liga

Rock around the clock
We three
Tutti frutti
I almost lost my mind
A mansion on the hill
Sheik of Araby

Also recorded during this period & now officially released;

Breathless (The Philip Morris Show, 1958)   STCD 2
Whole lotta shakin' goin' on (Cal's Corral, 1959)

                                                          STCD 2

Jerry Lee Lewis

HIS WORK AT SUN AS A SESSION PIANIST FOR OTHER ARTISTS

DECEMBER 4, 1956 (706 Union, Memphis)

Jerry Lee Lewis (pno), Carl Perkins (vcl, gtr), Jay B. Perkins (gtr), Clayton Perkins (bs), W.S. Holland (dms).

Matchbox	Sun Box 101
Put your cat clothes on	UNRELEASED
Your true love	Sun Box 101

DECEMBER 11, 1956 (706 Union, Memphis)

Jerry Lee Lewis (pno), Billy Riley (vcl, gtr), Roland Janes (gtr), Marvin Pepper (bs), Jimmy Van Eaton (dms).

Flyin' saucers rock 'n' roll (alt)	Sun Box 106
Flyin' saucers rock 'n' roll (master)	Sun 260
I want you baby (master)	Sun 260
I want you baby (alt)	Sun Box 106

JANUARY 5, 1957 (706 Union, Memphis)

Jerry Lee Lewis (pno), Kenneth Parchman (vcl), other details uncertain.

Love crazy	?
Treat me right	?

JANUARY 6, 1957 (706 Union, Memphis)

Jerry Lee Lewis (pno), Luke McDaniel (vcl), other details uncertain.

My baby don't rock	?
High high high	?
That's what I tell my heart	?

JANUARY 25, 1957 (706 Union, Memphis)

Jerry Lee Lewis (possibly pno), Jimmy Williams (vcl), Jimmy Wilson (possibly pno), other details uncertain.

Tomorrow	Sun Box 106
It all depends on you	Sun 270
Please don't cry over me	Sun 270
That's my desire (my one desire)	?

JANUARY 30, 1957 (706 Union, Memphis)

Jerry Lee Lewis (pno), Billy Riley (vcl, gtr), Roland Janes (gtr), Marvin Pepper (bs), Jimmy Van Eaton (dms), Johnny 'Ace' Cannon (sax).

Red hot (alt 1)	Sun Box 106
Red Hot (alt 2)	CDX 9
Red hot (master)	Sun 277
	Pearly Lee (master)
Pearly Lee (alt)	CDX 9

JANUARY 30, 1957 (706 Union, Memphis)

Jerry Lee Lewis (pno), other personnel as December 4, 1956.

Caldonia	6467.028
Her love rubbed off (alt 1)	Sun Box 101
Her love rubbed off (alt 2)	Sun LP 112
Her love rubbed off (alt 3)	BCD 15494
You can do no wrong	6467.028
Roll over Beethoven	6467.028
Matchbox	Sun 261
Your true love	Sun 261
Put your cat clothes on (alt 1)	Sun Box 101
Put your cat clothes on (alt 2)	JS 6013
Sweethearts or strangers (alt 1)	6467.028
Sweethearts or strangers (alt 2)	BCD 15494
Be honest with me (alt 1)	Sun Box 101
Be honest with me (alt 2)	BCD 15494
Try my heart out	BCD 15494
Keeper of the key	Sun Box 101

FEBRUARY, 1957 (706 Union, Memphis)

Jerry Lee Lewis (pno), other personnel as January 30, 1957 (Billy Riley session).

She's my baby (Red hot) (alt 1)		CR 30115
She's my baby (Red hot) (alt 2)		LP 1024

THE SMASH/MERCURY SESSIONS

SEPTEMBER 22, 1963 (Sam Phillips studio, Nashville), Producer; Shelby Singleton

Jerry Lee Lewis (voc, pno), more details unknown.

30093	Whole lotta shakin' goin' on	S 1412,SRS 67040
30094	Crazy arms	SRS 67040
30095	Great balls of fire	S 1413,SRS 67040
30096	High school confidential	S 1413,SRS 67040
30097	I'll make it all up to you	SRS 67040
30098	Break up	SRS 67040
30099	Down the line	SRS 67040
30100	Hit the road, Jack	S 1857
30101	End of the road	SRS 67040
30102	Your cheatin' heart	SRS 67040
30103	Wedding bells	SRS 67097
30104	Just because	SRS 67079

SEPTEMBER 24, 1963 (Sam Phillips studio, Nashville). Producer; Shelby Singleton.

Jerry Lee Lewis (voc, pno), more details unknown.

30105	Breathless	S 1412,SRS 67040
30106	He took it like a man	SRS 67097
30107	Drinkin' wine spo-dee-o-dee	SRS 67079
30108	Johnny B. Goode	SRS 67063
30109	Hallelujah, I love her so	SRS 67079
30110	You went back on your word	S 1930,SRS 67063
30111	Pen & paper	S 1857
30112	The hole he said he'd dig for me	S 1906
30112	The hole he said he'd dig for me (alt)	134 204 MCY(France)
30113	You win again	SRS 67040
30114	Fools like me	SRS 67040
30115	Hit the road, Jack	SRS 67052

FEBRUARY 14, 1964 (RCA Victor studio, Nashville). Producer; Shelby Singleton

Jerry Lee Lewis (voc, pno), more details unknown.

30338-1	I'm on fire (1)	134 204 MCY
30338-2	I'm on fire (2)	S 1886
30339	She was my baby (he was my friend)	S 1906
30340	Bread & butter man	S 1886
30341	I bet you're gonna like it	SRS 67097

APRIL 5, 1964 (The Starclub, Reperbahn, Hamburg, West Germany). Producer; Siggi Loch

Jerry Lee Lewis (voc, pno), & The Nashville Teens: Pete Shannon (gtr), John Allen (gtr), Ray Phillips (bass), John Hanken OR Barry Jenkins (dms).

Down the Line	148 005 STL
Mean woman blues	842 945 PY
High school confidential	842 945 PY
Money	842 945 PY
Matchbox	842 945 PY
What'd I say (part 1)	842 945 PY
What'd I say (part 2)	842 945 PY
Great balls of fire	842 945 PY
Good golly miss Molly	842 945 PY
Lewis boogie	842 945 PY
Your cheatin' heart	842 945 PY
Hound dog	842 945 PY
Long tall Sally	842 945 PY
Whole lotta shakin' goin' on	842 945 PY

Also possibly;

| You win again | UNRELEASED |
| I'm on fire | UNRELEASED |

JULY 1, 1964 (Municipal Auditorium, Birmingham, Alabama). Producer; Shelby Singleton & Jerry Kennedy

Jerry Lee Lewis (voc, pno), James Albert 'Buck' Hutcheson (gtr), Herman 'Hawk' Hawkins (bs), Morris 'Tarp' Tarrant (dms), Larry Nichols (org).

33790	Jenny Jenny	SRS 67056
33791	Who will the next fool be	SRS 67056
33792	Memphis, Tennessee	SRS 67056
33793	Hound dog	SRS 67056
33794	Mean woman blues	SRS 67056

33795	Hi-heel sneakers	S 1930(edit), SRS 67056
33796	No particular place to go	SRS 67056
33797	Together again	SRS 67056
33798	Long tall Sally	SRS 67056
33799	Whole lotta shakin' goin' on	SRS 67056

JANUARY 5, 1965 (Fred Foster studio, Nashville). Producer; Jerry Kennedy

Jerry Lee Lewis (voc, pno), more details unknown.

33359	Got you on my mind	SRS 67063
33360	Mathilda	SRS 67079
33361	Corrine, Corrina	SRS 67063
33362	Sexy ways	SRS 67063
33363	The Wild side of life	SRS 67071

JANUARY 6, 1965 (Fred Foster studio, Nashville). Producer; Shelby Singleton & Jerry Kennedy

Jerry Lee Lewis (voc, pno), more details unknown.

33369	Flip, flop & fly	SRS 67063
33370	Don't let go	SRS 67063
33371	Maybellene	SRS 67063
33372	Roll over Beethoven	SRS 67063
33373	Just in time	BFX 15210

JANUARY 7, 1965 (Fred Foster studio, Nashville). Producer; Shelby Singleton & Jerry Kennedy

Jerry Lee Lewis (voc, pno), details unknown.

33379	I believe in you	S 1969, SRS 67063
33380	Herman the Hermit	SRS 67063
33381	Baby, hold me close	S 1969, SRS 67063
33382	Skid row	BFX 15210

MAY 12, 1965 (Mirasound studios, New York). Producer; Shelby Singleton

Jerry Lee Lewis (voc, pno), more details unknown.

36121	This must be the place	S 1992
36122	Rockin' pneumonia & the boogie woogie flu	S 1992
36123	Wedding bells	UNRELEASED
36124	Seasons of my heart	SRS 67071
36125	Big boss man	SRS 67079

| 36126 | Too young | SRS 67079 |
| 36127 | Danny boy | BFX 15210 |

AUGUST 30, 1965 (RCA Victor studio, Nashville). Producer; Shelby Singleton

Jerry Lee Lewis (voc, pno), more details unknown.

33628	Crazy arms	SRS 67071
33629	City lights	SRS 67071
33630	Funny how time slips away	SRS 67071
33631	He'll have to go	UNRELEASED

AUGUST 31, 1965 (RCA Victor studio, Nashville). Producer; Shelby Singleton

Jerry Lee Lewis (voc, pno), Linda Gail Lewis (duet voc*), more details unknown.

33637	Ring of fire	SRS 67071
33638	Baby (you've got what it takes)*	S 2006
33639	Green green grass of home	S 2006,SRS 67071
33640	What a heck of a mess	UNRELEASED

JANUARY 5, 1966 (Sun studio, 639 Madison, Memphis). Producer; Jack Clement

Jerry Lee Lewis (voc, pno), Charlie Freeman (gtr), possibly Herman 'Hawk' Hawkins (bs), Morris 'Tarp' Tarrant (dms), possibly Danny Daniels (org).

37789	Sticks & stones	S 2027,SRS 67079
37790	What a heck of a mess	S 2027
37791	Lincoln limousine	SRS 67079
37792	Rockin' Jerry Lee	BFX 15210

JANUARY 6, 1966 (Sun studio, 639 Madison, Memphis). Producer; Jack Clement

Jerry Lee Lewis (voc, pno), Charlie Freeman (gtr), possibly Herman 'Hawk' Hawkins (bs), Morris 'Tarp' Tarrant (dms), possibly Danny Daniels (org).

37793	Memphis beat	SRS 67079
37794	The Urge	SRS 67079
37795	Whenever you're ready	SRS 67079
37796	She thinks I still care	SRS 67079

PROBABLY APRIL-MAY, 1966 (Unknown location, possibly a 'Catch My Soul' rehearsal session)

Jerry Lee Lewis (voc, pno), unknown bs & dms.

That's what you call love	EVCD 3001
The Cannikin clink	EVCD 3001

Note: The above titles were released as 'Lust of the blood' & 'Let a soldier drink' respectively. Gary Skala listed the correct (?) titles in 'Shaking Keyboard' issue 25.

JULY 2 (or possibly July 22), 1966 (Sun studio, 639 Madison, Memphis). Producer; Shelby Singleton

Jerry Lee Lewis (voc, pno), Charlie Freeman (gtr), possibly Herman 'Hawk' Hawkins (bs), Morris 'Tarp' Tarrant (dms), possibly Danny Daniels (org).

38195	Memphis beat	S 2053
38195	Memphis beat (alt)	134 204 MCY
38196	Twenty four hours a day (without strings)	BFX 15210
38196	Twenty four hours a day (with strings)	Pumpin' 1963 (bootleg)
38197	Swinging doors (without strings)	BFX 15210
48544	Swinging doors (with strings)	SR 61346
38198	If I had it all to do over (without strings)	BFX 15210
38198	If I had it all to do over (with strings)	S 2053

Note: Master 48544 is a new mix of master 38197. Also, the rehearsal sessions for the 'Memphis Beat' album were held at Roland Janes Sonic Studios in Memphis. Some of the rehearsal cuts were deemed better than the cuts obtained at the Sun studio & were therefore used on the album.

SEPTEMBER 7, 1966 (Panther Hall, Fort Worth, Texas). Producer; Shelby Singleton

Jerry Lee Lewis (vcl, pno), Charlie Freeman (gtr), Herman 'Hawk' Hawkins (bs), Morris 'Tarp' Tarrant (dms), Danny Daniels (org).

39012	Little queenie	SRS 67086
39013	How's me ex treating you	SRS 67086
39014	Johnny B. Goode	SRS 67086
39015	Green green grass of home	SRS 67086
39016	What'd I say (part 2)	SRS 67086
39017	You win again	SRS 67086
39018	I'll sail my ship alone	SRS 67086
39019	Cryin' time	SRS 67086
39020	Money	SRS 67086

| 39021 | Roll over Beethoven | SRS 67086 |

MAY 12, 1967 (American studio, Memphis). Producer; Jerry Kennedy

Jerry Lee Lewis (vcl, pno), more details unknown.

39525	Just dropped in	SRS 67097
39526	It's a hang up baby	S 2103,SRS 67097
39527	Holdin' on	S 2103,SRS 67097

AUGUST 9, 1967 (Columbia studio A, Nashville). Producer; Jerry Kennedy

Jerry Lee Lewis (vcl, pno), Kenneth Lovelace (gtr), more details unknown.

39545	Hey baby	SRS 67097
39546	Dream baby (how long must I dream)	SRS 67097
39547	Treat her right	SRS 67097
39548	Turn on your lovelight	S 2122,SRS 67097,SRM 1 637
39549	Shotgun man	S 2122,SRS 67097,SRM 1 637

JANUARY 5, 1968 (Columbia studio, Nashville). Producer; Jerry Kennedy

Jerry Lee Lewis (vcl, pno), Kenneth Lovelace (fiddle), probably Bob Moore (bs), probably Buddy Harman (dms), Chorus; Dorothy Ann Dillard, Priscilla Ann Hubbard, William Guilford Wright, Louis D. Nunley. More details unknown.

41057	All the good is gone	S 2164,SRS 67104,SRS 67131
41058	Another place another time	S 2146,SRS 67104,SRS 67131
41059	Walking the floor over you	S 2146,SRS 67104

APRIL 16, 1968 (Columbia studio, Nashville). Producer; Jerry Kennedy

Personnel as January 5, 1968, though substitute the following on masters 41122-41125; Chorus; Hurshel W. Wiginton, Dolores D. Edgin, June E. Page, Joseph T. Babcock. Also; Linda Gail Lewis (duet voc*).

41118	I'm a lonesome fugitive	SRS 67104
41119	Break my mind	SRS 67104
41120	Play me a song I can cry to	SRS 67104
41121	Before the next teardrop falls	SRS 67104
41122	All night long	SRS 67104
41123	We live in two different worlds*	S 2220,SRS 67104,SRS 67126

| 41124 | What's made Milwaukee famous | S 2164,SRS 67104,SRS 67131 |
| 41125 | On the back row | SRS 67104 |

AUGUST 14, 1968 (Columbia studio, Nashville). Producer; Jerry Kennedy

Jerry Lee Lewis (voc, pno), Kenneth Lovelace (fiddle), probably Bob Moore (bs), probably Buddy Harman (dms), more details unknown.

42981	Slippin' around	S 2186,SRS 67131
42982	(Grand old) Moon up above	UNRELEASED
42983	She still comes around	S 2186,SRS 67112,SRS 67131

Note: Master 42982 was re-recorded on June 13, 1969 as a duet with Linda Gail Lewis. The song was re-titled 'Earth up above'.

OCTOBER 21, 1968 (Columbia studio, Nashville). Producer; Jerry Kennedy

Personnel as August 14, 1968.

43017	Today I started loving you again	SRS 67112
43018	Louisiana man	SRS 67112,SRS 67131
43019	There stands the glass	SRS 67112
43020	I can't have a merry Christmas, Mary (without you)	73155
43021	Out of my mind	SRS 67112
43022	I can't get over you	SRS 67112
43023	Listen, they're playing my song	SRS 67112
43024	Echoes	S 2244,SRS 67112,SRS 67128
43025	Release me	SRS 67112

NOVEMBER 12, 1968 (Columbia studio, Nashville). Producer; Jerry Kennedy

Personnel as August 14, 1968.

43044	Let's talk about us	S 2202,SRS 67112,SRS 67131
43045	To make love sweeter for you	S 2202,SRS 6712,SRS 67131
43046	You're gettin' ready to hurt me	UNRELEASED

FEBRUARY 18, 1969 (Columbia studio, Nashville). Producer; Jerry Kennedy

Jerry Lee Lewis (vcl), Linda Gail Lewis (duet vcl), Hargus 'Pig' Robbins (pno), Kenneth Lovelace (fiddle), Chorus; Hurshel W. Wiginton, Dolores E. Edgin, June E. Page, Joseph T. Babcock. More details unknown.

| 43098 | Don't let me cross over | S 2220,SRS 67126 |

FEBRUARY 25, 1969 (Columbia studio, Nashville). Producer; Jerry Kennedy

Personnel as August 14, 1968.

43101	Born to lose	SRS 67117
43102	You belong to me	BFX 15228
52454	You belong to me (re-mix)	73872,SRMI 1109
43103	Oh lonesome me	SRS 67117
43104	Sweet dreams	SRS 67117
43105	Cold, cold heart	UNRELEASED

FEBRUARY 26, 1969 (Columbia studio, Nashville). Producer; Jerry Kennedy

Personnel as August 14, 1968.

43106	Cold, cold heart	SRS 67118
43107	Fraulein	SRS 67118
43108	Why don't you love me (like you used to do)	SRS 67118
43109	Four walls	SRS 67117
43110	It makes no difference now	SRS 67118
43111	I love you because	SRS 67117
43112	I'm so lonesome I could cry	SRS 67117
56680	I'm so lonesome I could cry (with strings)	76148
43113	Jambalaya	SRS 67117
43114	More & more	SRS 67118
43115	One has my name (the other has my heart)	S 2224,SRS 67118,SRS 67131
43116	Burning memories	SRS 67118
43117	Mom & dad's waltz	SRS 67117
43118	Pick me up on your way down	SRS 67118
43119	Heartaches by the number	SRS 67117
43120	I can't stop loving you	S 2224,SRS 67118
43121	My blue heaven	BFX 15228
52455	My blue heaven (re-mix)	UNRELEASED
43122	I wonder where you are tonight	SRS 67117

FEBRUARY 28, 1969 (Columbia Studio, Nashville). Producer; Jerry Kennedy

Personnel as August 14, 1968, with the addition of Linda Gail Lewis (duet vcl*).

43123	Jackson*	SRS 67117,SRS 67126
43124	Sweet thing*	SRS 67118,SRS 67126
43125	He'll have to go	SRS 67118
43126	You've still got a place in my heart	SRS 67117
43127	I get the blues when it rains	SRS 67118

JUNE 13, 1969 (Monument studio, Nashville). Producer; Jerry Kennedy

Personnel as August 14, 1968, with the addition of Linda Gail Lewis (duet vcl).

45438	Gotta travel on	SRS 67126
45439	Milwaukee here I come	SRS 67126
45440	Cryin' time	SRS 67126
45441	Roll over Beethoven	S 2254,SRS 67126
45442	Secret places	S 2254,SRS 67126
45443	Don't take it out on me	SRS 67126
45444	Earth up above	SRS 67126

AUGUST 4, 1969 (Monument studio, Nashville). Producer; Jerry Kennedy

Jerry Lee Lewis (vcl, pno), Harold Ray Bradley (gtr), Jerry 'Chip Young' Stembridge (gtr), Ray Edenton (gtr), Jerry Kennedy (gtr), Ned Gail Davis (st. gtr), Jerry W. Shock (gtr), Bob Moore (bs), Kenneth Lovelace (fiddle), Buddy Harman (dms), Hargus 'Pig' Robbins (org), Bergen D. White (string arrangements), Chorus; Unknown.

45479	Waiting for a train	SRS67128
45480	Love of all seasons	BFX 15228
45481	She even woke me up to say goodbye	S 2244,SRS 67128, SRS 67131

Note: Master 45480 was recorded 'solo' by Linda Gail Lewis (the song's composer) under the title 'Joy & love you bring'.

SEPTEMBER 13, 1969 (Varsity Stadium Toronto, Canada).

Jery Lee Lewis (vcl, pno, gtr*), Kenneth Lovelace (gtr, fiddle), possibly Ned Gail Davis (st. gtr), possibly Ed DeBruhl (bs), Russell Smith (dms).

| | Don't be cruel | RARE SOUND 1114 (bootleg) |
| | Hound dog | BFX 15228 |

Mean woman blues	BFX 15228
Great balls of fire	BFX 15228
Mystery train*	BFX 15228
Whole lotta shakin' goin' on	BFX 15228
Jailhouse rock	BFX 15228

OCTOBER 14, 1969 (Monument studio, Nashville). Producer; Jerry Kennedy

Personnel as August 4, 1969, *except* Bergen D. White (string arrangements).

45515	When the grass grows over me	SRS 67128
45516	Wine me up	SRS 67128
45517	Since I met you baby	SRS 67128
45518	Workin' man blues	SRS 67128

OCTOBER 15, 1969 (Monument studio, Nashville). Producer; Jerry Kennedy

Personnel as August 4, 1969, *except* Bergen D. White (string arrangements).

45519	Once more with feeling	BFX 15228
45520	In loving memories	BFX 15228
45521	You went out of your way (to walk on me)	S 2257,SRS 67128
45522	My only claim to fame	SRS 67128

NOVEMBER 18, 1969 (Monument studio, Nashville). Producer: Jerry Kennedy

Personnel as August 4, 1969, *except* Bergen D. White (string arrangements).

45537	Brown eyed handsome man	SRS 67128
45538	In loving memories	73155,SR 61318
45539	Once more with feeling	S 2257,SRS 67128,SRS 67131

Note: Personnel details for August 4/October 14/October 16/November 18, 1969 are taken from the LP SRS 67128, & may not be 100% correct.

MARCH 9, 1970 (Monument studio, Nashville). Producer; Jerry Kennedy

Jerry Lee Lewis (vcl, pno), Mamie Lewis (vcl*), Jerry 'Chip Young' Stembridge (gtr), Harold Ray Bradley (gtr), Ray Edenton (gtr), Jerry Kennedy (gtr), Ned Gail Davis (st. gtr), Kenneth Lovelace (fiddle), Bob Moore (bs), Ed DeBruhl (bs), Buddy Harman (dms), Chorus; Hugh Gordon Stoker, Neal Matthews jr, Raymond C. Walker, Ernest Duane West.

47053	Gather round children*	SR 61318
47054	I'd be talkin' all the time	SR 61323
47055	Alvin	SCPB 6816 125

47056   I forgot more than you'll ever know   SR 61323

MARCH 10, 1970 (Monument studio, Nashville). Producer; Jerry Kennedy

Personnel as March 10, 1970 except different Chorus; Dorothy Ann Dillard,
Jeannie M. Ogletree, William Guilford Wright, Louis D. Nunley.

47057   Bottles & barstools   SR 61323
47058   Life's little ups & downs   SR 61323
47059   There must be more to love than this   73099,SR 323,SRM 1
                                                     5006
47060   Sweet Georgia Brown   SR 61323,SRM 1 5006
47061   Home away from home   73099,SR 61323
47062   Woman, woman (get out of your way)   73192,SR 61323
47063   Reuben James   SR 61323

Note: The Tracksheet notes a vocal group overdub for masters 47057/58/59 on
April 1, 1970, & also notes a Jerry Lee Lewis vocal overdub for masters
47062/63 on October 24, 1970.

**MAY 22, 1970 (International Hotel (Show 1), Las Vegas). Producer: Jerry
Kennedy & Roy Dea**

Jerry Lee Lewis (vcl, pno), Linda Gail Lewis (duet vcl*/solo vcl**), James
Albert 'Buck' Hutcheson (gtr), Kenneth Lovelace (gtr/fiddle), Ned Gail Davis
(st. gtr), Ed DeBruhl (bs), Morris 'Tarp' Tarrant (dms), Jerry Lee Lewis
Junior (tambourine/vcl***).

             Intro   UNRELEASED
             Flip, flop & fly   UNRELEASED
             You win again   UNRELEASED
             Cold, cold heart   UNRELEASED
             Shoeshine man   UNRELEASED
             Homecoming   UNRELEASED
             Down the line*   UNRELEASED
             I wish you love**   UNRELEASED
             Johnny B. Goode**   UNRELEASED
             Once more with feeling   UNRELEASED
             She even woke me up to say goodbye   UNRELEASED
             Rip it up ***   UNRELEASED
             Great balls of fire/Whole lotta shakin' UNRELEASED
                goin' on
             Closing (instrumental)   UNRELEASED

**MAY 22, 1970 (International Hotel (Show 2), Las Vegas). Producer; Jerry
Kennedy & Roy Dea**

Personnel as May 22, 1970 (show 1).

	Intro	UNRELEASED
	Today I started loving you again	UNRELEASED
	Sweet little sixteen	BFX 15228
	Jenny Jenny/Long tall Sally/Tutti frutti	BFX 15228
	C. C. rider	BFX 15228
47119	Ballad of forty dollars	SR 61278
	Homecoming	UNRELEASED
	High school confidential	BFX 15228
	Great balls of fire	UNRELEASED
	Down the line/I'm movin' on*	BFX 15228
	Silver threads & golden needles**	UNRELEASED
	Got you on my mind again (1)*	UNRELEASED
	Got you on my mind again (2)*	UNRELEASED
	Whole lotta shakin' goin' on	BFX 15228

MAY 22, 1970 (International Hotel (Show 3), Las Vegas). Producer; Jerry Kennedy & Roy Dea

Personnel as May 22, 1970 (Show 1).

	Oh lonesome me	BFX 15228
	Your cheatin' heart	BFX 15228
	Smoke gets in your eyes (instrumental)	BFX 15228
	Jambalaya	UNRELEASED
	Invitation to your party	BFX 15228
	Blue suede shoes	BFX 15228
	When the grass grows over me	BFX 15228
	Jackson*	BFX 15228
	Take these chains from my heart**	UNRELEASED
	Proud Mary ***	UNRELEASED
	Drinkin' champagne	UNRELEASED
	Shoeshine man	UNRELEASED
	Closing (instrumental)	UNRELEASED

MAY 23, 1970 (International Hotel (Show 1), Las Vegas). Producer; Jerry Kennedy & Roy Dea

Personnel as May 22, 1970 (Show 1).

	Intro	SR 61278
	Ubangi stomp	UNRELEASED
	Cold, cold heart	UNRELEASED
47112	Jambalaya	SR 61278
47113	She still comes around	SR 61278
47114	Drinkin' champagne	SR 61278
	Got you on my mind again*	UNRELEASED

	Roll over Beethoven	UNRELEASED
	I wish you love**	UNRELEASED
47116	Once more with feeling	SR 61278
	I can't seem to say goodbye	UNRELEASED
	One minute past eternity	UNRELEASED
	Rip it up***	UNRELEASED
	Great balls of fire	UNRELEASED
	Whole lotta shakin' goin' on	UNRELEASED
	Homecoming	UNRELEASED

MAY 23, 1970 (International Hotel (Show 2), Las Vegas). Producer; Jerry Kennedy & Roy Dea

Personnel as May 22, 1970 (Show 1).

	Intro	BFX 15228
	Flip, flop & fly	SR 61278
	Today I started loving you again	BFX 15228
	San Antonio Rose (1)	UNRELEASED
	San Antonio Rose (2)	SR 61278
	Invitation to your party	UNRELEASED
	Down the line*	UNRELEASED
47117	When you wore a tulip & I wore a big red rose*	SR 61278
47111	She even woke me up to say goodbye	SR 61278
	Silver threads & golden needles**	UNRELEASED
	One has my name (the other has my heart)	BFX 15228
	Shoeshine man	BFX 15228
	Once more with feeling	UNRELEASED
	Great balls of fire	BFX 15228
	Ballad of forty dollars	UNRELEASED

MAY 23, 1970 (International Hotel (SHOW 3), Las Vegas). Producer; Jerry Kennedy & Roy Dea

Personnel as May 22, 1970 (Show 1).

	Intro	UNRELEASED
	Mean woman blues	BFX 15228
	You are my sunshine	BFX 15228
	Stagger Lee	UNRELEASED
	Homecoming	BFX 15228
	Got you on my mind again*	BFX 15228
47118	Take these chains from my heart**	SR 61278

Great balls of fire	UNRELEASED
What'd I say	BFX 15228
Mexcali rose (slow)	BFX 15228
Mexicali rose (fast)	BFX 15228
Whole lotta shakin' goin' on (closing)	UNRELEASED

JULY 16, 1970 (Mercury studio, Nashville)

Jerry Lee Lewis (duet vcl, gtr), Linda Gail Lewis (duet vcl), Harold Ray
Bradley (gtr), James Albert 'Buck' Hutcheson (gtr), Jerry 'Chip Young'
Stembridge (gtr), Jerry Kennedy (gtr), Ray Edenton (gtr), Ned Gail Davis
(st. gtr), Bob Moore (bs), Kenneth Lovelace (fiddle), Buddy Harman (dms),
Hargus 'Pig' Robbins (pno), Chorus; Dorothy Ann Dillard, Jeanine M.
Ogletree, William Guilford Wright, Louis D. Nunley.

47133	Before the snow flies	73113

OCTOBER 5, 1970 (Mercury studio, Nashville). Producer; Jerry Lee Lewis & Linda Gail Lewis

Jerry Lee Lewis (vcl, pno), Linda Gail Lewis (duet vcl*), Jerry 'Chip Young'
Stembridge (gtr), Harold Ray Bradley (gtr), Ray Edenton (gtr), James Albert
'Buck' Hutcheson (gtr), Ned Gail Davis (st. gtr), Kenneth Lovelace (fiddle),
Bob Moore (bs), Ed DeBruhl (bs), Buddy Harman (dms), Chorus; Hugh
Gordon Stoker, Neal Matthews jr, Raymond C. Walker, Hoyt H. Hawkins.

47191	Cheater pretend*	SCPB 6816 125
47192	He looked beyond my fault	SR 61318
47193	Handwriting on the wall*	73303
47194	The old rugged cross	SR 61318
47195	The 'lly of the valley	SR 61318
47196	I'll meet you in the morning (medley pt 2)	SR 61318
47197	If we never meet again (medley part 1)	SR 61318
47198	I'm longing for home	SR 61318
47199	Black mama	830 207-1
47208	I'll fly away	SR 61318

OCTOBER 6, 1970 (Mercury studio, Nashville). Producer; Jerry Lee Lewis & Linda Gail Lewis

Personnel as October 5, 1970, except different Chorus; Dorothy Ann Dillard,
Jeannie M. Ogletree, William Guilford Wright, Louis D. Nunley.

47200	I know that Jesus will be there*	SR 61318
47201	My God's not dead	SR 61318
47202	Foolaid	SR 61323

| 47203 | One more time | SR 61323 |
| 47204 | Too much to gain to lose | SR 61318 |

DECEMBER 15, 1970 (Fame recording studio, Memphis). Producer; Jerry Lee Lewis

Jerry Lee Lewis (vcl, pno), more details unknown.

Jealous heart	BFX 15228
The last letter	BFX 15228
Meeting in the air	830 207-1
Where he leads me	830 207-1
Living on the hallelujah side	830 207-1
A picture from life's other side	BFX 15228

DECEMBER, 1970 (Church Live recording, Memphis)

Jerry Lee Lewis (vcl, pno), Kenneth Lovelace (gtr, fiddle), Ed DeBruhl (bs), Jerry Lee Lewis jr (dms), Bill Strom (org), also unknown choir.

Looking for a city	BFX 15228
I'm longing for home	BFX 15228
Blessed saviour thou wilt guide us	BFX 15228
Someone who cares for you	BFX 15228
If we never meet again/I'll meet you in the morning	BFX 15228
Down the sawdust trail	BFX 15228
Peace in the valley	BFX 15228
Precious memories	BFX 15228
The old rugged cross	BFX 15228
It will be worth it all when we see Jesus	BFX 15228
I know that Jesus will be there	BFX 15228
I'm in the gloryland way	BFX 15228
Tomorrow may mean goodbye	BFX 15228
Amazing grace	BFX 15228
On the Jericho road	BFX 15228
I'll fly away	BFX 15228
My god is real	BFX 15228
When Jesus beckons me home	BFX 15228
I won't have to cross Jordan alone	BFX 15228
Keep on the firing line	BFX 15228

Note: 'Blessed saviour thou wilt guide us' was re-recorded on December 14, 1977 under the title 'Life's railway to heaven'.

FEBRUARY 3, 1971 (Mercury studio, Nashville). Producer; Jerry Kennedy

Jerry Lee Lewis (vcl, pno), Herman B. 'Pete' Wade (gtr), Dale Sellers (gtr), Ray Edenton (gtr), Jerry Kennedy (gtr), Pete Drake (st. gtr), Kenneth Lovelace (fiddle), Bob Moore (bs), Buddy Harman (dms), Chorus; Hugh Gordon Stoker, Neal Matthews jr, Raymond C. Walker, Hoyt H. Hawkins, Mildred Kirkham.

48419	The hurtin' part	SR 61346
48420	Touching home	73192,SR 61343,SRM 1 5006
48421	Comin' back for more	SR 61343
48422	When baby gets the blues	SR 61343

Note: The tracksheet notes a vocal group overdub on master 48421.

MARCH 23, 1971 (Mercury studio, Nashville). Producer; Jerry Kennedy

Jerry Lee Lewis (vcl, pno), Jerry 'Chip Young' Stembridge (gtr), Herman B 'Pete' Wade (gtr), Dale Sellers (gtr), Jerry Kennedy (gtr), Lloyd Green (st. gtr), Kenneth Lovelace (fiddle), Bob Moore (bs), Bill Strom (bs), Jerry K. Carrigan (dms), Chorus; Dorothy Ann Dillard, Mildred Kirkham, William Guilford Wright, Louis D. Nunley.

48437	Help me make it through the night	SR 61343
48438	Mother, the queen of my heart	SR 61343
48439	Time changes everything	SR 61343
48440	Hearts were made for beating	SR 61343

Note: The tracksheet notes a Jerry Lee Lewis vocal overdub for master 48440 on March 30, 1971.

MARCH 30, 1971 (Mercury studio, Nashville). Producer; Jerry Kennedy

Jerry Lee Lewis (vcl, pno), Ray Edenton (gtr), Jerry Kennedy (gtr), Harold Ray Bradley (gtr), Jerry W. Shook (gtr), Pete Drake (st. gtr), Kenneth Lovelace (fiddle), Bob Moore (bs), Bill Strom (bs), Buddy Harman (dms), Roy Dea (unknown), Chorus; Dorothy Ann Dillard, Mildred Kirkham, William Guilford Wright, Louis D. Nunley.

48445	When he walks on you (like you have walked on me)	73227,SR 61343
48447	Foolish kind of man	73227,SR 61343
48448	Another hand shakin' goodbye	SR 61346
48449	Please don't talk about me when I'm gone	SR 61343

JUNE 17, 1971 (Mercury studio, Nashville). Producer; Jerry Kennedy

Jerry Lee Lewis (vcl, pno), Jerry 'Chip Young' Stembridge (gtr), Ray
Edenton (gtr), Harold Ray Bradley (gtr), Jerry Kennedy (gtr), Pete Drake
(st. gtr), Kenneth Lovelace (fiddle), Bob Moore (bs), Buddy Harman (dms),
Bill Strom (org), Roy Dea (unknown), Chorus; Dorothy Ann Dillard,
Jeanine O. Walker, William Guilford Wright, Louis D. Nunley.

48509	The goodbye of the year	SR 61346
48510	Someday you'll want me to want you	SCPB 6816 125
48511	No honky tonks in heaven	73328
48512	Big blon' baby	SR 61346
48513	Lonesome fiddle man	SR 61346
48514	Things that matter most to me	SR 61346
48515	I don't know why, I just do	SCPB 6816 125
48516	Thirteen at the table	SR 61346

AUGUST 4, 1971 (Mercury studio, Nashville). Producer; Jerry Kennedy

Jerry Lee Lewis (vcl, pno), Jerry 'Chip Young' Stembridge (gtr), Ray
Edenton (gtr), Harold Ray Bradley (gtr), Pete Drake (st. gtr), Kenneth
Lovelace (fiddle), Bob Moore (bs), Buddy Harman (dms), Hargus 'Pig'
Robbins (pno), Bill Strom (org), Roy Dea (unknown), Chorus; Hurshel W.
Wiginton, Dolores D. Edgin, June E. Page, Joseph T. Babcock, Mildred
Kirkham, also String Section (arranged by Cam Mullins).

48530	For the good times	SR 61346
48531	Would you take another chance on me	73248,SR 61346,SRMI 5006
48532	Me & Bobby McGee	73248,SR 61346,SRMI 5006
48533	And for the first time	830 207-1

Note: The tracksheet notes a piano overdub for masters 48530/31 on August
5,1971.

JANUARY 14, 1972 (Mercury studio, Nashville). Producer; Jerry Kennedy

Jerry Lee Lewis (vcl, pno), Herman B. 'Pete' Wade (gtr), Harold Ray
Bradley (gtr), Jerry Kennedy (gtr), Dale Sellers (gtr), Pete Drake (st. gtr),
Bob Moore (bs), Buddy Harman (dms), Bill Strom (org), Roy Dea
(unknown), Chorus; Hurshel W. Wiginton, Dolores D. Edgin, June E. Page,
Joseph T. Babcock, Mildred Kirkham, also String Section (arranged by Cam
Mullins).

| 49751 | Think about it darlin' | 73273,SR 61366,SRMI 5006 |

| 49752 | No traffic out of Abilene | SR 61366 |
| 49753 | Chantilly lace | 73273,SRMI 637,SRMI 5006 |

Note: The tracksheet notes a vocal group overdub for master 49751 on January 26, 1972.

FEBRUARY 25, 1972 (Mercury studio, Nashville). Producer; Jerry Kennedy

Jerry Lee Lewis (vcl, pno), Jerry 'Chip Young' Stembridge (gtr), Ray Edenton (gtr), Harold Ray Bradley (gtr), Pete Drake (st. gtr), Jerry Kennedy (gtr), Kenneth Lovelace (fiddle), Norman Keith 'Buddy' Spicher (fiddle), Bob Moore (bs), Buddy Harman (dms), Bill Strom (org), Roy Dea (unknown), Chorus; Hurshel W. Wiginton, Dolores D. Edgin, June E. Page, Joseph T. Babcock, Mildred Kirkham, Anna Patricia Williams, also String Section (arranged by Cam Mullins).

49780	Lonely weekends	74296,SRM 637
49781	C. C. rider	SRMI 637
49782	Walk a mile in my shoes	SRMI 637
49783	Games people play	SRMI 637
49784	Don't be cruel	SRMI 637
49785	You can have her	SRMI 637
49786	I'm walkin'	SRMI 637
49787	You don't miss your water	SRMI 637

Note: The tracksheet notes Strings overdubs for masters 49781/82/83/87 on March 2, 1972.

MAY 31, 1972 (Mercury studio, Nashville). Producer; Roy Dea

Jerry Lee Lewis (vcl, pno), Linda Gail Lewis (duet vcl), Jerry 'Chip Young' Stembridge (gtr), Ray Edenton (gtr), Harold Ray Bradley (gtr), Jerry Kennedy (gtr), Pete Drake (st. gtr), Bob Moore (bs), Kenneth Lovelace (fiddle), Jerry K. Carrigan (dms), Hargus 'Pig' Robbins (pno, org), Chorus; Hurshel W. Wiginton, Dolores D. Edgin, June E. Page, Joseph T. Babcock.

| 49815 | Me & Jesus | 73303 |

JULY 19, 1972 (Mercury studio, Nashville). Producer; Jerry Kennedy

Jerry Lee Lewis (vcl, pno), Jerry 'Chip Young' Stembridge (gtr), Ray Edenton (gtr), Harold Ray Bradley (gtr), Jerry Kennedy (gtr), Pete Drake (st. gtr), Bob Moore (bs), Kenneth Lovelace (fiddle), Buddy Harman (dms), Hargus 'Pig' Robbins (pno), Bob Phillips (tpt), Albert Wayne Butler (tbn), Stephen Ralph Sefsik (clarinet), Chorus; Hurshel W. Wiginton, Sonja Carol

Montgomery, June E. Page, Joseph T. Babcock, Mildred Kirkham, Anna
Patricia Williams, also String Section (arranged by Cam Mullins).

49840	Too many rivers	SR 61366
49841	No more hanging on	SR 61366
49842	The mercy of a letter	SR 61366
49843	She's reachin' for my mind	SR 61366
49844	Wall around heaven	SR 61366
49845	We both know which one of us was wrong	SR 61366
49846	Parting is such sweet sorrow (instrumental)	SR 61366
49847	Who's gonna play this old piano	73328,SR 61366,SRM 1 5006
49848	Bottom dollar	SR 61366
49849	Parting is such sweet sorrow (vocal)	830 829-1

Note: The tracksheet notes Jerry Lee Lewis vocal overdubs for masters 49840/
41/42/43/47/48/49 (two overdubs on 49847) on July 26, 1972. A piano overdub
for master 49849 was also recorded on that date.
Note: The tracksheet notes further vocal overdubs for masters 49841/42/43 on
October 11, 1972. A bass & electric piano overdub was also recorded on that
date. At this session masters 49841/42/43 were given the new master numbers
of 49867/68/69 (respectively).

**JANUARY 8-11, 1973 (Advision studio, London, England). Producer; Steve
Rowland**

Jerry Lee Lewis (vcl, pno), Tony Ashton (percussion, pno, org), Andy Brown
(electric pno, org), Delaney Bramlett (gtr, bottleneck gtr), B. J. Cole (st.
gtr), Tony Colton (percussion), Drew Croon (acoustic gtr), Matthew Fisher
(percussion, org), Peter Frampton (gtr), Rory Gallagher (gtr, bottleneck gtr),
Pete Gavin (dms, percussion), John Gustafson (bs), Chas Hodges (vcl, gtr,
bs), Joe Jammer (gtr), Kenny Jones (dms, percussion), Mickey Jones (gtr),
Mick Kelly (dms, percussion), Albert Lee (acoustic gtr, gtr, electric pno),
Alvin Lee (gtr), Jerry Lee Lewis jr (percussion), Kenneth Lovelace (acoustic
gtr, fiddle), Brian Parrish (percussion, harmonica), Pete Robinson (electric
pno), Steve Rowland (percussion), Ray Smith (acoustic gtr, percussion), Gary
Taylor (acoustic gtr, percussion), Klaus Voormann (bs), Gary Wright (org),
Chorus; Thunder thighs (Karen Friedman, Dari Lallou, Casey Synge).

JANUARY 8, 1973

| I don't want to be lonely tonight | UNRELEASED |
| Let's get back to rock 'n roll | UNRELEASED |

| 50043 | Sixty minute man | SRM2 803 |

JANUARY 9, 1973

50033	Sea cruise	SRM2 803
	Early morning rain (instrumental)	SLP 1280 (bootleg)
50041	Early morning rain (vocal)	SRM2 803
50047	Pledging my love	SRM2 803
	Goldmine in the sky	BFX 15240
50038	Trouble in mind	SRM2 803
50032	Bad moon rising	SRM2 803
	Bad moon rising (alt. 1)	SLP 1280 (bootleg)
	Bad moon rising (alt. 2)	UNRELEASED
50035	No headstone on my grave	73402 (edit), SRM2 803

JANUARY 10, 1973

50030	Music to the man	SRM2 803
	Music to the man (alt.)	UNRELEASED
50034	Jukebox	SRM2 803
	Jukebox (alt.)	SLP 1280 (bootleg)
50039	Johnny B. Goode	SRM2 803
	Johnny B. Goode (alt.)	UNRELEASED
50042	Whole lotta shakin' goin' on	SRM2 803
	Singing the blues	BFX 15241
	Satisfaction	BFX 15240
	Waterloo	UNRELEASED
50044	Down the line	SRM2 803

JANUARY 11, 1973

50029	Drinkin' wine spo-dee-o-dee	73374, SRM2 803
	Drinkin' wine spo-dee-o-dee (alt.)	UNRELEASED
50046	Rock & roll medley; Good golly miss Molly / Long tall Sally / Jenny Jenny / Tutti frutti / Whole lotta shakin' goin' on	73374, SRM2 803
50037	Memphis, Tennessee	SRM2 803
50031	Baby what you want me to do	SRM2 803
50036	Big boss man	SRM2 803
50040	High school confidential (instrumental)	SRM2 803
50045	What'd I say	SRM2 803
	Be bop a lula	BFX 15241

JANUARY 8-11, 1973

Dungaree doll	BFX 15240
I can't give you anything but love, baby	BFX 15240

PROBABLY MID MARCH, 1973 (Trans Maximus inc. studio, Memphis). Producer; Tony Colton.

Jerry Lee Lewis (vcl, pno), Moetta Hill (duet vcl*), Steve Cropper (gtr), Cate (gtr), Donald 'Duck' Dunn (bs), Pete Gavin (dms).

49060	Jack Daniels (old number seven)	73402
49061	Why me lord	830 207-1
	Good time Charlie's got the blues*	UNRELEASED
	Lord what's left for me to do	UNRELEASED

JULY 10, 1973 (Mercury studio, Nashville). Producer; Stan Kesler

Jerry Lee Lewis (vcl, pno), Jerry 'Chip Young' Stembridge (gtr), Jerry W. Shook (gtr), Ray Edenton (gtr), Harold Ray Bradley (gtr), Pete Drake (st. gtr), Bob Moore (bs), Kenneth Lovelace (fiddle), Buddy Harman (dms), Jerry Lee Lewis jr (dms), Unknown (tambourine), Chorus; James W. Glaser, Neal Matthews jr, Raymond C. Walker, Hoyt H. Hawkins, Winifred S. Breast, also String Section (arranged by Cam Mullins).

50238	Ride me down easy	SRMI 677
50239	Cold, cold morning light	73491,SRMI 710
50240	The alcohol of fame	SRMI 710
50241	Tomorrow's taking baby away	73618,SRMI 710
50242	Mama's hands	SRMI 677
50243	What my woman can't do	SRMI 677

Note: The tracksheet notes a Jerry Lee Lewis vocal overdub for masters 50240/41/42/43 without a date. The liner notes for LPs SRMI 710 mention vocal overdubs at Phillips studio, Memphis.

JULY 11, 1973 (Mercury studio, Nashville). Producer; Stan Kesler

Jerry Lee Lewis (vcl, pno), Herman B. 'Pete' Wade (gtr), Jerry 'Chip Young' Stembridge (gtr), Ray Edenton (gtr), Harold Ray Bradley (gtr), Pete Drake (st. gtr), Bob Moore (bs), Kenneth Lovelace (fiddle), Buddy Harman (dms), Jerry Lee Lewis jr (dms), String Section (arranged by Cam Mullins).

50247	Tell tale signs	73491,SRMI 710
50248	The morning after baby let me down	SRMI 677
50249	I think I need to pray	73423,SRMI 677
50250	I hate goodbyes	SRMI 710
50251	Where would I be	SRMI 710

50252	My cricket & me	SRMI 677
50253	Falling to the bottom	73452,SRMI 677
50254	The gods were angry with me	830 829-1

Note: The tracksheet notes a Jerry Lee Lewis vocal overdub for masters 50247/48/49/50/51/52/53/54 (two overdubs for 50250 & 50254) without a date. A piano overdub for master 50254 was also recorded. The liner notes for LPs SRMI 710 mention vocal overdubs at Phillips studio, Memphis.

JULY 12, 1973 (Mercury studio, Nashville). Producer; Stan Kesler.

Jerry Lee Lewis (vcl, pno), Herman B. 'Pete' Wade (gtr), Billy R. Stanford (gtr), Jerry 'Chip Young' Stembridge (gtr), Ray Edenton (gtr), Harold Ray Bradley (gtr), Pete Drake (st. gtr), Bob Moore (bs), Kenneth Lovelace (fiddle), Buddy Harman (dms), String Section (arranged by Cam Mullins).

50255	Sometimes a memory ain't enough	73423,SRMI 677
50256	Bluer words	SRMI 710
50257	He can't fill my shoes	73618,SRMI 710
50258	I'm left, you're right, she's gone	73452,SRMI 677
50259	Keep me from blowing away	SRMI 677
50260	Honky tonk wine	SRMI 677
50261	Room full of roses	SRMI 710

Note: The tracksheet notes a Jerry Lee Lewis vocal overdub for masters 50255/56/57/58/59/60 (two overdubs for 50255/58) without a date, & a vocal overdub for master 50261 on July 13, 1973. The liner notes for LPs SRMI 677 & SRMI 710 mention vocal overdubs at Phillips studio, Memphis.

SEPTEMBER 24-26, 1973 (Trans Maximus inc. studio, Memphis, & Sugar Hill studio, Houston, Texas Producer; Huey Meaux.

Jerry Lee Lewis (vcl, pno), Steve Cropper (gtr), Carl Perkins (gtr), Tony Joe White (gtr), Kenneth Lovelace (gtr), Paul Cannon (gtr), Jim Tarbutton (gtr), Charles Owens (st. gtr), Donald 'Duck' Dunn (bs), Herman 'Hawk' Hawkins (bs), Tommy Cathy (bs), Al Jackson (dms), Morris 'Tarp' Tarrant (dms), Joel Williams (dms), Jerry Lee Lewis jr (percussion), Mack Vickery (harmonica), James Brown (org), Augie Meyers (org), J. L. 'Marty' Morrison (org), Mark Lindsey (horns), Bill Taylor (horns), Russ Carlton (horns), Memphis Horns (Wayne Jackson, James Mitchell, Jack Hale, Ed Logan, Andrew Love), Chorus; The Sugar Sweets (Houston).

51070	Meat man	73462 (edit), SRMI 690
51071	When a man loves a woman	SRMI 690
	When a man loves a woman (rehearsals)	BFX 15229
51072	Hold on I'm coming (slow)	SRMI 690

	Hold on I'm coming (fast)	BFX 15229
51073	Just a little bit	73462,SRMI 690
51074	Born to be a loser	SRMI 690
51075	The haunted house (edited)	SRMI 690
51075	The haunted house (full version)	BFX 15229
51076	Blueberry hill	SRMI 690
51077	The revolutionary man	SRMI 690
51078	Big blue diamonds	SRMI 690
	Big blue diamonds (rehearsal instrumental)	BFX 15229
51079	That old Bourbon Street church	SRMI 690
	Honey hush	BFX 15229
	All over hell & half of Georgia	BFX 15229
	I sure miss those good old times	BFX 15229
	I sure miss those good old times (rehearsals)	BFX 15229
	Cry	BFX 15229
	Cry (rehearsal instrumental)	BFX 15229
	Raining in my heart	BFX 15229
	Margie	BFX 15229
	Margie (rehearsal)	BFX 15229
	Silver threads among the gold	BFX 15229
	Take your time	BFX 15229

Also possibly;

	She's about a mover	UNRELEASED
	Tell it like it is	UNRELEASED
	You talk too much	UNRELEASED

NOVEMBER 28, 1973 (Unknown location)

Jerry Lee Lewis (vcl, pno), J. L. 'Marty' Morrison (org), more details unknown.

	Meat man (slow)	UNRELEASED
	Bad, bad Leroy Brown	UNRELEASED
	Don't pass me by	UNRELEASED

Also possibly recorded at this session,

	Sweet bye bye	UNRELEASED

FEBRUARY 21, 1974 (Mercury studio, Nashville). Producer; Stan Kesler

Jerry Lee Lewis (vcl, pno), Herman B. 'Pete' Wade (gtr), Jerry 'Chip Young' Stembridge (gtr), Thomas Sparkman (unknown), Jerry W. Shook (gtr),

Harold Ray Bradley (gtr), Pete Drake (st. gtr) Bob Moore (bs), Kenneth
Lovelace (fiddle), Buddy Harman (dms), String Section (arranged by Cam
Mullins).

| 50372 | A picture from life's other side | SRMI 710 |
| 50373 | I've forgot more about you than he'll ever know | SRMI 710 |

MARCH 13, 1974 (Probably Sam Phillips studio, Nashville)

Jerry Lee Lewis (vcl, pno), Mack Vickery (harmonica), more details
unknown.

Can't you hear the saviour	UNRELEASED
That kind of fool	UNRELEASED
I hate you	UNRELEASED
Rugged but right	UNRELEASED
Ramblin' man	UNRELEASED
Crawdad song	UNRELEASED

OCTOBER 2, 1974 (Mercury studio, Nashville). Producer; Jerry Kennedy

Jerry Lee Lewis (vcl, pno), Herman B. 'Pete' Wade (gtr), Jerry 'Chip Young'
Stembridge (gtr), Ray Edenton (gtr), Harold Ray Bradley (gtr), Jerry
Kennedy (gtr), John Lee Christopher jr (gtr), Pete Drake (st. gtr), Bob
Moore (bs), Kenneth Lovelace (fiddle), Charles R. 'Charlie' McCoy
(harmonica, vibes), Buddy Harman (dms), Unknown (harpsichord), Chorus;
Hugh Gordon Stoker, Neal Matthews jr, Raymond C. Walker, Hoyt H.
Hawkins, Mildred Kirkham, Anna Patricia Williams.

51478	Until the day forever ends	830 829-1
51479	Boogie woogie country man	73685,SRMI 1030,SRMI 5006
51480	I can still hear the music in the restroom	73661,SRMI 1030
51481	Speak a little louder to us Jesus	830 207-1
51482	Honey hush	SCPB 6816 125
51483	Jesus is on the main line (call him sometime)	SRMI 1030

Note: The tracksheet notes a Jerry Lee Lewis vocal overdub for master 51478
without a date, & a vocal overdub for master 51481 on November 12, 1974. A
vocal overdub for master 51482 was recorded on September 9, 1975 at the
Phillips Recording Service, Memphis.

OCTOBER 3, 1974 (Mercury studio, Nashville). Producer; Jerry Kennedy

Personnel as October 2, 1974.

51484	(Remember me) I'm the one who loves you	SRMI 1030
51485	Shake, rattle & roll	SRMI 1064
51486	Love inflation	SRMI 1030
51487	I don't want to be lonely tonight	SRMI 1064
51488	Forever forgiving	SRMI 1030
51489	A little peace & harmony	SRMI 1030
51490	No one knows me	830 829-1
51491	When I take my vacation in heaven	73729,SRMI 1064

Note: The tracksheet notes a Jerry Lee Lewis vocal overdub for master 51484 on November 12, 1974, & a vocal overdub for 51487 without a date. A vocal overdub for 51491 was recorded on September 9, 1975 at the Phillips Recording Service, Memphis. The liner notes to LP SRMI 1064 mention that vocal overdubs were supervised by Knox Phillips.

NOVEMBER 12, 1974 (Mercury studio, Nashville). Producer; Jerry Kennedy

Jerry Lee Lewis (vcl, pno), Tommy D. Allsup (gtr), Billy R. Sanford (gtr), Ray Edenton (gtr), Jerry Kennedy (gtr), John Lee Christopher jr (gtr), Pete Drake (st. gtr), Bob Moore (bs), Kenneth Lovelace (fiddle), Buddy Harman (dms), Hargus 'Pig' Robbins (org), Chorus; Hugh Gordon Stoker, Neal Natthews jr, Raymond C. Waker, Hoyt H. Hawkins, Mildred Kirkham, Anna Patricia Williams.

51515	I'm still jealous of you	73685,SRMI 1030
51516	You ought to see my mind	SRMI 1064
51517	Don't boogie woogie (when you say your prayers tonight)	73763,SRMI 1064

Note: A vocal overdub for master 51516 was recorded on September 9, 1975 at the Phillips Recording Service, Memphis. The liner notes to LP SRMI 1064 mention that the vocal overdubs were supervised by Knox Phillips.

JANUARY 15, 1975 (Mercury studio, Nashville). Producer; Jerry Kennedy

Jerry Lee Lewis (vcl, pno), Herman B. 'Pete' Wade (gtr), Jerry W. Shook (gtr), Ray Edenton (gtr), Harold Ray Bradley (gtr), Jerry Kennedy (gtr), Lloyd Green (st. gtr), Bob Moore (bs), Kenneth Lovelace (fiddle), Charles R. 'Charlie' McCoy (harmonica, vibes), Buddy Harman (dms), Hargus 'Pig' Robbins (org), Chorus; Hugh Gordon Stoker, Neal Matthews jr, Raymond C. Walker, Hoyt H. Hawkins, Mildred Kirkham, Anna Patricia Williams.

51537	Thanks for nothing	SRMI 1030
51538	Red hot memories (ice cold beer)	SRMI 1030
51539	I was sorta wonderin'	SRMI 1030

| 51540 | Jerry's place | SRMI 1064 |
| 51541 | That kind of fool | 73763,SRMI 1064 |

Note: The tracksheet notes a Jerry Lee Lewis vocal overdub for masters 51539 & 51541 on February 17, 1975, & a vocal overdub for master 51540 in Memphis, without a date. The liner notes to LP SRMI 1964 mention that the vocal overdubs were supervised by Knox Phillips.

FEBRUARY 17, 1975 (Mercury studio, Nashville). Producer; Jerry Kennedy

Jerry Lee Lewis (vcl, pno), Herman B. 'Pete' Wade (gtr), Jerry 'Chip Young' Stembridge (gtr), Ray Edenton (gtr), Harold Ray Bradley (gtr), Jerry Kennedy (gtr), Pete Drake (st. gtr), Michael A. Lee (bs), Kenneth Lovelace (fiddle), Charles R. 'Charlie' McCoy (harmonica, vibes), Buddy Harman (dms), Hargus 'Pig' Robbins (org), Unknown (harpsichord), Chorus; Hugh Gordon Stoker, Neal Matthews jr, Raymond C. Walker, Hoyt H. Hawkins, Mildred Kirkham, Anna Patricia Williams.

51556	Your cheatin' heart	SRMI 1064
51557	Crawdad song	SRMI 1064
51558	The House of blue lights	830 829-1
51559	Goodnight Irene	SRMI 1064

Note: The tracksheet notes a Jerry Lee Lewis vocal overdub for masters 51556/58/59 in Memphis, without a date. A vocal overdub for master 51557 was recorded on September 9, 1975 at the Phillips Recording Service, Memphis. The liner notes to LP SRMI 1064 mention that the vocal overdubs were supervised by Knox Phillips.

JUNE 19, 1975 (Mercury studio, Nashville). Producer; Jerry Kennedy

Jerry Lee Lewis (vcl, pno), Billy R. Sanford (gtr), Jerry W. Shook (gtr), Ray Edenton (gtr), Harold Ray Bradley (gtr), Don McMinn (gtr), Jerry Kennedy (gtr), Pete Drake (st. gtr), Bob Moore (bs), Kenneth Lovelace (fiddle), Buddy Harman (dms), Hargus 'Pig' Robbins (pno, org), Chorus; Hugh Gordon Stoker, Neal Matthews jr, Raymond C. Walker, Hoyt H. Hawkins, Mildred Kirkham, Anna Patricia Williams, Priscilla Ann Hubbard.

51610	A damn good country song	73729,SRMI 1064
51610	A damn good country song (alt.)	BFX 15229
51611	Lord what's left for me to do	830 829-1
51612	Great balls of fire	830 207-1
51613	The one rose that's left in my heart	BFX 15229

Note: The tracksheet notes a Jerry Lee Lewis vocal overdub for master 51611 in Memphis, without a date. Vocal overdubs for masters 51610/13 were recorded on September 9, 1975 at the Phillips Recording Service, Memphis.

The liner notes to LP SRMI 1064 mention that the vocal overdubs were supervised by Knox Phillips.

DECEMBER 15, 1975 (Soundshop studio, Nashville). Producer; Charlie Fach

Jerry Lee Lewis (vcl, pno), John Lee Christopher (gtr), Reggie Young (gtr), Michael A. Leech (bs), Kenneth Lovelace (fiddle), Ralph Gallant (dms), Bobby R. Wood (pno), Bobby G. Emmons (unknown)

52324	I'm knee deep in loving you	830 829-1
52325	Listen to the music	A vocal track was not recorded
52326-1	I can help (fast)	830 829-1
52326-2	I can help (slow)	830 207-1
52327	Slippin' & slidin'	830 207-I(xit), BFX 15229
52328-1	From a jack to a king	UNRELEASED
52328-2	From a jack to a king	UNRELEASED
52328-3	From a jack to a king (blues version)	BFX 15229
52328-4	From a jack to a king	UNRELEASED
52328-5	From a jack to a king (country version)	BFX 15229

DECEMBER 16, 1975 (US Recording studio, Nashville). Producer; Charlie Fach & Jerry Kennedy

Jerry Lee Lewis (vcl, pno), Herman B. 'Pete' Wade (gtr), Jerry 'Chip Young' Stembridge (gtr), Jerry W. Shook (gtr), Harold Ray Bradley (gtr), Jerry Kennedy (gtr), Pete Drake (st. gtr), Bob Moore (bs), Kenneth Lovelace (fiddle), Charles R. 'Charlie' McCoy (harmonica, vibes), Buddy Harman (dms), Hargus 'Pig' Robbins (pno, org), Chorus; Hugh Gordon Stoker, Bergen D. White, Neal Matthews jr, Herman C. Harper, Mildred Kirkham, Anna Patricia Williams.

52329	After the fool you've made of me	SRMI 1109
52330	The closest thing to you	73872,SRMI 1109,SRMI 5006
52331	I love it (when you love all over me)	UNRELEASED
52332	I can't keep my hands off of you	830 829-1
52333	The one rose that's left in my heart	SRMI 1109

Note: The tracksheet notes a Jerry Lee Lewis vocal overdub for masters 52329/30/33 (two overdubs for 52330) on May 20, 1976, & a 2nd vocal overdub & vocal chorus overdub for master 52329 without a date. The tracksheet also notes guitar & strings overdub (arranged by Cam Mullins) for master 52330 on June 11, 1976. Master 52331 was destroyed on the date of recording.

MAY 20, 1976 (US Recording studio, Nashville). Producer; Jerry Kennedy

Jerry Lee Lewis (vcl, pno), Herman B. 'Pete' Wade (gtr), Jerry 'Chip Young'
Stembride (gtr), Ray Edenton (gtr), Harold Ray Bradley (gtr), Jerry
Kennedy (gtr), Lloyd Green (st. gtr), Bob Moore (bs), Kenneth Lovelace
(fiddle), Buddy Harman (dms), Chorus; Hugh Gordon Stoker, Neal
Matthews jr, Raymond C. Walker, Hoyt H. Hawkins, Mildred Kirkham,
Anna Patricia Williams, Priscilla Ann Hubbard.

52400	Wedding bells	SRMI 1109
52401	The fifties	SCPB 6816 125
52402	No one will ever know	SRMI 1109
52403	Only love can get you in my door	SRMI 1109
52404	The old country church	SRMI 1109

Note: The tracksheet notes a vocal group (five girls) overdub for master 52401
on May 24, 1976, & guitar & Strings (arranged by Cam Mullins) overdubs for
master 52401 on June 11, 1976.

MAY 28, 1976 (US Recording studio, Nashville). Producer; Jerry Kennedy

Personnel as May 28, 1976, with the addition of Hargus 'Pig' Robbins (pno,
org).

52405	Harbour lights	830 829-1
52406	Jerry Lee's rock 'n' roll revival show	SRMI 1109
52407	I sure miss those good old times	SRMI 1109
52408	Let's put it back together again	73822,SRMI 1109

Note: The tracksheet notes Strings (arranged by Cam Mullins) overdubs for
masters 52406 & 52408 on June 11, 1976. Two guitar overdubs & a saxophone
overdub were also made on this date.

**AUGUST 3, 1977 (US Recording studio, Nashville). Producer; Jerry
Kennedy**

Jerry Lee Lewis (vcl, pno), Herman B. 'Pete' Wade (gtr), Jerry 'Chip Young'
Stembridge (gtr), Ray Edenton (gtr), Harold Ray Bradley (gtr), Jerry
Kennedy (gtr), Pete Drake (st. gtr), Bob Moore (bs), Kenneth Lovelace
(fiddle), Buddy Harman (dms), Hargus 'Pig' Robbins (pno, org), Harvey
Larry 'Duke' Faglier (unknown), Chorus; Hugh Gordon Stoker, Neal
Matthews jr, Louis D. Nunley, Hoyt H. Hawkins, Mildred Kirkham, Anna
Patricia Williams, Mary Holladay, Ginger Holladay.

53220	Country memories	SRMI 5004
53221	As long as we live	SRMI 5004
53222	Jealous heart	SRMI 5004
53223	(You'd think by now) I'd be over you	SRMI 5004

| 53224 | Come on in | SRMI 5004 |
| 53225 | Who's sorry now | SRMI 5004 |

Note: The tracksheet notes a Jerry Lee Lewis vocal overdub for master 53220 on September 2, 1977, & vocal overdubs for masters 53222/23/24 (two each for 23/34) on September 1, 1977. The tracksheet also notes Strings (arranged by Bergen D. White) overdubs for master 53222/44 on September 6, 1977.

AUGUST 4, 1977 (US Recording studio, Nashville). Producer; Jerry Kennedy

Jerry Lee Lewis (vcl, pno), Herman B. 'Pete' Wade (gtr), Jerry 'Chip Young' Stembridge (gtr), John Lee Christopher jr (gtr), Jerry Kennedy (gtr), Weldon Myrick (st. gtr), Michael A. Leech (bs), Kenneth Lovelace (fiddle), Jerry K. Carrigan (dms), Hargus 'Pig' Robbins (pno, org), Harvey Larry 'Duke' Faglier (unknown), Chorus; Hugh Gordon Stoker, Neal Matthews jr, Louis D. Nunley, Hoyt H. Hawkins, Mildred Kirkham, Anna Patricia Williams, Mary Holladay, Ginger Holladay.

53226	Let's say goodbye like we said hello	SRMI 5004
53227	Georgia on my mind	SRMI 5004
53228	What's so good about goodbye	SRMI 5004
53229	Tennessee Saturday night	SRMI 5004
53230	Ivory tears	830 207-1
53231	Middle age crazy	55011,SRMI 5004,SRMI 5006

Note: The tracksheet notes a Jerry Lee Lewis vocal overdub for masters 53226/27/28/31 (two overdubs for 28/31) on September 1, 1977, & Strings (arranged by Bergen D. White) overdubs for masters 53228/31 on September 6, 1977.

NOVEMBER 23, 1977 (US Recording studio, Nashville). Producer; Jerry Kennedy

Jerry Lee Lewis (vcl, pno), James D. Capps (gtr), Herman B. 'Pete' Wade (gtr), Jerry 'Chip Young' Stembridge (gtr), Harold Ray Bradley (gtr), John Lee Christopher jr (gtr), Jerry Kennedy (gtr), Pete Drake (st. gtr), Bob Moore (bs), Kenneth Lovelace (fiddle), Buddy Harman (dms), Hargus 'Pig' Robbins (pno, org), Harvey Larry 'Duke' Faglier (unknown), Chorus; Hugh Gordon Stoker, Neal Matthews Jr, Louis D. Nunley, Hoyt H. Hawkins, Mildred Kirkham, Anna Patricia Williams, Ginger Holladay.

53257	The last letter	SCPB 6816 125
53258	The last cheater's waltz	SRMI 5010
53259	Let's live a little	SCPB 6816 125

53260	I hate you	SRMI 5010
53261	Everybody needs a rainbow	A vocal track was not recorded
53262	Before the night is over	SRMI 5010
53263	Sittin' & thinkin'	SCPB 6816 125

Note: The tracksheet notes a Strings (arranged by Bergen D. White) overdub for master 53258 on January 4, 1978. Also Jerry Lee Lewis vocal overdubs for masters 53258 (March 18, 1978), 53260 (March 3, 1978) & 53263 (November 23, 1977).

DECEMBER 14, 1977 (US Recording studio, Nashville). Producer; Jerry Kennedy

Jerry Lee Lewis (vcl, pno), Jerry 'Chip Young' Stembridge (gtr), Jerry W. Shook (gtr), Thomas Grady Martin (gtr), Jerry Kennedy (gtr), Weldon M. Myrick (st. gtr), Michael A. Leech (bs), Kenneth Lovelace (fiddle), Jerry K. Carrigan (dms), Hargus 'Pig' Robbins (pno, org), Harvey Larry 'Duke' Faglier (unknown).

53273	By day by day	A vocal track was not recorded
53274	Blue suede shoes	SRMI 5010
53275	Lucille	SRMI 5010
53276	Corrine, Corrina	SCPB 6816 125
53277	Don't let the stars get in your eyes	55028,SRMI 5010
53278	Sweet little sixteen	SRMI 5010
53279	Life's railway to heaven	830 829-1
53280	Ivory tears	BFX 15229

Note: The tracksheet notes a Jerry Lee Lewis vocal overdub for master 53277 on March 10, 1978, & a vocal group overdub for master 53276 on January 1, 1978.

DECEMBER 15, 1977 (US Recording studio, Nashville). Producer; Jerry Kennedy

Jerry Lee Lewis (vcl, pno), Herman B. 'Pete' Wade (gtr), Jerry 'Chip Young' Stembridge (gtr), Ray Edenton (gtr), Jerry Kennedy (gtr), Harold Bradley (gtr), Pete Drake (st. gtr), Bob Moore (bs), Kenneth Lovelace (fiddle), Buddy Harman (dms), Hargus 'Pig' Robbins (pno, org), Harvey Larry 'Duke' Faglier (unknown), Chorus; Hugh Gordon Stoker, Neal Matthews jr, Louis D. Nunley, Hoyt H. Hawkins, Mildred Kirkham, Anna Patricia Williams, Ginger Holladay.

53281	You call everybody darling	SCPB 6816 125

53282	Wild & wooly ways	SRMI 5010
53283	I'll find it where I can	55028,SRMI 5010
53284	Lord, I've tried everything but you	830 829-1
53285	You're all too ugly tonight	830 829-1
53286	Arkansas seesaw	SRMI 5010
53287	Pee Wee's place	SRMI 5010

Note: The tracksheet notes a Jerry Lee Lewis vocal overdub for masters 53281/82 on March 10, 1978, & a Strings (arranged by Bergen D. White) overdub on January 31, 1978.

Note: The 1966 'Catch my soul' rehearsal & the Toronto, 1969 concert were NOT actually recorded for Smash/Mercury, but have been included for the sake of completion.

Note: There are *unconfirmed* rumours that the following titles were also recorded during the 1963-1977 Smash period;

My pumpkin & me (1963)	Forever yours
Remember me (1965-1966)	Kentucky fields
Hello memories (1965-1966)	Endless sleep
Lonely weekends (1965-1966)	Brownville
Duet Session with Roger Miller (late 60s)	Country styled
Goodtime Charlie's got the blues (1974 – solo?)	Only the grass
Hey rattlesnake	Muleskinner blues
Livin' lovin' wreck	Country fire
Battle of New Orleans	

SESSIONS FOR VARIOUS LABELS, 1977-1993

NOVEMBER, 1977 (The Wiltern Theatre, Los Angeles, California).

Jerry Lee Lewis (vcl, pno), Ira Newborn (gtr), Wolfgang Melz (bs), Don Poncher (dms), Al Aarons (tpt), Gary Barone (tpt), Jock Ellis (tbn), Anthony Brown (sax), Buddy Collette (sax), Steve Douglas (sax), Don Menza (sax).

Whole lotta shakin' goin' on	AMLM 66500
Great balls of fire	AMLM 66500
Great balls of fire (movie version)	UNRELEASED

JANUARY 4-7, 1979 (Filmways-Heider Recording, Hollywood, California). Producer; Bones Howe

Jerry Lee Lewis (vcl, pno), James Burton (gtr, dobro), Tim May (gtr), Kenneth Lovelace (gtr, fiddle), David Parlato (bs), Hal Blaine (dms), Chorus; The Ron Hicklin Singers (Ron Hicklin, Stan Farber, Gene Morford, John Bahler, Jim Haas). Strings arranged by Bob Alcivar.

Don't let go	6E-184
Rita May	E-46067,6E-184
Everyday I have to cry	6E-184
I like it like that	6E-184
Number one lovin' man	6E-184
Rockin' my life away	E-46030,6E-184
Who will the next fool be	E-46067(edit),6E-184
(You've got) personality	6E-184
I wish I was eighteen again	E-46030,6E-184
Rockin' little angel	6E-184

1979 (Roland Janes Studio, Memphis, TN). Producer; Roland Janes

Jerry Lee Lewis (vcl, pno), other personnel details unknown.

Silver threads among the gold	UNRELEASED
I can feel old age coming on	UNRELEASED
Beautiful dreamer	UNRELEASED
Green light	UNRELEASED
Pick me up on your way down	UNRELEASED
There stands the glass	UNRELEASED
That kind of fool	UNRELEASED
Ths world is not my home	UNRELEASED
Precious memories	UNRELEASED
Rockin' pneumonia & the boogie woogie flu	UNRELEASED
Autumn leaves	UNRELEASED
Who will the next fool be	UNRELEASED
Let's talk about us	UNRELEASED

JUNE 18/19/20, 1979 (Palomino, Hollywood, California) (2 shows each night)

Jerry Lee Lewis (vcl, pno), Kenneth Lovelace (gtr, fiddle), Harvey 'Duke' Eaglier (gtr), Joel Shumaker (bs), Ron Norwood (dms).

JUNE 18, 1979 (Palomino, Hollywood) (Show 1)

Sweet little sixteen	UNRELEASED
You win again	UNRELEASED
High school confidential	UNRELEASED
Middle age crazy	UNRELEASED
Boogie woogie country man	UNRELEASED
Who will the next fool be	UNRELEASED
Cold, cold heart	UNRELEASED
Crazy arms	UNRELEASED
Drinkin' wine spo-dee-o-dee	UNRELEASED

Harbour lights	UNRELEASED
Release me	UNRELEASED
Fraulein	UNRELEASED
Hound dog	UNRELEASED
Don't be cruel	UNRELEASED
Big legged woman	UNRELEASED
Great balls of fire	UNRELEASED
Whole lotta shakin' goin' on	UNRELEASED
You can have her	UNRELEASED

JUNE 18, 1979 (Palomino, Hollywood) (Show 2)

Drinkin' wine spo-dee-o-dee	SCR-785
Sweet little sixteen	SCR-785
You win again	UNRELEASED
I'm throwing rice	UNRELEASED
Boogie woogie country man	SCR-785
Me & Bobby McGee	SCR-785
Rockin' my life away	SCR-785
Harbour lights	UNRELEASED
Oh, lonesome me	UNRELEASED
Cold, cold heart	UNRELEASED
No headstone on my grave	SCR-785
Chantilly lace	SCR-785
A picture from life's other side	CD 2696742
Will the circle be unbroken	SCR-785, CD 2696742
Hey good lookin'	SCR-785, CD 2696742
Middle age crazy	CD 2696742
I'll find it where I can	SCR-785
I wish I was eighteen again	CD 2696742
Mexicali rose	CD 2696742
Great balls of fire	UNRELEASED
Whole lotta shakin' goin' on	SCR-785
You can have her	SCR-785

JUNE 19, 1979 (Palomino, Hollywood) (Show 1)

Roll over Beethoven	UNRELEASED
No headstone on my grave	UNRELEASED
Chantilly lace	UNRELEASED
You win again	UNRELEASED
Your cheatin' heart	UNRELEASED
Cold, cold heart	UNRELEASED
Rockin' my life away	UNRELEASED

Trouble in mind	UNRELEASED
High school confidential	CD 2696742
What's made Milwaukee famous	UNRELEASED
I was sorta wonderin'	UNRELEASED
Touching home	UNRELEASED
I wish I was eighteen again	UNRELEASED
I'll find it where I can	UNRELEASED
I can't stop loving you	UNRELEASED
Great balls of fire	UNRELEASED
Whole lotta shakin' goin' on	UNRELEASED
You can have her	UNRELEASED

JUNE 19, 1979 (Palomino, Hollywood) (Show 2)

No headstone on my grave	CD 2696742
Chantilly lace	CD 2696742
Middle age crazy	UNRELEASED
I'll find it where I can	CD 2696742
I can't stop loving you	UNRELEASED
Rockin' my life away	CD 2696742
Who's gonna play this old piano	CD 2696742
Trouble in mind	UNRELEASED
Hey good lookin'	UNRELEASED
You win again	UNRELEASED
Roll over Beethoven	CD 2696742
Great balls of fire	UNRELEASED
Johnny B. Goode/Whole lotta shakin'	CD 2696742

JUNE 20, 1979 (Palomino, Hollywood) (Show 1)

Roll over Beethoven	UNRELEASED
Harbour lights	UNRELEASED
No headstone on my grave	UNRELEASED
Chantilly lace	UNRELEASED
Trouble in mind	UNRELEASED
What'd I say	UNRELEASED
Memphis, Tennessee	UNRELEASED
Me & Bobby McGee	UNRELEASED
Help me make it through the night	UNRELEASED
Another place, another time	UNRELEASED
Middle age crazy	UNRELEASED
Great balls of fire	UNRELEASED
Whole lotta shakin' goin' on	UNRELEASED
You can have her	UNRELEASED

Meat man   UNRELEASED

JUNE 20, 1979 (Palomino, Hollywood) (Show 2).

You are my sunshine	CD 2696742
Big legged woman	CD 2696742
You win again	CD 2696742
Rockin' my life away	CD 2696742
What's made Milwaukee famous	CD 2696742
Bottles & barstools	CD 2696742
Another place, another time	CD 2696742
What'd I say	CD 2696742
I can't stop loving you	CD 2696742
Your cheatin' heart	CD 2696742
Who's gonna play this old piano	CD 2696672
Harbour lights	CD 2696742
You belong to me	CD 2696742
Great balls of fire	UNRELEASED
Whole lotta shakin' goin' on	UNRELEASED
You can have her	UNRELEASED
Meat man	UNRELEASED

Note: SCR-785 was issued on CD in 1991 as 'Live at the Vapor's Club' (ACE
CDCH 326). Many of the titles on CD 2696742 were issued on three previous
CDs (TOMATO 2696612/2696672/2696732). The TOMATO recordings
featured overdubbed guitar/drums, the latter probably played by Buddy
Harman.

**MID-LATE 1979 (Filmways-Heider Recording, Hollywood & possible other
locations). Producer; Bones Howe, possibly Eddie Kilroy on some tracks.**

Jerry Lee Lewis (vcl, pno), other personnel on some tracks possibly as
January 4-7, 1979

(Hot damn) I'm a one woman man	WB 2HS 3441
Milk cow blues	SLP 1260(bootleg)
Tossing & turning	SLP 1260(bootleg)
Old time rock & roll	SLP 1260(bootleg)
I ain't loved you	SLP 1260(bootleg)
Lovers honeymoon	UNRELEASED
Birds & the bees (or 'Boy meets girl')	UNRELEASED
C.C. rider	UNRELEASED
Old sweet music (or 'Sweet Jesus')	UNRELEASED
Coming back for more	UNRELEASED
Big legged woman	UNRELEASED

Whole lotta shakin' goin' on	UNRELEASED
Meat man	UNRELEASED

1979-1980 (details as above)

Phillipino baby	UNRELEASED
End of the road	UNRELEASED
That was the way it was then	UNRELEASED
Darktown strutter's ball	UNRELEASED
New Orleans	UNRELEASED

LATE 1979 (Fireside Studios, Nashville). Producer; Eddie Kilroy

Jerry Lee Lewis (vcl, pno), Kenneth Lovelace (gtr, fiddle), Bobby Thompson (gtr, banjo), Steve Chapman (gtr), Dave Kirby (gtr), Harvey 'Duke' Faglier (gtr), Stu Basore (st. gtr), Bobby Dyson (bs), Jimmy Isbell (dms), Bunky Keels (electric pno, org), Dennis Good (tbn), Dennis Solee (clarinet), Ronald Keller (tpt), George Tidwell (tpt), Chorus; The Lea Jane Singers. Strings arranged by Billy Strange.

Rockin' Jerry Lee	E-46642,6E-254
Who will buy the wine (It all depends)	6E-254
Love game	6E-254
Alabama Jubilee	6E-254
Good time Charlie's got the blues	6E-254
When two worlds collide	E-46591,6E-254
Good news travels fast	E-46591,6E-254
I only want a buddy not a sweetheart	6E-254
Honky tonk stuff	6E-254
Honky tonk stuff	E-46642
Toot, toot, tootsie goodbye	6E-254

SUMMER, 1980 (Fireside Studios, Nashville). Producer; Eddie Kilroy

Jerry Lee Lewis (vcl, pno), other personnel as late 1979 sessions, though with the addition of Russ Hicks (st. gtr) & with a different horn section (Rex Peer, John Gobe, Terry Mead).

Folsom prison blues	E-47026,6E-291
I'd do it all again	6E-291
Jukebox junky	6E-291
Too weak to fight	6E-291
Late night lovin' man	6E-291
Change places with me	E-47095,6E-291
Let me on	6E-291
Let me on (alt)	UNRELEASED

Thirty-nine & holding	E-47095,6E-291
Mama, this one's for you	6E-291
Over the rainbow	E-47026,6E-291

SUMMER-LATE 1980 (Locations uncertain). Producer; Probably Eddie Kilroy

Jerry Lee Lewis (vcl, pno), other personnel uncertain, possibly as Summer, 1980.

Mona Lisa	UNRELEASED
Fraulein	UNRELEASED
Flip, flop & fly	UNRELEASED
Tennessee waltz	UNRELEASED
Love me with all of your heart	UNRELEASED
Bourbon Street parade	UNRELEASED
Blue moon	UNRELEASED
Sticks & stones	UNRELEASED
Keep my motor running	UNRELEASED
Living legend	UNRELEASED

Note: 'Living legend' could just be an alternative title for 'I'd do it all again'. Reportedly, some forty titles were cut in Colorado on November, 1980, including several spiritual songs. Vocal overdubs were made for the Colorado sessions at least twice, in early 1981 & again in early 1982.

JANUARY 408, 1981 (Unknown location, probably in Texas). Producer; ?

Jerry Lee Lewis (vcl, pno), Mickey Gilley (vcl, pno). Other personnel & song details unknown.

APRIL 17, 1981 (Wembley Arena, London)

Jerry Lee Lewis (vcl, pno), Carl Perkins (gtr, duet vcl)*, Kenneth Lovelace (gtr, fiddle), Joel Shumaker (gtr), Randy Wilkes (bs), Ron Norwood (dms).

Keep my motor running	PWK CD 049
Middle age crazy	UNRELEASED
What'd I say	PWK CD 049
Over the rainbow	UNRELEASED
Folsom prison blues	UNRELEASED
High school confidential	PWK CD 049
Thirty-nine & holding	UNRELEASED
Great balls of fire	UNRELEASED
Whole lotta shakin' goin' on	UNRELEASED
Matchbox/Blue suede shoes*	MCP 001

APRIL 23, 1981 (Sporthall Boeblingen, Stuttgart)

Jerry Lee Lewis (vcl, pno), Carl Perkins (gtr, vcl)*, Johnny Cash (voc)*,
Kenneth Lovelace (gtr), Jerry Hensley (gtr), Marty Stuart (gtr, mandolin),
Robert 'Bob' Wootton (gtr), Henry Strzelecki (bs), W. S. Holland (dms),
Jack Hale Jnr, Robert Lewin (horns), June Carter-Cash (duet vcl on 'When
the saints go marching in').

I'll fly away*	FC 37961
Will the circle be unbroken*	FC 37961
Lawdy miss Clawdy / C.C. rider	UNRELEASED
Whole lotta shakin' goin' on	FC 37961 (also issued on a single)
Rockin' my life away	FC 37961
When the saints go marching in*	UNRELEASED
Peace in the valley*	FC 37961
I saw the light*	FC 37961

JUNE 30, 1981 (Fireside Studios, Nashville). Producer; Eddie Kilroy

Jerry Lee Lewis (pno, duet vcl on 'Honky tonkin''), Kenneth Lovelace (vcl,
gtr, fiddle), Dave Sellor (gtr), Dave Kirby (gtr), Steve Phillips (st. gtr),
Bobby Dyson (bs), Jim Isbell (dms), Bucky Keele (pno).

Honky tonkin'	EL-KJ-2950
Beer drinkin' honky tonkin' blues	UNRELEASED

Note: Although the main session was held on the above date, Jerry's pno/vcl
were added at a later date, probably late 1981.

NOVEMBER-DECEMBER, 1981 (Location unknown). Producer; Billy Sherill

Demonstration sessions for Columbia records, all details unknown.

1982 (Woodland Sound Studios & The Recording Company, Nashville). Producer; Ron Chancey

Jerry Lee Lewis (vcl, pno), Shane Keister (pno), Billy Sanford (gtr,
mandolin), Jerry Shook (gtr), Kenneth Lovelace (gtr, fiddle), James Capps
(gtr), Joe Osborn (bs), Jack Williams (bs), Gene Chrisman (dms &
percussion), Chorus; Lea Jane Berinati, Donna McElroy, Yvonne Hodges,
Sheri Huffman, Diane Tidwell, Lisa Silver, Karen Taylor, Judy Rodman,
Donna Sheridon. Horns; The Muscle Shoals Horns (Harvey Thompson,
Ronald Fades, Charles Rose, Harrison Calloway). Strings arranged by Bergen
D. White.

My fingers do the talkin'	MCA-52151,MCA-5387, CDCH 332
My fingers do the talkin' (alt)	CDCH 348
She sure makes leaving look easy	MCA-5387,CDCH 348
Why you been gone so long	MCA-52233,MCA-5387, SCR 386,CDCH 332
Why you been gone so long (alt)	CDCH 332
She sings amazing grace	MCA-52233,MCA-5387, SCR 386,CDCH 348
Better not look down	MCA-5387,SCR 386
Better not look down (alt)	CDCH 332
Honky tonk rock & roll piano man	MCA-5387,SCR 386-7,SCR 386,CDCH 332
Honky tonk rock & roll piano man (alt)	CDCH 348
Come as you were	MCA-52188,MCA-5387, SCR 386,CDCH 348
Circumstantial evidence	MCA-52188,MCA-5387
Circumstantial evidence (alt vcl overdub)	CDCH 332
Forever forgiving	MCA-52151,MCA 5387,SCR 386,CDCH 348
Forever forgiving (alt)	CDCH 332
Honky tonk heaven	MCA-5387
Honky tonk heaven (extended version)	SCR 386,CDCH 348
Rock & roll money	SCR 386,CDCH 332
Daughters of Dixie	CDCH 332
Daughters of Dixie (alt)	CDCH 348
Any old upright will do	UNRELEASED

1983-EARLY 1984 (Music City Hall, Woodland Sound Studios & The Soundshop Recording Studios, Nashville) Producer; Ron Chancey.

Jerry Lee Lewis (vcl, pno), David Briggs (pno), Hargus 'Pig' Robbins (pno, org), Steve Nathan (synthesizer), Kenneth Lovelace (gtr, fiddle), Reggie Young (gtr), Duncan Cameron (gtr), Billy Sanford (gtr), Jerry Shook (gtr), Jerry 'Chip Young' Stembridge (gtr), Pete Drake (st. gtr), Bob Moore (bs), Harold Ray Bradley (bs), Buddy Harman (dms), Chorus; Diane Tidwell, Wendy Suits, Lori Brooks, Linda Neal, Lisa Silver, Vicki Hampton, Hurshel Wiginton, Phillip Forest, Lewis Nunley, Dennie Wilson, Doug Clements. Strings arranged by Bergen D. White.

I am what I am	MCA-52369,MCA-5478, CDCH 332
I am what I am (alt)	CDCH 348

Only you (& you alone) (vcl overdub version)	MCA-5478
Only you (& you alone) (undubbed version)	CDCH 332
Get out your big roll daddy	MCA-5478,CDCH 332
Get out your big roll daddy (alt)	SCR 386-7,SCR 386
Have I got a song for you	MCA-5478,CDCH 348
Careless hands	MCA-5478,CDCH 348
Candy kisses	MCA-5478,CDCH 348
I'm looking over a four leaf clover	MCA-5478,CDCH 332
I'm looking under a skirt	CDCH 332
Send me the pillow that you dream on	MCA-5478,CDCH 348
Honky tonk heart	MCA-5478,SCR 386,CDCH 348
That was the way it was then	MCA-52369,MCA-5478, CDCH 348
Teenage queen	CDCH 332
She never said goodbye	CDCH 348

Note: All tracks on CDCH 332 & CDCH 348 have been remixed, & some feature guitar overdubs by Eddie Jones. Some tracks on SCR 386 have also been remixed.

NOVEMBER 17, 1983 (Music City Hall, Nashville). Producer; Ron Chancey

Jerry Lee Lewis (vcl, pno).

Ragtime doodle	STCD 2
Meat man	STCD 2
Lovin' up a storm	STCD 2
Ubangi stomp	STCD 2
Rock & roll Ruby	STCD 2
Piano doodle	STCD 2
House of blue lights	STCD 2
A damn good country song	STCD 2
Beautiful dreamer	STCD 2
Autumn leaves	STCD 2
Pilot baby	STCD 2
Room full of roses	STCD 2
Keep a knockin'	STCD 2
Silver threads among the gold	STCD 2
Alabama jubilee	STCD 2
Lazy river	STCD 2
Mama, this one's for you	STCD 2

Note: This was a vocal overdub session for 'Candy kisses' & 'Send me the pillow that you dream on'.

FEBRUARY 2, 1984 (Chelsea Recording Studio, Brentwood, TN). Producers; Joe Johnson & Max Powell

Jerry Lee Lewis (vcl, pno), Webb Pierce (vcl)*, Mel Tillis (vcl)**, Faron Young (vcl)***, other personnel unknown.

No love have I * ** ***	PL 1006
Medley; Back street affair/**	PL 1006
There stands the glass/	PL 1006
I ain't never/*	PL 1006
I don't care ***	PL 1006
Honky tonk song * ** ***	'PL 1006
Walkin' the dog * ** ***	PL 1006
Tupelo county jail * ** ***	PL 1006
It's been so long * ** ***	PL 1006
Memory number one	PL 1006
Softly & tenderly *	PL 1006
Merry-go-round world	UNRELEASED

Note: These recordings were originally older 8-rack Webb Pierce racks. They were transferred to 24-track, & new vocal & instrumental backing was added. All other overdubs were made January 25-Februay 4, 1984.

MARCH 17-21, 1984 (Gilley's Recording Studio, Pasedena, Texas). Producers; Jerry Lee Lewis & Mickey Gilley.

Jerry Lee Lewis (vcl, pno), Mickey Gilley (vcl, pno), James Burton (gtr), Kenneth Lovelace (gtr/fiddle), Conrad 'Rocky Stone' Durocher (accoustic gtr), Mark Oliverius (keyboards), Eli Nelson (st. gtr), poss. Cody Ward (fiddle), poss. Norman Carlson (sax), Bob Moore (bs), Murray 'Buddy' Harman (dms), poss. Byron Metcalf (dms). Unknown titles

NOVEMBER 23, 1984 (Gilley's Club, Pasedena, Texas)

Jerry Lee Lewis (vcl, pno), Mickey Gilley (vcl, pno), James Burton (gtr), Kenneth Lovelace (gtr/fiddle), Bob Moore (bs), Murray 'Buddy' Harman (dms). Unknown titles

1984-1988

Jerry reportedly cut sessions for Columbia, Atlantic, Capitol & RCA records during these years. All details are unknown.

1985 (Palomino, Hollywood, California)

Jerry Lee Lewis (vcl, pno), James Burton (gtr), Butch Baker (gtr), Kenneth Lovelace (gtr/fiddle), Bob Moore (bs), Murray 'Ruddy' Harman (dms).

She even woke me up to say goodbye	CD 2696742
Careless hands	CD 2696742
Who will the next fool be	CD 2696742
Thirty-nine & holding	CD 2696742
Over the rainbow	CD 2696742
Trouble in mind	CD 2696742
Boogie woogie country man	CD 2696742
Little queenie	CD 2696742
Lucille	CD 2696742
Georgia on my mind	CD 2696742
Meat man	CD 2696742
Touching home	CD 2696742
Cold, cold heart	CD 2696742
There must be more to love than this	CD 2696742
Brown eyed handsome man	CD 2696742
Great balls of fire	CD 2696742
Whole lotta shakin' goin' on	CD 2696742

Note: Many of the titles on CD 2696742 were issued on three previous CDs (TOMATO 2696612/2696672/2696732).

SEPTEMBER, 1985 (Sun Studio, 706 Union, Memphis). Producer; Chips Moman

Jerry Lee Lewis (vcl, pno), Kenneth Lovelace (gtr), Carl Perkins (acoustic gtr), Bob Moore (bs), Murray 'Buddy' Harman (dms), Horns (arranged by Mike Leech); Johnny 'Ace' Cannon, Wayne Jackson, Bob Lewin, Jack Hale jnr.

Keep my motor running	USAH 1
Keep my motor running (alt)	UNRELEASED
Sixteen candles	884-934-7,USAH 1

SEPTEMBER, 1985 (American Sound Studio, Memphis). Producer; Chips Moman

Jerry Lee Lewis (vcl), Johnny Cash (vcl, acoustic gtr), Carl Perkins (vcl), Roy Orbison (vcl), Reggie Young (gtr), Marty Stuart (gtr), Bobby Emmons (keyboards), Bobby Wood (keyboards), Bob Wootten (gtr), Mike Leech (bs), Gene Chrisman (dms), horns (arranged by Mike Leech); Johnny 'Ace'

Cannon, Wayne Jackson, Bob Lewin, Jack Hale jnr. Overdubbed strings;
Memphis Strings.

| We remember the king | USAH 1 |
| Waymore's blues | USAH 1 |

SEPTEMBER, 1985 (American Sound Studio, Memphis). Producer; Chips Moman

Jerry Lee Lewis (vcl), Johnny Cash (vcl, acoustic gtr), Carl Perkins (vcl), Roy
Orbison (vcl), Reggie Young (gtr), Marty Stuart (gtr), Bobby Emmons
(keyboards), Bobby Wood (keyboards), J. R. Cobb (gtr), Mike Leech (bs),
Gene Chrisman (dms), Horns (arranged by Mike Leech); Johnny 'Ace'
Cannon, Wayne Jackson, Bob Lewin, Jack Hale jnr, Chorus on 'Big train
(from Memphis)'; June Carter-Cash, Jack Clement, Dave Edmunds, Rebecca
Evans, John Fogerty, Wynonna Judd, Naomi Judd, Chips Moman, Rick
Nelson, Sam Phillips, Marty Stuart, Toni Wine.

Rock & roll (fais-do-do)	884-760-7, 884-934-7,
	USAH 1
Big train (from Memphis)	USAH 1

MAY 24, 1986 (Church Street Station, Orlando, Florida)

Jerry Lee Lewis (vcl, pno), Kenneth Lovelace (gtr, fiddle), Butch Baker (gtr),
Unknown (bs), Murray 'Buddy' Harman (dms).

Lucille	CD 15403
Great balls of fire	CD 15403,PLATCD 342
Rockin' my life away	CD 15403,PLATCD 342
Keep my motor running	PLATCD 342
Over the rainbow	PLATCD 342
You turn me on / Whole lotta shakin' goin' on / Good golly miss Molly / Tutti-frutti	PLATCD 342
Whole lotta shakin' goin' on (part only)	CD 15403

LATE 1986/EARLY 1987 (Location uncertain). Producer; Bob Moore

Jerry Lee Lewis (vcl, pno), Kenneth Lovelace (gtr, fiddle), Billy Sanford?
(gtr), Bob Moore (bs), Murray 'Buddy' Harman (dms), Chorus; The
Jordanaires (Hugh Gordon Stoker, Neal Matthews jnr, Louis D. Nunley,
Hoyt H. Hawkins).

Meat man	Bellaphon 260.07.121
Jailhouse rock	Bellaphon 260.07.121
House of blue lights	Bellaphon 260.07.121
Rock 'n' roll funeral	Bellaphon 260.07.121

Don't touch me	Bellaphon 260.07.121
Changing mountains	Bellaphon 260.07.121
Beautiful dreamer	Bellaphon 260.07.121
I'm alone because I love you	Bellaphon 260.07.121
Lucille	Bellaphon 260.07.121
Seventeen	Bellaphon 260.07.121
Mathilda	Bellaphon 260.07.121
Wake up little Susie	Bellaphon 260.07.121

MARCH/EARLY APRIL, 1987 (Location uncertain). Producer; Eddie Kilroy

Jerry Lee Lewis (vcl, pno), oher personnel unknown.

Rock 'n' roll is something special	UNRELEASED
What am I living for	UNRELEASED
One of those things we all go through	UNRELEASED
Hang up my rock & roll shoes	UNRELEASED
C.C. rider	UNRELEASED
This world is not my home	UNRELEASED
Blue Monday	UNRELEASED
Mona Lisa	UNRELEASED
Only the lonely	UNRELEASED
Autumn leaves	UNRELEASED

APRIL 7, 1987 (Rolling Stone Club, Milan, Italy). Producer; Kim 'Cadillac' Brown

Jerry Lee Lewis (vcl, pno), Linda Gail Lewis (duet vcl on 'Jackson', backing vcl), Phoebe Lewis (backing vcl), Moetta Stewart (keyboards, backing vcl), Kenneth Lovelace (gtr, fiddle, vcl), Joel Shumaker (gtr), Harvey 'Duke' Faglier (bs), Danny Harrison (dms).

Rockin' my life away	UNRELEASED
Trouble in mind	UNRELEASED
Boogie woogie country man	UNRELEASED
There must be more to love than this	GRP 3307
You win again	CDGLL 104
Jackson	GRP 3307
Over the rainbow	UNRELEASED
Mona Lisa	CDGLL 104
If I had my wings	UNRELEASED
One of those things we all go through	CDGLL 104
High school confidential	GRP 3307
Me & Bobby McGee	GRP 3307

Great balls of fire	CDGLL 104
You belong to me	UNRELEASED
I am what I am	CDGLL 104
Whole lotta shakin' goin' on	UNRELEASED

APRIL 8, 1987 (Palaeur, Rome, Italy). Producer; Kim 'Cadillac' Brown

Jerry Lee Lewis (vcl, pno), other personnel as April 7, 1987.

Rockin' my life away	UNRELEASED
Hang up my rock & roll shoes	CDGLL 104
C.C. rider	UNRELEASED
Hey baby	UNRELEASED
Rock 'n' roll is something special	UNRELEASED
Good news travels fast	UNRELEASED
To make love sweeter for you	UNRELEASED
What'd I say	GRP 3307
Jerry Lee's rock 'n' roll revival show	GRP 3307
Over the rainbow	GRP 3307
Crawdad song	GRP 3307
Middle age crazy	UNRELEASED
I am what I am	GRP 3307
Great balls of fire	GRP 3307
This world is not my home	UNRELEASED
Whole lotta shakin' goin' on	GRP 3307

JANUARY 25, 1988 (KIVA Studios, Memphis). Producers; Ronnie McDowell & Joe Meador

Jerry Lee Lewis (vcl), Ronnie McDowell (vcl), Greg Martin (gtr), Richard Lane (gtr), Douglas Phelps (bs), Martin Kicklitter (dms), Steve Shepherd (pno), Rich Ripani (keyboards).

| Never too old to rock & roll (single) | CURB 10521,d2-77414 |
| Never too old to rock & roll (album) | CRBD 10602 |

1988 (Unknown location, Memphis)

Jerry Lee Lewis (vcl, pno), other personnel unknown.

| Tom Dooley & me | UNRELEASED |

Note: Demo recording of song intended for inclusion in the film 'K-9 COP'.

MAY, 1988 (Unknown location). Producer; Eddie Kilroy

Jerry Lee Lewis (vcl, pno), other personnel & song details unknown. This was probably recorded for Mercury records.

OCTOBER-NOVEMBER, 1988 (Ocean Way Studios, Los Angeles, Memphis Sound, Memphis, & KIVA Studios, Memphis). Producer; T Bone Burnett, with additional production on 'Crazy arms' by Bob Schaper.

Jerry Lee Lewis (vcl, pno), Gerald McGee (gtr), Jerry Scheff (bs), David Kamper (dms), Dennis Quaid (duet vcl)*

Great balls of fire	889-312-7,889-798-7,839 516
High school confidential	873-006,839 516
High school confidential (movie version)	UNRELEASED
I'm on fire	839 516
Whole lotta shakin' goin' on	839 516
Whole lotta shakin' goin' on (alt)	EVCD 3001
Whole lotta shakin' goin' on (movie version)	UNRELEASED
Breathless	889-312-7,839 516
Crazy arms (solo version)	839 516,EVCD 3001
Crazy arms*	889-798-7,839 516
Wild one (Real wild child)	873-006,839 516
Wild one (Real wild child) (alt)	EVCD 3001
Wild one (Real wild child) (movie version)	UNRELEASED
That lucky old sun	839 516
My God is real	EVCD 3001
I'm throwing rice	EVCD 3001
I'm using my bible for a road map	EVCD 3001
There'll be no detour in heaven	EVCD 3001
I'm longing for home	EVCD 3001
Lewis boogie	UNRELEASED
April showers	UNRELEASED
Old black Joe	UNRELEASED
If I didn't care	UNRELEASED
Blue moon	UNRELEASED
Georgia on my mind	UNRELEASED
House of blue lights	UNRELEASED
Lady of Spain	UNRELEASED
Sweet dreams	UNRELEASED
As we travel along the Jericho road	UNRELEASED
The old rugged cross	UNRELEASED
Old piano roll blues	UNRELEASED
Softly & tenderly	UNRELEASED
Peach pickin' time in Georgia	UNRELEASED
Barrel house boogie (instrumental)	UNRELEASED
Jesus, Jesus, Jesus	UNRELEASED
Keep on the firing line	UNRELEASED

Note: Initial pressings of 839 516 featured the solo version of 'Crazy arms'. This was replaced by the duet version on later pressings.

JANUARY 30-FEBRUARY 1, 1990 (706 Union, Memphis). Producer; Andy Paley

Jerry Lee Lewis (vcl, pno), Michael Turk (harmonica), Stuart Gunn (tuba), Robert O. Turner (st. gtr), Yoshihiro Arita (banjo), Matthew Glaser (violin), John Curtis (mandolin), Andy Paley (dms), Chorus; Micheal Kernan, Billy West.

It was the whiskey talkin' (not me)	7-19809-4,7599-26279
It was the whiskey talkin' (not me) (alt)	FRLP 9001(bootleg)
It was the whiskey talkin' (not me) (alt)	UNRELEASED
Sixteen candles	FRLP 9001(bootleg)
Lucille	FRLP 9001(bootleg)
Rockin' my life away	FRLP 9001(bootleg)
Jimmy, Mickey & me	FRLP 9001(bootleg)
Breathless	FRLP 9001(bootleg)
The one rose that's left in my heart	FRLP 9001(bootleg)
Down the sawdust trail	FRLP 9001(bootleg)
Roomful of roses	FRLP 9001(bootleg)
Rockin' rollin' Jerry Lee / Shine on harvest moon	FRLP 9001(bootleg)
San Antonio rose	FRLP 9001(bootleg)
Mona Lisa	FRLP 9001(bootleg)
For the good times	UNRELEASED
A damn good country song	UNRELEASED

Note: The backing track for 'It was the whiskey talkin' (not me)' features all musicians except Andy Paley, & was recorded in California in the winter of 1989-1990.

FEBRUARY, 1990 (706 Union, Memphis). Producer; Andy Paley

Jerry Lee Lewis (vcl, pno), Bobby B. Keyes (gtr), Russell Keyes (bs), Andy Paley (dms/rhythm gtr).

It was the whiskey talkin' (not me) (rock & roll version)	7-19809-4,7599-26279

NOVEMBER, 1990 (706 Union, Memphis). Producer; Gary Hardy

Jerry Lee Lewis (vcl, pno), other personnel unknown.

Mexicali rose	UNRELEASED

Before the night is over   UNRELEASED

(three others, titles unknown)

AUGUST 14, 1992 (Unknown TV studio, Paris, France). Producer; ?

Jerry Lee Lewis (vcl, pno), Dorothee (duet vcl)*, Kenneth Lovelace (gtr),
Tommy McClure (bs), Jimmy Isbell (dms).

End of the road   UNRELEASED
Whole lotta shakin' goin' on   UNRELEASED
Great balls of fire*   AB 0153 2 BM 650

JERRY LEE LEWIS

Discography

PART ONE – THE SUN SESSIONS

SUN SINGLES, 1956-1965

	USA	UK	(USA numbers refer to SUN, UK numbers refer to LONDON)
Dec '56	259	Unissued	Crazy arms / End of the road
Apr '57	267	HLS.8457	Whole lotta shakin' goin' on / It'll be me
Nov '57	281	Unissued	Great balls of fire / You win again
Dec '57	Unissued	HLS.8529	Great balls of fire / Mean woman blues
Feb '58	Unissued	HLS.8559	You win again / I'm feeling sorry
Feb '58	288	HLS.8592	Breathless / Down the line
May '58	296	HLS.8780	High school confidential / Fools like me
Jun '58	301	Unissued	The return of Jerry Lee / Lewis boogie
Aug '58	303	HLS.8700	Break up / I'll make it all up to you
Nov '58	312	HLS.9083	I'll sail my ship alone / It hurt me so
Feb '59	317	HLS.8840	Lovin' up a storm / Big blon' baby
Jun '59	324	HLS.8941	Let's talk about us / The ballad of Billy Joe
Sep '59	330	HLS.8993	Little queenie / I could never be ashamed of you
Mar '60	337	HLS.9131	Baby, baby bye bye / Old black Joe
Aug '60	344	HLS.9202	Hang up my rock 'n' roll shoes / John Henry
Oct '60	3559	Unissued	In the mood / I get the blues when it rains
Nov '60	352	Unissued	Love made a fool of me / When I get paid
Feb '61	356	HLS.9335	What'd I say / Livin' lovin' wreck

Jun '61	364	HLS.9414	It won't happen with me / Cold, cold heart
Sep '61	367	Unissued	Save the last dance with me / As long as I live
Oct '61	Unissued	HLS.9446	As long as I live / When I get paid
Nov '61	371	Unissued	Money / Bonnie B
Jan '62	374	HLS.9526	I've been twistin' / Ramblin' rose
Jul '62	379	HLS.9584	Sweet little sixteen / How's my ex treating you
Nov '62	382	HLS.9688	Good golly miss Molly / I can't trust me (in your arms anymore)
Apr '63	384	HLS.9722	Teenage letter / Seasons of my heart (with Linda Gail Lewis)
Mar '64	Unissued	HLS.9867	Lewis boogie / Bonnie B
Mar '65	396	HLS.9980	Carry me back to old Virginia / I know what it means

SUN EPS, 1957-1965

USA	1957	EPA.107	Mean woman blues / I'm feeling sorry / Whole lotta shakin' goin' on / Turn around
USA	1958	EPA.108	Don't be cruel / Goodnight Irene / Put me down / It all depends
USA	1958	EPA.109	Ubangi stomp / Crazy arms / Jambalaya / Fools like me
USA	1958	EPA.110	High school confidential / When the saints go marching in / Matchbox / It'll be me
UK	1958	RES.1140	It'll be me / Whole lotta shakin' goin' on / Great balls of fire / You win again
UK	1959	RES.1186	Don't be cruel / Put me down / It all depends / Crazy arms
UK	1959	RES.1187	Jambalaya / Fools like me / High school confidential / When the saints go marching in
UK	1961	RES.1296	What'd I say / Livin' lovin' wreck / John Henry / Hang up my rock 'n' roll shoes
UK	1962	RES.1336	Money / Save the last dance for me / Turn around / Hello Josephine
UK	1963	RES.1351	Sweet little sixteen / How's my ex treating you / Lovin' up a storm / I've been twistin'
UK	1963	RES.1378	Good golly miss Molly / I can't trust me (in your arms anymore) / Teenage letter / Seasons of my heart (with Linda Gail Lewis)

US SUN INTERNATIONAL SINGLES, 1969-1973

1969 S.I.1101 Invitation to your party / I could never be ashamed of you
1969 S.I.1107 One minute past eternity / Frankie & Johnny
1970 S.I.1115 I can't seem to say goodbye / Goodnight Irene
1970 S.I.1119 Waiting for a train / Big legged woman
1971 S.I.1125 Love on broadway / Matchbox
1972 S.I.1128 Your lovin' ways / I can't trust me (in your arms anymore)
1973 S.I.1130 I can't trust me (in your arms anymore) / Good rockin'
tonight

EPS RELEASED BY THE JERRY LEE LEWIS INTERNATIONAL FAN-CLUB, 1984-1985

1984 JLL EP 001 Break up / Breathless / High school confidential / Down
the line
1985 JLL EP 002 Put me down / I'll sail my ship alone / Let's talk about us
/ Great balls of fire

THE SUN ALBUMS, 1958-1989

All of the following albums featured at least one previously unissued track
(though a handful had already appeared on bootlegs) with the exception of;
HAS.8251/HAS.8323/S.I.LP 102/S.I.LP 103.

SUN 1230/HAS.2138. JERRY LEE LEWIS. USA/UK, 1958

Don't be cruel / Goodnight Irene / Put me down / It all depends / Ubangi
stomp / Crazy arms / Jambalaya / Fools like me / High school confidential /
When the saints go marching in / Matchbox / It'll be me.

SUN 1265/HAS.2440. JERRY LEE'S GREATEST. USA/UK, 1961

Money / As long as I live / Frankie & Johnny / Home / Hello hello baby /
Hillbilly music / Let's talk about us / What'd I say / Break up / Great balls of
fire / Cold, cold heart / Hello Josephine.

HAS.8251.WHOLE LOTTA SHAKIN' GOIN' ON. UK, 1966

Whole lotta shakin' goin' on / Turn around / Mean woman blues / You win
again / Lovin' up a storm / Big blon' baby / It hurt me so / Little queenie /
John Henry / Hang up my rock 'n' roll shoes / Sweet little sixteen / Lewis
boogie / I know what it means / Carry me back to old Virginia.

HAS.8323. BREATHLESS. UK, 1967

Breathless / I've been twistin' / Good golly miss Molly / Livin' lovin' wreck /

It won't happen with me / Teenage letter / Save the last dance for me / Ramblin' rose / When I get paid / How's my ex treating you / Seasons of my heart (with Linda Gail Lewis) / I can't trust me (in your arms anymore) / Love made a fool of me / End of the road.

S.I.LP 102. ORIGINAL GOLDEN HITS VOLUME ONE. USA, 1969

Crazy arms / You win again / Lewis boogie / Great balls of fire / Down the line / End of the road / Little queenie / Teenage letter / Whole lotta shakin' goin' on / Breathless / It'll be me.

S.I.LP 103. ORIGINAL GOLDEN HITS VOLUME TWO. USA, 1969

Fools like me / I'll sail my ship alone / How's my ex treating you / Money / High school confidential / I could never be ashamed of you / Save the last dance for me / Mean woman blues / Break up / I'll make it all up to you / What'd I say.

S.I.LP 107. ROCKIN' RHYTHM & BLUES. USA, 1969

C.C. Rider / What'd I say / Little queenie / Big legged woman / Good rockin' tonight / Good golly miss Molly / Save the last dance for me / Sweet little sixteen / Hang up my rock 'n' roll shoes / Hello Josephine / Johnny B. Goode.

S.I.LP 108. GOLDEN CREAM OF THE COUNTRY. USA, 1969

Invitation to your party / Cold, cold heart / Ramblin' rose / One minute past eternity / Frankie & Johnny / Home / Jambalaya / How's my ex treating you / Seasons of my heart (with Linda Gail Lewis) / I can't trust me (in your arms anymore) / As long as I live.

S.I.LP 114. A TASTE OF COUNTRY. USA, 1969

I can't seem to say goodbye / I love you so much it hurts / I'm throwing rice / Goodnight Irene / Your cheating heart / Am I to be the one (with Charlie Rich) / Crazy arms / Night train to Memphis / As long as I live / You win again / It hurt me so.

S.I.LP 119. SUNDAY DOWN SOUTH. USA, 1970.

Will the circle be unbroken / Old time religion / Carry me back to old Virginia / When the saints go marching in / Silver threads. (Other tracks by JOHNNY CASH)

S.I.LP 121. OLE TYME COUNTRY MUSIC. USA, 1970

All around the watertank (Waiting for a train) / Carry me back to old Virginia / John Henry / Old black Joe / My blue heaven / You're the only star (in my blue heaven) / The Crawdad song / Hand me down my walkin' cane / You are my sunshine / If the world keeps on turning (I'll keep on loving you) / Deep Elem blues.

S.I.LP 124. MONSTERS. USA, 1970

Don't be cruel / Your cheating heart / Save the last dance for me / Pink pedal pushers / Good golly miss Molly / Matchbox / Be bop a lula / Jailhouse rock / Drinkin' wine spo-dee-o-dee / Honey hush / Singing the blues.

S.I.LP 125. SING HANK WILLIAMS. USA, 1971

Lovesick blues / You win again / Your cheating heart / Jambalaya / Settin' the woods on fire. (other tracks by JOHNNY CASH)

S.I.LP 128. ORIGINAL GOLDEN HITS VOLUME THREE. USA, 1971

One minute past eternity / Let's talk about us / Your lovin' ways / I can't trust me (in your arms anymore) / Lovin' up a storm / Love on Broadway / Sweet little sixteen / Invitation to your party / I love you because / As long as I live / Good golly miss Molly.

6467.029. ROCKIN' & FREE. UK, 1974

Pumpin' piano rock / Sixty minute man / Ooby dooby / Mexicali rose / Shame on you / When my blue moon turns to gold again / Tomorrow night / Ole pal of yesterday / All night long / Come what may / Release me / Wild one (Real wild child) / Hound dog / Rock 'n' roll Ruby / Born to lose / Little green valley / Crazy heart / Long gone lonesome blues / My Carolina sunshine girl / Friday night / Sick & tired / So long I'm gone.

NY 6. COLLECTORS EDITION. HOLLAND, 1974

I don't love nobody / Milkshake Mademoiselle / Just who is to blame / Rockin' the boat of love / Set my mind at ease / Ooby dooby / Carrying on / My pretty quadroon / Rock 'n' roll Ruby / Wild one (real wild child) / Slippin' around / My Bonnie.

CHARLY CR 30002. JERRY LEE LEWIS & HIS PUMPING PIANO. UK, 1974

Friday night / Wild one (real wild child) / Whole lotta twistin' / Dixie (instrumental) / Rock 'n' roll Ruby / Carrying on / Sail away (with Charlie Rich) / Pumpin' piano rock / Hound dog / Hong kong blues / Rockin' the boat of love / Near you (instrumental) / Cool, cool ways / Ooby dooby / Someday (you'll want me to want you) / (Just a shanty in old) Shanty town.

CHARLY CR 30006. 16 SONGS NEVER RELEASED BEFORE: RARE JERRY LEE LEWIS VOL.1. UK, 1974

Sixty minute man / Release me / Sick & tired / Let the good times roll / Slippin' around / Little green valley / So long I'm gone / Crazy heart / Set my mind at ease / I know what it means / High powered woman / Billy boy / Wild side of life / When my blue moon turns to gold again / Instrumental (The Marines' hymn) / My pretty quadroon.

CHARLY CR 30007. 16 SONGS NEVER RELEASED BEFORE: RARE JERRY LEE LEWIS VOL.2. UK, 1974

Mexicali rose / Lucky old sun / Ole pal of yesterday / All night long / Come what may / I don't love nobody / Tomorrow night / Shame on you / Carolina sunshine girl / Instrumental (Lewis workout) / I forgot to remember to forget / No more than I get / Nothin' shakin' (sung by Linda Gail Lewis) / Just who is to blame / Born to lose / Long gone lonesome blues.

CHARLY CR 30129. NUGGETS VOLUME TWO. UK, 1977

Crazy arms / Hillbilly music / Turn around / Night train to Memphis / My blue heaven / It hurt me so / I can't help it / When the saints go marching in / Whole lotta twistin' / I'll sail my ship alone / Friday night / Just who is to blame / I can't trust me (in your arms anymore) / Hello hello baby / High powered woman / The Crawdad song.

S.I.LP 1000. GOLDEN ROCK 'N' ROLL. USA, 1977

Whole lotta twistin' / Rock 'n' roll Ruby / Sick & tired / When I get paid / The return of Jerry Lee / Milkshake mademoiselle / Pumpin' piano rock / Let the good times roll / Livin' lovin' wreck / I've been twistin' (1) / High powered woman / Hello hello baby / My Bonnie / Ubangi stomp / Hong kong blues / I've been twistin' / Ooby dooby / My pretty quadroon / Rockin' the boat of love / Lewis boogie.

UK SUN 1003. GOOD ROCKIN' TONITE. UK, 1979

Waiting for a train / Be bop a lula / I could never be ashamed of you / Drinkin' wine spo-dee-o-dee / Settin' the woods on fire / Pink pedal pushers / Johnny B. Goode / Matchbox / Big legged woman / Bonnie B. / Good rockin' tonight / Hand me down my walkin' cane / Let's talk about us / Honey hush / Old black Joe / Deep Elem blues.

UK SUN 1006. THE MILLION DOLLAR QUARTET. UK, 1981

Just a little talk with Jesus / Walk that lonesome valley / I shall not be moved / Peace in the valley / Down by the riverside / I'm with the crowd but oh so alone / Farther along / Blessed Jesus hold my hand / As we travel along the Jericho road / I just can't make it by myself / Little cabin on the hill / Summertime has passed & gone / I hear a sweet voice calling / And now sweetheart you've done me wrong / Keeper of the key / Crazy arms / Don't forbid me.

SUN 102. THE SUN YEARS (12 LP BOX SET) UK, 1983

RECORD ONE

End of the road / Crazy arms / You're the only star (in my blue heaven) / Born to lose / Tomorrow night / Silver threads (amongst the gold) / I'm throwing rice / I love you so much it hurts / Deep Elem blues / Hand me down my walking cane / The Crawdad song / Dixie (inst) / The Marine's hymn (inst) / Goodnight Irene (2 takes) / Will the circle be unbroken / Old time religion / When the saints go marching in.

RECORD TWO

Turn around / That lucky old sun / I love you because / I can't help it / Cold, cold heart / Shame on you / I'll keep on loving you / You're the only star (in my blue heaven) / Whole lotta shakin' goin' on / Ole pal of yesterday / It'll be me / Pumpin' piano rock / You win again / Love letters in the sand / Little green valley / It'll be me (2 takes) / Whole lotta shakin' goin' on.

RECORD THREE

Lewis boogie / It'll be me / All night long / Sixty minute man / I don't love nobody / My Carolina sunshine girl / Long gone lonesome blues / You are my sunshine / Lewis boogie / Drinkin' wine spo-dee-o-dee / Honey hush / Singing the blues / Rockin' with red / Matchbox (2 takes) / Ubangi stomp / Rock 'n' roll Ruby / So long I'm gone.

RECORD FOUR

Ooby dooby / I forgot to remember to forget / You win again / I'm feeling sorry (2 takes) / Mean woman blues / Why should I cry over you / Great balls of fire (3 takes) / You win again / Sexy ways (false start) / Cool, cool ways / Milkshake mademoiselle / Down the line / I'm sorry I'm not sorry / Down the line.

RECORD FIVE

Milkshake mademoiselle (2 takes) / Breathless / Down the line / Breathless / High school confidential (3 takes) / Good rockin' tonight / Pink pedal pushers / Jailhouse rock / Hound dog / Don't be cruel / Someday (you'll want me to want you) / Jambalaya / Friday night / Big legged woman.

RECORD SIX

Hello hello baby / Frankie & Johnny / It all depends / Your cheating heart / Lovesick blues / Goodnight Irene / Matchbox / Put me down / Fools like me / Wild one (Real wild child) / Carrying on / Crazy heart / Put me down / Let the good times roll / Slippin' around / I'll see you in my dreams (inst) / Put me down / High school confidential.

RECORD SEVEN

Memory of you / Come what may / Live & let live / Break up / Crazy heart / I'll make it all up to you / Johnny B. Goode / Crazy arms / Break up / The Return of Jerry Lee / Settin' the woods on fire / Break up / Johnny B. Goode / Break up / I'll make it all up to you (2 takes + overdub excerpt) / Drinkin' wine spo-dee-o-dee.

RECORD EIGHT

I'll sail my ship alone (2 takes) / It hurt me so (2 takes) / You're the only star (in my blue heaven) / Lovin' up a storm (2 takes) / Big blon' baby / Sick & tired / (Just a shanty in old) Shanty town / Release me / I could never be ashamed of you / Near you (inst) / I could never be ashamed of you / Hillbilly music.

RECORD NINE

My blue heaven (2 takes) / Let's talk about us / Home / Night train to Memphis / The ballad of Billy Joe / Let's talk about us / Sail away (with Charlie Rich) / Am I to be the one (with Charlie Rich) / I'm the guilty one / Let's talk about us / Little queenie / Lewis workout (inst) / The wild side of life / Billy boy / Mexicali rose / I get the blues when it rains (inst) / In the mood (inst).

RECORD TEN

Old black Joe / Baby, baby bye bye / As long as I live / Bonnie B. / What'd I say / C.C. rider / Hang up my rock 'n' roll shoes / John Henry / When my blue moon turns to gold again / When I get paid / Love made a fool of me / No more than I get / My Bonnie / I forgot to remember to forget / Cold, cold heart / Livin' lovin' wreck / What'd I say.

RECORD ELEVEN

It won't happen with me / C.C. rider / I love you because / Save the last dance for me / Hello Josephine / High powered woman / Ramblin' rose / Rockin' the boat of love / Money / I've been twistin' / Whole lotta twistin' goin' on / High powered woman / I know what it means / Sweet little sixteen (2 takes) / Hello Josephine / Set my mind at ease / Waiting for a train.

RECORD TWELVE

Waiting for a train / Good rockin' tonight / Be bop a lula / How's my ex
treating you / Good golly miss Molly / I can't trust me (in your arms anymore)
/ My pretty quadroon / Seasons of my heart (with Linda Gail Lewis) /
Teenage letter / Your lovin' ways / Just who is to blame (2 takes) / Hong
Kong blues / Love on Broadway / One minute past eternity / Invitation to
your party / I can't seem to say goodbye / Carry me back to old Virginia.

CHARLY CD 102. THE COMPLETE MILLION DOLLAR SESSION. UK, 1987

You belong to my heart / When god dips his love in my heart / Just a little talk
with Jesus / Walk that lonesome valley / I shall not be moved / Peace in the
valley / Down by the riverside / I'm with the crowd but oh so alone / Farther
along / Blessed Jesus hold my hand / As we travel along the Jericho road / I
just can't make it by myself / Little cabin on the hill / Summertime has passed
& gone / I hear a sweet voice calling / Sweetheart you done me wrong /
Keeper of the key / Crazy arms / Don't forbid me / Brown eyed handsome
man / Out of sight, out of mind / Brown eyed handsome man / Don't be cruel
(2 takes) / Paralysed / Don't be cruel / There is no place like home / When the
saints go marching in / Softly & tenderly / Is it so strange / That's when your
heartaches begin / Brown eyed handsome man / Rip it up / I'm gonna bid my
blues goodbye / Crazy arms / That's my desire / End of the road / Jerry's
boogie / You're the only star (in my blue heaven) / Elvis farewell.

CHARLY CD 70. RARE & ROCKIN'. UK, 1987

It won't happen with me / Teenage letter / Pink pedal pushers / Hillbilly music
/ Deep Elem blues / You win again / I'm feeling sorry / I'm the guilty one / It
hurt me so / I love you because / Cold, cold heart / Whole lotta shakin' goin'
on / In the mood / Great balls of fire / I forget to remember to forget / Turn
around / It all depends / It'll be me (2 takes) / Sixty minute man / Lovin' up a
storm / Rockin' with red / Honey hush / Hound dog / Hang up my rock 'n' roll
shoes.

ZU-ZAZZ Z 2003. KEEP YOUR HANDS OFF OF IT! UK, 1987

Keep your hands off of it! (Birthday cake) / Bonnie B. / Your cheating heart /
Gettin' in the mood / I get the blues when it rains / As long as I live / Baby,
baby bye bye / Mexicali rose (parts 1 & 2) / Old black Joe / Bonnie B. / You
can't help it (I can't help it) / Waiting for a train.

ZU-ZAZZ Z 2004. DON'T DROP IT! UK, 1988

Don't drop it / Hound dog / Great speckled bird (2 takes) / Baby, baby bye

bye / I can't trust me (in your arms anymore) / What'd I say / Bonnie B. / As
long as I live / Old black Joe / You can't help it (I can't help it) / Waiting for a
train.

SUN BOX 109. SUN INTO THE SIXTIES (8 ALBUM VARIOUS ARTISTS SET, INCLUDES ONE ALBUM ON JERRY). UK, 1989

As long as I live / Bonnie B. / What'd I say / Don't drop it / Great speckled
bird / You can't help it (I can't help it) / Old black Joe / Baby, baby bye bye /
My blue heaven (2 takes) / I've been twistin' / Good golly miss Molly /
Waiting for a train / I can't trust me (in your arms anymore) / I can't seem to
say goodbye / Carry me back to old Virginia.

SUN CD BOX 4. JERRY LEE LEWIS, THE ULTIMATE

318 tracks on 12 CDs. Released by Charly Records, U.K.

CHARLY CD BOX 1. THE SUN YEARS (8 CD BOX SET). UK, 1989

Track listing is the same as the LP box set (Sun 102), though with different
takes of two songs: High school confidential / Near you (inst) & with the
addition of the following: Keep your hands off of it (Birthday cake) / Don't
drop it / Great speckled bird / Old black Joe / Carry me back to old Virginia /
I can't trust me (in your arms anymore) / Bonnie B. / As long as I live / Good
golly miss Molly / You can't help it (I can't help it) / What'd I say / I can't
seem to say goodbye / I've been twistin' / Sittin' & thinkin' (Linda Gail Lewis)
/ Nothin' shakin' (Linda Gail Lewis).

BEAR FAMILY BCD 15420. CLASSIC JERRY LEE LEWIS (8 CD BOX SET). GERMANY, 1989

Crazy arms / End of the road / You're the only star (in my blue heaven) /
Born to lose / Silver threads / I'm throwing rice / I love you so much it hurts /
Deep Elem blues / Goodnight Irene (2 takes) / Honey hush / The Crawdad
song / Dixie (inst) / The Marines' hymn (inst) / That lucky old sun / Hand me
down my walking cane / You're the only star (in my blue heaven) / Lewis
boogie / I love you because / I can't help it / Cold, cold heart / Shame on you /
I'll keep on loving you / You are my sunshine / Tomorrow night / Sixty minute
man / It all depends / I don't love nobody / Whole lotta shakin' goin' on / It'll
be me (2 takes) / Whole lotta shakin' goin' on / It'll be me (2 takes) / Ole pal
of yesterday / You win again / Love letters in the sand / Little green valley /
Lewis boogie / Pumpin' piano rock / It'll be me / All night long / Old time
religion / When the saints go marching in / My Carolina sunshine girl / Long
gone lonesome blues / Drinkin' wine spo-dee-o-dee / Singing the blues /
Rockin' with Red / Matchbox (2 takes) / Ubangi stomp / Rock 'n' roll Ruby /
So long I'm gone / Ooby dooby / I forgot to remember to forget / You win

again / I'm feeling sorry (4 takes) / Mean woman blues / Turn around / Great balls of fire (2 takes) / Why should I cry over you / Great balls of fire / You win again / Down the line (2 takes) / I'm sorry, I'm not sorry / Down the line / Sexy ways (false start) / Cool, cool ways / Milkshake mademoiselle / Breathless / Milkshake mademoiselle (2 takes) / Breathless / High school confidential (4 takes) / Put me down / Good rockin' tonight / Pink pedal pushers / Jailhouse rock / Hound dog / Don't be cruel / Someday (you'll want me to want you) / Jamabalaya / Friday night / Big legged woman / Hello, hello baby / Frankie & Johnny / Your cheating heart / Lovesick blues / Goodnight Irene / When the saints go marching in / Matchbox / It all depends / Put me down / Fools like me / Carrying on / Crazy heart / Put me down (2 takes) / High school confidential / Slippin' around / I'll see you in my dreams (inst) / Wild one (Real wild child) / Let the good times roll / Fools like me / Settin' the woods on fire / Memory of you / Come what may / Break up / Crazy heart / Live & let live / I'll make it all up to you / Crazy arms / Johnny B. Goode / Break up / The Return of Jerry Lee / Break up / I'll make it all up to you / Break up / Johnny B. Goode / Break up / I'll make it all up to you / Drinkin' wine spo-dee-o-dee / I'll sail my ship alone / It hurt me so / You're the only star (in my blue heaven) / It hurt me so / Lovin' up a storm (2 takes) / Big blon' baby / Sick & tired / (Just a shanty in old) Shanty town / Release me / I could never be ashamed of you / Near you (inst) / I could never be ashamed of you / Hillbilly music / My blue heaven (2 takes) / Let's talk about us / Little queenie / Home / Will the circle be unbroken / The ballad of Billy Joe / Sail away (with Charlie Rich) / Am I to be the one (with Charlie Rich) / Night train to Memphis / I'm the guilty one / Let's talk about us / The Wild side of life / Billy boy / My Bonnie / Mexicali rose (2 takes) / Gettin' in the mood / In the mood / I get the blues when it rains (2 takes) / Don't drop it / The great speckled bird (2 takes) / Bonnie B. / Baby, baby bye bye (2 takes) / You can't help it (I can't help it) / Old black Joe / Your cheating heart / Old black Joe / Bonnie B. / As long as I live / Hound dog / As long as I live / What'd I say / Keep your hands off of it (Birthday cake) / Hang up my rock 'n' roll shoes / John Henry / What'd I say / C.C. rider / When my blue moon turns to gold again / Lewis workout / When my blue moon turns to gold again / When I get paid / Love made a fool of me / No more than I get / Livin' lovin' wreck / What'd I say / Cold, cold heart / I forgot to remember to forget / It won't happen with me / C.C. rider / I love you because / Save the last dance for me / Hello Josephine / High powered woman / My blue heaven (2 takes) / Sweet little sixteen / Ramblin' rose / Money / Rockin' the boat of love / Ramblin' rose / I've been twistin' / Whole lotta twistin' goin' on / I've been twistin' / I know what it means / High powered woman / Sweet little sin / Hello Josephine / Set my mind at ease / Waiting for a train / Sweet little sixteen / Waiting for a train / How's my ex treating you / Good rockin' tonight / Be bop a lula / Hello Josephine / How's my ex treating you / Good golly miss Molly / I can't trust me (in your arms anymore) / Good golly miss Molly / My pretty quadroon / Waiting for a train / Teenage letter / Seasons of my heart (with Linda Gail Lewis) / Your lovin' ways / Just who is to blame (2 takes) / Hong Kong blues / Love on Broadway / One minute past eternity / Invitation to your party (2 takes) / I can't seem to say goodbye / Carry me back to old Virginia (3 takes).

The following albums also featured previously unissued Sun tracks for the first time:

W.B. JAM ½. JAMBOREE MOVIE SOUNDTRACK. USA, 1957? (various artists album)

Great balls of fire (movie version).

JS-6120. RURAL ROUTE 2. USA. 1972.

Billy boy.

6467.025. PUT YOUR CAT CLOTHES ON. UK, 1973 (VARIOUS ARTISTS COMPILATION)

Milkshake mademoiselle.

6467.027. CARRYIN' ON. UK, 1974. (VARIOUS ARTISTS COMPILATION)

Carrying on.

POWER PAK 247. FROM THE VAULTS OF SUN. USA, 1974.

The wild side of life.

HALLMARK SHM 823. GREAT BALLS OF FIRE. UK, 1974.

I've been twistin' (alternative take).

CHARLY CR 30116. MORE REBEL ROCKABILLY. UK, 1976. (VARIOUS ARTISTS COMPILATION)

It won't happen with me (alternative take).

HALLMARK SHM 864. KINGS OF COUNTRY – VOLUME ONE. UK, 1976. (VARIOUS ARTISTS COMPILATION)

Sail away (alternative take).

SUN LP 1004. WILD ONE AT THE HIGH SCHOOL HOP. UK, 1982

High school confidential (alternative take).

BEAR FAMILY BFX 15211. THE COUNTRY YEARS. GERMANY, 1986 (VARIOUS ARTISTS BOX SET)

I'm feeling sorry (2 takes) / Goodnight Irene / Fools like me / I'll sail my ship alone (all alternative takes).

PICKWICK PCD 840. THE GREATEST HITS VOLUME TWO. UK, 1986

I'll sail my ship alone (alternative take).

SUN BOX 106. SUN – THE ROCKIN' YEARS. UK, 1987. (VARIOUS ARTISTS BOX SET)

Whole lotta shakin' goin' on (alternative take).

PICKWICK PWK 015. THE COUNTRY SOUND OF JERRY LEE LEWIS. UK, 1987

Set me mind at ease (alternative take).

The following bootlegs feature alternative takes that haven't been officially released:

REDITA 103. (TITLE UNKNOWN)
BOP CAT 100. GOOD ROCKIN' TONIGHT
SUN STAR Q02. OUTTAKES

A CD of dubious legality was released in 1991

ELECTROVERT EVCD 3001. THE KILLER'S PRIVATE STASH

This didn't actually feature any SUN recordings, but DID include the following tracks; I don't hurt anymore (KWKH demo, 1954) / (If I ever needed you) I need you now (KWKH demo, 1954) / Lust of the blood (That's what you call love) (CATCH MY SOUL rehearsal, circa 1966) / My god is real (1988 outtake) / Wild one (Real wild child) (1988 outtake) / I'm throwing rice (1988 outtake) / Crazy arms (solo version, 1988) / Whole lotta shakin' goin' on (1988 outtake) / I'm using my bible for a road map – There'll be no detour in heaven (1988 outtake) / I'm longing for home (1988 outtake).

PART TWO – THE SMASH/MERCURY SESSIONS

US SMASH/MERCURY SINGLES, 1963-1978

Oct '63	1857	Hit the road, Jack / Pen & paper
Feb '64	1886	I'm on fire / Bread & butterman
Jun '64	1906	She was my baby / The hole he said he'd dig for me
Sep '64	1930	High heel sneakers / You went back on your word

Jan '65	1969	Baby, hold me close / I believe in you
Jun '65	1992	Rockin' pneumonia & the boogie-woogie flu / This must be the place
Sep '65	2006	Green green grass of home / Baby, you've got what it takes (with Linda Gail Lewis)
Mar '66	2027	Sticks & stones / What a heck of a mess
Aug '66	2053	Memphis beat / If I had it all to do over
Jun '67	2103	It's a hang up baby / Holdin' on
Sep '67	2122	Turn on your lovelight / Shotgun man
Feb '68	2146	Another place, another time / Walkin' the floor over you
May '68	2164	What's made Milwaukee famous / All the good is gone
Sep '68	2186	She still comes around / Slippin' around
Nov '68	2002	To make love sweeter for you / Let's talk about us
Apr '69	2220	Don't let me cross over / We live in two different worlds (both with Linda Gail Lewis)
Apr '69	2224	One has my name / I can't stop loving you
Sep '69	2244	She even woke me up to say goodbye / Echoes
Nov '69	2254	Roll over Beethoven / Secret places (both with Linda Gail Lewis)
Dec '69	2257	Once more with feeling / You went out of your way
Jul '70	73099	There must be more to love than this / Home away from home
Nov '70	73113	Before the snow flies (with Linda Gail Lewis) / What is love (Linda Gail *only*)
Nov '70	73155	I can't have a merry Christmas, Mary (without you) / In loving memories
'71	73192	Touching home / Woman, woman
'71	73227	When he walks on you / Foolish kind of man
Oct '71	73248	Would you take another chance on me / Me & Bobby McGee
Feb '72	73273	Chantilly lace / Think about it darlin'
May '72	73296	Lonely weekends / Turn on your lovelight
Jun '72	73303	Me & Jesus / Handwriting on the wall (both with Linda Gail Lewis)
Sep '72	73328	Who's gonna play this old piano / No honky tonks in heaven
Jan '73	73361	No more hanging on / The Mercy of a letter
Feb '73	73374	Drinkin' wine spo-dee-o-dee / Rock medley
'73	73402	No headstone on my grave / Jack Daniel's (old number seven)
Aug '73	73423	Sometimes a memory ain't enough / I need to pray
'73	73452	Falling to the bottom / I'm left, you're right, she's gone

Feb '74	73462	Just a little bit / Meat man
May '74	73491	Telltale signs / Cold, cold morning light
Sep '74	73618	He can't fill my shoes / Tomorrow's taking baby away
Jan '75	73661	I can still hear the music in the rest room / (Remember me) I'm the one who loves you
May '75	73685	Boogie-woogie country man / I'm still jealous of you
Oct '75	73729	A damn good country song / When I take my vacation in heaven
Jan '76	73763	Don't boogie-woogie / That kind of fool
Jun '76	73822	Let's put it back together again / Jerry Lee's rock 'n' roll revival show
Nov '76	73872	The closest thing to you / You belong to me
Oct '77	55011	Middle-age crazy / Georgia on my mind
Feb '78	55021	Come on in / Who's sorry now
May '78	55028	I'll find it where I can / Don't let the stars get in your eyes
'82	76148	I'm so lonesome I could cry* / Pick me up on your way down

I have *not* included details of the Smash all time hits or Mercury Country Celebrity singles.

(* with added strings)

THE SMASH/MERCURY ALBUMS, 1964-1987

SRS 67040. THE GOLDEN HITS OF JERRY LEE LEWIS. USA, 1964

Whole lotta shakin' goin' on / Fools like me / Great balls of fire / I'll make it all up to you / Down the line / End of the road / Breathless / Crazy arms / You win again / High school confidential / Break up / Your cheatin' heart.

SRS 67052. ALL TIME SMASH HITS. USA, 1964 (VARIOUS ARTISTS ALBUM)

Hit the road, Jack (alt)

SRS 67056. THE GREATEST LIVE SHOW ON EARTH. USA, 1964

Jenny, Jenny / Who will the next fool be / Memphis, Tennessee / Hound dog / Mean woman blues / Hi heel sneakers / No particular place to go / Together again / Long tall Sally / Whole lotta shakin' goin' on.

PHILLIPS 842 945 PY. LIVE AT THE STARCLUB, HAMBURG, GERMANY, 1964.

Mean woman blues / High school confidential / Money / Matchbox / What'd I say (parts 1 & 2) / Great balls of fire / Good golly miss Molly / Lewis boogie /

Your cheatin' heart / Hound dog / Long tall Sally / Whole lotta shakin' goin' on.

PHILIPS 148 005 STL. STARCLUB SHOW, 6. GERMANY, 1965? (VARIOUS ARTISTS ALBUM)

Down the line (live)

SRS 67063. THE RETURN OF ROCK. USA, 1965

I believe in you / Maybelline / Flip, flop & fly / Roll over Beethoven / Don't let go / Herman the hermit / Baby, hold me close / You went back on your word / Corrine, Corrina / Sexy ways / Johnny B. Goode / Got you on my mind.

SRS 67071. COUNTRY SONGS FOR CITY FOLKS. USA, 1965

Green green grass of home / Wolverton mountain / Funny how time slips away / North to Alaska (with Linda Gail Lewis) / The wild side of life / Walk right in / City lights / Ring of fire / Detroit city / Crazy arms / King of the road / Seasons of my heart.

SRS 67079. MEMPHIS BEAT. USA, 1966

Memphis beat / Mathilda / Drinkin' wine spo-dee-o-dee / Hallelujah, I love her so / She thinks I still care / Just because / Sticks & stones / Whenever you're ready / Lincoln Limousine / Big boss man / Too young / The urge.

SRS 67086. BY REQUEST (MORE OF THE GREATEST LIVE SHOW ON EARTH). USA, 1966

Little queenie / How's my ex treating you / Johnny B. Goode / Green green grass of home / What'd I say (part 2) / You win again / I'll sail my ship alone / Cryin' time / Money / Roll over Beethoven.

SRS 67097. SOUL MY WAY. USA, 1967

Turn on your love light / It's a hang up baby / Dream baby (How long must I dream) / Just dropped in / Wedding bells / He took it like a man / Hey baby / Treat her right / Holdin' on / Shotgun man / I betcha gonna like it.

SRS 67104. ANOTHER PLACE, ANOTHER TIME. USA, 1968

What's made Milwaukee famous / Play me a song I can cry to / On the back row / Walking the floor over you / All night long / I'm a lonesome fugitive / Another place, another time / Break my mind / Before the next teardrop falls / All the good is gone / We live in two different worlds (with Linda Gail Lewis).

SRS 67112. SHE STILL COMES AROUND (TO LOVE WHAT'S LEFT OF ME). USA, 1968

To make love sweeter for you / Let's talk about us / I can't get over you / Out of my mind / Today I started loving you again / She still comes around / Louisiana man / Release me / Listen they're playing my song / There stands the glass / Echoes.

SRS 67117. THE COUNTRY MUSIC HALL OF FAME HITS, VOLUME ONE. USA, 1969

I wonder where you are tonight / I'm so lonesome I could cry / Jambalaya / Four walls / Heartaches by the number / Mom & dad's waltz / Sweet dreams / Born to lose / Oh lonesome me / You've still got a place in my heart / I love you because / Jackson (with Linda Gail Lewis).

SRS 67118. THE COUNTRY MUSIC HALL OF FAME HITS, VOLUME TWO. USA, 1969

I can't stop loving you / Fraulein / He'll have to go / More & more / Why don't you love me (like you used to do) / It makes no difference now / Pick me up on your way down / One has my name (the other has my heart) / I get the blues when it rains / Cold, cold heart / Burning memories / Sweet thing (with Linda Gail Lewis).

SRS 67126. TOGETHER (WITH LINDA GAIL LEWIS). USA, 1969

Milwaukee here I come / Jackson / Don't take it out on me / Cryin' time / Sweet thing / Secret places / Don't let me cross over / Gotta travel on / We live in two different worlds / Earth up above / Roll over Beethoven.

SRS 67128. SHE EVEN WOKE ME UP TO SAY GOODBYE. USA, 1969

Once more with feeling / Workin' man blues / Waiting for a train / Brown eyed handsome man / My only claim to fame / Since I met you baby / She even woke me up to say goodbye / Wine me up / When the grass grows over me / You went out of your way (to walk on me) / Echoes.

134 204 MCY. I'M ON FIRE. UK/EUROPE, 1969

Memphis beat / Pen & paper / I'm on fire / She was my baby / This must be the place / What a heck of a mess / The rockin' pneumonia & the boogie-woogie flu / If I had it all to do over / Hit the road, Jack / The hole he said he'd dig for me / Bread & butter man / Baby, you've got what it takes (with Linda Gail Lewis).
Note: The FRENCH issue featured a different take of 'The hole he said he'd dig for me'.

SRS 67131. THE BEST OF JERRY LEE LEWIS. USA, 1970

What's made Milwaukee famous / Another place, another time / She even woke me up to say good-bye / Louisiana man / Slippin' around / All the good is gone / To make love sweeter for you / One has my name (the other has my heart) / She still comes around (to love what's left of me) / Once more with feeling / Let's talk about us.

SR 61278. LIVE AT THE INTERNATIONAL HOTEL, LAS VEGAS. USA, 1970

She even woke me up to say goodbye / Jambalaya / She still comes around (to love what's left of me) / Drinkin' champagne / San Antonio Rose / Once more with feeling / When you wore a tulip & I wore a big red rose (with Linda Gail Lewis) / Take these chains from my heart (Linda Gail Lewis) / The Ballad of forty dollars / Flip, flop & fly.

SR 61318. IN LOVING MEMORIES. USA, 1970

In loving memories / The lily of the valley / Gather round children / My god's not dead / He looked beyond my fault / The old rugged cross / I'll fly away / I'm longing for home / I know that Jesus will be there (with Linda Gail Lewis) / Too much to gain to lose / If we never meet again – I'll meet you in the morning (medley).

SR 61323. THERE MUST BE MORE TO LOVE THAN THIS. USA, 1970

There must be more to love than this / Bottles & barstools / Reuben James / I'd be talkin' all the time / One more time / Sweet Georgia Brown / Woman, woman (get out of our way) / I forgot more than you'll ever know / Foolaid / Home away from home / Life's little ups & downs.

SR 61343. TOUCHING HOME. USA, 1971

When he walks on you (like you have walked on me) / Time changes everything / Help me make it through the night / Mother, the queen of my heart / Hearts were made for beating / Foolish kind of man / Touching home / Please don't talk about me when I'm gone / You helped me up (when the world let me down) / When baby gets the blues / Coming back for more.

SR 61346. WOULD YOU TAKE ANOTHER CHANCE ON ME. USA, 1971

Would you take another chance on me / Another hand shakin' goodbye / Swinging doors / Thirteen at the table / Big blon' baby / Lonesome fiddle man / Me & Bobby McGee / For the good times / Things that matter most to me / The hurtin' part / The goodbye of the year.

SRM 1 637. THE KILLER ROCKS ON. USA, 1972

Don't be cruel / You can have her / Games people play / Lonely weekends / You don't miss your water / Turn on your lovelight / Chantilly lace / C.C. rider / Walk a mile in my shoes / Me & Bobby McGee / Shotgun man / I'm walkin'.

SR 61366. WHO'S GONNA PLAY THIS OLD PIANO (THINK ABOUT IT, DARLIN'). USA, 1972

Who's gonna play this old piano / She's reachin' for my mind / Too many rivers / We both know which one of us was wrong / Wall around heaven / No more hanging on / Think about it, darlin' / Bottom dollar / No traffic out of Abilene / Parting is such sweet sorrow (instrumental) / The mercy of a letter.

SRM 2 803. THE SESSION. (DOUBLE ALBUM) USA, 1973

Drinkin' wine spo-dee-o-dee / Music to the man / Baby what you want me to do / Bad moon rising / Sea cruise / Jukebox / No headstone on my grave / Big boss man / Pledging my love / Memphis, Tennessee / Trouble in mind / Johnny B. Goode / High school confidential (instrumental, does NOT feature Jerry) / Early morning rain / Whole lotta shakin' goin' on / Sixty minute man / Down the line / What'd I say / Rock 'n' roll medley.

SRM 1 677. SOMETIMES A MEMORY AIN'T ENOUGH. USA, 1973

Sometimes a memory ain't enough / Ride me down easy / Mama's hands / What my woman can't do / My cricket & me / I'm left, you're right, she's gone / Honky tonk wine / Falling to the bottom / I think I need to pray / The morning after baby let me down / Keep me from blowing away.

SRM 1 690. SOUTHERN ROOTS. USA, 1973

Meat man / When a man loves a woman / Hold on I'm coming / Just a little bit / Born to be a loser / The haunted house / Blueberry hill / The revolutionary man / Big blue diamonds / That old Bourbon Street church.

SRM 1 710. 1-40 COUNTRY. USA, 1974

He can't fill my shoes / Tell tale signs / A picture from life's other side / I hate goodbyes / I've forgot more about you (than he'll ever know) / Tomorrow's taking baby away / Cold, cold morning light / The alcohol of fame / Where would I be / Bluer words / Room full of roses.

SRM 1 1030. BOOGIE WOOGIE COUNTRY MAN. USA, 1975

I'm still jealous of you / A little peace & harmony / Jesus is on the main line (call him sometime) / Forever forgiving / (Remember me) I'm the one who loves you / Red hot memories (ice cold beer) / I can still hear the music in the restroom / Love inflation / I was sorta wonderin' / Thanks for nothing / Boogie woogie country man.

SRM 1 1964. ODD MAN IN. USA, 1975

Don't boogie woogie (when you say your prayers tonight) / Shake, rattle & roll / You ought to see my mind / I don't want to be lonely tonight / That kind of fool / Goodnight Irene / A damn good country song / Jerry's place / When I take my vacation in heaven / The Crawdad song / Your cheatin' heart.

SRM 1 1109. COUNTRY CLASS. USA, 1976

Let's put it back together again / No one will ever know / You belong to me / I sure miss those good old times / That old country church / After the fool you've made of me / Jerry Lee's rock 'n' roll revival show / Wedding bells / Only love can get you in my door / The one rose that's left in my heart / The closest thing to you.

SRM 1 5004. COUNTRY MEMORIES. USA, 1977

Middle age crazy / Let's say goodbye like we said hello / Who's sorry now / Jealous heart / Georgia on my mind / Come on in / As long as we live / (You'd think by now) I'd be over you / Country memories / What's so good about goodbye / Tennessee Saturday night.

SRM 1 5006. THE BEST OF JERRY LEE LEWIS VOLUME TWO. USA, 1978

Chantilly lace / Think about it, darlin' / Sweet Georgia Brown / Touching home / Would you take another chance on me / There must be more to love than this / Middle age crazy / Me & Bobby McGee / Let's put it back together / Who's gonna play this old piano / The closest thing to you / Boogie woogie country man.

SRM 1 5010. KEEPS ROCKIN'. USA, 1978

I'll find it where I can / Blue suede shoes / I hate you / Arkansas seesaw / Lucille / The last cheater's waltz / Wild & woolly ways / Sweet little sixteen / Don't let the stars get in your eyes / Pee Wee's place / Before the night is over.

SCPB 6816 125. THE MERCURY SESSIONS. HOLLAND, 1985

Alvin / Cheater pretend (with Linda Gail Lewis) / Corrine, Corrina / I can't have a merry Christmas (Mary without you) / You call everybody darling / The last letter / Let's live a little / Sittin' & thinkin' /Someday (you'll want me to want you) / The fifties / Honey hush / I don't know why.

BFX 15240, THE COMPLETE SESSION VOLUME ONE. GERMANY, 1986

Drinkin' wine spo-dee-o-dee / Music to the man / Baby what you want me to do / Bad moon rising / Sea cruise / Satisfaction / Jukebox / No headstone on my grave / Big boss man / Pledging my love / Dungaree doll / Memphis, Tennessee / I can't give you anything but love, baby.

BFX 15241. THE COMPLETE SESSION VOLUME TWO. GERMANY, 1986

Be-bop-a-lula / Trouble in mind / Johnny B. Goode / High school confidential (instrumental) / Early morning rain / Singing the blues / Goldmine in the sky / Whole lotta shakin' goin' on / Sixty minute man / Down the line / What'd I say / Rock 'n' roll medley.

830 207-1. 30th ANNIVERSARY ALBUM. HOLLAND, 1986

Black mama / And for the first time / Ivory tears / Where he leads me I'll follow / Living on the hallelujah side / Meeting in the air / Speak a little louder to us Jesus / Why me Lord (with Moetta Hill) / Great balls of fire / I can help / Slippin' & slidin' / Dungaree doll / I can't give you anything but love, baby / Goldmine in the sky / Singing the blues / Be-bop-a-lula / Satisfaction.

830 829-1. FROM THE VAULTS. HOLLAND, 1986

House of blue lights / I'm knee deep in loving you / Nobody knows me / I can help / My blue heaven / You belong to me / You're all too ugly tonight / I can't keep my hands off of you / Life's railway to heaven / The Crawdad song / Until the day forever ends / Lord, I've tried everything but you / Harbour lights / Oh lord, what's left for me to do / The Gods were angry with me / Parting is such sweet sorrow.

BEAR FAMILY BFX 15210. THE KILLER: 1963-1968 (10 LP BOX SET). GERMANY, 1986

RECORD ONE

Whole lotta shakin' goin' on / Crazy arms / Great balls of fire / High school confidential / I'll make it all up to you / Break up / Down the line / Hit the road, Jack / End of the road / Your cheatin' heart / Wedding bells / Just because / Breathless / He took it like a man / Drinkin' wine spo-dee-o-dee / Johnny B. Goode / Hallelujah, I love her so.

RECORD TWO

You went back on your word / Pen & paper / The hole he said he'd dig for me / You win again / Fools like me / Hit the road, Jack / I'm on fire (2 takes) /

She was my baby (he was me friend) / Bread & butterman / I betcha gonna like it / Got you on my mind / Mathilda / Corrine, Corrina / Sexy ways / The wild side of life.

RECORD THREE (LIVE AT THE STARCLUB, HAMBURG)

Mean woman blues / High school confidential / Money / Matchbox / What'd I say (parts 1 & 2) / Down the line / Great balls of fire / Good golly miss Molly / Lewis boogie / Your cheatin' heart / Hound dog / Long tall Sally / Whole lotta shakin' goin' on.

RECORD FOUR (THE GREATEST LIVE SHOW ON EARTH)

Jenny, Jenny / Who will the next fool be / Memphis, Tennessee / Hound dog / Mean woman blues / Hi-heel sneakers / No particular place to go / Together again / Long tall Sally / Whole lotta shakin' goin' on.

RECORD FIVE

Flip, flop & fly / Don't let go / Maybelline / Roll over Bethoven / Just because / I believe in you / Herman the Hermit / Baby, hold me close / Skid row / This must be the place / Rockin' pneumonia & the boogie woogie flu / Seasons of my heart / Big boss man / Too young / Danny boy / Crazy arms / City lights / Funny how time slips away.

RECORD SIX

North to Alaska (with Linda Gail Lewis) / Walk right in / Wolverton mountain / King of the road / Detroit city / Ring of fire / Baby (you've got what it takes) (with Linda Gail Lewis) / Green green grass of home / Sticks & stones / What a heck of a mess / Lincoln limousine / Rockin' Jerry Lee / Memphis beat / The Urge / Whenever you're ready / She thinks I still care / Memphis beat (2 takes) / Twenty four hours a day / Swinging doors.

RECORD SEVEN (BY REQUEST, MORE OF THE GREATEST LIVE SHOW ON EARTH)

Little queenie / How's my ex treating you / Johnny B. Goode / Green green grass of home / What'd I say (part two) / You win again / I'll sail my ship slone / Cryin' time / Money / Roll over Beethoven.

RECORD EIGHT

Swingin' doors / If I had it all to do over / Just dropped in / It's a hang up baby / Holdin' on / Hey baby / Dream baby / Treat her right / Turn on your lovelight / Shotgun man / All the good is gone / Another place, another time / Walking the floor over you / I'm a lonesome fugitive / Break my mind / Play me a song I can cry to / Before the next teardrop falls.

RECORD NINE

All night long / We live in two different worlds (with Linda Gail Lewis) / What's made Milwaukee famous / On the back row / Slipping around / She still comes around / Today I started loving you again / Louisiana man / There stands the glass / I can't have a merry Christmas, Mary (without you) / Out of my mind / I can't get over you / Listen, they're playing my song / Echoes / Release me / Let's talk about us / To make love sweeter for you.

RECORD TEN (LIMITED EDITION BONUS ALBUM)

Jerry Lee Lewis interview with Dave Booth (recorded in Toronto, 1976).

BEAR FAMILY BFX 15228. THE KILLER: 1969-1972 (11 LP BOX LET). GERMANY, 1986

RECORD ONE

Don't let me cross over (with Linda Gail Lewis) / Born to lose / You belong to me (2 takes) / Oh lonesome me / Sweet dreams / Cold, cold heart / Fraulein / Why don't you love me (like you used to do) / Four walls / It makes no difference now / I love you because / I'm so lonesome I could cry / Jambalaya / More & more / One has my name (the other has my heart) / Burning memories / Mom & dad's waltz.

RECORD TWO

Pick me up on your way down / Heartaches by the number / I can't stop loving you / My blue heaven / I wonder where you are tonight / Jackson (with Linda Gail Lewis) / Sweet thing (with Linda Gail Lewis) / He'll have to go / You've still got a place in my heart / I get the blues when it rains / Gotta travel on (with Linda Gail Lewis) / Milwaukee here I come (with Linda Gail Lewis) / Cryin' time (with Linda Gail Lewis) / Roll over Beethoven (with Linda Gail Lewis) / Secret places (with Linda Gail Lewis) / Don't take it out on me (with Linda Gail Lewis) / Earth up above (with Linda Gail Lewis).

RECORD THREE

Waiting for a train / Love of all seasons / She even woke me up to say goodbye / When the grass grows over me / Wine me up / Since I met you baby / Workin' man blues / Once more with feeling / In loving memories / You went out of your way (to walk on me) / My only claim to fame / Brown eyed handsome man / In loving memories / Once more with feeling / Gather round children / I'd be talkin' all the time / Alvin / I forgot more than you'll ever know.

RECORD FOUR

Bottles & barstools / Life's little ups & downs / There must be more to love than this / Sweet Georgia Brown / Home away from home / Woman, woman (get out of our way) / Reuben James / Before the snow flies (with Linda Gail Lewis) / Cheater pretend (with Linda Gail Lewis) / He looked beyond my fault / Handwriting on the wall (with Linda Gail Lewis) / The old rugged cross / The lily of the valley / If we never meet again – I'll meet you in the morning (medley) / I'm longing for home / Black Mama / I'll fly away.

RECORD FIVE (LIVE AT THE INTERNATIONAL HOTEL, LAS VEGAS, 1)

She even woke me up to say goodbye / Jamabalaya / She still comes around / Drinkin' champagne / San Antonio rose / Once more with feeling / When you wore a tulip (with Linda Gail Lewis) / Take these chains from my heart (Linda Gail Lewis) / Ballad of forty dollars / Flip, flop & fly / Sweet little sixteen / Jenny Jenny-Long tall Sally-Tutti frutti (medley) / C.C. rider / High school confidential / Down the line – I'm movin' on (medley, with Linda Gail Lewis) / Whole lotta shakin' goin' on / Oh lonesome me / Your cheatin' heart / Smoke gets in your eyes / Invitation to your party.

RECORD SIX (LIVE AT THE INTERNATIONAL HOTEL, LAS VEGAS, 2)

Blue suede shoes / When the grass grows over me / Jackson (with Linda Gail Lewis) / Staggerlee / Today I started loving you again / One has my name (the other has my heart) / Shoeshine man / Great balls of fire / Mean woman blues / You are my sunshine / Homecoming / Got you on my mind again (with Linda Gail Lewis) / What'd I say / Mexicali rose (slow & fast versions).

RECORD SEVEN

I know that Jesus will be there (with Linda Gail Lewis) / My God's not dead / Foolaid / One more time / Too much to gain to lose / Jealous heart / The last letter / Meeting in the air / Where he leads me I'll follow / Living on the hallelujah side / A picture from life's other side / The hurtin' part / Touching home / Coming back for more / When my baby gets the blues / Help me make it through the night / Mother, the queen of my heart / Time changes everything / Hearts were made for beating.

RECORD EIGHT (CHURCH LIVE RECORDING)

Looking for a city / I'm longing for home / Blessed saviour thou will guide us / Someone who cares for you / If we never meet again – I'll meet you in the morning (medley) / Down the sawdust trail / Peace in the valley / Precious memories / The old rugged cross / It will be worth it all when we see Jesus /

I know that Jesus will be there / I'm in the gloryland way / Tomorrow may mean goodbye / Amazing grace / On the Jericho road / I'll fly away / My God is real / What will the answer be / I won't have to cross Jordan alone / Keep on the firing line.

RECORD NINE

When he walks on you (like you walked on me) / You helped me up (when the world let me down) / Foolish kind of man / Another handshakin' goodbye / Please don't talk about me when I'm gone / The goodbye of the year / 'Someday, you'll want me to want you / No honky tonks in heaven / Big blon' baby / Lonesome fiddle man / Things that matter most to me / I don't know why, I just do / Thirteen at the table / For the good times / Would you take another chance on me / Me & Bobby McGee / And for the first time /Think about it, darlin' / No traffic out of Abilene.

RECORD TEN

Chantilly lace / Lonely weekends / C.C. rider / Walk a mile in my shoes / Games people play / Don't be cruel / You can have her / I'm walkin' / You don't miss your water / Me & Jesus (with Linda Gail Lewis) / Too many rivers / Wall around heaven / We both know which one of us was wrong / Parting is such sweet sorrow (instrumental) / Who's gonna play this old piano / Bottom dollar / Parting is such sweet sorrow (vocal) / No more hanging on / The mercy of a letter / She's reachin' for my mind.

RECORD ELEVEN (LIMITED EDITION BONUS ALBUM)

1969 Open end interview + the following songs recorded in Toronto '69: Hound dog / Mean woman blues / Great balls of fire / Mystery train / Whole lotta shakin' goin' on / Jailhouse rock.

BEAR FAMILY BFX 15229. THE KILLER: 1973-1977 (12 LP BOX SET). GERMANY, 1987

RECORD ONE

Drinkin' wine spo-dee-o-dee / Music to the man / Baby, what you want me to do / Bad moon rising / Sea cruise / (I can't get no) Satisfaction / Jukebox / No headstone on my grave / Big boss man / Pledging my love / Dungaree doll / Memphis, Tennessee / I can't give you anything but love, baby.

RECORD TWO

Be bop a lula / Trouble in mind / Johnny B. Goode / High school confidential (instrumental) / Early morning rain / Singing the blues / Goldmine in the sky / Whole lotta shakin' goin' on / Sixty minute man / Down the line / What'd I say / Rock 'n' roll medley.

RECORD THREE

Jack Daniel's / Why me Lord (with Moetta Hill) / Ride me down easy / Cold, cold morning light / Alcohol of fame / Tomorrow's taking baby away / Mama's hands / What my woman can't do / Tell tale signs / The morning after baby let me down / I think I need to pray / I hate goodbyes / Where would I be / My cricket & me / Falling to the bottom / The gods were angry with me / Sometimes a memory ain't enough / Bluer words.

RECORD FOUR

Meat man / When a man loves a woman / Hold on I'm coming / Just a little bit / Born to be a loser / The haunted house / Blueberry hill / Revolutionary man / Big blue diamonds / That old Bourbon Street church.

RECORD FIVE

All over hell & Georgia / Take your time / The haunted house / I sure miss those good old times / Margie / Raining in my heart / Hold on I'm coming / Cry / Honey hush / Silver threads among the gold.

RECORD SIX

Meat man / Big blue diamonds / I sure miss those good old times (2 takes) / When a man loves a woman / Silver threads among the gold / Hold on I'm coming (2 takes) / Cry (instrumental) / Margie + chat.

RECORD SEVEN

He can't fill my shoes / I'm left, you're right, she's gone / Keep me from blowing away / Honky tonk wine / Room full of roses / A picture from life's other side / I've forgot more about you (than he'll ever know) / Until the day forever ends / Boogie woogie country man / I can still hear the music in the restroom / Speak a little louder to us Jesus / Honey hush / Jesus is on the main line / Remember me / Shake, rattle & roll / Love inflation / I don't want to be lonely tonight / Forever forgiving.

RECORD EIGHT

A little peace & harmony / No one knows me / When I take my vacation in heaven / I'm still jealous of you / You ought to see my mind / Don't boogie woogie (when you say your prayers tonight) / Thanks for nothing / Red hot memories / I was sorta wonderin' / Jerry's place / That kind of fool / Your cheatin' heart / The Crawdad song / The house of blue lights / Goodnight Irene / A damn good country song (2 takes) / Lord what's left for me to do.

RECORD NINE

Great balls of fire / The one rose that's left in my heart / I'm knee deep in loving you / I can help (2 takes) / Slippin' & slidin' / From a jack to a king (2 takes) / After the fool you've made of me / The closest thing to you / I can't keep my hands off of you / The one rose that's left in my heart / Wedding bells / The fifties / No one will ever know / Only love can get you in my door.

RECORD TEN

That old country church / Harbour lights / Jerry Lee's rock 'n' roll revival show / I sure miss those good old times / Let's put it back together again / Country memories / As long as we live / Jealous heart / (You'd think by now) I'd be over you / Come on in / Who's sorry now / Let's say goodbye like we said hello / Georgia on my mind / What's so good about goodbye / Tennessee Saturday night / Ivory tears / Middle age crazy / The last letter / The last cheater's waltz.

RECORD ELEVEN

Let's live a little / I hate you / Before the night is over / Sittin' & thinkin' / Blue suede shoes / Corrine, Corrina / Don't let the stars get in your eyes / Sweet little sixteen / Life's railway to heaven / Ivory tears / You call everybody darling / Wild & woolly ways / I'll find it where I can / Lord I've tried everything but you / You're all too ugly tonight / Arkansas seesaw / Pee Wee's place.

RECORD TWELVE. (LIMITED EDITION BONUS ALBUM)

Open end interview to promote Southern Roots, 1973.

The following bootlegs feature alternate takes from this period that haven't been officially released:

RARE SOUND 1114. ROCK & ROLL WITH JERRY LEE.
PUMPIN' 1963. THE GREAT JERRY LEE LEWIS (EP).
SUN SLP-1280. ALIVE & ROCKIN'.

See also the SUN section for the track listing of 'The Killer's Private Stash' (Electrovert EVCD 3001). This features two recordings from this period.

PART THREE – THE POST-MERCURY SESSIONS

US POST-MERCURY SINGLES, 1979-1990

| '79 | E-46030 | Rockin' my life away / I wish I was eighteen again |
| '79 | E-46067 | Who will the next fool be / Rita May |

'80	E-46591	When two worlds collide / Good news travels fast
'80	E-46642	Honky tonk stuff/Rockin' Jerry Lee
'80	E-47026	Folsom prison blues / Over the rainbow
'81	E-47095	Thirty-nine & holding / Change places with me
'82	?	(Get rhythm) (Johnny Cash) / Whole lotta shakin' goin' on
'82	MCA 52151	My fingers do the talkin' / Forever forgiving
'83	MCA 52188	Circumstantial evidence / Come as you were
'83	MCA 52233	Why you been gone so long / She sings amazing grace
'84	MCA 52369	I am what I am / That was the way it was then
'86	SCR 386-7	Get out your big roll daddy / Honky tonk rock & roll piano man
'86	884-760-7	(Birth of rock & roll) (Carl Perkins) / Rock 'n' roll fais do do
'86	884-934-7	Sixteen candles / Rock 'n' roll fais do do
'88	CRB 10521	Never too old to rock & roll (with Ronnie McDowell) / (Rock & roll kiss) (Ronnie McDowell)
'89	889-312-7	Great balls of fire / Breathless (Also cassette single 889-312-4)
'89	889-798-7	Crazy arms (with Dennis Quaid) / Great balls of fire
'89	873-006	High school confidential / Wild one (Real wild child)
'90	7-19809-4	It was the whiskey talkin' (not me) / It was the whiskey talkin' (not me) (Rock & roll version)

POST-MERCURY ALBUMS, 1978-1992

AMLM 66500. AMERICAN HOT WAX. USA, 1978 (VARIOUS ARTISTS DOUBLE ALBUM)

Whole lotta shakin' goin' on / Great balls of fire.

ELEKTRA 6E-254. JARRY LEE LEWIS. USA, 1979

Don't let go / Rita May / Everyday I have to cry / I like it like that / Number one lovin' man / Rockin' my life away / Who will the next fool be / (You've got) Personality / I wish I was eighteen again / Rocking little angel.

WB 2HS 3441. ROADIE. USA, 1980 (VARIOUS ARTISTS DOUBLE ALBUM)

(Hot damn) I'm a one woman man.

ELEKTRA 6E-254. WHEN TWO WORLDS COLLIDE. USA, 1980

Rockin' Jerry Lee / Who will buy the wine / Love game / Alabama jubilee /

Good time Charlie's got the blues / When two worlds collide / Good news
travels fast / I only want a buddy not a sweetheart / Toot, toot tootsie
goodbye.

ELEKTRA 6e-291. KILLER COUNTRY. USA, 1980

Folsom prison blues / I'd do it all again / Jukebox junky / Too weak to fight /
Late night lovin' man / Change places with me / Let me on / Thirty-nine &
holding / Mama, this one's for you / Over the rainbow.

MERVYN CONN MCP 001. SILK CUT FESTIVAL. UK, 1982 (VARIOUS ARTISTS DOUBLE ALBUM)

Matchbox-Blue suede shoes (medley, with Carl Perkins).

COLUMBIA FC 37961. THE SURVIVORS USA, 1982

I'll fly away / Whole lotta shakin' goin' on / Rockin' my life away / Peace in
the valley / Will the circle be unbroken / I saw the light (other tracks by
JOHNNY CASH & CARL PERKINS).

MCA-5387. MY FINGERS DO THE TALKIN'. USA, 1982

My fingers do the talkin' / She sure makes leaving look easy / Why you been
gone so long / She sings amazing grace / Better not look down / Honky tonk
rock & roll piano man / Come as you were / Circumstantial evidence / Forever
forgiving / Honky tonk heaven.

MCA-5478. I AM WHAT I AM. USA, 1984

I am what I am / Only you (& you alone) / Get out your big roll daddy / Have
I got a song for you / Careless hands / Candy kisses / I'm looking over a four
leaf clover / Send me the pillow that you dream on / Honky tonk heart / That
was the way it was then.

PULSATION PL 1006. FOUR LEGENDS: JERRY LEE LEWIS, FARON YOUNG, MEL TILLIS & WEBB PIERCE. USA, 1985

No love have I / There stands the glass / Honky tonk song / Walkin' the dog /
Tupelo county jail / It's been so long / Memory number one / Softly &
tenderly. (other tracks by Faron Young, Mel Tillis & Webb Pierce).

SCR-785. SIX OF ONE, HALF DOZEN OF THE OTHER. USA, 1985

No headstone on my grave / Chantilly lace / I'll find it where I can / Drinkin'
wine spo-dee-o-dee / Sweet little sixteen / Boogie woogie country man / Me &
Bobby McGee / Rockin' my life away / Whole lotta shakin' goin' on / You can
have her / Hey good lookin' / Will the circle be unbroken.

SCR-386, GET OUT YOUR BIG ROLL DADDY. USA, 1986

Get out your big roll daddy / Honky tonk heart / Forever forgiving / Why you been gone so long / She sings amazing grace / Rock 'n' roll money / Honky tonk heaven / Better not look down / Honky tonk rock & roll piano man / Come as you were.

SMASH USAH-1. CLASS OF '55. USA, 1986

Sixteen candles / Keep my motor running / Waymore's blues / Rock 'n' roll fais do do/Big train (from Memphis). (other songs by Johnny Cash, Carl Perkins & Roy Orbison).

ELITE EL-KJ-2950. TWENTY YEARS OVERNIGHT. USA, 1987

Honky tonkin' (with Kenny Lovelace). (other tracks by Kenny Lovelace).

GREENLINE GRP 3307. LIVE IN ITALY. ITALY, 1987

Roll in my sweet baby's arms (band) / High school confidential / Me & Bobby McGee / Jackson (with Linda Gail Lewis) / There must be more to love than this / Great balls of fire / What'd I say / Jerry Lee's rock 'n' roll revival show / Over the rainbow / The Crawdad song / I am what I am / Whole lotta shakin' goin' on.

BELLAPHON 260.07.121. ROCKET. GERMANY, 1988

Meat man / Jailhouse rock / House of blue lights / Rock 'n' roll funeral / Don't touch me / Changing mountains / Beautiful dreamer / I'm alone because I love you / Lucille / Seventeen / Mathilda / Wake up little Susie.

GREENLINE CDGLL 104. LIVE IN ITALY. ITALY, 1988

Great balls of fire / I am what I am / You win again / Jackson (with Linda Gail Lewis) / Mona Lisa / Over the rainbow / The Crawdad song / What'd I say / High school confidential / Me & Bobby McGee / One of those things we all go through / Jerry Lee's rock 'n' roll revival show / Hang up my rock 'n' roll shoes / There must be more to love than this / Whole lotta shakin' goin' on.

PICKWICK PWK CD 049. HIGHLIGHTS FROM THE WEMBLEY COUNTRY MUSIC FESTIVALS. UK, 1988 (VARIOUS ARTISTS CD)

Keep my motor running / High school confidential / What'd I say.

POLYDOR 839 516. GREAT BALLS OF FIRE. USA, 1989

Great balls of fire / High school confidential / Big legged woman (Booker T. Laury) / I'm on fire / Rocket 88 (Jackie Brenston & the Delta Cats) / Whole lotta shakin' goin' on / Whole lotta shakin' goin' on (Valerie Wellington) /

Breathless / Crazy arms (with Dennis Quaid) / Wild one (Real wild child) / That lucky old sun / Great balls of fire (original version).

SIRE 7599-26279. DICK TRACY. USA, 1990. (VARIOUS ARTISTS ALBUM)

It was the whiskey talkin' (not me) / It was the whiskey talkin' (not me) (rock & roll version).

TOMATO CD 2996742. THE COMPLETE PALOMINO CLUB RECORDINGS (2 CD SET). HOLLAND, 1991

You win again / What's made Milwaukee famous / What'd I say / Meat man / Another place, another time / I can't stop loving you / Your cheating heart / Big legged woman / Whole lotta shakin' goin' on / Great balls of fire / Rockin' my life away / Harbour lights / Bottles & barstools / You belong to me / Who's gonna play this old piano / Careless hands / Trouble in mind / Who will the next fool be / Touching home / There must be more to love than this / Cold, cold heart / Thirty-nine & holding / She even woke me up to say goodbye / I wish I was eighteen again / Lucille / Brown eyed handsome man / Hey good lookin' / Roll over Beethoven / Chantilly lace / Little queenie / Johnny B. Goode – Whole lotta shakin' goin' on (medley) / No headstone on my grave / Georgia on my mind / Mexicali rose / Will the circle be unbroken / I'll find it where I can / High school confidential / Boogie woogie country man / Middle age crazy / You are my sunshine / A picture from life's other side / Over the rainbow.
Note: Many of the above tracks were previously issued on three earlier CDs in 1989; Rockin' My Life Away (2696612), Heartbreak (2696672) & Rocket 88 (2696732). 2696672 featured an alternate 'Who's gonna play this old piano'.

ACE CDCH-332. HONKY TONK ROCK & ROLL PIANO MAN. UK, 1991

My fingers do the talkin' / Why you been gone so long / Daughters of Dixie / Teenage queen / I'm looking over a four leaf clover / I am what I am / Better not look down / Only you (& you alone) / Honky tonk rock & roll piano man / Circumstantial evidence / I'm looking under a skirt / Rock 'n' roll money / Forever forgiving / Why you been gone so long / Get out your big roll daddy.

DELTA 15403. COUNTRY ROCKERS LIVE. GERMANY, 1991 (VARIOUS ARTISTS CD)

Lucille / Great balls of fire / Rockin' my life away / Whole lotta shakin' goin' on (part only).

PRISM LEISURE PLATCD 342. ROCK & ROLL LEGENDS. UK, 1991 (VARIOUS ARTISTS CD)

Keep my motor running / Over the rainbow / Rock & roll medley / Great balls of fire / Rockin' my life away.

CURB CRBD-10602. UNCHAINED MELODY. USA, 1991

Never too old to rock & roll (with Ronnie McDowell). (other tracks by Ronnie McDowell).

ACE CDCH-348. PRETTY MUCH COUNTRY. UK, 1992

Honky tonk heaven / She never said goodbye / That was the way it was then / Candy kisses / I am what I am / Come as you were / She sings amazing grace / Have I got a song for you / Daughters of Dixie / Send me the pillow you dream on / She sure makes leaving look easy / My fingers do the talkin' / Honky tonk heart / Careless hands / Honky tonk rock & roll piano man / Forever forgiving.

STOMPERTIME STCD 2. NERVOUS AND SHAKIN' ALL OVER. UK, 1992

Ragtime doodle / Meat man / Lovin' up a storm / Ubangi stomp / Rock & roll Ruby / Piano doodle / House of blue lights / A damn good country song / Beautiful dreamer / August leaves / Pilot baby / Room full of roses / Keep a knockin' / Silver threads amongst the gold / Alabama jubilee / Lazy river / Mama, this one's for you / Breathless (live 1958) / Whole lotta shakin' goin' on (live 1959)

The following bootlegs feature tracks from this period that haven't been officially released:

SUN SLP-1280. ALIVE & ROCKIN'
ELECTROVERT EVCD 3001. THE KILLER'S PRIVATE STASH
JERRY LEE LEWIS JOKES & SINGS MONA LISA

Songs recorded with Jerry Lee Lewis for his new Sire album are:

It Was The Whiskey Talking (Not Me) – written by Andy Paley, Jonathan Paley, Ned Claflin and Mike Kernan
Restless Heart – written by Andy Paley, Kenny Lovelace, and James Burton
Goosebumps – written by Andy Paley and Al Anderson
Crown Victoria Custom 51 – written by Andy Paley, Jerry Lee Lewis, James Burton and Kenny Lovelace
I'll Never Get Out Of This World Alive – written by Hank Williams

Miss The Mississippi – written by Jimmie Rodgers
Poison Love – old song by Johnny and Jack (writer not known)
High Blood Pressure – written by Huey Piano Smith
Young Blood – written by Jerry Lieber and Mike Stoller
I'll Hold You In My Heart – sung by Eddy Arnold
One Of Them Old Things We All Go Through – writer and singer unknown
That's My Desire' – writer unknown, lots have sung it
Things – written by Bobby Darin
House Of Blue Light – writer unknown
Down The Road Apiece – written by Chuck Berry

Musicians:
Drums: Glen Colson, Andy Paley, Tommy Ardolino, Buddy Harman, Don
   Allen
Bass: Bob Glaub, Dave Rowe (Rorick), Joey Spampinato, Alvin M. Byrd, Jr,
   Jonathan Paley, Jeff Berlin
Guitars: Bobby Keyes, Elliot Easton, James Burton, Kenny Lovelace, Andy
   Paley, Mike Kernan
Steel Guitar: Robby Turner
Fiddle: Danny Weinstein, Kenny Lovelace
Harmonica: Mike Turk
Horns: Danny Weinstein, Bob Efford, Stuart Aptekar
Accordian: Frank Morocco
Background voices: Andy Paley, Billy West, Mike Kernan
Recording Studios: Kiva Recording / Memphis, Tennessee (House of Blues
   Studios)
   Sun Studio / Memphis, Tennessee
   Your Place Or Mine / Los Angeles, California
   Sunset Sound Factory / Los Angeles, California
Producer: Andy Paley
Executive Producer: Seymour Stein

JERRY LEE LEWIS

Video Discography (UK)

THE IMMORTAL JERRY LEE LEWIS SPECTACULAR SHOW (MUSIC VIDEO 233)

Recorded in the Fulcrum Centre, Slough, 14.2.80 (1st show). Kenneth
Lovelace (gtr/fiddle), Joel Shumaker (gtr), Duke Faglier (bass), Ron
Norwood (dms).

MUSIC PROGRAMME EIGHT (INTER VISION)

Originally filmed for In Concert in Los Angeles, 8-9.1.74 (broadcast 18.1.74).
Linda Gail Lewis (vcls, 1 song only), Kenneth Lovelace (gtr), J. W. Brown
(bass), Marty Morrison (org) Gene Fitzgerald? (dms), Atlanta James (Mack
Vickery) (harmonica), Bill Taylor (tpt), Mike Thomas (tpt) Russ Carlton
(sax).
(Also featured on this tape are Little Anthony & The Imperials, Rufus
Thomas, Freddy Cannon & Del Shannon).

THE LONDON ROCK 'N' ROLL SHOW (?)

Recorded at Wembley Stadium, London, 5.8.72.
Linda Gail Lewis (vcls), Kenneth Lovelace (gtr, vcls), Buddy Church (gtr),
Herman 'Hawk' Hawkins (bass,) Bill Strom (organ), Charlie Owens (steel
gtr), Jo Jo Tate (dms).

JERRY LEE LEWIS LIVE (CBS FOX 6340-50)

Recorded at The Hammersmith Odeon, London, 16.4.83
Kenneth Lovelace (gtr/fiddle), Joel Shumaker (gtr), Randy Wilkes (bass), Bill
Strom (organ), Ron Norwood (dms).

JERRY LEE LEWIS THE KILLER PERFORMANCE (VIRGIN VVD 053)

Features one song from the Steve Allen Show, 28.7.57, remainder recorded at
The Colston Hall, Bristol, 19.4.83
(Steve Allen show); J. W. Brown (bass), Russell Smith (dms).
(Bristol); Kenneth Lovelace (gtr/fiddle), Joel Shumaker (gtr), Randy Wilkes
(bass), Bill Strom (organ), Ron Norwood (dms).

WEMBLEY COUNTRY FESTIVALS (correct title??) (BBC video???)

Features selections from Jerry's appearances at The Wembley Country
Festivals, 17.4.81/11.4.XX/7.4.85. Also features Carl Perkins.
(17.4.81/11.4.82); Kenneth Lovelace (gtr/fiddle), Joel Shumaker (gtr), Randy
Wilkes (bass), Ron Norwood (dms).
(7.4.85); Kenneth Lovelace (gtr/fiddle), James Burton (gtr), Bob Moore
(bass), Buddy Harman (dms).

I AM WHAT I AM (CHARLY VIDJAM 21)

Documentary featuring archive footage + interviews.

FATS & FRIENDS (CHANNEL 5)

TV special recorded in New Orleans, 25.7.86. Also features Fats Domino & Ray Charles. Linda Gail Lewis (vcls), Kenneth Lovelace (gtr, vcls), Butch Baker (gtr), Ron Wood (gtr), Sugar Blue (gtr), Bob Moore (Bass), Buddy Harman (dms).

COUNTRY ROCKERS (PRISM PLA TV 354)

Filmed at Church Street Station, Orlando, Florida, 24.5.86.
Kenneth Lovelace (gtr/fiddle), Butch Baker (gtr), Unknown (bass), Buddy Harman (dms). (Also featured on this tape are Roger McGunn & Nitty Gritty Band).

THE KILLER LIVE! – JERRY LEE LEWIS & AN ALL STAR BAND! (TELSTAR)

Recorded at The Hammersmith Odeon, London, 21.11.89
Van Morrison (vcls, 1 song only), Kenneth Lovelace (gtr), James Burton (gtr), Dave Edmunds (gtr), Brian May (gtr), Stuart Adamson (gtr), Dave Davies (gtr), Phil Chen (bass), John Lodge (bass), Jim Isbell (dms).

LIVE KILLER (CHARLY VIDJAM 42)

Recorded at The Stockyard Lounge, Nashville, late March, 87 & at The Royal York Hotel, Toronto, May, 87.
(Nashville); Linda Gail Lewis (vcls), Kenneth Lovelace (gtr, vcls), Joel Shumaker (bass), Danny Harrison (dms), Moetta Stewart (organ/piano, vcls). (Toronto); Kenneth Lovelace (gtr, fiddle), Joel Shumaker (gtr), Duke Faglier (bass), Jim Isbell (dms).

JERRY LEE LEWIS – THE STORY OF ROCK 'N' ROLL (BMG VIDEO 791 096)

Documentary, includes clips from the following shows; The Steve Allen Show, 28.7.57, The Dewey Phillips Show, Dec. 57, Dick Clark's Beechnut Show, 15.2.58, Granada TV Special, 19.3.64, Shindig, 14.4.65, Shindig, 23.9.65, Toronto Peace Festival, 13.9.69.
Jerry is also featured on the following video releases;
The Best of American Bandstand Volume 1 (???) (Great balls of fire, Beechnut, 15.2.58) Ready Steady Go! Volume Two (MVP99 1002 2) (Whole lotta shakin' goin' on, 20.11.64) Ready Steady Go! Volume Three (MVP99 1006 2) (Hi-heel sneakers, 20.11.64).

THE JERRY LEE LEWIS SHOW, 71 (MAGNUM FORCE MMGV 030)

JERRY LEE LEWIS

The Radio Transcriptions

Editor: Charles White
European editor: Thomas Sobezak, Schanzenbarg 6, D-2060 Bad Oldesloe,
Germany.

Main source of information is from Austrian fan, Peter Molecz, who definitely
is the only one who possesses a complete collection of Jerry Lee Lewis radio
transcription discs.

Radio transcription discs are NOT bootlegs. They are specially made for disc
jockeys with the note 'FOR RADIO PLAY ONLY – NOT FOR SALE'. The
discs are pressed in small quantities and that is why they are so valuable for
record collectors. The sound quality is usually very good.

Some of the rare radio transcription discs are re-issued on bootleg albums
with poor sound quality. Uusually these bootlegs are incomplete.

JUNE 21-25, 1971 – Nashville, Tennessee

The Ralph Emery Show featuring guest star Jerry Lee Lewis
Producer: Show Biz, Inc., Nashville, Tennessee.
For Radio Play Only – Not For Sale

Different Interviews with Ralph Emery + announcements to the airplayed
songs by Jerry Lee Lewis
Show 1050-1054

SEPTEMBER 1, 1980 – Wheeling, WVA

Jamboree In The Hills – The Superball Of Country Music
Producer: Mutual Broadcasting System, Arlington, Virginia
For Radio Play Only – Not For Sale

Jerry Lee Lewis (vcl, pno)
Jerry Lee Lewis Band from 1980

Great Balls Of Fire/	Jamboree In The Hills/Labor Day 1980
Whole Lotta Shakin' Goin' On/	Jamboree In The Hills/Labor Day 1980
Country Music Is Here To Stay	Jamboree In The Hills/Labor Day 1980
Other Songs unknown and	
unreleased.	

LATE 1980/EARLY 1981 – Location unknown, prob. different shows Illinois and Merryville/Indiana

Producer: NBC Radio Network, two different discs
For Radio Play Only – Not For Sale

Jerry Lee Lewis (vcl/piano)
Jerry Lee Lewis Band from 1980, 1981

Rockin' My Life Away	Country Sessions Week 107, Week 18
Over The Rainbow	Country Sessions Week 107, Week 18
Tennessee Saturday Night	Country Sessions Week 107, Week 18
Georgia On My Mind	Country Sessions Week 107, Week 18
Drinkin' Wine Spo Dee O Dee	Country Sessions Week 107, Week 18
You Win Again	Country Sessions Week 107, Week 18
What'd I Say	Country Sessions Week 107, Week 18
Come On In	Country Sessions Week 18
Sweet Georgia Brown	Country Sessions Week 18
Send Me The Pillow That You Dream On	Country Sessions Week 107
There Must Be More To Love Than This	Country Sessions Week 107
Don't Be Cruel	Country Sessions Week 107
High School Confidential	Country Sessions Week 107, Week 18
Great Balls Of Fire	Country Sessions Week 107, Week 18
Whole Lotta Shakin' Goin' On/	Country Sessions Week 107, Week 18
Meat Man/	Country Sessions Week 107, Week 18
You Can Have Her/	Country Sessions Week 18
Good Golly Miss Molly	Country Sessions Week 18
Folsom Prison Blues	Country Sessions Week 18

JANUARY 3, 1981 – Gilley's Club, Pasadena, Texas

Producer: Westwood One, Culver City, CA.
For Radio Play Only – Not For Sale

Jerry Lee Lewis (vcl, pno)
Jerry Lee Lewis Band from 1981

Rockin' My Life Away	Live From Gilley's Show 81 08
You Win Again	Live From Gilley's Show 81 08
Who Will The Next Fool Be	Live From Gilley's Show 81 08
Another Place Another Time	Live From Gilley's Show 81 08
What'd I Say	Live From Gilley's Show 81 08

Middle Age Crazy	Live From Gilley's Show 81 08
I'll Find It Where I Can	Live From Gilley's Show 81 08
Good News Travels Fast	Live From Gilley's Show 81 08
Sweet Little Sixteen	Live From Gilley's Show 81 08
Blue Suede Shoes	Live From Gilley's Show 81 08
No Headstone On My Grave	Live From Gilley's Show 81 08
Harbour Lights	Live From Gilley's Show 81 08
I'm So Lonesome I Could Cry	Live From Gilley's Show 81 08
Rockin' Jerry Lee	Live From Gilley's Show 81 08

Note: There exists a bootleg release of this show, but the sound quality is poor in comparison to the original disc.

APRIL 17, 1981 – Wembley Arena, London, England

The International Festival Of Country Music 1981
Producer: Mutual Broadcasting System, Arlington, Virginia
For Radio Play Only – Not For Sale

Jerry Lee Lewis (cl, pno)
Jerry Lee Lewis Band from 1981

Keep My Motor Running	Int. Festival Of Country Music 1981
Middle Age Crazy	Unreleased
What'd I Say	Int. Festival Of Country Music 1981
Over The Rainbow	Unreleased
Folsom Prison Blues	Unreleased
High School Confidential	Int. Festival Of Country Music 1981
Thirty Nine And Holding	Unreleased
Great Balls Of Fire	Int. Festival Of Country Music 1981
Whole Lotta Shakin' Goin' On	Unreleased
Matchbox/Blue Suede Shoes	Int. Festival Of Country Music 1981

DECEMBER 3, 1981 – Opryland, Nashville, Tennessee

Silver Eagle Cross Country Music Show
Producer: ABC Radio Networks, DIR Broadcasting Corp., New York
For Radio Play Only – Not For Sale

Jerry Lee Lewis (vcl, pno)
Jerry Lee Lewis Band from 1981

Good News Travels Fast	Silver Eagle, February 6, 1982
Memory Number One	Silver Eagle, February 6, 1982
There Stands The Glass	Silver Eagle, February 6, 1982

Middle Age Crazy	Silver Eagle, February 6, 1982
Chantilly Lace	Silver Eagle, February 6, 1982
What'd I Say	Silver Eagle, February 6, 1982
You Win Again	Silver Eagle February 6, 1982
You Are The One Rose	Silver Eagle, February 6, 1982
Great Balls Of Fire	Silver Eagle, February 6, 1982
Let's Have A Party/Jailhouse Rock	Silver Eagle, February 6, 1982
When Two Worlds Collide	Silver Eagle, February 6, 1982
Over The Rainbow	Silver Eagle, February 6, 1982
Hadacol Boogie	Silver Eagle, February 6, 1982
White Christmas/Blue Christmas	Silver Eagle, February 6, 1982
Mexicali Rose	Silver Eagle, February 6, 1982
Rockin' My Life Away	Silver Eagle, February 6, 1982
Whole Lotta Shakin' Goin' On	Silver Eagle, February 6, 1982
Good Golly Miss Molly/Tutti Frutti	Silver Eagle, February 6, 1982
	Note: There exists a bootleg release of only a part of this show, but the sound quality of the bootleg is very poor in comparison to the original disc.

APRIL 11, 1982 – Wembley Arena, London, England

The International Festival Of Country Music 1982
Producer: Mutual Broadcasting System, Arlington, Virginia
Airplay Weekend of October 30-31, 1982
For Radio Play Only – Not For Sale

Jerry Lee Lewis (vcl, pno)
Jerry Lee Lewis Band from 1982

Rockin' My Life Away	Int. Festival Of Country Music 1982
You Are The One Rose	Unreleased
Thirty Nine And Holding	Int. Festival Of Country Music 1982
You Win Again	Int. Festival Of Country Music 1982
Me And Bobby McGee	Unreleased
Good News Travels Fast	Int. Festival Of Country Music 1982
Georgia On My Mind	Unreleased
What'd I Say	Int. Festival Of Country Music 1982
C.C. Rider	Unreleased
She Even Woke Me Up To Say Goodbye	Unreleased
Would You Take Another Chance On Me	Unreleased

Pick Me Up On Your Way Down	Unreleased
Drinkin' Wine Spo Dee O Dee	Int. Festival Of Country Music 1982
Old Black Joe	Unreleased
Chantilly Lace	Unreleased
I'm So Lonesome I Could Cry	Int. Festival Of Country Music 1982
Great Balls Of Fire	Int. Festival Of Country Music 1982
Whole Lotta Shakin' Goin' On/	Unreleased
You Can Have Her	Unreleased
	Note: The original US radio transcription disc includes also interviews with Jerry Lee Lewis by DJ Lee Arnold.

JUNE 1982 – Gilley's Club, Pasadena, Texas

Producer: Westwood One, Culver City, CA.
For Radio Play Only – Not For Sale

Jerry Lee Lewis (vcl, pno)
Jerry Lee Lewis Band from 1982

Rockin' My Life Away	Live From Gilley's Show 82 33
No Headstone On My Grave	Live From Gilley's Show 82 33
Help Me Make It Through The Night	Live From Gilley's Show 82 33
Me And Bobby McGee	Live From Gilley's Show 82 33
I Can Still Hear The Music In The Restroom	Live From Gilley's Show 82 33
My Fingers Do The Talkin'	Live From Gilley's Show 82 33
Great Balls Of Fire	Live From Gilley's Show 82 33
Whole Lotta Shakin' Goin' On	Live From Gilley's Show 82 33
	Note: Whole Lotta Shakin' Going On is a duet with Jerry's cousin Mickey Gilley; at the time of writing this is the only duet beween Jerry and Mickey released on disc.

NOVEMBER 27, 1982 – Orpyland, Nashville, Tennesse

The Silver Eagle Cross Country Music Show ("MCA Show")
Producer: ABC Radio Networks, DIR Broadcasting Corp., New York
For Radio Play Only – Not For Sale

Jerry Lee Lewis (vcl, pno)

Jerry Lee Lewis Band from 1982

Rockin' My Life Away	Silver Eagle, November 27, 1982
Who Will The Next Fool Be	Silver Eagle, November 27, 1982
Boogie Woogie Country Man	Silver Eagle, November 27, 1982
She Even Woke Me Up To Say Goodbye	Silver Eagle, November 27, 1982
C.C. Rider	Silver Eagle, November 27, 1982
Chantilly Lace	Silver Eagle, November 27, 1982
She Sure Makes Leaving Look Easy	Silver Eagle, November 27, 1982
Middle Age Crazy	Silver Eagle, November 27, 1982
Thirty Nine And Holding	Silver Eagle, November 27, 1982
Great Balls Of Fire	Silver Eagle, November 27, 1982
When I Take My Vacation In Heaven/	Silver Eagle, November 27, 1982
Mama, This One's For You	Silver Eagle, November 27, 1982
Whole Lotta Shakin' Goin' On/	Silver Eagle, November 27, 1982
Meat Man	Silver Eagle, November 27, 1982

Note: There was another Silver Eagle Country Music Show released in 1983 featuring 'Jerry Lee Lewis Live From The New York Ritz Hotel', but this show is only a mixture of parts from both Nashville Shows.

APRIL 29, 1983 – Fort Worth, Texas

Producer: Mutual Broadcasting System, Arlington, Virginia
For Radio Play Only – Not For Sale

Jerry Lee Lewis (vcl, pno)
Jerry Lee Lewis Band from 1983

I Don't Want To Be Lonely Tonight	Lee Arnold On A Country Road, Weekend Of May 28, 1983
You Win Again	Lee Arnold On A Country Road, Weekend Of May 28, 1983
Middle Age Crazy	Lee Arnold On A Country Road, Weekend Of May 28, 1983
I Can't Help It	Lee Arnold On A Country Road, Weekend Of May 28, 1983
Keep My Motor Running	Lee Arnold On A Country Road, Weekend Of May 28, 1983

Pledging My Love	Lee Arnold On A Country Road, Weekend Of May 28, 1983
Thirty Nine And Holding	Lee Arnold On A Country Road, Weekend Of May 28, 1983
Chantilly Lace	Lee Arnold On A Country Road, Weekend Of May 28, 1983
She Even Woke Me Up To Say Goodbye	Lee Arnold On A Country Road, Weekend Of May 28, 1983
Sweet Georgia Brown	Lee Arnold On A Country Road, Weekend Of May 28, 1983
Drinkin' Wine Spo Dee O Dee	Lee Arnold On A Country Road, Weekend Of May 28, 1983
Whole Lotta Shakin' Goin' On/	Lee Arnold On A Country Road, Weekend Of May 28, 1983
Meat Man	Lee Arnold On A Country Road, Weekend Of May 28, 1983

Note: This is probably the rarest of all Jerry Lee Lewis radio shows. The sound quality of the original disc is perfect.

APRIL 30, 1983 – Gilley's Club, Pasadena, Texas

Producer: Westwood One, Culver City, CA.
For Radio Play Only – Not For Sale

Jerry Lee Lewis (vcl, pno)
Jerry Lee Lewis Band from 1983

I Don't Want To Be Lonely Tonight	Live From Gilley's Show 83 24
Rockin' Jerry Lee	Live From Gilley's Show 83 24
Trouble in Mind	Live From Gilley's Show 83 24
Crazy Arms	Live From Gilley's Show 83 24
Chantilly Lace	Live From Gilley's Show 83 24
Georgia On My Mind	Live From Gilley's Show 83 24
Tennessee Saturday Night	Live From Gilley's Show 83 24
Keep My Motor Running	Live From Gilley's Show 83 24
You Win Again	Live From Gilley's Show 83 24
Drinkin' Wine Spo Dee O Dee	Live From Gilley's Show 83 24
Middle Age Crazy	Live From Gilley's Show 83 24
Sweet Georgia Brown	Live From Gilley's Show 83 24
Rockin' My Life Away	Live From Gilley's Show 83 24
Great Balls Of Fire	Live From Gilley's Show 83 24
Whole Lotta Shakin' Goin' On	Live From Gilley's Show 83 24

MARCH 1984 – Gilley's Club, Pasadena, Texas

Producer: Westwood One, Culver City, CA.
For Radio Play Only – Not For Sale

Jerry Lee Lewis (vcl, pno)
Jerry Lee Lewis Band from 1984

Drinkin' Wine Spo Dee O Dee	Live From Gilley's Show 84 19
Over The Rainbow	Live From Gilley's Show 84 19
You Win Again	Live From Gilley's Show 84 19
Middle Age Crazy	Live From Gilley's Show 84 19
Sweet Little Sixteen	Live From Gilley's Show 84 19
No Headstone On My Grave	Live From Gilley's Show 84 19
Chantilly Lace	Live From Gilley's Show 84 19
I Am What I Am	Live From Gilley's Show 84 19
C.C. Rider	Live From Gilley's Show 84 19
Great Balls Of Fire	Live From Gilley's Show 84 19
Whole Lotta Shakin' Goin' On	Live From Gilley's Show 84 19

Note: There exists a bootleg release of this show. The sound quality of the bootleg is very good but the sound of the original disc is even slightly better.

AUGUST/SEPTEMBER 1984 – Gilley's Club, Pasadena, Texas

Producer: Westwood One, Culver City, CA.
For Radio Play Only – Not For Sale

Jerry Lee Lewis (vcl, pno)
Jerry Lee Lewis Band from 1984

Rockin' My Life Away	Live From Gilley's Show 84 42
Rock And Roll Money	Live From Gilley's Show 84 42
Who Will The Next Fool Be	Live From Gilley's Show 84 42
Chantilly Lace	Live From Gilley's Show 84 42
Over The Rainbow	Live From Gilley's Show 84 42
Room Full Of Roses	Live From Gilley's Show 84 42
Who's Gonna Play This Old Piano	Live From Gilley's Show 84 42
Middle Age Crazy	Live From Gilley's Show 84 42
I'm Looking Over A Four Leaf Clover	Live From Gilley's Show 84 42
Thirty Nine And Holding	Live From Gilley's Show 84 42
Boogie Woogie Country Man	Live From Gilley's Show 84 42
Great Balls Of Fire	Live From Gilley's Show 84 42

Whole Lotta Shakin' Goin' On
Live From Gilley's Show 84 42
Note: There exists a bootleg release of this show. The sound quality of the bootleg is very good but the sound of the original disc is even slightly better.

SEPTEMBER 1984 – E.M. Loew's Theatre, Worcester, Mass.

The Silver Eagle Cross Counry Music Show
Producer: ABC Radio Networks, DIR Broadcasting Corp., New York
For Radio Play Only – Not For Sale

Jerry Lee Lewis (vcl, pno)
Jerry Lee Lewis Band from 1984

Rockin' My Life Away	Silver Eagle 178, December 8, 1984
C.C. Rider	Silver Eagle 178, December 8, 1984
Good News Travels Fast	Silver Eagle 178, December 8, 1984
Georgia On My Mind	Silver Eagle 178, December 8, 1984
Circumstantial Evidence	Silver Eagle 178, December 8, 1984
How Great Thou Art	Silver Eagle 178, December 8, 1984
I Saw The Light	Silver Eagle 178, December 8, 1984
Coming Back For More	Silver Eagle 178, December 8, 1984
Let's Talk About Us	Silver Eagle 178, December 8, 1984
Careless Hands	Silver Eagle 178, December 8, 1984
Who Will The Next Fool Be	Silver Eagle 178, December 8, 1984
Chantilly Lace	Silver Eagle 178, December 8, 1984
You Are The One Rose	Silver Eagle 178, December 8, 1984
Mean Woman Blues	Silver Eagle 178, December 8, 1984
You Win Again	Silver Eagle 178, December 8, 1984
Sweet Little Sixteen	Silver Eagle 178, December 8, 1984
Over The Rainbow	Silver Eagle 178, December 8, 1984
Who's Gonna Play This Old Piano	Silver Eagle 178, December 8, 1984
Lucille	Silver Eagle 178, December 8, 1984
Great Balls Of Fire	Silver Eagle 178, December 8, 1984
Silver Eagle 178, December 8, 1984	
Meat Man	Silver Eagle 178, December 8, 1984

Note: There exists a bootleg release of this show. The sound quality of the bootleg is extremely poor in comparison to the original disc.

FEBRUARY 28, 1986 – Palomino Club, Hollwood, California

Producer: Westwood One, Culver City, CA.

For Radio Play Only – Not For Sale

Jerry Lee Lewis (vcl, pno)
Jerry Lee Lewis Band from 1986

Lewis Boogie	Live From Gilley's 86 13
Brown Eyed Handsome Man	Live From Gilley's 86 13
Over The Rainbow	Live From Gilley's 86 13
She Even Woke Me Up To Say Goodbye	Live From Gilley's 86 13
Great Balls Of Fire (slow)	Live From Gilley's 86 13
High Heel Sneakers	Live From Gilley's 86 13
Chantilly Lace	Live From Gilley's 86 13
Think About It Darling	Live From Gilley's 86 13
Sweet Georgia Brown	Live From Gilley's 86 13
Memphis Tennessee	Live From Gilley's 86 13
Great Balls Of Fire (fast)	Live From Gilley's 86 13
Whole Lotta Shakin' Goin' On	Live From Gilley's 86 13

Note: There exists a bootleg release of this show. The sound quality of the bootleg is very good but the sound of the original disc is even slightly better.

OCTOBER 1987 – Gilley's Club, Pasadena, Texas

Producer: Westwood One, Culver City, CA.
For Radio Play Only – Not For Sale

Jerry Lee Lewis (vcl, pno)
Jerry Lee Lewis Band from 1987

Roll Over Beethoven	Live From Gilley's 88 28
You Win Again	Live From Gilley's 88 28
Sweet Little Sixteen	Live From Gilley's 88 28
Another Place, Another Time	Live From Gilley's 88 28
High School Confidential	Live From Gilley's 88 28
Me And Bobby McGee	Live From Gilley's 88 28
She Even Woke Me Up To Say Goodbye	Live From Gilley's 88 28
Chantilly Lace	Unreleased
What'd I Say	Unreleased
Trouble In Mind	Unreleased
Coming Back For More	Unreleased
Corrine, Corrina	Unreleased
Cold Cold Heart	Unreleased

Great Balls Of Fire   Unreleased
Lucille   Unreleased
Whole Lotta Shakin' Goin' On   Unreleased

CHART POSITIONS

U.S.A. POP

Debut date	Peak pos.	Wks chr.	Title	Label & number
24 Jun '57	3	29	Whole lotta shakin' goin' on Best seller No. 3/Top 100 No. 3/ Jockey No. 9	Sun 267
25 Nov '57	2	21	Great balls of fire Best seller No. 2/Top 100 No. 2/ Jockey No. 9	Sun 281
17 Feb '58	95	1	You win again	Sun 281
3 Mar '58	7	15	Breathless Best seller No. 9/Top 100 No. 7/ Jockey No. 23	Sun 288
2 June '58	21	11	High school confidential Best seller No. 22/Top 100 No. 21	Sun 296
15 Sep '58	52	5	Break up/	
8 Sep '58	85	1	I'll make it all up to you	Sun 303
19 Jan '59	93	1	I'll sail my ship alone	Sun 312
3 Apr '61	30	8	What'd I say	Sun 356
15 Sep '62	95	3	Sweet little sixteen	Sun 379
11 Apr '64	98	1	I'm on fire	Smash 1886
21 Nov '64	91	1	High heel sneakers	Smash 1930
30 Mar '68	97	2	Another place another time	Smash 2146
6 Jul '68	94	3	What's made Milwaukee famous (has made a loser out of me)	Smash 2164
27 Nov '71	40	10	Me and Bobby McGee	Mercury 73248
4 Mar '72	43	10	Chantilly lace	Mercury 73273
22 Jul '72	95	3	Turn on your love light	Mercury 73296
7 Apr '73	41	10	Drinking wine spo-dee-o-dee	Mercury 73374

RHYTHM & BLUES SINGLES

Date	Pos.	Wks.	Title	Label & number
24 Aug '57	1	8	Whole lotta shakin' goin' on	Sun 267
30 Nov '57	3	12	Great balls of fire	Sun 281
8 Mar '58	5	7	Breathless	Sun 288
14 Jun '58	16	4	High school confidential	Sun 296
29 May '61	26	1	What'd I say	Sun 356

COUNTRY CHARTS

Debut date	Peak pos.	Wks chr.	Title	Pop pos.	Label & number
17 Jun '57	1	23	Whole lotta shakin' goin' on Best seller No. 1/Jockey No. 6	3	Sun 267
2 Dec '57	1	19	Great balls of fire Best seller No. 1/Jockey No. 4	2	
23 Dec '57	2	10	You win again Best seller No. 2/Jockey No. 4	95	Sun 281
17 Mar '58	4	13	Breathless Best seller No. 4/Jockey No. 12	7	Sun 288
9 June '58	9	10	High school confidential Best seller No. 9	21	Sun 296
13 Oct '58	19	1	I'll make it all up to you Best seller No. 19	85	Sun 303
8 May '61	27	1	What'd I say	30	Sun 356
7 Aug '61	22	5	Cold cold heart		Sun 364
1 Feb '64	36	2	Pen and paper flip side 'Hit the road Jack' No. 103 on the pop charts		Smash 1857
9 Mar '68	4	17	Another place another time	97	Smash 2164
8 Jun '68	2	16	What's made Milwaukee famous (has made a loser out of me)	94	Smash 2164
28 Sep '68	2	12	She still comes around (to love what's left of me)		Smash 2186
28 Dec '68	1	15	To make love sweeter for you		Smash 2202
24 May '69	9	11	Don't let me cross over Jerry Lee Lewis & Linda Gail Lewis		Smash 2220
31 May '69	3	15	One has my name (the other has my heart)		Smash 2224

16 Aug '69	6	12	Invitation to your party		Sun 1101
4 Oct '69	2	13	She even woke me up to say goodbye		Smash 2244
29 Nov '69	2	16	One minute past eternity		Sun 1107
10 Jan '70	71	2	Roll over Beethoven		Smash 2254

Jerry Lee Lewis & Linda Gail Lewis

No. 29 pop hit for Chuck Berry in '56

21 Feb '70	2	14	Once more with feeling		Smash 2257
25 Apr '70	7	15	I can't seem to say goodbye		Sun 1115
22 Aug '70	1	15	There must be more to love than this		Mercury 73099
21 Nov '70	11	12	Waiting for a train (all around the watertank)		Sun 1119

No. 14 pop hit for Jimmie Rodgers in '29

30 Jan '71	48	8	In loving memories		Mercury 73155
27 Mar '71	3	6	Touching home	110	Mercury 73192
26 Jun '71	31	9	Love on Broadway		Sun 1125
24 July '71	11	13	When he walks on you (like you have walked on me)		Mercury 73227
6 Nov '71	1	17	Would you take another chance on me/		
		15	Me and Bobby McGee	40	Mercury 73248
11 Mar '72	1	15	Chantilly lace	43	

No. 6 pop hit for Big Boppa in '58

		15	Think about it darlin'		Mercury 73272
17 Jun '72	11	11	Lonely weekend		Mercury 73296

flip side 'Turn on your lover light' hit No. 95 in pop charts

7 Oct '72	14	13	Who's gonna play this old piano		Mercury 73328

17 Feb '73	19	10	No more hanging on		Mercury 73361
21 Apr '73	20	11	Drinking wine spo-dee-o-dee	41	Mercury 73374
			No. 2 R&B hit for Stick McGhee in '49		
4 Aug '73	60	6	No headstone on my grave	104	Mercury 73402
29 Sep '73	6	14	Sometimes a memory ain't enough		Mercury 73402
9 Feb '74	21	12	I'm left, you're right, she's gone		Mercury 73452
			recorded by Elvis Presley in '55		
22 Jun '74	18	12	Tell tale signs		Mercury 73491
19 Oct '74	8	12	He can't fill my shoes		Mercury 73618
22 Feb '75	13	12	I can still hear the music in the restroom		Mercury 73661
28 Jun '75	24	13	Boogie Woogie Country Man		Mercury 73685
6 Dec '75	68	5	A damn good country song		Mercury 73729
14 Feb '76	58	6	Don't boogie woogie		Mercury 73763
7 Aug '76	6	15	Let's put it back together again		Mercury 73822
18 Dec '76	27	11	The closest thing to you		Mercury 73872
29 Oct '77	4	18	Middle age crazy		Mercury 55011
			title of 1980 film based on this song		
11 Mar '78	10	12	Come on in		Mercury 55021
24 Jun '78	10	12	I'll find it where I can		Mercury 55028
15 Dec '78	26	13	Save the last dance for me		Sun 1139
7 Apr '79	84	3	Cold, cold heart		Sun 1141
7 Apr '79	18	11	Rockin' my life away / I wish I was eighteen again	101	Elektra 46030

21 Jul '79	20	11	Who will the next fool be	Elektra 46067
9 Feb '80	1	12	When two worlds collide	Elektra 46591
24 May '80	28	12	Honky tonk stuff	Elektra 46642
6 Sep '80	10	12	Over the rainbow	Elektra 47026
17 Jan '81	4	15	Thirty nine and holding	Elektra 47095
24 Apr '82	43	11	I'm so lonesome I could cry	Mercury 76148
25 Sep '82	52	7	I'd do it all again	Elektra 69962
18 Dec '82	44	10	My fingers do the talkin'	MCA 52151
19 Mar '83	66	6	Come as you were	MCA 52188
9 Jul '83	65	5	Why you been gone so long	MCA 52233
23 Aug '86	61	6	Sixteen candles	Amer.S.884934

USA ALBUM CHARTS

Date chart'd	Peak pos.	Wks. chart'd	Album title	Label & number
28 Jan '64	116	8	The golden hits of Jerry Lee Lewis	Smash 67040
5 Dec '64	71	17	The greatest live show on earth	Smash 67056
5 Jun '65	121	5	The return of rock	Smash 67063
14 May '66	145	3	Memphis beat	Smash 67079
29 Jun '68	160	12	Another place another time	Smash 67104
8 Feb '69	149	7	She still comes around (to love what's left of me)	Smash 67112
10 May '69	127	10	Jerry Lee Lewis sings the Country Music Hall of Fame, Vol. 1	Smash 67117
10 May '69	127	10	Jerry Lee Lewis sings the Country Music Hall of Fame, Vol. 2	Smash 67118
27 Sep '69	119	4	Original golden hits – Vol. 1	Sun 102
27 Sep '69	122	5	Original golden hits – Vol. 2	Sun 103
28 Feb '70	186	2	She even woke me up to say goodbye	Smash 67128
9 May '70	114	14	The best of Jerry Lee Lewis	Smash 67131
10 Oct '70	149	6	Live at the International, Las Vegas	Mercury 61278
30 Jan '71	190	6	There must be more to love than this	Mercury 61323
24 Jul '71	152	3	Touching home	Mercury 61343
27 Nov '71	115	12	Would you take another chance on me?	Mercury 61346

22 Apr '72	105	12	The 'Killer' rocks on		Mercury 637
17 Mar '73	37	19	The session		Mercury 803(2)
28 Apr '79	186	3	Jerry Lee Lewis		Elektra 184

UK SINGLES

Date	Pos.	Wks.	Title	Label
27 Sep '57	8	10	Whole lotta shakin' goin' on	London HLS.8457
20 Dec '57	1	12	Great balls of fire	London HLS.8529
27 Dec '57	26	1	Whole lotta shakin' goin' on (re-entry)	London HLS.8457
11 Apr '58	8	7	Breathless	London HLS.8592
23 Jan '59	12	6	High school confidential	London HLS.8780
1 May '59	28	1	Lovin' up a storm	London HLS.8840
9 Jun '60	47	1	Baby baby bye bye	London HLS.9131
4 May '61	10	12	What'd I say	London HLS.9335
3 Aug '61	49	2	What'd I say (re-entry)	London HLS.9335
6 Sep '62	38	5	Sweet little sixteen	London HLS.9584
14 Mar '63	31	6	Good golly Miss Molly	London HLS.9688
6 May '72	33	5	Chantilly lace	Mercury 6052 141

Bibliography

by
Chas 'Dr Rock' White and Professor B. Lee Cooper

Much has been written about Jerry Lee Lewis. The most comprehensive source of day-to-day photographs, concert reviews, interviews, newspaper clippings, magazine articles, record reviews and other print items is Wim de Boer's bi-monthly *Fire-Ball Mail*. This slim magazine has been the keeper of Jerry Lee's literary flame since 1962. The following bibliography selects the most popular, most influential and most available print resources on the personal life and professional music career of 'The Killer'.

Sun Records: The Memphis Launching Pad

Barbara Barnes, 'Sun Records: An Insider's View', *New Kommotion*, II (Spring 1977), pp.30–31.

Robert Becker, 'The Sun Sound', *Record Exchanger*, III (February 1973), pp. 12–14.

B. Lee Cooper and James A. Creeth, 'Present At the Creation: The Legend Of Jerry Lee Lewis On Record, 1956-1963', *Fire-Ball Mail*, XXII (May/June 1984), pp. 9–12.

Peter Doggett, 'Sun Records: The Golden Years', *Record Collector*, No. 92 (April 1987), pp. 24–25.

Peter Doggett, 'Sun Records On CD', *Record Collector* No. 95 (July 1987), pp. 15–18.

Colin Escott and Martin Hawkins, *Sun Records: The Brief History Of The Legendary Record Label*. New York: Quick Fox, 1980.

Colin Escott and Martin Hawkins (comps), *Sun Records: The Discography*. Bremen, West Germany: Bear Family Records, 1987.

Robert Finnis, 'The Rise and Set of Sun', *Rock*, XI (December 14, 1970), pp. 9–10, 31.

Peter Guralnick, 'The Million Dollar Quartet', *New York Times Magazine*, (25 March 1979), pp. 28–30, 41–45.

Claude Hall, 'Phillips, Presley, Cash, Sun', *Billboard*, LXXXI (27 December 1969), p. 110.

Cub Koda, 'The Rockin' Sun Year: Sumpin' for Cool-In-The-Know Folks', *Goldmine*, No. 182 (17 July 1982), pp. 78–79.

Cub Koda, 'The Sun Blues Box: A Killer By Any Standard', *Goldmine*, No. 151 (9 May 1986), pp. 68, 70.

'Memphis Spurs Country/Blues Merger', *Billboard*, LXXXI (29 March 1969), p. 24.

John Pugh, 'Rise and Fall of Sun Records', *Country Music*, II (November 1973), pp. 26–32.

Joe Sasfy, 'Sunrise At Memphis', *Musician*, No. 88 (February 1986) pp. 96–100, 110.

Paul Vernon, *The Sun Legend*. London: Steve Lane, 1969.

Biographical Studies

Robert Cain, *Whole Lotta Shakin' Goin' On: Jerry Lee Lewis – The Rock Years, The Country Years, The Triumphs, And The Tragedies*. New York: Dial Press, 1981.

Alan Clark, *Jerry Lee Lewis: The Ball of Fire*. West Covina, California: Alan Clark Productions, 1980.

Colin Escott, *Jerry Lee Lewis: The Killer 1953–1968*. Bremen, West Germany: Bear Family Records, 1986.

Colin Escott, *Jerry Lee Lewis: The Killer 1973–1977*. Bremen, West Germany: Bear Family Records, 1987.

Tania A. LeFebvre, *Jerry Lee Lewis: The Killer's Story*. Paris, France: Horus Books, 1980.

Myra Lewis, with Murray Silver, *Great Balls of Fire: The Uncensored Story of Jerry Lee Lewis*. New York: Quill Books, 1982.

Robert Palmer, *Jerry Lee Lewis Rocks!* New York: Delilah Books, 1981.

Nick Tosches, *Hellfire: The Jerry Lee Lewis Story*, New York: Dell Publishing Company, Inc., 1982.

Articles and Essays

Stuart Colman, 'Jerry Lee Lewis: The Killer Himself', in *They Kept On Rockin': The Giants Of Rock 'N' Roll* (Poole, Dorset, England: Blandford Press, 1982), pp. 53–65.

Phil Cook, 'Jerry Lee Lewis,' *Record Collector*, No. 17 (January 1981), pp. 13–19.

B. Lee Cooper, 'Jerry Lee Lewis And Little Richard: Career Parallels In The Lives Of The Court Jesters Of Rock 'N' Roll', *Music World And Record Digest*, No. 46 (23 May 1979), p. 6.

B. Lee Cooper, 'Jerry Lee Lewis: Rock 'N' Roll's Living Legend', *Music World*, No. 90 (October 1981), pp. 28–36.

Howard Elson, 'Jerry Lee Lewis', in *Early Rockers* (New York: Proteus Books, 1982), pp. 78–89.

Colin Escott and Martin Hawkins, 'Jerry Lee Lewis' and 'The Lewis Style', in *Sun Records: The Brief History Of The Legendary Record Label* (New York: Quick Fox, 1980), pp. 103–108 and 109–115.

Paul Gambaccini, 'Jerry Lee Lewis', in *Track Records: Profiles Of 22 Rock Stars* (North Pomfret, Vermont: David and Charles, 1986), pp. 93–100.

Ren Grevatt, 'Jerry Lee Lewis Is The Wildest Of Them All!', *Melody Maker*, XXXIII (25 January 1958), pp. 8–9.

John Grissim, 'Jerry Lee Lewis: Higher Than Most . . . And Getting Higher', *Rolling Stone*, No. 66 (17 September 1970), pp. 30–33.

John Grissim, 'Whole Lotta Shakin' At the D.J. Hop', in *Country Music: White Man's Blues* (New York: Paperback Library, 1970), pp. 271–296.

Peter Guralnick, 'Jerry Lee Lewis: The Greatest Rocker Of Them All', *Fire-Ball Mail*, XXII (January/February 1984), pp.10–11.

Peter Guralnick, 'Jerry Lee Lewis: Hang Up My Rock 'N' Roll Shoes', in *Feel Like Coming Home: Portraits In Blues And Rock 'N' Roll* (New York: Outerbridge and Dienstfrey, 1971), pp.146–162.

John Hubner, 'Jerry Lee Lewis', *Goldmine*, No. 62 (July 1981), pp.23–25.

Mark Humphrey, 'Jerry Lee Lewis: Where The Lord And The Devil Both Have Their Way', *Esquire*, XCVII (June 1982), pp. 106–108.

Bob Kinder, 'Jerry Lee Lewis', *Record Exchanger*, No. 21 (1975), pp. 4–11.

Bill Littleton, 'Jerry Lee Lewis: There's Still "A Whole Lotta Shakin' Goin' On"', *Country Style*, No.69 (August 1981), pp. 28–31.

Jim Miller, 'Jerry Lee Lewis', in *The Rolling Stone Illustrated History of Rock 'N' Roll*, revised edition (New York: Random House/Rolling Stone Press Book, 1980), pp. 66–71.

Steve Scott, 'Jerry Lee Lewis', *Record Collector*, No. 41 (January 1983), pp. 20–26.

David Seay, 'The King and the Killer', in *Stairway to Heaven: The Spiritual Roots Of Rock 'N' Roll From The King And Little Richard To Prince And Amy Grant* (New York: Ballantine Books, 1986), pp. 45–69.

Arnold Shaw, 'Jerry Lee Lewis Interview', in *The Rockin' 50's: The Decade That Transformed The Pop Music Scene* (New York: Hawthorn Books, 1974), pp. 190–193.

Murray M. Silver, Jnr., 'Jerry Lee Lewis Update: Dubs, Recent Discoveries, And Black Waxen Frisbees', *Goldmine*, No. 71 (April 1982), pp. 178–179.

Irwin Stambler, 'Jerry Lee Lewis', in *The Encyclopaedia Of Pop, Rock And Soul* (New York: St Martin's Press, 1974), pp. 306–308.

Nick Tosches, 'Behold A Shaking: Jerry Lee Lewis, 1953–1956', *Journal Of Country Music*, IX (October 1981), pp. 4–11.

Nick Tosches, 'The Coming of Jerry Lee Lewis', *Journal Of Country Music*, IX, No. 2 (1982), pp. 16–25.

Nick Tosches, 'Loud Covenants', in *Country: The Biggest Music In America* (New York: Dell Publishing Company, Inc., 1977), pp. 23–97.

Nick Tosches, 'Nashville Babylon – Loud Covenants: Jerry Lee Lewis, God's Garbage Man', *Creem*, IX (March 1978), pp. 48–51 ff.

Nick Tosches, 'Whole Lotta Shakin' Goin' On', *Goldmine*, No. 76 (September 1982), p. 19.

Stephen R. Tucker, 'Pentecostalism And Popular Culture In The South: A Study Of Four Musicians', *Journal Of Popular Culture*, XVI (Winter 1982), pp. 68–80.

Cliff White, 'The Killer Speaks: An Interview', *New Kommotion*, No. 24 (1980), pp. 22–24.

Timothy White, 'Jerry Lee Lewis', in *Rock Stars* (New York: Stewart, Tabori and Chang, 1984), pp. 66–71.

Bill Williams, 'Jerry Lee Lewis: Super Showman/Paradox', *Billboard*, (31 March 1973), pp. 39–46.

Interviews and Commentaries

Robert Cain, 'Steve Allen: An Interview', 'Mickey Gilley: An Interview', 'Sun Records Today: An Interview With Shelby Singleton', 'Tom Jones And The "Killer": An Interview', and 'The Country Years: An Interview With Jerry Kennedy', in *Whole Lotta Shakin' Goin' On: Jerry Lee Lewis – The Rock Years, The Country Years, The Triumphs And The Tragedies* (New York: Dial Press, 1981), pp. 61–69, 35–40, 103–108, 109–113, and 115–126.

Ben Ferguson, 'Speaking to The Killer: Jerry Lee Lewis Interview', *Paperback Writer*, I (July 1979), p.8.

Dan Forte, 'Kenny Lovelace: Two Decades With Jerry Lee Lewis', *Guitar Players*, XVII (December 1983), pp. 80–82, 154.

Bill Fugate and Jerry Lee Lewis, 'Much Too Much', *Bop*, No. 1 (1982), pp. 32–37.

Bill Kaval, 'Exclusive Interview', *Music World And Record Digest*, No. 41 (May 16, 1979), p. 1.

Jerry P. Osborrne and Shelby Singleton, 'Million Dollar Quartet!', in

Our Best To You – From Record Digest (Prescott, Arizona: O'Sullivan, Woodside and Company, 1981), pp. 39–44.

Nick Tosches, 'Linda Gail Lewis', *Goldmine*, No. 67 (December 1981), p. 162.

Book Reviews

Jay Cocks, 'A Few Rounds With The Killer', *Time*, CXXI (14 March 1983), p. 98.

B. Lee Cooper, 'In Search Of Jerry Lee Lewis', *JEFM Quarterly*, XVIII (Fall 1982/Winter 1983), pp. 192–193.

B. Lee Cooper, 'Review of *Whole Lotta Shakin' Goin' On: Jerry Lee Lewis Rocks* by Robert Palmer; *Hellfire: The Jerry Lee Lewis Story* by Nick Tosches; and *Great Balls Of Fire: The Uncensored Story of Jerry Lee Lewis* by Myra Lewis, with Murray Silver', *American Music*, III (Summer 1985), pp. 236–238.

Robert Hilburn, 'Review of Three Books About Jerry Lee Lewis', *Journal of Country Music*, IX, No. 2 (1982), pp. 126–129.

Jack Hurst, 'Child Bride Tells Jerry Lee's Story', *Detroit Free Press*, (4 July 1982), pp. F 1, 5.

Paul Nelson, '"Hellfire": Devil's Music and Jerry Lee Lewis,' *Rolling Stone*, No. 374 (22 July 1982), p. 42.

Robert Santelli, 'Review of *Hellfire* by Nick Tosches', *Goldmine*, No. 75 (August 1982), p. 177.

James Wolcott, 'Review of *Hellfire* by Nick Tosches', *Esquire*, XCVII (July 1982), p. 120.

Catherine Yronwode, 'Review', *Bop*, No. 1 (1982), pp. 38–39.

Concert Reviews

Billy Miller, '88 Keys Of Fury: The Killer Slays New York!' *Kicks*, No. 2 (1979), pp. 43–44.

Robert Palmer, 'Jerry Lee's Shrine', *Rolling Stone*, No. 321 (10 July 1980), p. 68.

Paul Sandford, 'Jerry Lee – Almost Back To Being Brilliant', *New Kommotion*, II (Spring 1977), p. 16.

Record Reviews

B. Lee Cooper and James A. Creeth, 'Present At The Creation: The Legend of Jerry Lee Lewis On Record, 1956-1963', *JEFM Quarterly*, XIX (Summer 1983), pp. 122–129.

Colin Escott, 'Jerry Lee Lewis: Huey P. Meaux, and The "Southern Roots" Sessions', *Goldmine*, No. 196 (29 January 1988), pp. 38, 40.

Cub Koda, '200-Plus Sun Sides by The Killer Hizzownself', *Goldmine*, No.
131 (2 August 1985), p. 60.

Adam Komorowski, 'Jerry Lee Lewis Sun Box', *New Kommotion*, No. 27
(1983), pp. 5–8.

Tony Neale, Bill Humphreys, and Dave Oksanen, 'Reviews and Previews –
The Million Dollar Quartet', *Music World*, No. 84 (April 1981), pp.
56–58.

'Record Collector's Album Of The Month – The Million Dollar Quartet
(Charly/Sun 1006)', *Record Collector*, No. 25 (September 1981), pp. 50–51.

'Review of Jerry Lee Lewis – The Killer, 1963–1968 (Bear Family BFX
15210)', *Record Collector*, No. 88 (December 1986), pp. 53–54.

Nick Tosches, 'Review Of Jerry Lee Lewis Album', *High Fidelity*, XXIX
(June 1979), p. 109.

Joel Vance, 'Jerry Lee Lewis: Doing All He Can To Become A Legend In
His Own Time', *Stereo Review*, XLV (July 1980), p. 71.

Discographies

Wim de Boer (comp.), *Breathless: The Jerry Lee Lewis Long Play Album
Guide*. Best, Holland: De Witte Publications, 1983.

Robert Cain, 'Discography', in *Whole Lotta Shakin' Goin' On: Jerry Lee
Lewis*, (New York: Dial Press, 1981), pp. 127–141.

Phil Cook, 'Jerry Lee Lewis U.K. Discography, 1957–67', *Record Collector*,
No. 17 (January 1981), pp. 18–19.

B. Lee Cooper, 'The Charted 45 R.P.M. Hits of Jerry Lee Lewis, 1957-1980'
and 'Selected Discography Of Jerry Lee Lewis Albums, 1958-1980', *Music
World*, No. 90 (October 1981), pp. 32–34 and 34–36.

Colin Escott and Martin Hawkins (comps.), *Sun Records: The Discography*.
Bremen, West Germany: Bear Family Records, 1987.

Barrie Gamblin, 'Jerry Lee Lewis – a Post-1970 Discography', *New
Kommotion*, No. 6 (Summer 1974, pp. 22–23.

Barrie Gamblin, 'Jerry Lee Lewis, 1970–1974: Part 2', *New Kommotion*, No.
7 (Fall 1974), pp. 10–11.

Barrie Gamblin, 'Jerry Lee Lewis, 1970–1974: Part 3', *New Kommotion*, No.
8 (Winter 1975), pp. 8–9.

Barrie Gamblin, 'The Mercury Sessions: Jerry Lee Lewis Unreleased
Masters', *Fire-Ball Mail*, XXIII (July/August 1985), pp. 4–6.

Bob Kinder, 'Jerry Lee Lewis Discography', *Record Exchanger*, No. 21
(1975), p. 11.

Jon McAuliffe, 'Jerry Lee Lewis: Another Place, Another Time – The
Smash Years', *Goldmine*, No. 176 (April 24, 1987), p. 16.

Steve Scott, 'Jerry Lee Lewis Discography: The Sun Releases', *Record
Collector*, No. 41 (January 1983), p. 26.

Nick Tosches, 'Session Recordings', *Goldmine*, No. 112 (9 November 1984), pp. 6–22.

Nick Tosches, 'Jerry Lee Lewis: The Smash Mercury Years – Part 2', *Goldmine*, No. 113 (23 November 1984), pp. 30–38.

Richard Weize (comp.), 'A Preliminary Jerry Lee Lewis Discography', in *Jerry Lee Lewis: The Killer, 1963–1968* by Colin Escott (Bremen, West Germany: Bear Family Records, 1986), pp. 81–127.

Richard Weize (comp.), 'A Preliminary Jerry Lee Lewis Discography', in *Jerry Lee Lewis: The Killer, 1969–1972* by Colin Escott (Bremen, West Germany: Bear Family Records, 1986), pp. 65–120.

Richard Weize (comp.), 'A Preliminary Jerry Lee Lewis Discography' (revised edition)', in *Jerry Lee Lewis: The Killer, 1973–1977* by Colin Escott (Bremen, West Germany: Bear Family Records, 1987), pp. 65–120.